JESUS
in Context

JESUS
in Context

Background Readings for Gospel Study

EDITED BY

DARRELL L. BOCK
and GREGORY J. HERRICK

Baker Academic
Grand Rapids, Michigan

Published by Baker Academic
a division of Baker Publishing Group
P.O. Box 6287, Grand Rapids, MI 49516-6287
www.bakeracademic.com

Printed in the United States of America

Library of Congress Cataloging-in-Publication Data
Jesus in context : background readings for Gospel study / edited by Darrell L. Bock and Gregory J. Herrick.
    p.   cm.
Includes bibliographical references and indexes.
ISBN 0-8010-2719-5 (pbk.)
1. Bible. N.T. Gospels—Criticism, interpretation, etc. I. Bock, Darrell L. II. Herrick, Gregory J., 1964–
BS2555.52.J47 2005
226′.095—dc22   2005007946

Permission to quote extensively from the following sources is appreciated and acknowledged:

The Dead Sea Scrolls Translated: The Qumran Texts in English, by Florentino García Martínez, translated by Wilfred G. E. Watson, 2nd ed. (Leiden: E. J. Brill; Grand Rapids: Eerdmans, 1996). ©1994, 1996 E. J. Brill, used by permission of Wm. B. Eerdmans Publishing Co., Grand Rapids, MI. All rights reserved.

The Mishnah: A New Translation, translated by Jacob Neusner (New Haven, CT: Yale University Press, 1988). Used by permission. Copyright ©1988 by Yale University. All rights reserved.

The Old Testament Pseudepigrapha, edited by James H. Charlesworth, 2 vols. (Garden City, NY: Doubleday, 1983–85). Copyright ©1983 and 1985 by James H. Charlesworth. Used by permission of Doubleday, a division of Random House, Inc.

Contents

Canonical Guide
to the Readings

The primary Gospel passages elucidated by the *good reference index* readings are identified in the section headings throughout the book and are listed in canonical order in the table below. Page numbers indicate where a section of readings begins, but the section may extend over several pages.

Matthew	section	page	Matthew	section	page	Matthew	section	page
1:1–17	2.2	40	8:18–22	6.4	95	15:1–20	7.7	110
1:18–25	2.5	49	8:18–22	9.1	123	16:1–2a	6.18	105
2:1–12	2.7	51	8:28–34	6.5	96	16:4	6.18	105
2:13–21	2.8	52	9:1–8	4.5	76	17:1–9	8.1	118
2:22–23	2.9	54	9:9–13	4.6	79	17:10–13	8.2	119
3:1–6	3.2	57	9:14–17	4.7	80	17:14–21	8.3	119
3:11–12	3.4	66	9:18–26	6.6	97	17:24–27	8.4	119
3:13–17	3.6	70	9:27–31	6.7	98	18:10–14	8.5	120
4:18–22	4.1	72	10:1–16	6.8	98	18:12–14	9.13	134
4:23	4.4	74	10:17–25	6.9	99	18:15	9.16	137
5:3–12	5.1	83	10:34–36	6.10	100	18:15–18	8.6	120
5:14–16	5.2	84	10:34–36	9.6	128	18:21–22	8.7	121
5:17–20	5.3	84	10:37–39	6.11	101	19:16–22	10.1	145
5:27–30	5.4	85	11:2–6	6.12	101	19:30	9.8	131
5:31–32	5.5	85	11:28–30	6.13	101	20:20–28	10.2	146
5:33–37	5.6	86	12:1–8	4.8	80	20:29–34	6.7	98
6:1–4	5.7	87	12:9–14	4.9	80	21:1–9	10.4	146
6:16–18	5.8	88	12:15–21	6.14	102	21:10–19	11.1	150
6:19–21	5.9	88	12:22–30	6.17	103	22:1–14	9.12	133
6:24	5.10	89	12:38–42	6.18	105	22:1–14	11.2	156
7:13–14	5.12	91	13:18–23	7.1	107	22:15–22	11.3	157
7:13–14	9.8	131	13:31–32	7.2	107	22:23–33	11.4	158
7:22–23	9.8	131	13:36–43	7.3	108	22:34–40	9.3	125
7:24–27	5.13	92	13:44–46	7.4	108	22:34–40	11.5	161
7:7–11	5.11	90	14:1–2	7.5	109	22:41–46	11.6	161
8:5–13	6.1	93	14:3–4	3.5	67	23:1–36	11.7	162
8:11–12	9.8	131	14:3–12	7.6	110	23:4	9.4	126
8:16–17	6.3	94	15:1–9	9.4	126	23:6–7	9.4	126

Matthew	section	page
23:13	9.4	126
23:25–32	9.4	126
23:34–36	9.4	126
23:37–39	9.9	132
23:37–39	11.8	165
24:1–2	11.9	165
24:9–14	11.10	176
24:15–22	11.11	176
24:29–31	11.12	177
24:42–51	9.5	128
25:1–13	11.13	181
25:14–30	10.3	146
25:14–30	11.14	183
25:31–46	11.15	183
26:1–5	11.16	185
26:6–13	6.15	102
26:21–25	14.2	238
26:26–29	11.17	185
26:30–35	11.18	186
26:36–46	11.19	187
26:57–75	11.20	188
27:11–14	11.21	193
27:15–23	11.22	195
27:24–26	11.23	196
27:27–31a	11.24	197
27:33–37	11.25	199

Mark	section	page
1:1	3.1	57
1:2–6	3.2	57
1:7–8	3.4	66
1:9–11	3.6	70
1:16–20	4.1	72
1:21–22	4.2	72
1:23–28	4.3	73
1:32–34	6.3	94
1:39	4.4	74
2:1–12	4.5	76
2:13–17	4.6	79
2:18–22	4.7	80
2:23–28	4.8	80
3:1–6	4.9	80
3:7–12	6.14	102
3:13–19a	6.8	98

Mark	section	page
3:22–27	6.17	103
4:13–20	7.1	107
4:21	5.2	84
4:30–32	7.2	107
5:1–20	6.5	96
5:21–43	6.6	97
6:7–11	6.8	98
6:14–16	7.5	109
6:17–18	3.5	67
6:17–29	7.6	110
7:1–9	9.4	126
7:1–23	7.7	110
8:11–12	6.18	105
9:2–10	8.1	118
9:11–13	8.2	119
9:14–29	8.3	119
9:43	5.4	85
9:45	5.4	85
9:47	5.4	85
10:17–22	10.1	145
10:35–45	10.2	146
10:38	9.6	128
10:46–52	6.7	98
11:1–10	10.4	146
11:11–17	11.1	150
12:13–17	11.3	157
12:18–27	11.4	158
12:28–34	9.3	125
12:28–34	11.5	161
12:35–37a	11.6	161
12:37b–40	11.7	162
13:1–2	11.9	165
13:9–13	6.9	99
13:9–13	11.10	176
13:14–20	11.11	176
13:24–27	11.12	177
13:33–37	9.5	128
13:34	10.3	146
14:1–2	11.16	185
14:3–9	6.15	102
14:18–21	14.2	238
14:22–25	11.17	185
14:26–31	11.18	186
14:32–42	11.19	187

Mark	section	page
14:53–72	11.20	188
15:2–5	11.21	193
15:6–14	11.22	195
15:15	11.23	196
15:16–20a	11.24	197
15:22–26	11.25	199

Luke	section	page
1:1–4	2.1	37
1:5–25	2.3	44
1:26–38	2.4	47
2:8–20	2.6	51
2:39–40	2.9	54
3:1–6	3.2	57
3:10–14	3.3	58
3:15–18	3.4	66
3:19–20	3.5	67
3:19–20	7.6	110
3:21–22	3.6	70
4:31–32	4.2	72
4:33–37	4.3	73
4:40–41	6.3	94
4:44	4.4	74
5:17–26	4.5	76
5:27–32	4.6	79
5:33–39	4.7	80
6:1–5	4.8	80
6:6–11	4.9	80
6:12–16	6.8	98
6:17–19	6.14	102
6:20b–26	5.1	83
6:39	11.7	162
6:40	6.9	99
6:47–49	5.13	92
7:1–10	6.1	93
7:11–17	6.2	94
7:18–23	6.12	101
7:36–50	6.15	102
8:1–3	6.16	102
8:11–15	7.1	107
8:16	5.2	84
8:26–39	6.5	96
8:40–56	6.6	97
9:1–5	6.8	98

9

Cross-Reference Table

The table below indicates where a unit from *Jesus according to Scripture* (*JaS*) appears in *Jesus in Context* (*JiC*). Only *JaS* units that contain extrabiblical references are covered in *JiC*, therefore gaps in the numbering occur. Page numbers indicate where a section of readings begins, but the section may extend over several pages.

JaS unit	JiC section	page	JaS unit	JiC section	page	JaS unit	JiC section	page
1	2.1	37	45	5.2	84	100	6.14	102
2	2.2	40	46	5.3	84	101	6.15	102
3	2.3	44	48	5.4	85	102	6.16	102
4	2.4	47	49	5.5	85	104	6.17	103
7	2.5	49	50	5.6	86	106	6.18	105
9	2.6	51	53	5.7	87	112	7.1	107
11	2.7	51	56	5.8	88	116	7.2	107
12	2.8	52	57	5.9	88	119	7.3	108
13	2.9	54	59	5.10	89	120	7.4	108
15	3.1	57	63	5.11	90	129	7.5	109
16	3.2	57	65	5.12	91	130	7.6	110
18	3.3	58	68	5.13	92	135	7.7	110
19	3.4	66	72	6.1	93	145	8.1	118
20	3.5	67	73	6.2	94	146	8.2	119
21	3.6	70	75	6.3	94	147	8.3	119
26	4.1	72	76	6.4	95	149	8.4	119
27	4.2	72	78	6.5	96	153	8.5	120
28	4.3	73	82	6.6	97	154	8.6	120
32	4.4	74	83	6.7	98	156	8.7	121
35	4.5	76	86	6.8	98	160	9.1	123
36	4.6	79	87	6.9	99	162	9.2	123
37	4.7	80	89	6.10	100	164	9.3	125
38	4.8	80	90	6.11	101	175	9.4	126
39	4.9	80	93	6.12	101	184	9.5	128
43	5.1	83	97	6.13	101	185	9.6	128

JaS unit	*JiC* section	page	*JaS* unit	*JiC* section	page	*JaS* unit	*JiC* section	page
189	9.7	128	248	11.11	176	J11	13.8	215
192	9.8	131	250	11.12	177	J12	13.9	215
194	9.9	132	255	11.13	181	J14	13.10	216
195	9.10	132	256	11.14	183	J16	13.11	217
196	9.11	132	257	11.15	183	J17	13.12	218
197	9.12	133	259	11.16	185	J18	13.14	223
200	9.13	134	264	11.17	185	J19	13.15	227
206	9.14	134	267	11.18	186	J20	13.16	230
208	9.15	135	269	11.19	187	J21	13.17	230
210	9.16	137	271	11.20	188	J22	13.18	231
214	9.17	137	274	11.21	193	J23	13.19	235
221	10.1	145	277	11.22	195	J24	13.20	235
225	10.2	146	278	11.23	196	J25	13.21	236
228	10.3	146	279	11.24	197	J26	14.1	237
229	10.4	146	281	11.25	199	J27	14.2	238
230	10.5	148	291	11.26	200	J30	14.3	239
231	11.1	150	294	11.27	200	J34	14.4	239
237	11.2	156	J1	12.1	205	J36	14.5	239
238	11.3	157	J2	12.2	206	J41	14.6	240
239	11.4	158	J4	13.1	208	J43	14.7	242
240	11.5	161	J5	13.2	209	J44	14.8	243
241	11.6	161	J6	13.3	210	J45	14.9	244
242	11.7	162	J7	13.4	211	J46	14.10	246
243	11.8	165	J8	13.5	211	J47	14.11	247
245	11.9	165	J9	13.6	212	J50	14.12	248
247	11.10	176	J10	13.7	213			

Preface

Too often the view persists that somehow the Bible (and therefore the Gospels) simply fell out of heaven into our laps and that it has no real historical context other than our own twenty-first century. At least this is the manner in which the Bible is often read in the church. While this approach correctly recognizes the timelessness of the Bible and its ability to speak across cultures and centuries, it is neither the best nor the safest avenue for penetrating the meaning of these ancient texts.

The truth is, of course, that the Gospels (our primary concern here) came to expression in a real historical context, and that fully to understand their message they must be read and studied with an understanding of this historical context. Real people wrote these texts about Jesus for real people (e.g., churches), describing the work of God in Christ using concepts and language understandable to those audiences.

The Gospels describe the coming, ministry, death, resurrection, ascension, and exaltation of Jesus Christ, and they do so according to first-century customs, language, culture, and conventions. Living in a time and culture quite distinct from theirs, however, we in the twenty-first century must investigate this original setting in order better to understand Jesus' ministry and teachings. Both *Jesus according to Scripture* and *Jesus in Context* are intended to help further our understanding of Jesus' original historical situation.

Jesus according to Scripture travels through the Gospels, scene by scene, explaining the meaning of the text with reference to the words and works of Jesus. In the course of the discussion, many Greco-Roman and Jewish sources are referred to that offer relevant background to the biblical text. However, due to space limitations, the extrabiblical texts themselves could not be included in that volume. The present companion volume, *Jesus in Context,* supplies the texts cited in *Jesus according to Scripture* and, to facilitate cross-referencing, includes the number of the unit where the reference appears in *Jesus according to Scripture.*[1] It is intended for those who do not have access to these extrabiblical texts or are unfamiliar with how to find them. By quoting this material rather than simply giving a list of references, its relevance to a given biblical passage is immediately obvious. To our knowledge, no resource like this exists in English.

By reading this background material, we gain a better understanding of first-century Jewish customs such as corban, hand washing, tithing, marriage, death, and festivals. We also learn about the theological environment in which Jesus ministered, including Jewish concerns

1. The unit number from *Jesus according to Scripture* appears at the end of the relevant heading in the present work and is accompanied by the label *JaS.* Units from *Jesus according to Scripture* that do not contain extrabiblical references are omitted here, therefore gaps in the numbering occur.

13

about God, his kingdom, law keeping, and messianic hopes prevalent at the time. We also gain an appreciation for how Jesus' message might have been perceived and what opinions or expectations his audience held about the topics he addressed. These expectations, often growing out of contemporary theological reflection within first-century Judaism, cannot be illumined by a study of their Old Testament roots alone.

How to Use This Book

The bulk of the material in this collection comes from Jewish texts dating to centuries before or after the time of Jesus. The general nature and character of these works is discussed in the introduction. To gain a more detailed understanding of these sources, consult the works cited in the notes. Some of these texts, like the Mishnah (AD 200) and Talmud (c. AD 500), were written after the time of Jesus and the New Testament (i.e., after AD 100). Quotations from these later texts are marked with an asterisk (*) as a way of signaling caution in the appeal to these texts because of their age. Nevertheless, they are included in this collection because they are often appealed to by New Testament commentators to provide historical or

conceptual background, and in some cases the traditions they record may actually go back to a time near or before the time of Jesus and the production of the canonical Gospels.

The selection of texts reflects sources often connected with important events or topics in the study of Jesus. The short introductory notes preceding the excerpts seek to orient the reader to the point of connection. In many cases, the relevance of the material will be obvious; in others, the excerpt provides more general background to the Gospel passage. Some texts are included merely because they have traditionally been associated with Jesus' activity, even though there may be some doubt as to their relevance. One benefit of this collection is the opportunity it affords readers to assess firsthand the merits and relevance of these texts.

We hope that *Jesus in Context* will help attentive students of the Bible to better appreciate Jesus' message by setting it more clearly in its original historical-cultural context. It is further hoped that this appreciation will move readers of the Gospels to reflect on and respond to the content of Jesus' message and its potential impact on their lives.

Darrell L. Bock
Greg Herrick

Acknowledgments

We wish to thank Baker Academic for their decision to undertake a "poor man's Strack-Billerbeck." For years we have said to students that it was worth learning German just to be able to use Strack-Billerbeck and the information it provides.[1] German is still worth learning, but the present work reflects the students' desire for an English compilation of background writings for the Gospels, especially the relevant Jewish materials. Our thanks go to the many students who have asked for such a work. We hope it meets their expectations.

We offer special thanks to the administration of Dallas Theological Seminary and to Mark Bailey, John Grassmick, and Buist Fanning, in particular, for their willingness to allow a graduate assistant to help with this project as we were gathering the texts. Brittany Burnette filled this role admirably and also helped proofread an early draft.

We have used older translations for Josephus and Philo but have modernized the English style of these renderings where necessary. We appreciate the permission to use translations of the Old Testament Pseudepigrapha (Doubleday), Mishnah (Yale University Press), and Dead Sea Scrolls (William B. Eerdmans Publishing Company). Computer programs and the World Wide Web have made our work easier, both in compiling these texts and in checking them for accuracy. We thank OakSoft software, makers of Accordance; Logos Software and their Libronics program; and Davka Software, which has a full collection of Jewish sources from the rabbinic period. You can learn more online about these companies and their products.

1. H. L. Strack and Paul Billerbeck, *Kommentar zum Neuen Testament aus Talmud und Midrasch*, 6 vols. (Munich: Beck, 1922–28).

Introduction

Sources Predating or Contemporary with Jesus' Ministry

Numerous sources contribute to our understanding of the first-century world of Judaism, and numerous other materials trace the history of Judaism in the period following the life of Jesus. These sources tell us what we know about the world of Jesus, the history of Judaism, Jewish religious practice, the customs of everyday Jewish life, and the impact on Israel of Roman occupation and that of other nations before them. It is important to divide these sources into various periods to avoid anachronism in their study and use. Thus we group together the sources that predominantly predate or are contemporary with the arrival of Jesus and those that follow him. Our goal is simply to note what these sources are, where they can be located and referenced, and what they contribute to our study of Jesus and his world.

Old Testament Apocrypha, or Deuterocanonical Books

The Old Testament Apocrypha, or deuterocanonical books, is a collection

of fifteen works. These texts cover the period of history between the Testaments. They contain wisdom literature (Sirach, Wisdom of Solomon) as well as the history that leads directly into the first century AD (1 and 2 Maccabees). They cover the crucial period of the Maccabean War, when Judaism faced one of the greatest challenges to its existence. Most important for our study are 1 and 2 Maccabees, which cover this key period in some detail. To understand first-century Judaism, one must appreciate the impact of the events these books describe.

The books of the Apocrypha are important because they show us how Jews

---

1. Craig A. Evans (*Noncanonical Writings and New Testament Interpretation* [Peabody, MA: Hendrickson, 1992]) gives a full survey of the nature of these sources. More scholarly sources can be found by consulting the bibliography in Evans's work. A solid, more complete introductory overview to this literature and to the Judaism of this period is James C. VanderKam, *An Introduction to Early Judaism* (Grand Rapids:

Eerdmans, 2000). For a concise bibliography of key Jewish intertestamental and rabbinic literature, see David W. Chapman and Andreas J. Köstenberger, "Jewish Intertestamental and Early Rabbinic Literature: An Annotated Bibliographic Resource," *Journal of the Evangelical Theological Society* 43 (2000): 577–618.

2. Some translations of the Bible (e.g., NRSV, JB) contain these books. A good translation is *The Oxford Annotated Apocrypha,* ed. Bruce M. Metzger (New York: Oxford University Press, 1977). Standard abbreviations for these books can be found in *The SBL Handbook of Style,* ed. Patrick H. Alexander et al. (Peabody, MA: Hendrickson, 1999), 74. Roman Catholics accept these texts as part of the canonical Old Testament. This is the reason for the name *deuterocanonical.* Josephus gives an ancient Jewish view that no Scripture was written after Artaxerxes (*Against Apion* 1.8.40–41). Though these works were often included in important Jewish manuscript collections and were respected Jewish literature, they did not emerge within Judaism as part of the recognized Jewish canon. These books are cited by chapter and verse like biblical books.

of the Greek and Hasmonean eras tried to make sense of their faith and how they attempted to express the importance of the role of the law and the nature of Israel's hope in a period just preceding Jesus. Thus these texts give us a window into how certain strands within Judaism tried to make sense of their faith, especially at a time when Jewish identity was under pressure from other national groups.

Old Testament Pseudepigrapha

Another source of Jewish material is the Old Testament Pseudepigrapha. It contains a variety of texts reflecting an array of genres: apocalyptic, wisdom, testaments, prayers, hymns, and texts expanding on the Old Testament. This corpus of texts spans a period from about the sixth century BC to the ninth century AD. Yet the bulk of the important material comes from the period between the second century BC and the second century AD. Many of the concepts and customs mentioned only briefly in the Old Testament are elaborated on in these texts, showing Jewish views on subjects that the Gospels also discuss. This literature was not always widely circulated, but it does reflect what some Jewish groups were thinking at various times about important religious issues, and it helps us to appreciate the complexity and concerns of Judaism at this time. In fact, this literature shows that Judaism was not monolithic in this period but had many substreams and strands. Particularly important among these books are the apocalyptic or eschatologically oriented works like 1 Enoch, 4 Ezra, and the Psalms of Solomon. Other texts, such as Jubilees, show that legal concerns were important. Still another type of text tried to show that Jews and Gentiles could get along, best exemplified by the Letter of Aristeas, which also describes the traditional view of the origin of the Septuagint, the Greek translation of the Old Testament.

Dead Sea, or Qumran, Scrolls

Perhaps the most dramatic archaeological discovery of the twentieth century involved the texts found in caves at Qumran overlooking the Dead Sea. These texts probably belonged to a community of Essene Jewish separatists who had become disenchanted with temple practices in the second century BC. The texts became known as the Dead Sea Scrolls.[4] These works are the remains of the library of this separatist community, which came into existence as a result of the Maccabean War and lasted until AD 68. Included within these texts are not only copies of ancient Old Testament manuscripts but also various religious texts, including some of the Pseudepigrapha. Many of these texts describe the practices of this unique community.

---

6. The current standard edition is James H. Charlesworth, ed., *The Old Testament Pseudepigrapha*, 2 vols. (New York: Doubleday, 1983–85). Pseudepigrapha means "falsely inscribed," indicating their pseudonymous and noncanonical character. However, these works are still of value as historical sources that reflect the thinking of the time, in much the same way as the previous category of sources. Citations are by chapter and verse like biblical references. For standard abbreviations for these works, see *SBL Handbook of Style*, 74–75.

4. See Florentino García Martínez, *The Dead Sea Scrolls Translated*, 2nd ed. (Leiden: Brill; Grand Rapids: Eerdmans, 1996). It is usually easy to spot a reference to a Dead Sea Scroll text, as its sigla normally has a number (of the cave), the designation Q for Qumran, and a manuscript number (e.g., 4Q175). A few texts are known by other names as well. A diglot version of these texts exists in Hebrew/Aramaic and English: Florentino García Martínez and Eibert J. C. Tigchelaar, *The Dead Sea Scrolls Study Edition*, 2 vols. (Leiden: Brill; Grand Rapids: Eerdmans, 2000). Standard abbreviations and identifications can be found in the works by García Martínez and in *SBL Handbook of Style*, 75–77, 176–233.

which had chosen not to risk any compromise with Hellenism or with official Judaism, which they believed had been tainted by Hellenism. They went to the desert to be a pure community and wait for God to deliver them and vindicate their stand as God's true people. The importance of ritual and religious calendars is also evident from this material, revealing an approach to religious practice that is far different from much religious expression today but that reflects concerns that existed within first-century Judaism. Much has been written about these texts and how they have revolutionized New Testament study.[5]

Philo

Another Jewish source contemporary with Jesus' time is Philo of Alexandria (c. 20 BC–AD 50). His primary value lies in the information he gives us about how Jews in the Diaspora (that is, Jews scattered throughout the Roman Empire) viewed their faith, and we learn little from him about the views of Jews within Israel/Palestine. Nevertheless, Philo is still significant for revealing how some intellectually oriented Jews thought.[6] He gives us a glimpse of how some Jews borrowed from the world of Hellenism and yet still vigorously defended their faith and people. Many of Philo's expositions attempt to make sense of key narratives of Hebrew Scripture and relate them to the cultural-philosophical environment of the Greco-Roman context as found in Egypt at this time. As such, his work is of limited importance to our study.

Josephus

When we think about the history of Judaism during the first century AD and about the first century in general, pride of place goes to the pro-Roman, Jewish general and historian Josephus (AD 37– c. 100).[7] Without him, we would know far less about this period. His four works give an account ranging from the time of Genesis to Jerusalem's fall in AD 70 and the resulting political fallout. *Antiquities* surveys Israel's history from Genesis to the time of Josephus's writing around AD 90. *The Wars of the Jews* (also called *The Jewish War*) covers the period from the Maccabean War and the controversial Syrian ruler Antiochus Epiphanes up to the time of his writing. *Against Apion* is a work defending Judaism against Greek critics. Finally, *The Life of Flavius Josephus* is an autobiography extolling the merits of his life. These texts are crucial because they give us insight into how a major figure living in Jesus' day viewed Israel's history and key political events.

5. For a good initial reading list, see García Martínez, *Dead Sea Scrolls Translated,* lvii.

6. For an English translation, see *The Works of Philo: Complete and Unabridged,* trans. C. D. Yonge, new updated ed. (Peabody, MA: Hendrickson, 1993). The Greek texts with English translations can be found in F. H. Colson et al., eds., *Philo,* Loeb Classical Library, 10 vols. plus 2 supplemental vols. (Cambridge: Harvard University Press, 1929–53). The Latin names of Philo's works appear in the Loeb volumes. Both English and Latin titles appear in the Hendrickson edition. Standard abbreviations can be found in *SBL Handbook of Style,* 78.

7. For an English translation, see *The Works of Josephus: Complete and Unabridged,* trans. William Whiston, new updated ed. (Peabody, MA: Hendrickson, 1987). The technical diglot edition (Greek text with English translation on facing pages) of Josephus is H. St. J. Thackeray et al., eds., *Josephus,* Loeb Classical Library, 10 vols. (Cambridge: Harvard University Press, 1926–65). Often the titles of Josephus's works appear in Latin. The Hendrickson edition lists the Latin titles, but both Latin and English names and their abbreviations can be found in *SBL Handbook of Style,* 79. Citations from the works of Philo and Josephus typically include book, chapter, paragraph, and sentence numbers, though their shorter works may have only two or three of these divisions. At the very least, numbers for the highest and lowest levels must be given when citing specific passages (e.g., *Ant.* 12.1.3 is inadequate, but either 12.1.3 §§119–53 or 12.119–53 is sufficient).

His discussions are full of treatments of everyday life and give examples of how terms were regularly used. The study of Josephus is a branch of Jewish studies all its own, for one must consider and weigh his testimony and the varying perspectives his works reflect.[8] At one time in the West's educational system, Josephus was the text read most after the Bible. Josephus is usually fairly reliable as a source, but his perspective needs critical assessment.

Greco-Roman Sources

Greco-Roman sources also abound for this period. One collection of texts that are often related to New Testament study is edited by M. Eugene Boring, Klaus Berger, and Carsten Colpe.[9] This collection has both Jewish and Hellenistic sources in it, but many references cite Greco-Roman literature, Hermetica texts,[10] inscriptions, papyri, and letters.[11]

Sources Postdating the Time of Jesus

After Josephus, we cross a major boundary in our sources. Most sources mentioned up to this point come from the first century or earlier (some pseudepigraphic texts are later). All the sources after this point postdate the time of Jesus. Because we cannot be sure that ideas from a later period were also present in an earlier period, information coming from these sources needs to be used with caution to avoid the danger of projecting concepts back into an earlier period.[12] On the other hand, because Judaism is a conservative religious tradition, many practices, especially those relating to the temple, would have little reason to be altered since the temple no longer existed when these works were written. That is, it is unlikely that traditional practices that could no longer be observed would be altered or added to. Hence, it is likely that the descriptions

8. The study of Josephus and his historical reliability is not without controversy. For discussion and more detail, see Evans, *Noncanonical Writings*, 86–96.

9. *Hellenistic Commentary on the New Testament* (Nashville: Abingdon, 1995).

10. The Corpus Hermeticum is a collection of seventeen tractates written in Greek and dating from the mid–first to the mid–third centuries AD. The texts reflect religious and philosophical teachings present in mystical forms of Gnosticism. For discussion and introductory bibliography, see Everett Ferguson, *Backgrounds of Early Christianity*, 2nd ed. (Grand Rapids: Eerdmans, 1993).

11. In the index to Boring, Berger, and Colpe, citations of Greco-Roman sources cover seven pages while citations of Jewish texts cover only four pages. While both contexts are important to the history and culture of the region, the Jewish sources are in general more important.

12. For a consideration of the difficulties in deriving reliable historical data from these sources as well as from Josephus, see John P. Meier, *A Marginal Jew: Rethinking the Historical Jesus*, vol. 3, *Companions and Competitors*, Anchor Bible Reference Library (New York: Doubleday, 2001), 299–310. Meier notes that information attested in multiple ancient Jewish sources is more likely to be historically accurate, but he is a little too skeptical of the New Testament Gospels' ability to reach back to the time of Jesus—rather than reflect merely an early church perspective—when addressing issues related to the Pharisees. That the New Testament perspective reflects a polemical situation does not nullify the fact that these writers were closer to the events than we are as we attempt to reconstruct the historical details. Many of these conflicts best explain why Jesus ran into opposition from official Judaism. Such perspectives may not require a choice between a Jesus setting or an early church setting. Still, Meier's point is valid that these later sources need to be handled carefully. Despite these difficulties, the wealth of Jewish material and the Jewish setting of Jesus' ministry requires that these Jewish sources be carefully examined and appreciated for their contribution to our understanding of Jesus' life and times. Despite his cautions about their use, Meier points out that using Jewish materials with care provides a needed corrective to reading Jesus' life exclusively through Greco-Roman sources and in only a Greco-Roman light.

of temple practices would be preserved rather than changed. Thus this later material can still have value for us, especially in describing religious practice and custom.

Midrashim

A key source for Jewish understanding of Scripture is the midrashim, the Hebrew plural form for *midrash*, which means "searching out." These texts, most of which postdate our period, are collections of rabbinic interpretations of biblical texts. The Midrash Rabbah is the most important, covering the Pentateuch plus Song of Songs, Esther, Ecclesiastes, Ruth, and Lamentations. It was compiled from AD 450 to 1110. Material dating from AD 750 to 800 also exists for the Psalms.

Earlier collections of midrashim exist for Exodus (*Mekilta*), Leviticus (*Sipra* [*Sifra*]), Numbers (*Sipre* [*Sifre*]), and Deuteronomy (*Sipre* [*Sifre*]).[13] *Mekilta* dates from the second century; the others date to the fourth century. We gain insight here into how later Jews read their Scripture and how tradition talked about it.[14] However, the use of the midrashim for Gospel study requires caution because of their later date and because the likelihood of later reflection embellishing scriptural interpretations increases over time. Thus, we cannot be certain that ideas expressed in the midrashim really go back to Jesus' time. When readings in this material are simi-

lar to material found in earlier sources, then these readings can be treated with more confidence. However, one should always note when later extrabiblical material is being cited.

Mishnah

A major source of Jewish religious practice and rabbinic legal reflection is the Mishnah.[15] This work contains a series of legal discussions covering the whole of Jewish religious practice. It represents an official codification of the oral law. Six major topics are covered in the six main divisions (also called orders or volumes) of this work: seeds (*Zeraᶜim*), feasts (*Moᶜed*), women (*Našim*), damages (*Neziqin*), holy things (*Qodašim*), and cleannesses (*Teharot*, i.e., purity). Subdivisions of these six orders are called tractates, which have chapters and paragraphs. Two types of material appear in the Mishnah: *halakah* (legal rulings) and *haggadah* (stories intended to illustrate or edify). Though we must be careful how we use this material (tradition says that it was codified c. AD 170 under the lead-

---

13. Alternate spellings for the names of these books appear in brackets.

14. We have noted only the more prominent sources, which as a whole comprise many volumes of material. These works are variously organized and divided, so citations come in varying forms, but usually the name of the specific midrashic work is included. For details and bibliography on individual texts and translations, see Evans's discussion of the midrashim in *Noncanonical Writings*, 128–39. For abbreviations, see *SBL Handbook of Style*, 81.

15. Two capable translations of this material are Herbert Danby, *The Mishnah: Translated from the Hebrew and with Introduction and Brief Explanatory Notes* (Oxford: Oxford University Press, 1933); and Jacob Neusner, *The Mishnah: A New Translation* (New Haven: Yale University Press, 1988). A solid bilingual source is Philip Blackman, *Mishnayoth*, 6 vols. plus supplement (reprint, Gateshead: Judaica, 1977). The word *mishnah* means "repetition," indicating that this work is a codifying of oral tradition, which was learned by being repeated. Some additional tractates and remarks were added later and constitute the Tosepta (Tosefta), which means "addition." The standard method of citing the Mishnah begins with *m.*, followed by the tractate name (often abbreviated), and the chapter and paragraph number (e.g., *m. Sanh.* 7.2). Citations from the Tosepta are similar in form to those of the Mishnah, but *t.* instead of *m.* precedes the tractate name (e.g., *t. Ber.* 5.18). For details, see Evans, *Noncanonical Writings*, 118–25. For abbreviations, see *SBL Handbook of Style*, 79–80.

ership of Rabbi Judah Ha-Nasi), there is often much insight into Jewish attitudes and practices within a faith that was concerned to preserve its traditions and pass on its practices. This source is often the most helpful regarding ancient Jewish practices. Its roots lie within the sect of the Pharisees, however, while the period of Jesus' ministry was controlled by the Sadducees, who rejected oral tradition. Thus the practices described here would not be agreed on or practiced by all Jews in Jesus' time.

Talmud

The final major Jewish source, the Talmud, comes from the fifth and sixth centuries AD.[16] There are two major versions of the Talmud, a Palestinian edition (fifth century, also called the Jerusalem Talmud) and the official rabbinic edition known as the Babylonian Talmud (sixth century). The Talmud is a legal rabbinic text that includes the Mishnah and the gemara, a rabbinic commentary (gemara means "completion") on the Mishnah and an anthology of competing rabbinic views on specific matters. If care needs to be exercised in using the Mishnah, even more care is called for in appealing

to the Talmud because of the late dates of these sources.[17] These texts can still help us appreciate Jewish sensitivities and the history of later discussion on various points.

Non-Jewish Sources

There are also some significant non-Jewish sources dating to this period. Most of these texts are by major Roman historians, giving us a sense of Greco-Roman life, ideas, expressions, and attitudes as well as literary genres.[18] Roman sources spend little time on Judea, since it was too small a part of the empire to be considered significant from their perspective. Nonetheless, details about Greco-Roman culture abound in these sources, so they give us a glimpse into Hellenistic perspectives. Given the mix of Jewish and Greco-Roman elements in first-century Israel, both Jewish and Greco-Roman sources are important. The impact of a foreign presence in Israel—of Hellenism—was an important issue for the Jews, who were surrounded by it. These Jews wanted to be faithful to God and had distinct practices to mark out their uniqueness. Jewish history leading to the time of Jesus reflects a constant struggle over how to be unique.

---

16. The Talmud consists of many volumes of material. For the Palestinian Talmud, see Jacob Neusner, ed., *The Talmud of the Land of Israel*, 35 vols. (Chicago: University of Chicago Press, 1982–94); for the Babylonian Talmud, see Israel Epstein, ed., *The Babylonian Talmud*, 35 vols. (London: Soncino, 1935–48). The word *talmud* means "studying." The form of talmudic citations varies depending on which talmud is being cited. The Palestinian Talmud does not come with a uniform citation method. It is introduced with either *y.* or *j.* for Yerushalmi/Jerusalem. Often the numeration parallels the Mishnah, though Neusner's edition uses its own system. Citations from the Babylonian Talmud have a prefixed *b.* followed by the tractate name and folio number, which consists of a numeral and a letter (the letter indicating which side of the page is intended), making it easy to recognize a reference to the Babylonian Talmud (e.g., *b. Sanh.* 22ᵃ).

17. This is one of the failings of the old classic by Alfred Edersheim, *The Life and Times of Jesus the Messiah*, 2 vols. (1883; reprint, Grand Rapids: Eerdmans, 1953), for he depended heavily on talmudic material. His work reflected the best that scholarship could offer in his time, but our knowledge of sources has grown in the century since he wrote.

18. For solid introductions to the Greco-Roman background, see Ferguson, *Backgrounds of Early Christianity*; and James S. Jeffers, *The Greco-Roman World of the New Testament Era* (Downers Grove, IL: InterVarsity, 1999). For sources, see David Aune, *Greco-Roman Literature and the New Testament: Selected Forms and Genres*, SBL Sources for Biblical Study 21 (Atlanta: Scholars Press, 1988); as well as the bibliography in Boring, Berger, and Colpe, eds., *Hellenistic Commentary*, 594–601.

and faithful to God in the midst of what seemed a divine judgment that had brought the nations into Jewish land.

A final, important source of material is the works of the church fathers. The church fathers wrote to, or in defense of, the church in the generations after Jesus. Although these texts were written after the Gospels, they sometimes contain traditions from the apostolic period. The writings of the church fathers are available in collections grouped by time period. The earliest post–New Testament writings are the New Testament Apocrypha and the ante-Nicene fathers (fathers who lived and wrote before the Council of Nicea in AD 325, which includes the Apostolic Fathers).[19] Another extensive collection is that of the Nicene and post-Nicene fathers.[20] Since patris-tic texts are later than the Gospels, they must be used with care, but they do tell us how the Gospel material was interpreted by those in the early church. Most patristic citations in the present volume pertain to the origins of the various Gospels or to debates about key features in Jesus' life, such as his virgin birth.

Conclusion

Sources relevant to the study of Jesus are largely Jewish in nature. Fortunately, these sources have become the object of renewed study and interest since the mid–twentieth century and the discovery of the Dead Sea Scrolls. This renewed study of Judaism has marked out a fresh and potentially fruitful path for the study of Jesus. Many students have little familiarity with such sources and may even be unaware that they exist, but the background they provide is important to the study of Jesus. The value of these extrabiblical sources lies not in any claim to canonical authority but in their providing a barometer of cultural feelings and expectations concerning God's promise. Every culture has its "cultural script" that is assumed as its members communicate. These sources help us get a reading of the cultural script prevalent in the time of Jesus. They help us understand people's reactions to Jesus and his ministry as well as deepen our own perception of Jesus' claims.

19. Standard English editions of the New Testament Apocrypha are Wilhelm Schneemelcher, ed., *New Testament Apocrypha*, trans. R. McL. Wilson, rev. ed., 2 vols. (Cambridge: Clarke; Louisville: Westminster/John Knox, 1991–92); and J. K. Elliott, ed., *The Apocryphal New Testament: A Collection of Apocryphal Christian Literature in an English Translation* (Oxford: Clarendon; New York: Oxford University Press, 1993). English translations of the ante-Nicene fathers are available in Alexander Roberts and James Donaldson, eds., *The Ante-Nicene Fathers*, 10 vols. (1885–87; repr., Grand Rapids: Eerdmans, n.d.). A more recent edition of only the Apostolic Fathers is Michael W. Holmes, ed., *The Apostolic Fathers: Greek Texts and English Translations* (Grand Rapids: Baker, 1999).

20. Standard English editions are Philip Schaff, ed., *A Select Library of Nicene and Post-Nicene Fathers of the Christian Church*, 1st series, 14 vols. (New York: Christian Literature Co., 1887–1900; repr., Grand Rapids: Eerdmans, 1979), containing works by Augustine and Chrysostom; and Philip Schaff and Henry Wace, eds., *A Select Library of Nicene and Post-Nicene Fathers of the Christian Church*, 2nd series, 14 vols. (New York: Christian Literature Co., 1890–1900; repr., Grand Rapids: Eerdmans, 1982), containing works by a variety of later church fathers. The Fathers of the Church series published by Catholic University of America Press includes works by both early and later church fathers.

Abbreviations

*	Indicates a source postdating the time of Jesus
b.	Indicates a tractate from the Babylonian Talmud
JaS	Indicates a unit from *Jesus according to Scripture*, by Darrell L. Bock (Grand Rapids: Baker, 2002)
m.	Indicates a tractate from the Mishnah
PGM	*Papyri graecae magicae: Die griechischen Zauberpapyri*, ed. K. Preisendanz (Berlin: Teubner, 1928)
t.	Indicates a tractate from the Tosefta
y.	Indicates a tractate from the Palestinian, or Jerusalem, Talmud

The Four Gospels: Distinctive Voices

1

Overviews of Matthew, Mark, Luke, and John

This chapter provides traditional, historical background on the authorship and contents of the four canonical Gospels. As we shall see, some elements in these traditions do not always agree, while others seem to be widely circulated and held.

1.1 Matthew

Eusebius, Ecclesiastical History 3.39.16*

Papias's comment, along with other church tradition, has led many to associate the Gospel of Matthew with the apostle by the same name.

But concerning Matthew he writes as follows: "So then Matthew wrote the oracles in the Hebrew language, and every one interpreted them as he was able."

Ignatius, To the Smyrnaeans 1.1.1–2*

In Matthew 3:15, Jesus requests that John baptize him "in order to fulfill all righteousness." Ignatius, bishop of Antioch, picks up that comment in his letter to the Smyrnaeans as he relates to them the certainties of the traditions they have received concerning Jesus' genuine humanity, deity, virgin birth, crucifixion under Pontius Pilate (and Herod), and resurrection. The fact that Ignatius cites Matthew (here in his comments to the Smyrnaeans and later in his comments to Polycarp) makes a date

around AD 107 necessary for Ignatius's remarks (the approximate dates of Ignatius's death run from 107 to 139, with the earlier date reflecting tradition).

[1] I [Ignatius] glorify Jesus Christ, the God who made you [the Smyrnaeans] so wise, for I have observed that you are established in an unshakeable faith . . . totally convinced with regard to our Lord that he is truly of the family of David with respect to human descent, Son of God with respect to the divine will and power, truly born of a virgin, baptized by John in order that *all righteousness might be fulfilled* by him, [2] truly nailed in the flesh for us under Pontius Pilate and Herod the tetrarch . . . in order that he might life up a banner for the ages through his resurrection for his saints and faithful people . . . (italics added).

Ignatius, To Polycarp 2.1–2*

Ignatius is exhorting Polycarp, "bishop of the church of the Smyrnaeans," to fulfill all the duties of his ministry, caring for both the physical and spiritual needs of his people. He is to give diligence to his office, promoting unity, prayer, and alertness (1.1–3). He urges Polycarp to love even those disciples who are perhaps harder to deal with and unruly. But, in doing so, Polycarp is to be vigilant for those who teach strange doctrines (cf. 3.1–2). In this context, somewhat reminiscent of Paul's advice to Timothy (2 Timothy), Ignatius alludes to a saying of Jesus found in Matthew 10:16. Again, this would indicate that Matthew was written before the year Ignatius died (probably AD 107).

¹If you love good disciples, it is no credit to you; rather with gentleness bring the troublesome ones into submission. "Not every wound is healed by the same treatment"; "relieve inflammations with cold compresses." ²"*Be as shrewd as snakes*" in all circumstances, yet always "*innocent as doves*" (italics added).

Irenaeus, **Against Heresies 3.1.1–2***

This text from Irenaeus suggests that Matthew wrote the Gospel that bears his name while Peter and Paul were preaching in Rome. This would date the Gospel in the early to mid-sixties. See also Eusebius's comments below.

¹We have learned from none others the plan of our salvation, than from those through whom the Gospel has come down to us, which they did at one time proclaim in public, and, at a later period, by the will of God, handed down to us in the Scriptures, to be the ground and pillar of our faith. For it is unlawful to assert that they preached before they possessed "perfect knowledge," as some do even venture to say, boasting themselves as improvers of the apostles. For, after our Lord rose from the dead, [the apostles] were invested with power from on high when the Holy Spirit came down [upon them], were filled from all [His gifts], and had perfect knowledge: they departed to the ends of the earth, preaching the glad tidings of the good things [sent] from God to us, and proclaiming the peace of heaven to men, who indeed do all equally and individually possess the Gospel of God. Matthew also issued a written Gospel among the

Hebrews in their own dialect, while Peter and Paul were preaching at Rome, and laying the foundations of the Church. After their departure, Mark, the disciple and interpreter of Peter, did also hand down to us in writing what had been preached by Peter. Luke also, the companion of Paul, recorded in a book the Gospel preached by him. ²Afterwards, John, the disciple of the Lord, who also had leaned upon His breast, did himself publish a Gospel during his residence at Ephesus in Asia.

Eusebius, **Ecclesiastical History 5.8.2***

Matthew published his Gospel among the Hebrews in their own language, while Peter and Paul were preaching and founding the church in Rome.

Josephus, **Antiquities 20.9.1 §§197–203**

This citation from Josephus suggests that the stoning of Stephen, which took place in AD 62, was carried out illegally and led to fear of repercussion from Roman authorities.

¹⁹⁷And now Caesar, upon hearing the death of Festus, sent Albinus into Judea, as procurator; but the king deprived Joseph of the high priesthood, and bestowed the succession to that dignity on the son of Ananus, who was also himself called Ananus. ¹⁹⁸Now the report goes that this elder Ananus proved a most fortunate man; for he had five sons who had all performed the office of a high priest to God, and who had himself enjoyed that dignity a long time formerly, which had never happened to any other of our high priests: ¹⁹⁹but this younger Ananus, who, as we have told you already, took the high priesthood, was a bold man in his temper, and very insolent; he was also of the sect of the Sadducees, who are very

rigid in judging offenders, above all the rest of the Jews, as we have already observed; [200]when, therefore, Ananus was of this disposition, he thought he had now a proper opportunity [to exercise his authority]. Festus was now dead, and Albinus was but upon the road; so he assembled the sanhedrin of judges, and brought before them the brother of Jesus, who was called Christ, whose name was James, and some others, [or, some of his companions]; and when he had formed an accusation against them as breakers of the law, he delivered them to be stoned: [201]but as for those who seemed the most equitable of the citizens, and such as were the most uneasy at the breach of the laws, they disliked what was done; they also sent to the king [Agrippa], desiring him to send to Ananus that he should act so no more, for that what he had already done was not to be justified; [202]nay, some of them went also to meet Albinus, as he was upon his journey from Alexandria, and informed him that it was not lawful for Ananus to assemble a sanhedrim without his consent;—[203]whereupon Albinus complied with what they said, and wrote in anger to Ananus, and threatened that he would bring him to punishment for what he had done; on which king Agrippa took the high priesthood from him, when he had ruled but three months, and made Jesus, the son of Damneus, high priest.

1.2 Mark

Eusebius, Ecclesiastical History 3.39.14–15*

In this text from Eusebius, who himself is following Aristion, we read that Mark was Peter's

interpreter. According to Aristion, Mark wrote accurately about Jesus.

[14]But now we must add to the words of his [Aristion] which we have already quoted the tradition which he gives in regard to Mark, the author of the Gospel. [15]It is in the following words: "This also the presbyter said: Mark, having become the interpreter of Peter, wrote down accurately, though not indeed in order, whatsoever he remembered of the things done or said by Christ. For he neither heard the Lord nor followed him, but afterward, as I said, he followed Peter, who adapted his teaching to the needs of his hearers, but with no intention of giving a connected account of the Lord's discourses, so that Mark committed no error while he thus wrote some things as he remembered them. For he was careful of one thing, not to omit any of the things which he had heard, and not to state any of them falsely." These things are related by Papias concerning Mark.

Anti-Marcionite Prologue*

. . . Mark declared, who is "stump-fingered," because he had rather small fingers in comparison with the stature of the rest of his body. He was the interpreter of Peter. After the death of Peter himself he wrote down this same gospel in the regions of Italy.

Irenaeus, Against Heresies 3.1.1–2*

See section 1.1. above for the text. Note that Irenaeus says Mark handed down to us in writing the preaching of Peter.

Eusebius, Ecclesiastical History 6.14.5–7*

According to Eusebius, Clement of Alexandria (c. AD 150–215) claims that Mark wrote a

Gospel sourced in Peter's preaching. See also the citation from Justin Martyr below.

[5]Again, in the same books, Clement gives the tradition of the earliest presbyters, as to the order of the Gospels, in the following manner: The Gospels containing the genealogies, he says, were written first. [6]The Gospel according to Mark had this occasion: As Peter had preached the Word publicly at Rome, and declared the Gospel by the Spirit, many who were present requested that Mark, who had followed him for a long time and remembered his sayings, should write them out. And having composed the Gospel he gave it to those who had requested it. When Peter learned of this, he neither directly forbade nor encouraged it.

Justin Martyr, **Dialogue with Trypho 106***

The remainder of the Psalm makes it manifest that He knew His Father would grant to Him all things which He asked, and would raise Him from the dead; and that He urged all who fear God to praise Him because He had compassion on all races of believing men, through the mystery of Him who was crucified; and that He stood in the midst of His brethren the apostles (who repented of their flight from Him when He was crucified, after He rose from the dead, and after they were persuaded by Himself that, before His passion He had mentioned to them that He must suffer these things, and that they were announced beforehand by the prophets), and when living with them sang praises to God, as is made evident in *the memoirs of the apostles . . . And when it is said that He changed the name of one of the apostles to Peter; and when it is written in the memoirs of Him that this so happened,* as well as

that He changed the names of other two brothers, the sons of Zebedee, to Boanerges, which means sons of thunder . . . (italics added).

Eusebius, **Ecclesiastical History 2.15.1–2***

This text indicates that Peter, according to a revelation, announced his pleasure with the production of Mark's Gospel. This would date the Gospel no later than the mid-sixties since, according to tradition, Peter died in the mid-sixties.

[1]And thus when the divine word had made its home among them, the power of Simon was quenched and immediately destroyed, together with the man himself. And so greatly did the splendor of piety illumine the minds of Peter's hearers that they were not satisfied with hearing once only, and were not content with the unwritten teaching of the divine Gospel, but with all sorts of entreaties they besought Mark, a follower of Peter, and the one whose Gospel is extant, that he would leave them a written monument of the doctrine which had been orally communicated to them. Nor did they cease until they had prevailed with the man, and had thus become the occasion of the written Gospel which bears the name of Mark. [2]And they say that Peter when he had learned, through a revelation of the Spirit, of that which had been done, was pleased with the zeal of the men, and that the work obtained the sanction of his authority for the purpose of being used in the churches. Clement in the eighth book of his Hypotyposes gives this account, and with him agrees the bishop of Hierapolis named Papias. And Peter makes mention of Mark in his first epistle which they say that he wrote in Rome itself, as is indicated by him, when he

calls the city, by a figure, Babylon, as he does in the following words: "The church that is at Babylon, elected together with you, salutes you; and so does Marcus my son."

John Chrysostom, Homilies on Matthew 1.7*

Chrysostom seems to reflect a tradition that Mark wrote his Gospel in Egypt at the request of certain disciples.

Of Matthew again it is said, that when those who from amongst the Jews had believed came to him, and besought him to leave to them in writing those same things, which he had spoken to them by word, he also composed his Gospel in the language of the Hebrews. And Mark too, in Egypt, is said to have done this self-same thing at the entreaty of the disciples.

1.3 Luke

Justin Martyr, Dialogue with Trypho 103.19*

Justin notes how the "memoirs" of Jesus were drawn up by the apostles and their followers.

For in the memoirs which I say were drawn up by His apostles and those who followed them, [it is recorded] that His sweat fell down like drops of blood while He was praying, and saying, "If it be possible, let this cup pass." His heart and also His bones trembling; His heart being like wax melting in His belly: in order that we may perceive that the Father wished His Son really to undergo such sufferings for our sakes, and may not say that He, being the Son of God, did not feel what was happening to Him and inflicted on Him. Further, the expression, "My strength is dried

up like a potsherd, and my tongue has cleaved to my throat," was a prediction, as I previously remarked, of that silence, when He who convicted all your teachers of being unwise returned no answer at all.

Muratorian Canon, lines 2–8*

The Muratorian Canon claims Luke the doctor as the author of the Gospel by his name.

The third Gospel book, that according to Luke. This physician Luke after Christ's ascension (resurrection?), since Paul had taken him with him as an expert in the way (of the teaching), composed it in his own name according to (his) thinking. Yet neither did he himself see the Lord in the flesh; and therefore, as he was able to ascertain it, so he begins to tell the story from the birth of John.[1]

Irenaeus, Against Heresies 3.1.1; 3.14.1*

Irenaeus closely associates Luke with Paul in the work of ministry and clearly ascribes a Gospel to Luke (for 3.1.1, see section 1.1 above).

3.14.1 But that this Luke was inseparable from Paul, and his fellow-laborer in the Gospel, he himself clearly evinces, not as a matter of boasting, but as bound to do so by the truth itself. For he says that when Barnabas, and John who was called Mark, had parted company from Paul, and sailed to Cyprus, "we came to Troas;" and when Paul had beheld in a dream a man of Macedonia, saying, "Come into Macedonia,

1. Wilhelm Schneemelcher, ed., *New Testament Apocrypha*, vol. 1, *Gospels and Related Writings*, Eng. trans. ed. R. McL. Wilson, rev. ed. (Cambridge: Clarke; Louisville: Westminster/John Knox, 1991), 34.

Paul, and help us," "immediately," he says, "we endeavored to go into Macedonia, understanding that the Lord had called us to preach the Gospel unto them. . . ." Paul has himself declared also in the Epistles, saying: "Demas has forsaken me, . . . and is departed unto Thessalonica; Crescens to Galatia, Titus to Dalmatia. Only Luke is with me." From this he shows that he was always attached to and inseparable from him. And again he says, in the Epistle to the Colossians: "Luke, the beloved physician, greets you." But surely if Luke, who always preached in company with Paul, and is called by him "the beloved," and with him performed the work of an evangelist, and was entrusted to hand down to us a Gospel, learned nothing different from him (Paul), as has been pointed out from his words, how can these men, who were never attached to Paul, boast that they have learned hidden and unspeakable mysteries?

Tertullian, Against Marcion 4.2.2; 4.5.3*

Tertullian, in his battle with Marcion, clearly ascribes authorship of a Gospel to Luke, the companion of Paul. In the second excerpt, he closely links Luke's Gospel with Paul and indicates that it is "received" among the churches.

4.2.2 You have now our answer to the *Antitheses* compendiously indicated by us. I pass on to give a proof of the Gospel—not, to be sure, of Jewry, but of Pontus—having become meanwhile adulterated; and this shall indicate the order by which we proceed. We lay it down as our first position, that the evangelical Testament has apostles for its authors, to whom was assigned by the Lord Himself this office of publishing the gospel. Since, however, there are apostolic men also,

they are yet not alone, but appear with apostles and after apostles; because the preaching of disciples might be open to the suspicion of an affectation of glory, if there did not accompany it the authority of the masters, which means that of Christ, for it was that which made the apostles their masters. Of the apostles, therefore, John and Matthew first instill faith into us; whilst of apostolic men, Luke and Mark renew it afterwards . . . Now, of the authors whom we possess, Marcion seems to have singled out Luke for his mutilating process. Luke, however, was not an apostle, but only an apostolic man; not a master, but a disciple, and so inferior to a master—at least as far subsequent to him as the apostle whom he followed (and that, no doubt, was Paul) was subsequent to the others; so that, had Marcion even published his Gospel in the name of St. Paul himself, the single authority of the document, destitute of all support from preceding authorities, would not be a sufficient basis for our faith. There would be still wanted that Gospel which St. Paul found in existence, to which he yielded his belief, and with which he so earnestly wished his own to agree, that he actually on that account went up to Jerusalem to know and consult the apostles, "lest he should run, or had been running in vain;" in other words, that the faith which he had learned, and the gospel which he was preaching, might be in accordance with theirs. Then, at last, having conferred with the (primitive) authors, and having agreed with them touching the rule of faith, they joined their hands in fellowship, and divided their labors thenceforth in the office of preaching the gospel, so that they were to go to the Jews, and St. Paul to the Jews and the Gentiles. Inasmuch, therefore, as the enlightener of St. Luke himself desired the authority of his predecessors for both his own faith and preaching, how much more may not I require for Luke's Gospel that which was necessary for the Gospel of his master.

4.5.3 For even Luke's form of the Gospel men usually ascribe to Paul. And it may well seem that the works which disciples publish belong to their masters. Well, then, Marcion ought to be called to a strict account concerning these (other Gospels) also, for having omitted them, and insisted in preference on Luke; as if they, too, had not had free course in the churches, as well as Luke's Gospel, from the beginning. Nay, it is even more credible that they existed from the very beginning; for, being the work of apostles, they were prior, and coeval in origin with the churches themselves. But how comes it to pass, if the apostles published nothing, that their disciples were more forward in such a work; for they could not have been disciples, without any instruction from their masters? . . . For if the (Gospels) of the apostles have come down to us in their integrity, whilst Luke's, which is received amongst us, so far accords with their rule as to be on a par with them in permanency of reception in the churches, it clearly follows that Luke's Gospel also has come down to us in like integrity until the sacrilegious treatment of Marcion.

Eusebius, **Ecclesiastical History 3.4.7***

Eusebius tells us that Luke was of "Antiochian parentage" and that he authored two volumes, a Gospel and the Acts.

But Luke, who was of Antiochian parentage and a physician by profession, and who was especially intimate with Paul and well acquainted with the rest of the apostles, has left us, in two inspired books, proofs of that spiritual healing art which he learned from them. One of these books is the Gospel. . . . The other book is the Acts of the Apostles which he composed not from the accounts of others, but from what he had seen himself.

1.4 John

Eusebius, **Ecclesiastical History 5.20.6***

Eusebius reports the testimony of Irenaeus, a famous church father and a pupil of Polycarp, about his time with Polycarp. He mentions Polycarp's contact with John.

I am able to describe the very place in which the blessed Polycarp sat as he discoursed, and his goings out and comings in, and the manner of his life, and physical appearance and his discourses to the people, and the accounts which he gave of his intercourse with John and with the others who had seen the Lord. And as he remembered their words, and what he heard from them concerning the Lord, and concerning his miracles and his teaching, having received them from the eyewitnesses of the Word of Life, Polycarp related all things in harmony with the Scriptures.

Irenaeus, **Against Heresies 3.1.2***

See section 1.1 above for the text. Note that Irenaeus says the disciple John, the one who leaned on Jesus' breast, did indeed publish a Gospel.

33

PART

2

Jesus according to the Synoptists

2

The Birth and Childhood
of Jesus

2.1 The Prologue to Luke (Luke 1:1–4) (*JaS* 1)

2 Maccabees 2:19–32

The following text shows how an ancient writer might begin a literary work with a preface or word of introduction. It also highlights the selectivity of some writers in the events they record.

[19]The story of Judas Maccabeus and his brothers, and the purification of the great temple, and the dedication of the altar, [20]and further the wars against Antiochus Epiphanes and his son Eupator, [21]and the appearances that came from heaven to those who fought bravely for Judaism, so that though few in number they seized the whole land and pursued the barbarian hordes, [22]and regained possession of the temple famous throughout the world, and liberated the city, and reestablished the laws that were about to be abolished, while the Lord with great kindness became gracious to them—[23]all this, which has been set forth by Jason of Cyrene in five volumes, we shall attempt to condense into a single book. [24]For considering the flood of statistics involved and the difficulty there is for those who wish to enter upon the narratives of history because of the mass of material, [25]we have aimed to please those who wish to read, to make it easy for those who are inclined to memorize, and to profit all readers. [26]For us who have undertaken the toil of abbreviating, it is no light matter but calls for sweat and loss of sleep, [27]just as it is not easy for one who prepares a banquet and seeks the benefit of others. Nevertheless, to secure the gratitude of many we will gladly endure the uncomfortable toil, [28]leaving the responsibility for exact details to the compiler, while devoting our effort to arriving at the outlines of the condensation. [29]For as the master builder of a new house must be concerned with the whole construction, while the one who undertakes its painting and decoration has to consider only what is suitable for its adornment, such in my judgment is the case with us. [30]It is the duty of the original historian to occupy the ground, to discuss matters from every side, and to take trouble with details, [31]but the one who recasts the narrative should be allowed to strive for brevity of expression and to forego exhaustive treatment. [32]At this point therefore let us begin our narrative, without adding any more to what has already been said; for it would be foolish to lengthen the preface while cutting short the history itself.

Josephus, **Antiquities** *preface 1–4*
§§1–26

Josephus, the first-century Jewish historian, writes the following introduction for his work titled *The Antiquities of the Jews.*

[1]Those who undertake to write histories do not, I perceive, take that trouble on one and the same account, but for many reasons, and those such as are very different one from another; [2]for some of them apply themselves to this part of learning to show their skill in composition, and that they may therein acquire a reputation for speaking finely; others of them there are, who write histories, in order to gratify those that happened to be concerned in them, and on that account have spared no pains, but rather go beyond their own abilities in the performance; [3]but others there are, who, of necessity and by force, are driven to write history, because they are concerned in the facts, and so cannot excuse themselves from committing them to writing, for the advantage of posterity; nay, there are not a few who are induced to draw their historical facts out of darkness into light, and to produce them for the benefit of the public on account of the great importance of the facts themselves with which they have been concerned. [4]Now of these several reasons for writing history, I must profess the two last were my own reasons also; for since I was myself interested in that war which we Jews had with the Romans, and knew myself its particular actions, and what conclusion it had, I was forced to give the history of it, because I saw that others perverted the truth of those actions in their writings. [5]Now I have undertaken the present work, as thinking it will appear to all the Greeks worthy of their study; for it will contain all our antiquities, and the constitution of our government, as interpreted out of the Hebrew Scriptures . . . [7]but because this work would take up a great compass, I separated it into a set treatise by itself, with a beginning of its own, and its own conclusion. . . . [10]I found, therefore, that the second of the Ptolemies was a king who was extraordinarily diligent in what concerned learning and the collection of books; that he was also peculiarly ambitious to procure a translation of our law, and of the constitution of our government therein contained, into the Greek tongue. . . . [17]As I proceed, therefore, I shall accurately describe what is contained in our records, in the order of time that belongs to them; for I have already promised so to do throughout this undertaking; and this without adding anything to what is therein contained, or taking away anything therefrom. . . . [24]I exhort, therefore, my readers to examine this whole undertaking in that view; for thereby it will appear to them, that there is nothing therein disagreeable either to the majesty of God, or to his love to mankind; for all things have here a reference to the nature of the universe; while our legislator speaks some things wisely, but enigmatically, and others under a decent allegory, but still explains such things as required a direct explication plainly and expressly. [25]However, those that have a mind to know the reasons of everything, may find here a very curious philosophical theory, which I now indeed shall waive the explication of; but if God afford me time for it, I will set about writing it after I have finished the present work. [26]I shall now betake myself to the history before me, after I have first mentioned what Moses says of the creation of the world, which I find described in

the sacred books after the manner following.

Letter of Aristeas 1–8

In the opening words of the *Letter of Aristeas*, the ancient writer claims that he produced his work with great care.

[1]A trustworthy narrative has been compiled, Philocrates, of the meeting which we had with Eleazer, high priest of the Jews, arising out of your attaching great importance to hearing a personal account of our mission, its content and purpose. By detailing each aspect I have tried to give you a clear exposition of it, realizing your scholarly disposition, [2]which is a supreme quality in any man who has tried continually to increase his learning and understanding, whether from the accounts (of others) or by actual experience. . . . [8]But lest we prolong the introduction and indulge in idle chatter, we will proceed to the main part of the narrative.

Lucian of Samosata, How to Write History 53–55*

Lucian here gives us a snapshot of his perspective on how history is to be properly written.

[53]Whenever he does use a preface, he will make a two points only, not three like the orators. He will omit the appeal for a favorable hearing and give his audience what will interest and instruct them. For they will give him their attention if he shows that what he is going to say will be important, essential, personal, or useful. [54]He will make what is to come easy to understand and quite clear, if he sets forth the causes and outlines the main events. The best historians have written prefaces of this sort: Herodotus, writing history to preserve events

from time's decay, great and glorious as they were, telling of Greek victories and barbarian defeat; Thucydides too, with his expectation that the war would be great, more memorable, and more important than any that had gone before; and in fact that sufferings in that war were considerable.

[55]After the preface, long or short in proportion to its subject matter, let the transition to the narrative be gentle and easy. For all the body of the history is simply a long narrative. So let it be adorned with the virtues proper to narrative, progressing smoothly, evenly and consistently, free from humps and hollows. Then let its clarity be limpid, achieved, as I have said, both by diction and the interweaving of the matter. For he will make everything distinct and complete, and when he has finished the first topic he will introduce the second, fastened to it and linked with it like a chain, to avoid breaks and a multiplicity of disjointed narratives; no, always the first and second topics must not merely be neighbors but have common matter and overlap.

Thucydides, History of the Peloponnesian War 1.21–22

In this text, we note the careful attention to accuracy that governed Thucydides in his written reconstruction of the Peloponnesian Wars. Similar attention to detail can be found in the introduction to Luke's Gospel (1:1–4). Note how he preferred accuracy to "romance" and "interest," even short-term popularity.

[21]On the whole, however, the conclusions I have drawn from the proofs quoted may, I believe, safely be relied on. Assuredly they will not be disturbed either by the lays of a poet displaying the exaggeration of his craft, or by the compositions of the chroniclers that are attractive at

truth's expense; the subjects they treat of being out of the reach of evidence, and time having robbed most of them of historical value by enthroning them in the region of legend. Turning from these, we can rest satisfied with having proceeded upon the clearest data, and having arrived at conclusions as can be expected in matters of such antiquity. To come to this war: despite the known disposition of the actors in a struggle to overrate its importance, and when it is over to return to their admiration of earlier events, yet an examination of the facts will show that it was much greater than the wars which preceded it.

[22]With reference to the speeches in this history, some were delivered before the war began, others while it was going on; some I heard myself, others I got from various quarters; it was in all cases difficult to carry them word for word in one's memory, so my habit has been to make the speakers say what was in my opinion demanded of them by the various occasions, of course adhering as closely as possible to the general sense of what they really said. And with reference to the narrative of events, far from permitting myself to derive it from the first source that came to hand, I did not even trust my own impressions, but it rests partly on what I saw myself, partly on what others saw for me, the accuracy of the report being always tried by the most severe and detailed test possible. My conclusions have cost me some labor from the want of coincidence between accounts of the same occurrences by different eyewitnesses, arising sometimes from imperfect memory, sometimes form undue partiality for one side or the other. The absence of romance in my history will, I fear, detract somewhat from its interest; but if it be judged useful by those inquirers who desire

an exact knowledge of the past as an aid to the interpretation of the future, which in the course of human things must resemble if it does not reflect it, I shall be content. In fine, I have written my work, not as essay which is to win the applause of the moment, but as a possession for all time.

2.2 Matthew's Genealogy of Jesus (Matt. 1:1–17) (JaS 2)

Josephus, **Life of Flavius Josephus 1** §§1–6

In this autobiographical work, Josephus records his own family line and the availability of "public records" for such a task.

[1]The family from which I am derived is not an ignoble one, but has descended all along from the priests; and as nobility among several people is of a different origin, so with us to be of the sacerdotal dignity, is an indication of the splendor of a family. [2]Now, I am not only sprung from a sacerdotal family in general, but from the first of the twenty-four courses; and as among us there is not only a considerable difference between one family of each course and another, I am of the chief family of that first course also; nay, further, by my mother I am of the royal blood; for the children of Asamoneus, from whom that family was derived, had both the office of the high priesthood, and the dignity of a king, for a long time together. [3]I will accordingly set down my progenitors in order. My grandfather's father was named Simon, with the addition of Psellus: he lived at the same time with that son of Simon the high priest, who first of all the high priests was named Hyrcanus. This Simon Psellus had nine sons, [4]one of whom was Matthias, called Ephlias;

he married the daughter of Jonathan the high priest; which Jonathan was the first of the sons of Asamoneus, who was high priest, and was the brother of Simon the high priest also. This Matthias had a son called Matthias Curtus, and that in the first year of the government of Hyrcanus: [5]his son's name was Joseph, born in the ninth year of the reign of Alexandra: his son Matthias was born in the tenth year of the reign of Archelaus; as was I born to Matthias in the first year of the reign of Caius Caesar. I have three sons: Hyrcanus, the eldest, was born in the fourth year of the reign of Vespasian, as was Justus born in the seventh, and Agrippa in the ninth. [6]Thus have I set down the genealogy of my family as I have found described in the public records, and so bid adieu to those who calumniate me [as of a lower original].

Eusebius, Ecclesiastical History 1.7.1–17*

In this text from Eusebius, Julius Africanus seeks to explain the differences between Matthew and Luke and also reports how some families kept genealogical records.

[1]Matthew and Luke in their gospels have given us the genealogy of Christ differently, and many suppose that they are at variance with one another. Since as a consequence every believer, in ignorance of the truth, has been zealous to invent some explanation which shall harmonize the two passages, permit us to subjoin the account of the matter which has come down to us, and which is given by Africanus, who was mentioned by us just above, in his epistle to Aristides, where he discusses the harmony of the gospel genealogies. After refuting the opinions of others as forced and deceptive, he gives the account which he

had received from tradition in these words: [2]"For whereas the names of the generations were reckoned in Israel either according to nature or according to law;—according to nature by the succession of legitimate offspring, and according to law whenever another raised up a child to the name of a brother dying childless; for because a clear hope of resurrection was not yet given they had a representation of the future promise by a kind of mortal resurrection, in order that the name of the one deceased might be perpetuated;—[3]whereas then some of those who are inserted in this genealogical table succeeded by natural descent, the son to the father, while others, though born of one father, were ascribed by name to another, mention was made of both—of those who were progenitors in fact and of those who were so only in name. [4]Thus neither of the gospels is in error, for one reckons by nature, the other by law. For the line of descent from Solomon and that from Nathan were so involved, the one with the other, by the raising up of children to the childless and by second marriages, that the same persons are justly considered to belong at one time to one, at another time to another; that is, at one time to the reputed fathers, at another to the actual fathers. So that both these accounts are strictly true and come down to Joseph with considerable intricacy indeed, yet quite accurately. [5]But in order that what I have said may be made clear I shall explain the interchange of the generations. If we reckon the generations from David through Solomon, the third from the end is found to be Matthan, who begat Jacob the father of Joseph. But if, with Luke, we reckon them from Nathan the son of David, in like manner the third from the end is Melchi, whose son Eli was the father of Joseph. For Joseph was the son of Eli, the son of Melchi. [6]Joseph therefore being the object proposed to us, it must be shown how it is that each is recorded to be his father, both Jacob, who derived his descent from Solomon, and Eli, who derived his from Nathan; first how it is that these two, Jacob and Eli, were brothers, and then how it is that their fathers, Matthan and Melchi, although of different families, are declared to be grandfathers of Joseph. [7]Matthan and Melchi having married in succession the same woman, begat children who were uterine brothers, for the law did not prohibit a widow, whether such by divorce or by the death of her husband, from marrying another. [8]By Estha then (for this was the woman's name according to tradition) Matthan, a descendant of Solomon, first begat Jacob. And when Matthan was dead, Melchi, who traced his descent back to Nathan, being of the same tribe but of another family, married her as before said, and begat a son Eli. [9]Thus we shall find the two, Jacob and Eli, although belonging to different families, yet brethren by the same mother. Of these the one, Jacob, when his brother Eli had died childless, took the latter's wife and begat by her a son Joseph, his own son by nature and in accordance with reason. Wherefore also it is written: 'Jacob begat Joseph.' But according to law he was the son of Eli, for Jacob, being the brother of the latter, raised up seed to him. [10]Hence the genealogy traced through him will not be rendered void, which the evangelist Matthew in his enumeration gives thus: 'Jacob begat Joseph.' But Luke, on the other hand, says: 'Who was the son, as was supposed' (for this he also adds), 'of Joseph, the son of Eli, the son of Melchi'; for he could not more clearly express the generation according to law. And the expression 'he begat' he has omitted

in his genealogical table up to the end, tracing the genealogy back to Adam the son of God. This interpretation is neither incapable of proof nor is it an idle conjecture. [11]For the relatives of our Lord according to the flesh, whether with the desire of boasting or simply wishing to state the fact, in either case truly, have banded down the following account: Some Idumean robbers, having attacked Ascalon, a city of Palestine, carried away from a temple of Apollo which stood near the walls, in addition to other booty, Antipater, son of a certain temple slave named Herod. And since the priest was not able to pay the ransom for his son, Antipater was brought up in the customs of the Idumeans, and afterward was befriended by Hyrcanus, the high priest of the Jews. [12]And having been sent by Hyrcanus on an embassy to Pompey, and having restored to him the kingdom which had been invaded by his brother Aristobulus, he had the good fortune to be named procurator of Palestine. But Antipater having been slain by those who were envious of his great good fortune was succeeded by his son Herod, who was afterward, by a decree of the senate, made King of the Jews under Antony and Augustus. His sons were Herod and the other tetrarchs. These accounts agree also with those of the Greeks. [13]But as there had been kept in the archives up to that time the genealogies of the Hebrews as well as of those who traced their lineage back to proselytes, such as Achior the Ammonite and Ruth the Moabitess, and to those who were mingled with the Israelites and came out of Egypt with them, Herod, inasmuch as the lineage of the Israelites contributed nothing to his advantage, and since he was goaded with the consciousness of his own ignoble extraction, burned all the genealogical records, thinking that he might appear of noble origin if no one else were able, from the public registers, to trace back his lineage to the patriarchs or proselytes and to those mingled with them, who were called Georae. [14]A few of the careful, however, having obtained private records of their own, either by remembering the names or by getting them in some other way from the registers, pride themselves on preserving the memory of their noble extraction. Among these are those already mentioned, called Desposyni, on account of their connection with the family of the Saviour. Coming from Nazara and Cochaba, villages of Judea, into other parts of the world, they drew the aforesaid genealogy from memory and from the book of daily records as faithfully as possible. [15]Whether then the case stand thus or not no one could find a clearer explanation, according to my own opinion and that of every candid person. And let this suffice us, for, although we can urge no testimony in its support, we have nothing better or truer to offer. In any case the Gospel states the truth." [16]And at the end of the same epistle he adds these words: "Matthan, who was descended from Solomon, begat Jacob. And when Matthan was dead, Melchi, who was descended from Nathan begat Eli by the same woman. Eli and Jacob were thus uterine brothers. Eli having died childless, Jacob raised up seed to him, begetting Joseph, his own son by nature, but by law the son of Eli. Thus Joseph was the son of both." [17]Thus far Africanus. And the lineage of Joseph being thus traced, Mary also is virtually shown to be of the same tribe with him, since, according to the law of Moses, inter-marriages between different tribes were not permitted. For the command is to marry one of the same family and lineage, so that the inheritance may not pass from tribe to tribe.

Origen, Against Celsus 1.28, 32, 33, 39*

The following selections from Origen's work *Against Celsus* deal with the question of Jesus' unusual birth. It is here that we learn of a Jewish theory about Mary's relationship with a soldier named Panthera.

[28]And since, in imitation of a rhetorician training a pupil, he introduces a Jew, who enters into a personal discussion with Jesus, and speaks in a very childish manner, altogether unworthy of the gray hairs of a philosopher, let me endeavor, to the best of my ability, to examine his statements, and show that he does not maintain, throughout the discussion, the consistency due to the character of a Jew. For he represents him disputing with Jesus, and confuting Him, as he thinks, on many points; and in the first place, he accuses Him of having "invented his birth from a virgin," and upbraids Him with being "born in a certain Jewish village, of a poor woman of the country, who gained her subsistence by spinning, and who was turned out of doors by her husband, a carpenter by trade, because she was convicted of adultery; that after being driven away by her husband, and wandering about for a time, she disgracefully gave birth to Jesus, an illegitimate child, who having hired himself out as a servant in Egypt on account of his poverty, and having there acquired some miraculous powers, on which the Egyptians greatly pride themselves, returned to his own country, highly elated on account of them, and by means of these proclaimed himself a God." Now, as I cannot allow anything said by unbelievers to remain unexamined, but must investigate everything from the beginning, I give it as my opinion that all these things worthily harmonize

with the predictions that Jesus is the Son of God. . . .

[32]But let us now return to where the Jew is introduced, speaking of the mother of Jesus, and saying that "when she was pregnant she was turned out of doors by the carpenter to whom she had been betrothed, as having been guilty of adultery, and that she bore a child to a certain soldier named Panthera;" and let us see whether those who have blindly concocted these fables about the adultery of the Virgin with Panthera, and her rejection by the carpenter, did not invent these stories to overturn His miraculous conception by the Holy Ghost: for they could have falsified the history in a different manner, on account of its extremely miraculous character, and not have admitted, as it were against their will, that Jesus was born of no ordinary human marriage. It was to be expected, indeed, that those who would not believe the miraculous birth of Jesus would invent some falsehood. And their not doing this in a credible manner, but (their) preserving the fact that it was not by Joseph that the Virgin conceived Jesus, rendered the falsehood very palpable to those who can understand and detect such inventions. . . .

[33]. . . And if there be any truth in the doctrine of the physiognomists, whether Zopyrus, or Loxus, or Polemon, or any other who wrote on such a subject, and who profess to know in some wonderful way that all bodies are adapted to the habits of the souls, must there have been for that soul which was to dwell with miraculous power among men, and work mighty deeds, a body produced, as Celsus thinks, by an act of adultery between Panthera and the Virgin?! Why, from such unhallowed intercourse there must rather have been brought forth some fool to do injury to mankind,—a teacher of licentiousness and wickedness, and other evils; and not of temperance, and righteousness, and the other virtues! . . .

[39]I do not think it necessary to grapple with an argument advanced not in a serious but in a scoffing spirit, such as the following: "If the mother of Jesus was beautiful, then the god whose nature is not to love a corruptible body, had intercourse with her because she was beautiful;" or, "It was improbable that the god would entertain a passion for her, because she was neither rich nor of royal rank, seeing no one, even of her neighbors, knew her." And it is in the same scoffing spirit that he adds: "When hated by her husband, and turned out of doors, she was not saved by divine power, nor was her story believed. Such things, he says, have no connection with the kingdom of heaven." In what respect does such language differ from that of those who pour abuse on others on the public streets, and whose words are unworthy of any serious attention?

2.3 The Announcement of John the Baptist's Birth (Luke 1:5–25) (JaS 3)

m. Tamid 5–7*

The point of the following selections from the Mishnah tractate *Tamid* is to give a general idea of how the national sacrifice might have been offered.

[5.1]A. The superintendent said to them, "Say one blessing."

B. They said a blessing, pronounced the Ten Commandments, the *Shema* [Hear O Israel (Dt. 6:4–9)], *And it shall come to pass if you shall hearken* (Dt. 11:13–21), and *And the Lord spoke to Moses* (Num. 15:37–41).

C. They blessed the people with three blessings: *True and sure, Abodah,* and the blessing of priests.

D. And on the Sabbath they add a blessing for the outgoing priestly watch.

²A. [The superintendent] said to them, "Those who are new to [the preparation of] the incense, come and cast lots."

B. They cast lots.

C. Whoever won won.

D. "Those who are new with those who have had a chance [compare Song of Songs 7:14], come and cast lots on who will bring up the limbs from the ramp to the altar."

E. R. Eliezer b. Jacob says, "He who brings up the limbs to the ramp [without another lottery] is the one who brings them up onto the altar."

³A. They handed them [who had no assignment] to the ministers.

B. They did remove their clothing from them.

C. And they left them only their underpants alone.

D. And there were wall niches there, on which were written [the names] of the various pieces of clothing.

⁴A. He who won [the right to offer] the incense did take the spoon. . . .

⁵A. He who won [the right to the ashes with] the firepan took the silver firepan and went up to the top of the altar and cleared away the cinders in either side and scooped up [ashes with the firepan].

B. He came down and emptied them out into that [firepan] of gold. . . .

⁶A. [When] they reached the area between the porch and the altar, one man took the shovel and tosses it between the porch and the altar.

B. No one in Jerusalem hears the voice of his fellow on account of the noise of the shovel.

C. And three purposes did it serve: (1) a priest who hears its sound knows

that his brethren the priests enter in to prostrate themselves, and he then runs and comes along; (2) and a son of a Levite who hears its noise knows that his brethren, the Levites, enter to say their song, and he then runs and comes along; (3) and the head of the priestly watch then had the unclean people stand at the eastern gate.

⁶·¹A. They [the priests who were in charge of the incense and of removing the ashes] began to go up onto the steps of the porch.

B. Those who had won [the right to remove] the ashes of the inner altar and the candlestick went before them [= M. 3:6A].

C. He who had won [the right to clean] the ashes of the inner altar went in and took the basket [left at M. 3:9] and prostrated himself and went out.

D. He who had won [the right to remove] the ashes of the candlestick entered in.

E. And [if] he found the two easternmost lamps still flickering, he clears out the eastern one and leaves the western one flickering,

F. for from it did he kindle the candlestick at twilight.

G. [If] he found that it had gone out, he cleaned it out and kindled it from the altar of the whole offering [M. 3:9E–F].

H. He took the oil jar from the second step [M. 3:9I] and prostrated himself and went out.

²A. He who had won [the right to make use of] the firepan heaped up the cinders on the [inner] altar and tamped them down with the back of the firepan and prostrated himself and went out.

³A. He who had won [the right to prepare] the incense did take the dish from the middle of the ladle and gave it [the ladle] to his friend or his relative. . . .

F. If he was a high priest, the superintendent says, "My lord, high priest, offer the incense."

G. The people departed, and he offered the incense and prostrated himself and went out.

7.1 A. When the high priest enters to prostrate himself, three [priests] support him: one by the right hand, one by the left, and one by the precious stones [on the shoulder pieces of the ephod, Ex. 28:9].

B. And as soon as the superintendent heard the sound of the feet of the high priest, that he goes out [of the *heikhal*], he raised the curtain for him.

C. He went in and prostrated himself and went out.

D. And his brethren the priests went in and prostrated themselves and went out.

2 A. They [the priests who had participated] came and stood on the steps of the porch.

B. They who were first [the one who removed the ashes of the inner altar, and the one who cleaned up the candlestick, the one who carried the shovel and the one who offered the incense and his associate] took up a position at the south of their brethren, the priests.

C. And five utensils were in their hand: (1) the ash bin in the hand of one, and (2) the oil jar in the hand of one, and (3) the fire shovel in the hand of one, and (4) the [incense] dish in the hand of one, and (5) the ladle and its cover [M. 5:4] in the hand of one.

D. They said one [priestly] blessing for the people [Num. 6:24–26].

E. But: In the provinces they say it as three blessings, and in the sanctuary, as one blessing.

F. In the sanctuary they would pronounce the [divine] name as it is written, and in the provinces, by an epithet.

G. In the provinces the priests raise up the palms of their hands as high as their shoulders, and in the sanctuary, over their heads,

H. except for the high priest, who does not raise his hands higher than the frontlet.

I. R. Judah says, "Even the high priest raises his hands above the frontlet,

J. "since it is said, *And Aaron lifted up his hands toward the people and blessed them* (Lev. 9:22)" [M. Sot. 7:6].

3 A. When the high priest wants to burn the offerings, he would go up on the ramp, with the prefect at his right.

B. [When] he reached the half way point of the ramp, the prefect took him by the right hand and led him up and led him up.

C. The first [of the nine priests, M. 4:3] handed him the head and the hind leg, and he laid his hands on them and tossed them [into the altar fire].

D. The second handed over to the first the two forelegs. He gives them to the high priest. And he laid his hands on them and tossed them [into the altar fire].

E. The second departed, going on his way.

F. And so did they hand over to him all the rest of the limbs, and he lays his hands on them, and tosses them [into the altar fires].

G. And when he wants, he lays on his hands, but others throw [the pieces into the fire].

H. He comes then to walk around the altar [toward the right, to the southwestern corner].

I. From what point does he begin?

J. From the southeastern corner, then northeastern one, northwestern, and southwestern [see M. Zeb. 5:3].

K. They gave him wine to pour out.

L. The prefect stands at the corner, with a flag in his hand, and two priests stand at the table of the fat pieces, with two silver trumpets in their hands.

M. They sounded a prolonged sound, a wavering sound, and a prolonged sound.

N. They came and stood near Ben Arza, one on his right, one on his left.

O. He stepped down to pour out the wine, and the prefect waved the flag, and Ben Arza dashed the cymbal, and the Levites broke out in song.

P. [When] they reached a break [in the singing], they sounded a prolonged sound, and the people prostrated themselves.

Q. At every break [in the singing] was a prolonged blast, and at every prolonged blast, a prostration.

R. This is the order of the daily whole offering in the liturgy of the house of our God. May it be [his] will that it be rebuilt, soon, in our own days. Amen.

⁴A. The singing which the Levites did sing in the sanctuary:

B. On the first day they did sing, *The earth is the Lord's and the fulness thereof, the world and they who live therein* (Ps. 24).

C. On the second day they did sing, *Great is the Lord and highly to be praised in the city of our God, even upon his holy hill* (Ps. 48).

Letter of Aristeas 95

The number of priests involved in presenting the daily sacrifices is estimated at seven hundred in the *Letter of Aristeas*, though the total number of priests at the time was probably several thousand.

A general silence reigns, so that one might think that there was not a single man in the place although the number of ministers in attendance is more than seven hundred, in addition to a large number of assistants bringing forward the animals for sacrifice.

2.4 The Birth Announcement to Mary (Luke 1:26–38) (*JaS* 4)

Plutarch, Life of Alexander *II*

It is often suggested that the report of Jesus' divine birth was not so unusual for his culture. For comparison purposes, we present here the account of Plutarch on the divine birth of Alexander. The simplicity of the account in Luke should be compared to this text.

As for the lineage of Alexander, on his father's side he was a descendant of Heracles through Caranus, and on his mother's side a descendant of Aeacus through Neoptolemus; this is accepted without any question. And we are told that Philip, after being initiated into the mysteries of Samothrace at the same time with Olympias, he himself being still a youth and she an orphan child, fell in love with her and betrothed himself to her at once with the consent of her brother, Arymbas. Well, then, the night before that on which the marriage was consummated, the bride dreamed that there was a peal of thunder and that a thunder-bolt fell upon her womb, and that thereby much fire was kindled, which broke into flames that travelled all about, and then was extinguished. At a later time, too, after the marriage, Philip dreamed that he was putting a seal upon his wife's womb; and the device of the seal, as he thought, was the figure of a lion. The other seers, now, were led by the vision to suspect that Philip needed to put a closer watch upon his marriage relations; but Aristander of Telmessus said that the woman was pregnant, since no seal was put upon what was empty, and pregnant of a son whose nature would be bold and lion-like. Moreover, a serpent was once seen lying stretched out by the side of Olympias as she slept, and we are told that this, more than anything else, dulled the ardour of Philip's attentions to his wife, so that he no longer came often to sleep by her side, either because he feared that some spells and enchantments might be practised upon him by her, or because he shrank for her embraces in the conviction that she was the partner of a superior being.

The following selections suggest an early and widespread tradition that Mary was from the line of David.

Justin Martyr, Dialogue with Trypho 43, 45, 100*

[43]As, then, circumcision began with Abraham, and the Sabbath and sacrifices and offerings and feasts with Moses, and it has been proved they were enjoined on account of the hardness of your people's heart, so it was necessary, in accordance with the Father's will, that they should have an end in Him who was born of a virgin, of the family of Abraham and tribe of Judah, and of David; in Christ the Son of God, who was proclaimed as about to come to all the world, to be the everlasting law and the everlasting covenant, even as the aforementioned prophecies show. . . .

[45]. . . Since those who did that which is universally, naturally, and eternally good are pleasing to God, they shall be saved through this Christ in the resurrection equally with those righteous men who were before them,

namely Noah, and Enoch, and Jacob, and whoever else there be, along with those who have known this Christ, Son of God, who was before the morning star and the moon, and submitted to become incarnate, and be born of this virgin of the family of David, in order that, by this dispensation, the serpent that sinned from the beginning, and the angels like him, may be destroyed, and that death may be contemned. . . .

[100]. . . Accordingly He revealed to us all that we have perceived by His grace out of the Scriptures, so that we know Him to be the first-begotten of God, and to be before all creatures; likewise to be the Son of the patriarchs, since He assumed flesh by the Virgin of their family, and submitted to become a man without comeliness, dishonored, and subject to suffering. Hence, also, among His words He said, when He was discoursing about His future sufferings: "The Son of man must suffer many things, and be rejected by the Pharisees and Scribes, and be crucified, and on the third day rise again." He said then that He was the Son of man, either because of His birth by the Virgin, who was, as I said, of the family of David, and Jacob, and Isaac, and Abraham; or because Adam was the father both of Himself and of those who have been first enumerated from whom Mary derives her descent. . . .

Irenaeus, Against Heresies 3.21.5*

And when He says, "Hear, O house of David," He performed the part of one indicating that He whom God promised David that He would raise up from the fruit of his belly (ventris) an eternal King, is the same who was born of the Virgin, herself of the lineage of David.

Tertullian, An Answer to the Jews 9*

And that the virgin of whom it behooved Christ to be born (as we have above mentioned) must derive her lineage of the seed of David, the prophet in subsequent passages evidently asserts. "And there shall be born," he says, "a rod from the root of Jesse"—which rod is Mary—"and a flower shall ascend from his root: and there shall rest upon him the Spirit of God, the spirit of wisdom and understanding, the spirit of discernment and piety, the spirit of counsel and truth; the spirit of God's fear shall fill Him." For to none of men was the universal aggregation of spiritual credentials appropriate, except to Christ; paralleled as He is to a "flower" by reason of glory, by reason of grace; but accounted "of the root of Jesse," whence His origin is to be deduced,—to wit, through Mary. For He was from the native soil of Bethlehem, and from the house of David; as, among the Romans, Mary is described in the census, of whom is born Christ.

Martyrdom and Ascension of Isaiah 11.2

And I saw a woman of the family of David the prophet whose name (was) Mary, and she (was) a virgin, and was betrothed to a man whose name (was) Joseph, a carpenter, and he also (was) of the seed and family of the righteous David of Bethlehem in Judah.

Gospel of the Nativity of Mary 1.1*

The blessed and glorious ever-virgin Mary, sprung from the royal stock and family of David, born in the city of Nazareth, was brought up at Jerusalem in the temple of the Lord. Her father was named Joachim, and her mother Anna. Her father's house was from Galilee and the city of Nazareth, but her mother's family from Bethlehem. . . .

Psalms of Solomon 17–18 (excerpts)

Several verses from *Psalms of Solomon* 17–18 (17.1–4, 21–23, 25–26, 30, 35–37; 18.3, 5) reveal that a nationalistic deliverer/messiah was anticipated who would destroy Israel's enemies and reign over subjugated Gentiles as well as the Israelite nation, bringing cleansing, purity, and blessing. This messiah is a Son of David. See section 9.17 below for all of *Psalms of Solomon* 17–18.

2.5 Joseph's Concern over Mary's Condition and the Announcement to Him (Matt. 1:18–25) (JaS 7)

m. Soṭah 1.1, 5; 5.1*

The following selections from the Mishnah tractate *Soṭah* reveal how shameful public trials could become. For the text of 5.1, see section 5.5 below.

[1.1]A. He who expresses jealousy to his wife [concerning her relations with another man (Num 5:14)]—

B. R. Eliezer says, "He expresses jealousy before two witnesses, and he imposes on her the requirement of drinking the bitter water on the testimony of a single witness or even on his own evidence. . . ."

[1.5]A. [Now] if she said, "I am unclean," she gives a quittance for her marriage contract [which is not paid over to her], and goes forth [with a writ of divorce].

B. And if she said, "I am clean," they bring her up to the eastern gate, which is at the entrance to Nicanor's Gate.

C. There it is that they force accused wives to drink the bitter water,

D. and they purify women after childbirth and purify lepers.

E. And a priest grabs her clothes—if they tear, they tear, and if they are ripped up, they are ripped up—until he bears her breast.

F. And he tears her hair apart [Num 5:18].

G. R. Judah says, "If she had pretty breasts, he did not let them show. And if she had pretty hair, he did not pull it apart."

m. Gittin 2.5; 9.3–4, 8*

These selections from Mishnah tractate *Gittin* reveal something of the process for securing a divorce, including the writ, witnesses, and the conditions, or terms, in general.

2.5A. All are valid for the writing of a writ of divorce,

B. even a deaf-mute, an idiot, or a minor.

C. A woman may write her own writ of divorce, and a man may write his quittance [a receipt for the payment of the marriage contract],

D. for the confirmation of the writ of divorce is solely through its signatures [of the witnesses = M. 2:1I].

E. All are valid for delivering a writ of divorce,

F. except for a deaf-mute, an idiot, and a minor,

G. a blind man, and a gentile.

9.3A. The text of the writ of divorce [is as follows]:

B. "Lo, you are permitted to any man."

C. R. Judah says, "[In Aramaic]: Let this be from me your writ of divorce, letter of dismissal, and deed of liberation, that you may marry anyone you want."

D. The text of a writ of emancipation [is as follows]:

E. "Lo, you are a free girl, lo, you are your own [possession]" [cf. Dt. 21:14].

9.4A. There are three writs of divorce which are invalid,

B. but if the wife [subsequently] remarried [on the strength of those documents],

C. the offspring is [nonetheless] valid:

I D. [If] he wrote it in his own handwriting, but there are no witnesses on it;

II E. there are witnesses on it, but it is not dated;

III F. it is dated, but there is only a single witness—

G. lo, these are the three kinds of invalid writs of divorce;

H. but if the wife [subsequently] remarried,

I. the offspring is valid.

J. R. Eleazar says, "Even though there are no witnesses on it [the document itself], but he handed it over to her in the presence of witnesses,

K. "it is valid.

L. "And she collects [her marriage contract] from mortgaged property,

M. "For witnesses sign the writ of divorce only for the good order of the world."

9.8A. A writ of divorce which one wrote in Hebrew with its witnesses' signing in Greek,

B. [or which he wrote in] Greek, with its witnesses' signing in Hebrew,

C. [or which] one witness [signed] in Hebrew and one in Greek,

D. [or which] the scribe wrote which one witness [signed, with the scribe as the second witness],

E. is valid.

F. [If it was written], "Mr. So-and-so, a witness" it is valid.

G. "The son of Mr. So-and so, a witness," it is valid.

H. "Mr. So-and-so, son of Mr. So-and-so," but he did not write, "a witness," it is valid.

I. And thus did the scrupulous in Jerusalem do.

J. [If] he wrote [only] his family name and her family name, it is valid.

K. A writ of divorce imposed by a court—

L. in the case of an Israelite court, it is valid.

M. And in the case of a gentile court, it is invalid.

N. In the case of gentiles, they beat him and say to him, "Do what the Israelites tell you to do," and it is valid.

2.6 The Adoration by the Shepherds (Luke 2:8–20) (JaS 9)

In both of the following selections from the Qumran text 1QH, the expression "people with whom he is pleased" refers to the elect of God.

1QH 4.31–35 (= col. 12); 11.7, 9 (= col. 19)

[4.31]To God Most High belong all the acts of justice, and the path of man is not secure except by the spirit which God creates for him [32]to perfect the path of the sons of man so that all his creatures come to know the strength of his power and the extent of his compassion with all the sons of his approval. [33]And dread and dismay have gripped me, all my /bones/ have fractured, my heart has melted like wax in front of the fire, my knees give way like water which flows down a slope/ [34]for I have remem-

bered my faults with the disloyalty of my ancestors, when the wicked rose up against your covenant [35]and the doomed against your word. . . .

[11.7]I know that truth is in your mouth, and justice in your hand. . . . [9]and in your goodness, abundance of forgiveness, and your compassion for all the sons of your approval. For you have taught them the basis of your truth.

Shemoneh Esreh, *benediction 17**

The people of God, according to this text, is Israel. Specifically, it refers to those within the nation who long for God to restore worship to the temple and who will receive his mercy when he does return.

Be pleased, Lord our God, with your people Israel and with their prayer. Bring back the worship into the Holy of Holies of your house and accept in love and pleasure the sacrifices of Israel and her prayer. And may the worship offered by Israel your people be pleasing to you always. O that our eyes might see your return with mercy to Zion. Blessed are you, Lord, who causes your presence to return to Zion.

2.7 The Visit of the Magi to Bethlehem (Matt. 2:1–12) (JaS 11)

b. Qiddušin 70*ᵃ**

This Talmud text discusses the *mamzer* as the illegitimate child of a slave or a Gentile. Only if a tradition like that of Panthera were true (noted in the Origen excerpt, 2.2 above), could this be applied to Jesus, and that is not the case.

MAMZERIM. How do we know it?—Because it is written: And Sanballat the Horonite, and Tobiah the slave, the Ammonite, heard it: and it is [also] written, [Moreover in those days the nobles of Judah sent many letters unto Tobiah . . .] For there were many in Judah sworn unto him, because he [Tobiah] was the son-in-law of Shechaniah the son of Arah; and his son Jehohanan had taken the daughter of Meshullam the son of Berchiah to wife. Now he [the Tanna of our Mishnah] holds that if a heathen or a slave has intercourse with the daughter of an Israelite, the issue is mamzer.

2.8 A Reenactment of Israel's Journey: Jesus to Egypt and Back alongside Unjust Suffering (Matt. 2:13–21) (JaS 12)

In the following selections from *Antiquities*, Josephus records Herod's vicious treatment of his family, friends, acquaintances, and subjects when they appeared to challenge him in any way or to take lightly his right to rule. Mariamne was Herod's wife.

Josephus, Antiquities 15.7.4 §§218–231; 16.5.4 §§150–159

15.7.4 [218]Upon these new acquisitions, he grew more magnificent, and conducted Caesar as far as Antioch; but upon his return, as much as his prosperity was augmented by the foreign additions that had been made him, so much the greater were the distresses that came upon him in his own family, and chiefly in the affair of his wife, wherein he formerly appeared to have been most of all fortunate; for the affection he had for Mariamne was in no way inferior to the affections of such as are on that account celebrated in history, and this very justly. [219]As for her, she was in other respects a chaste

woman, and faithful to him; yet had she somewhat of a woman rough by nature, and treated her husband imperiously enough, because she saw he was so fond of her as to be enslaved to her. She did not also consider seasonably with herself that she lived under a monarchy, and that she was at another's disposal, and accordingly would behave herself after a saucy manner to him, which yet he usually put off in a jesting way, and bore with moderation and good temper. [220]She would also expose his mother and his sister openly on account of the meanness of their birth, and would speak unkindly of them, insomuch, that there was before this a disagreement of unpardonable hatred among the women, and it was now come to greater reproaches of one another than formerly, [221]which suspicions increased, and lasted a whole year after Herod returned from Caesar. However, these misfortunes, which had been kept under some decency for a great while, burst out all at once upon such an occasion as was now offered; [222]for as the king was one day about noon lain down on his bed to rest him, he called for Mariamne, out of the great affection he had always for her. She came in accordingly, but would not lie down by him; and when he was very desirous of her company, she showed her contempt of him; and added, by way of reproach, that he had caused her father and her brother to be slain; [223]and when he took this injury very unkindly, and was ready to use violence to her in a precipitate manner, the king's sister, Salome, observing that he was more than ordinarily disturbed, sent in to the king his cupbearer who had been prepared long beforehand for such a design, and bade him tell the king how Mariamne had persuaded him to give his assistance in preparing a love potion for him; [224]and if he appeared to be greatly concerned, and to ask what that love potion was, to tell him that she had the potion, and that he was desired only to give it him; but that in case he did not appear to be much concerned at this potion, to let the thing drop; and that if he did so no harm should thereby come to him. When she had given him these instructions, she sent him in at this time to make such a speech. [225]So he went in after a composed manner, to gain credit to what he should say, and yet somewhat hastily; and said, that Mariamne had given him presents, and persuaded him to give him a love potion; and when this moved the king, he said that this love potion was a composition that she had given him, whose effects he did not know, which was the reason of his resolving to give him this information, as the safest course he could take, both for himself and for the king. [226]When Herod heard what he said, and was in an ill disposition before, his indignation grew more violent; and he ordered that eunuch of Mariamne, who was most faithful to her, to be brought to torture about this potion, as well knowing it was not possible that anything small or great could be done without him; [227]and when the man was under the utmost agonies, he could say nothing concerning the thing he was tortured about, but so far he knew, that Mariamne's hatred against him was occasioned by somewhat that Sohemus had said to her. [228]Now as he was saying this, Herod cried out aloud, and said, that Sohemus, who had been at all other times most faithful to him, and to his government, would not have betrayed what injunctions he had given him unless he had had a nearer conversation than ordinary, with Mariamne. [229]So he gave order that Sohemus should be

seized on and slain immediately; but he allowed his wife to take her trial; and got together those that were most faithful to him, and laid an elaborate accusation against her for this love potion and composition, which had been charged upon her by way of calumny only. However, he kept no temper in what he said, and was in too great a passion for judging well about this matter. Accordingly, when the court was at length satisfied that he was so resolved, they passed the sentence of death upon her; [230]but when the sentence was passed upon her, this temper was suggested by himself, and by some others of the court, that she should not be thus hastily put to death, but be laid in prison in one of the fortresses belonging to the kingdom; [231]but Salome and her party labored hard to have the woman put to death; and they prevailed with the king to do so, and advised this out of caution, lest the multitude should be tumultuous if she were suffered to live; and thus was Mariamne led to execution.

16.5.4 [150]Now some there are who stand amazed at the diversity of Herod's nature and purposes; for when we have respect to his magnificence, and the benefits which he bestowed on all mankind, there is no possibility for even those that had the least respect for him to deny, or, not openly to confess, that he had a nature vastly beneficent: [151]but when anyone looks upon the punishments he inflicted, and the injuries he did not only to his subjects, but to his nearest relations, and takes notice of his severe and unrelenting disposition there, he will be forced to allow that he was brutish, and a stranger to all humanity; [152]insomuch that these men suppose his nature to be different, and sometimes at contradiction

53

with itself; but I am myself of another opinion, and imagine that the occasion of both these sort of actions was one and the same; [153]for being a man ambitious of honor, and quite overcome by that passion, he was induced to be magnificent, wherever there appeared any hopes of a future memorial, or of reputation at present; [154]and as his expenses were beyond his abilities, he was necessitated to be harsh to his subjects; for the persons on whom he expended his money were so many, that they made him a very bad procurer of it; [155]and because he was conscious that he was hated by those under him, for the injuries he did them, he thought it not an easy thing to amend his offenses, for that it was inconvenient for his revenues; he therefore strove on the other side to make their ill will an occasion of his gains. [156]As to his own court, therefore, if any one was not very obsequious to him in his language, and would not confess himself to be his slave, or but seem to think of any innovation in his government, he was not able to contain himself, but prosecuted his very kindred and friends, and punished them as if they were enemies; and this wickedness he undertook out of a desire that he might be himself alone honored. [157]Now for this my assertion about that passion of his, we have the greatest evidence, by what he did to honor Caesar and Agrippa, and his other friends; for with what honors he paid his respects to them who were his superiors, the same did he desire to be paid to himself; and which he thought the most excellent present he could make another, he discovered an inclination to have the like presented to himself; [158]but now the Jewish nation is by their law a stranger to all such things, and accustomed to prefer righteousness to

glory; for which reason that nation was not agreeable to him, because it was out of their power to flatter the king's ambition with statues or temples, or any other such performances; [159]and this seems to me to have been at once the occasion of Herod's crimes as to his own courtiers and counsellors, and of his benefactions as to foreigners and those that had no relation to him.

2.9 To Nazareth in Galilee (Matt. 2:22–23; Luke 2:39–40) (JaS 13)

Josephus, Antiquities 17.11.1–4 §§299–317 (excerpts)

In this text, Josephus records the hatred and distrust the Jews had for Archelaus. They sent an entourage to Rome to request Archelaus be deposed, indicting both him and his father for serious crimes against the Jewish people. Nicolaus tried to defend Archelaus, but it was all for naught.

[299]So when Varus had settled these affairs, and had placed the former legion at Jerusalem, he returned back to Antioch; but as for Archelaus, he had new sources of trouble come upon him at Rome, on the occasions following: [300]for an embassage of the Jews was come to Rome, Varus having permitted the nation to send it, that they might petition for the liberty of living by their own laws. Now the number of the ambassadors that were sent by the authority of the nation were fifty, to which they joined above eight thousand of the Jews that were at Rome already. [301]Hereupon Caesar assembled his friends, and the chief men among the Romans, in the temple of Apollo, which he had built at a vast charge; whither the ambassadors came, and a multitude of the Jews that were there already came with them,

as did also Archelaus and his friends; [302]but as for the several kinsmen which Archelaus had, they would not join themselves with him, out of their hatred to him; and yet they thought it too gross a thing for them to assist the ambassadors [against him], as supposing it would be a disgrace to them in Caesar's opinion to think of thus acting in opposition to a man of their own kindred: [303]Philip also was come hither out of Syria, by the persuasion of Varus, with this principal intention to assist his brother [Archelaus]: for Varus was his great friend; but still so, that if there should any change happen in the form of government (which Varus suspected there would), and if any distribution should be made on account of the number that desired the liberty of living by their own laws, that he might not be disappointed, but might have his share in it. . . .

[304]Now upon the liberty that was given to the Jewish ambassadors to speak, they who hoped to obtain a dissolution of kingly government betook themselves to accuse Herod of his iniquities. . . . [309]. . . That Herod had put such abuses upon them as a wild beast would not have put on them, if he had power given him to rule over us; [310]and that although their nation had passed through many subversions and alterations of government, their history gave no account of any calamity they had ever been under, that could be compared with this which Herod had brought upon their nation: [311]that it was for this reason that they thought they might justly and gladly salute Archelaus as king, upon this supposition, that whosoever should be set over their kingdom, he would appear more mild to them than Herod had been; and that they had joined with him in the mourning for his father, in order to gratify him, and were ready

to oblige him in other points also, if they could meet with any degree of moderation from him: [312]but that he seemed to be afraid lest he should not be deemed Herod's own son; and so, without any delay, he immediately let the nation understand his meaning and this before his dominion was well established, since the power of disposing of it belonged to Caesar, who could either give it to him or not as he pleased. [313]That he had given a specimen of his future virtue to his subjects, and with what kind of moderation and good administration he would govern them, by that his first action which concerned them, his own citizens, and God himself also, when he made the slaughter of three thousand of his own countrymen at the temple. How, then could they avoid the just hatred of him, who, to the rest of his barbarity, has added this as one of our crimes, that we have opposed and contradicted him in the exercise of his authority? . . .

[315]Now when the Jews had said this, Nicolaus vindicated the kings from those accusations. . . . [317]When Caesar had heard these pleadings, he dissolved the assembly; but a few days afterwards he appointed Archelaus, not indeed to be king of the whole country, but ethnarch of one half of that which had been subject to Herod, and promised to give him the royal dignity hereafter, if he governed his part virtuously. . . .

Midrash on Psalms §8 on Psalm 2:6

This passage is an example of wordplay in Jewish writings. The wordplays are noted in italicized parentheses. They are all based on variations of the word *anoint*.

Truly it is I that have set (naskati) My King (Ps 2:6). What else can *nasakti* mean? "Anointed" as in the verse

Neither did I anoint (sakti) myself at all (Dan 10:3). Or "melted," as in the verse *A molten (massekah) calf* (Ex 32:4). Or "made great," as in the verse *Eight great (nasik) ones among men* (Micah 5:4), and in the verse *The greatness (nasik) of the north* (Ezek. 32:30). And where have I made my king great? *Upon My holy hill of Zion* (Ps 2:6), as the verse concludes.

3

The Backdrop
to Jesus' Ministry

3.1 The Introduction to Mark (Mark 1:1) (*JaS* 15)

Justin Martyr, **First Apology 66; 67***

Justin's comments represent his description of the gospel genre. He calls it "the memoirs of the apostles." It is our earliest description of the authorial roots of the literary term from the second century. Interestingly, he refers to Luke here in chapter 66 of his *First Apology*. Later in this same work (67.3), as he describes a weekly worship service of the early church, he uses the phrase to refer to the Gospels in general.

⁶⁶And this food is called among us Εὐχαριστία [the Eucharist] of which no one is allowed to partake but the man who believes that the things which we teach are true, and who has been washed with the washing that is for the remission of sins, and unto regeneration, and who is so living as Christ has enjoined. For not as common bread and common drink do we receive these; but in like manner as Jesus Christ our Savior, having been made flesh by the Word of God, had both flesh and blood for our salvation, so likewise have we been taught that the food which is blessed by the prayer of His word, and from which our blood and flesh by transmutation are nourished, is the flesh and blood of that Jesus who was made flesh. For the apostles, in the memoirs composed by them, which are called Gospels,

have thus delivered unto us what was enjoined upon them; that Jesus took bread, and when He had given thanks, said, "This do ye in remembrance of Me, this is My body"; and that, after the same manner, having taken the cup and given thanks, He said, "This is My blood"; and gave it to them alone. Which the wicked devils have imitated in the mysteries of Mithras, commanding the same thing to be done. For, that bread and a cup of water are placed with certain incantations in the mystic rites of one who is being initiated; you either know or can learn.

⁶⁷. . . And on the day called Sunday, all who live in cities or in the country gather together to one place, and the memoirs of the apostles or the writings of the prophets are read, as long as time permits. . . .

3.2 John the Baptist and Scripture (Mark 1:2–6; Matt. 3:1–6; Luke 3:1–6) (*JaS* 16)

Sirach 48:10

Malachi's image of the Elijah-like figure and his ministry, a person who would turn the hearts of the parents to their children, is reflected in the Synoptic Gospels and in the intertestamental Jewish work Sirach.

At the appointed time, it is written,
you are destined to calm the wrath
of God before it breaks out in fury,
to turn the hearts of parents to their
children, and to restore the tribes of
Jacob.

1QS 8.12–16; 9.17–21

The following two citations from *The Rule of
the Community* at Qumran reveal the community's use of Isaiah 40 to express their hope for
divine deliverance at some future time (****
stands for the divine name).

[8.12]And when these exist /as a com-
munity/ in Israel [13]/in compliance
with these arrangements/ they are
to be segregated from within 'the
dwelling of the men of sin to walk to
the desert in order to open there His
path. [14]As it is written: "In the desert,
prepare the way of ****, straighten in
the steppe a roadway for our God."
[15]This is the study of the law which
he commanded through the hand of
Moses, in order to set in compliance
with all that has been revealed from
age to age, [16]and according to what
the prophets have revealed through
his holy spirit.

[9.17]He [the Instructor] should reproach
(with) truthful knowledge and (with)
just judgment those who choose [18]the
path, each one according to his spirit,
according to the circumstances of
the time. He should lead them with
knowledge and in this way teach them
the mysteries of wonder and of truth
in the midst of [19]the men of the Community, so that they walk perfectly,
each one with his fellow, in all that
has been revealed to them. This is the
time for making ready the path [20]to the
desert and he will teach them about
all that has been discovered so that
they can carry it out in this moment
and so that they will be detached from

anyone who has not withdrawn his
path [21]from all wickedness.

Josephus, **Jewish War** *2.13.4–5 §§258–
261*

Josephus tells us how certain movements involving political rebellion were often associated
with "calls to the wilderness" and claims of
divine inspiration. They were quickly quashed
by the Roman authorities.

[258]There was also another body of
wicked men gotten together, not so
impure in their actions, but more
wicked in their intentions, who laid
waste the happy state of the city no
less than did these murderers. [259]These
were such men as deceived and deluded the people under pretense of
divine inspiration, but were for pro-
curing innovations and changes of the
government, and these prevailed with
the multitude to act like madmen, and
went before them into the wilderness,
as pretending that God would there
show them the signals of liberty; [260]but
Felix thought this procedure was to be
the beginning of a revolt; so he sent
some horsemen and footmen, both
armed, who destroyed a great num-
ber of them. [261]But there was an Egyptian false
prophet that did the Jews more mis-
chief than the former; for he was a
cheat, and pretended to be a prophet
also, and got together thirty thousand
men that were deluded by him.

3.3 What, Then, Shall We Do? (Luke 3:10–14) (*JaS* 18)

Josephus, **Antiquities** *18.5.2 §§116–
119; 12.4.2–9 §§160–222*

Josephus records the ministry of John and
how Herod Antipas unjustly put him to death.
Many of the Jews believed that Herod was

punished by God for what he did. The second, rather lengthy selection from the *Antiquities* reveals how people viewed toll collectors.

18.5.2 [116]Now some of the Jews thought that the destruction of Herod's army came from God, and that very justly, as a punishment of what he did against John, who was called the *Baptist*; [117]for Herod slew him, who was a good man, and commanded the Jews to exercise virtue, both as to righteousness towards one another, and piety towards God, and so to come to baptism; for that the washing [with water] would be acceptable to him, if they made use of it, not in order to the putting away [or the remission] of some sins [only], but for the purification of the body; supposing still that the soul was thoroughly purified beforehand by righteousness. [118]Now, when [many] others came in crowds about him, for they were very greatly moved [or pleased] by hearing his words, Herod, who feared lest the great influence John had over the people might put it into his power and inclination to raise a rebellion (for they seemed ready to do anything he should advise), thought it best, by putting him to death, to prevent any mischief he might cause, and not bring himself into difficulties, by sparing a man who might make him repent of it when it should be too late. [119]Accordingly he was sent a prisoner, out of Herod's suspicious temper, to Macherus, the castle I before mentioned, and was there put to death. Now the Jews had an opinion that the destruction of this army was sent as a punishment upon Herod, and a mark of God's displeasure against him.

12.4.2–9 [160]There was now one Joseph, young in age, but of great reputation among the people of Jerusalem, for gravity, prudence, and justice. His father's name was Tobias; and his mother was the sister of Onias the high priest, who informed him of the coming of the ambassador; for he was then sojourning at a village named Phicol, where he was born. [161]Hereupon he came to the city [Jerusalem], and reproved Onias for not taking care of the preservation of his countrymen, but bringing the nation into dangers, by not paying this money. For which preservation of them, he told him he had received the authority over them, and had been made high priest; [162]but that, in case he was so great a lover of money, as to endure to see his country in danger on that account, and his countrymen suffer the greatest damages, he advised him to go to the king, and petition him to remit either the whole or a part of the sum demanded. [163]Onias's answer was this:—That he did not care for his authority, and that he was ready, if the thing were practicable, to lay down his high priesthood; and that he would not go to the king, because he troubled not himself at all about such matters. Joseph then asked him if he would not give him leave to go ambassador on behalf of the nation; [164]he replied, that he would give him leave. Upon which Joseph went up into the temple, and called the multitude together to a congregation, and exhorted them not to be disturbed nor affrighted, because of his uncle Onias's carelessness, but desired them to be at rest, and not terrify themselves with fear about it; for he promised them that he would be their ambassador to the king, and persuade him that they had done him no wrong; [165]and when the multitude heard this, they returned thanks to Joseph. So he went down from the temple, and treated Ptolemy's ambassador in a hospitable manner. He also presented him with rich gifts, and feasted him magnificently for many days, and then sent him to the king before him, and told him that he would soon follow him; [166]for he was now more willing to go to the king, by the encouragement of the ambassador, who earnestly persuaded him to come into Egypt, and promised him that he would take care that he should obtain everything that he desired of Ptolemy; for he was highly pleased with his frank and liberal temper, and with the gravity of his deportment.

[167]When Ptolemy's ambassador was come into Egypt, he told the king of the thoughtless temper of Onias; and informed him of the goodness of the disposition of Joseph; and that he was coming to him to excuse the multitude, as not having done him any harm, for that he was their patron. In short, he was so very large in his encomiums upon the young man, that he disposed both the king and his wife Cleopatra to have a kindness for him before he came. [168]So Joseph sent to his friends at Samaria, and borrowed money of them; and got ready what was necessary for his journey, garments and cups, and beasts for burden, which amounted to about twenty thousand drachmae, and went to Alexandria. [169]Now it happened that at this time all the principal men and rulers went up out of the cities of Syria and Phoenicia, to bid for their taxes; for every year the king sold them to the men of the greatest power in every city. [170]So these men saw Joseph journeying on the way, and laughed at him for his poverty and meanness; but when he came to Alexandria, and heard that king Ptolemy was at Memphis, he went up thither to meet with him; [171]which happened as the king was sitting in his chariot, with his wife, and with his friend Athenion, who was the very

person who had been ambassador at Jerusalem, and had been entertained by Joseph. As soon therefore as Athenion saw him, he presently made him known to the king, how good and generous a young man he was. [172]So Ptolemy saluted him first, and desired him to come up into his chariot; and as Joseph sat there, he began to complain of the management of Onias: to which he answered, "Forgive him, on account of his age; for you cannot certainly be unacquainted with this, that old men and infants have their minds exactly alike; but you shall have from us, who are young men, everything you desire, and shall have no cause to complain." [173]With this good humor and pleasantry of the young man, the king was so delighted, that he began already, as though he had had long experience of him, to have a still greater affection for him, insomuch that he bade him take his diet in the king's palace, and be a guest at his own table every day; [174]but when the king was come to Alexandria, the principal men of Syria saw him sitting with the king, and were much offended at it.

[175]And when the day came on which the king was to let the taxes of the cities to farm, and those that were the principal men of dignity in their several countries were to bid for them, the sum of the taxes together, of Celesyria and Phoenicia, and Judea, with Samaria [as they were bidden for], came to eight thousand talents. [176]Hereupon Joseph accused the bidders, as having agreed together to estimate the value of the taxes at too low a rate; and he promised that he would himself give twice as much for them: but for those who did not pay, he would send the king home their whole substance; for this privilege was sold together with the taxes themselves. [177]The king was pleased to hear that offer; and,

cf Zacchaeus

because it augmented his revenues, he said he would confirm the sale of the taxes to him; but when he asked him this question whether he had any sureties that would be bound for the payment of the money, he answered very pleasantly, "I will give such security, and those of persons good and responsible, and which you shall have no reason to distrust": [178]And when he bade him name them, who they were he replied, "I give you no other persons, O king, for my sureties, than thyself, and this your wife; and you shall be security for both parties." So Ptolemy laughed at the proposal, and granted him the farming of the taxes without any sureties. [179]This procedure was a sore grief to those that came from the cities into Egypt, who were utterly disappointed; and they returned every one to their own country with shame.

[180]But Joseph took with him two thousand foot soldiers from the king, for he desired he might have some assistance, in order to force such as were refractory in the cities to pay. And borrowing of the king's friends at Alexandria five hundred talents, he made haste back into Syria. [181]And when he was at Askelon, and demanded the taxes of the people of Askelon, they refused to pay anything, and affronted him also: upon which he seized upon about twenty of the principal men, and slew them, and gathered what they had together, and sent it all to the king; and informed him what he had done. [182]Ptolemy admired the prudent conduct of the man, and commended him for what he had done; and gave him leave to do as he pleased. When the Syrians heard of this, they were astonished: and having before them a sad example in the men of Askelon that were slain, they opened their gates, and willingly admitted Joseph, and paid their taxes. [183]And when the inhabitants of Scythopolis attempted to affront him, and would not pay him those taxes which they formerly used to pay, without disputing about him, he slew also the principal men of that city, and sent their effects to the king. [184]By this means he gathered great wealth together, and made vast gains by this farming of the taxes; and he made use of what estate he had thus gotten, in order to support his authority, as thinking it a piece of prudence to keep what had been the occasion and foundation of his present good fortune; and this he did by the assistance of what he was already possessed of, [185]for he privately sent many presents to the king, and to Cleopatra, and to their friends, and to all that were powerful about the court, and thereby purchased their good will to himself.

[186]This good fortune he enjoyed for twenty-two years; and was become the father of seven sons, by one wife; he had also another son, whose name was Hyrcanus, by his brother Solymius's daughter, [187]whom he married on the following occasion. He once came to Alexandria with his brother, who had along with him a daughter already marriageable, in order to give her in wedlock to some of the Jews of chief dignity there. He then supped with the king, and falling in love with an actress that was of great beauty, and came into the room where they feasted, he told his brother of it, and entreated him, because a Jew is forbidden by their law to come near to a foreigner, to conceal his offense, and to be kind and subservient to him, and to give him an opportunity of fulfilling his desires. [188]Upon which his brother willingly entertained the proposal of serving him, and adorned his own daughter, and brought her to him by night, and put her into his bed. And Joseph, being disordered

with drink, knew not who she was, and so lay with his brother's daughter; and this did he many times, and loved her exceedingly; and said to his brother that he loved this actress so well, that he should run the hazard of his life [if he must part with her], and yet probably the king would not give him leave [to take her with him]. [189]But his brother bade him be in no concern about that matter, and told him he might enjoy her whom he loved without any danger, and might have her for his wife; and opened the truth of the matter to him, and assured him that he chose rather to have his own daughter abused, than to overlook him, and see him come to [public] disgrace. So Joseph commended him for this his brotherly love, and married his daughter; and by her begot a son whose name was Hyrcanus, as we said before. [190]And when this his youngest son showed, at thirteen years old, a mind that was both courageous and wise, and was greatly envied by his brethren, as being of a genius much above them, and such a one as they might well envy, [191]Joseph had once a mind to know which of his sons had the best disposition to virtue; and when he sent them severally to those that had then the best reputation for instructing youth, the rest of his children, by reason of their sloth and unwillingness to take pains, returned to him foolish and unlearned. [192]After them he sent out the youngest, Hyrcanus, and gave him three hundred yoke of oxen, and bid him go two days' journey into the wilderness, and sow the land there, and yet kept back privately the yokes of the oxen that coupled them together. [193]When Hyrcanus came to the place, and found he had no yokes with him, he condemned the drivers of the oxen, who advised him to send some to his father, to bring them some yokes; but

he thinking that he ought not to lose his time while they should be sent to bring him the yokes, he invented a kind of stratagem, and what suited an age elder than his own; [194]for he slew ten yoke of the oxen, and distributed their flesh among the laborers, and cut their hides into several pieces, and made him yokes, and yoked the oxen together with them; by which means he sowed as much land as his father had appointed him to sow, and returned to him. [195]And when he was come back, his father was mightily pleased with his sagacity, and commended the sharpness of his understanding, and his boldness in what he did. And he still loved him the more, as if he were his only genuine son, while his brethren were much troubled at it. [196]But when one told him that Ptolemy had a son just born, and that all the principal men of Syria, and the other countries subject to him, were to keep a festival, on account of the child's birthday, and went away in haste with great retinues to Alexandria, he was himself indeed hindered from going by old age; but he made trial of his sons, whether any of them would be willing to go to the king. [197]And when the elder sons excused themselves from going, and said they were not courtiers good enough for such conversation, and advised him to send their brother Hyrcanus, he gladly hearkened to that advice, and called Hyrcanus, and asked him, whether he would go to the king; and whether it was agreeable to him to go or not. [198]And upon his promise that he would go, and his saying that he should not want much money for his journey, because he would live moderately, and that ten thousand drachmas would be sufficient, he was pleased with his son's prudence. [199]After a little while, the son advised his father not to send his presents to the king from thence, but to give him a letter to his steward at Alexandria, that he might furnish him with money, for purchasing what should be most excellent and most precious. [200]So he thinking that the expense of ten talents would be enough for presents to be made the king, and commending his son, as giving him good advice wrote to Arion his steward, that managed all his money matters at Alexandria; which money was not less than three thousand talents on his account, [201]for Joseph sent the money he received in Syria to Alexandria. And when the day appointed for the payment of the taxes to the king came, he wrote to Arion to pay them. [202]So when the son had asked his father for a letter to the steward, and had received it, he made haste to Alexandria. And when he was gone, his brethren wrote to all the king's friends, that they should destroy him.

[203]But when he was come to Alexandria, he delivered his letter to Arion, who asked him how many talents he would have (hoping he would ask for no more than ten, or a little more); he said he wanted a thousand talents. At which the steward was angry, and rebuked him, as one that intended to live extravagantly; and he let him know how his father had gathered together his estate by painstaking and resisting his inclinations, and wished him to imitate the example of his father: he assured him withal, that he would give him but ten talents, and that for a present to the king also. [204]The son was irritated at this, and threw Arion into prison. But when Arion's wife had informed Cleopatra of this, with her entreaty, that she would rebuke the child for what he had done (for Arion was in great esteem with her), Cleopatra informed the king of it. [205]And Ptolemy sent for Hyrcanus, and told him that he wondered, when he was sent to him by his father, that he had not yet come into his presence, but had laid the steward in prison. And he gave order, therefore, that he should come to him, and give an account of the reason of what he had done. [206]And they report that the answer he made to the king's messenger was this; That "there was a law of his that forbade a child that was born to taste of the sacrifice, before he had been at the temple and sacrificed to God. According to which way of reasoning he did not himself come to him in expectation of the present he was to make to him, as to one who had been his father's benefactor; [207]and that he had punished the slave for disobeying his commands, for that it mattered not whether a master was little or great: so that unless we punish such as these, you yourself may also expect to be despised by your subjects." Upon hearing this his answer, he fell a-laughing, and wondered at the great soul of the child.

[208]When Arion was apprised that this was the king's disposition, and that he had no way to help himself, he gave the child a thousand talents, and was let out of prison. So after three days were over Hyrcanus came and saluted the king and queen. [209]They saw him with pleasure, and feasted him in an obliging manner, out of the respect they bare to his father. So he came to the merchants privately, and bought a hundred boys that had learning, and were in the flower of their ages, each at a talent apiece; as also he bought a hundred maidens, each at the same price as the other. [210]And when he was invited to feast with the king among the principal men in the country, he sat down the

lowest of them all, because he was little regarded, as a child in age still; and this by those who placed every one according to their dignity. [211]Now when all those that sat with him had laid the bones of the several parts on a heap before Hyrcanus (for they had themselves taken away the flesh belonging to them), till the table where he sat was filled full with them, [212]Trypho, who was the king's jester, and was appointed for jokes and laughter at festivals, was now asked by the guests that sat at the table [to expose him to laughter]. So he stood by the king, and said, "Do you not see, my lord, the bones that lie by Hyrcanus? by this similitude you may conjecture that his father made all Syria as bare as he has made these bones." [213]And the king laughing at what Trypho said, and asking of Hyrcanus, how he came to have so many bones before him? he replied, "Very rightfully, my lord; for they are dogs that eat the flesh and the bones together, as these your guests have done (looking in the mean time at those guests), for there is nothing before them; but they are men that eat the flesh and cast away the bones as I, who am also a man have now done." [214]Upon which the king admired at his answer, which was so wisely made; and bade them all make an acclamation, as a mark of their approbation of his jest, which was truly a facetious one. [215]On the next day Hyrcanus went to every one of the king's friends, and of the men powerful at court, and saluted them; but still inquired of the servants what present they would make the king on his son's birthday; [216]and when some said that they would give twelve talents, and that others of greater dignity would everyone give according to the quantity of their riches, he pretended to every one of them to be grieved that he was not able to bring so large a present; for that he had no more than five talents. And when the servants heard what he said, they told their masters; [217]and they rejoiced in the prospect that Joseph would be disapproved, and would make the king angry, by the smallness of his present. When the day came, the others, even those that brought the most, offered the king not above twenty talents; but Hyrcanus gave to every one of the hundred boys and hundred maidens that he had bought a talent apiece, for them to carry, and introduced them, the boys to the king and the maidens to Cleopatra; [218]everybody wondering at the unexpected richness of the presents, even the King and queen themselves. He also presented those that attended about the king with gifts to the value of a great number of talents, that he might escape the danger he was in from them; for to these it was that Hyrcanus's brethren had written to destroy him. [219]Now Ptolemy admired at the young man's magnanimity, and commanded him to ask what gift he pleased. But he desired nothing else to be done for him by the king than to write to his father and brethren about him. [220]So when the king had paid him very great respects, and had given him very large gifts, and had written to his father and his brethren, and all his commanders and officers, about him, he sent him away. [221]But when his brethren heard that Hyrcanus had received such favors from the king, and was returning home with great honor, they went out to meet him, and to destroy him, and that with the privity of their father: for he was angry at him for the [large] sum of money that he bestowed for presents, and so had no concern for his preservation. However, Joseph concealed the anger he had at his son, out of fear of the king. [222]And when Hyrcanus's brethren came to fight him, he slew many others of those that were with them, as also two of his brethren themselves; but the rest of them escaped to Jerusalem to their father. But when Hyrcanus came to the city, where nobody would receive him, he was afraid for himself, and retired beyond the river Jordan, and there abode; but obliging the Barbarians to pay their taxes.

The following texts from Suetonius and Dio Cassius depict Tiberius as an ideal ruler, a good shepherd.

Suetonius, Tiberius 32*

He rebuked some ex-consuls in command of armies, because they did not write their reports to the senate, and for referring to him the award of some military prizes, as if they had not themselves the right to bestow everything of the kind. He highly complimented a praetor, because on entering upon his office he had revived the custom of eulogizing his ancestors before the people. He attended the obsequies of certain distinguished men, even going to the funeral-pyre. He showed equal modesty towards the person of lower rank and in matters of less moment. When he had summoned the magistrates of Rhodes, because they had written him letters on public business without the concluding formula, he uttered not a word of censure, but merely dismissed them with orders to supply the omission. The grammarian Diogenes, who used to lecture every Sabbath at Rhodes, would not admit Tiberius when he came to hear him on a different day, but sent a message by a common slave of his, putting him off to the seventh day. When this man waited before the Emperor's door at Rome to pay his respects, Ti-

berius took no further revenge than to bid him return seven years later. To the governors who recommended burdensome taxes for his provinces, he wrote in answer that it was the part of a good shepherd to shear his flock, not skin it.

Dio Cassius, Roman History 57.10.5*

All these expenditures, moreover, he made from the regular revenues; for he neither put anyone to death for his money nor confiscated, at this time, anybody's property, nor did he even resort to tricky methods of obtaining funds. In fact, when Aemilius Rectus once sent him from Egypt, which he was governing, more money than was stipulated, he sent back to him the message: "I want my sheep shorn, not shaven."

Sirach 4:1, 4, 8; 7:32; 10:23; 11:12

These citations from Sirach reflect a concern for the poor, a practical outworking of one's professed commitment to the Lord.

4:1My child, do not cheat the poor of their living, and do not keep needy eyes waiting. . . . 4Do not reject a suppliant in distress, or turn your face away from the poor. . . . 8Give a hearing to the poor, and return their greeting politely.

7:32Stretch out your hand to the poor, so that your blessing might be complete.

10:23It is not right to despise one who is intelligent but poor, and it is not proper to honor one who is sinful.

11:12There are others who are slow and need help, who lack strength and about in poverty.

3.4 The One Mightier to Come (Matt. 3:11–12; Mark 1:7–8; Luke 3:15–18) (JaS 19)

Mekilta de Rabbi Ishmael, Nezikin 1 on Exodus 21:2*

According to this text from *Mekilta de Rabbi Ishmael*, it was beneath a Hebrew, though he be a slave, to put shoes on his master.

Six Years He Shall Serve. I might understand this to mean in any kind of service, but Scripture says: "You shall not make him to serve as a bondservant" (Lev. 25.39). Hence the sages say: A Hebrew slave must not wash the feet of his master, nor put his shoes on him, nor carry his things before him when going to the bath-house, nor support him by the hips when ascending steps, nor carry him in a litter or a chair or a sedan chair as slaves do. For it is said: "But over your brethren the children of Israel ye shall not rule, one over another, with rigour."

The following texts reveal the widespread use of "fire" imagery to speak of divine anger and judgment.

Jubilees 9.15; 36.10

9.15 And they all said, "So be it and so let it be to them and to their sons forever in their generations until the day of judgment in which the Lord God will judge them with a sword and with fire on account of all the evil of the pollution of their errors which have filled the earth with sin and pollution and fornication and transgression."

36.10 And on the day of turmoil and execration and indignation and wrath, (then) with devouring burning fire just as he burned Sodom so too he will burn up his land and his city and everything which will be his.

1 Enoch 10.6; 54.6; 90.24–27

10.6 And he [Raphael] covered his [Azaz'el's] face in order that he may not see light; and in order that he may be sent into the fire on the great day of judgment.

54.6 Then Michael, Raphael, Gabriel, and Phanuel themselves shall seize them on that great day of judgment and cast them into the furnace (of fire) that is burning that day, so that the Lord of the Spirits may take vengeance on them on account of their oppressive deeds which (they preformed) as messengers of Satan, leading astray those who dwell upon the earth.

90.24 Then his judgment took place. First among the stars, they received their judgment and were found guilty, and they went to the place of condemnation; and they were thrown into an abyss, full of fire and flame and full of the pillar of fire. 25 Then those seventy shepherds were judged and found guilty; and they were cast into that fiery abyss. 26 In the meantime I saw how another abyss like it, full of fire, was opened wide in the middle of the ground; and they brought those blinded sheep, all of which were judged, found guilty, and cast into this fiery abyss, and they were burned—the abyss is to the right of that house; 27 thus I saw those sheep while they were burning—their bones also were burning.

4 Ezra (= 2 Esdras) 7:36–38; 13:4

7:36 The pit of torment shall appear, and opposite it shall be the place of rest; and the furnace of hell shall be disclosed, and opposite it the paradise of delight. 37 Then the Most High will say to the nations that have been raised from the dead, "Look now, and understand whom you have denied, whom you have not served, whose commandments you have despised. [38]Look on this side and on that; here are delight and rest, and there are fire and torments." Thus he will speak to them on the day of judgment.

[13:4]And whenever his voice issued from his mouth, all who heard his voice melted as wax melts when it feels the fire.

Psalms of Solomon 15.4–7

[15:4]The one who does these things will never be disturbed by evil; the flame of fire and anger against the unrighteous shall not touch him [5]when it goes out from the Lord's presence against sinners to destroy the sinners' every assurance. [6]For God's mark is on the righteous for (their) salvation. [7]Famine and sword and death shall be far from the righteous; for they will retreat from the devout like those pursued by famine.

1QH 3.28–31 (= col. 11)

[28]And the outburst of wrath against the hypocrites, and the period of anger against Belial, and the ropes of death approach with no escape, [29]then the torrents of Belial will overthrow their high banks like a fire which devours all those drawing water(?) destroying every tree, green or dry, from its canals. [30]He revolves like flames of fire until none of those who drink are left. He consumes the foundations of clay [31]and the tract of dry land; the bases of the mountains does he burn and converts the roots of flint rock into steams of lava. It consumes right to the great deep.

1QS 2.4, 8, 15; 4.13

[2:4]Accursed are you for all your wicked, blameworthy deeds. May he (God) hand you over to dread . . . [8]to the gloom of everlasting fire. . . . [15]May God's anger and the wrath of his verdicts consume him [a man of Belial] for everlasting destruction. . . .

. . .[4:13]without end with the humiliation of destruction by the fire of the dark regions. And all the ages of their generations they shall spend in bitter weeping and harsh evils in the abysses of darkness.

3.5 John's Imprisonment (Luke 3:19–20; Matt. 14:3–4; Mark 6:17–18) (JaS 20)

Josephus, Antiquities 18.5.1 §§109–115; 18.5.2 §§116–119

Josephus describes how Herod Antipas fell in love with and married Herodias, the wife of his half brother, Philip. Many Jews believed that the destruction of Herod's army was God's punishment for Herod's beheading of John the Baptist and for his marrying his brother's wife (see section 3.3 above for the second reading).

18.5.1 [109]About this time Aretas (the king of Arabia Petres) and Herod had a quarrel, on the account following: Herod the tetrarch had married the daughter of Aretas, and had lived with her a great while; but when he was once at Rome, he lodged with Herod, who was his brother indeed, but not by the same mother; for this Herod was the son of the high priest Simon's daughter. [110]However, he fell in love with Herodias, this last Herod's wife, who was the daughter of Aristobulus their brother, and the sister of Agrippa the Great. This man ventured to talk to her about a marriage between them; which address when she admitted, an agreement was made for her to change her habitation, and come to him as soon as he should return from Rome; one article of this marriage also was this, that he should divorce Aretas's daughter. [111]So Antipas, when he had made this agreement, sailed to Rome; but when he had done there the business he went about, and was returned again, his wife having discovered the agreement he had made with Herodias, and having learned it before he had notice of her knowledge of the whole design, she desired him to send her to Macherus, which is a place on the borders of the dominions of Aretas and Herod, without informing him of any of her intentions. [112]Accordingly Herod sent her thither, as thinking his wife had not perceived anything; now she had sent a good while before to Macherus, which was subject to her father, and so all things necessary for her journey were made ready for her by the general of Aretas's army and by that means she soon came into Arabia, under the conduct of the several generals, who carried her from one to another successively; and she soon came to her father, and told him of Herod's intentions. [113]So Aretas made this the first occasion of his enmity between him and Herod, who had also some quarrel with him about their limits at the country of Gamalitis. So they raised armies on both sides, and prepared for war, and sent their generals to fight instead of themselves; [114]and when they had joined battle, all Herod's army was destroyed by the treachery of some fugitives, who, though they were of the tetrarchy of Philip, joined with Aretas's army. [115]So Herod wrote about these affairs to Tiberius; who being very angry at the attempt made by Aretas, wrote to

Vitellius, to make war upon him, and either to take him alive, and bring him to him in bonds, or to kill him, and send him his head. This was the charge that Tiberius gave to the president of Syria.

The following texts reveal Josephus's sensitivity to the Greek concept of virtue, which included the themes of justice and personal righteousness.

Josephus, Antiquities 16.2.3 §§41–43; 16.2.4 §§58–65; 7.14.2 §§338, 342; 7.14.5 §§355–356; 7.14.8 §374; 7.15.1 §384; 9.11.2 §236

16.2.3 [41]Now the privileges we desire, even when we are in the best circumstances, are not such as deserve to be envied, for we are indeed in a prosperous state by your means, but this is only in common with others; and it is no more than this which we desire, to preserve our religion without any prohibition, which as it appears not in itself a privilege to be envied us, so it is for the advantage of those that grant it to us: [42]for if the Divinity delights in being honored, he must delight in those that permit him to be honored. And there are none of our customs which are inhuman, but all tending to piety, and devoted to the preservation of justice; [43]nor do we conceal those injunctions of ours by which we govern our lives, they being memorials of piety, and of a friendly conversation among men.

16.2.4 [58]When Nicolaus had made this speech, there was no opposition made to it by the Greeks, for this was not an inquiry made, as in a court of justice, but an intercession to prevent violence to be offered to the Jews any longer; [59]nor did the Greeks make any defense of themselves, nor deny what it was supposed they had done. Their pretense was no more than this, that while the Jews inhabited in their country, they were entirely unjust to them [in not joining in their worship]; but they demonstrated their generosity in this that though they worshipped according to their own institutions, they did nothing that ought to grieve them. [60]So when Agrippa perceived that they had been oppressed by violence, he made this answer:—That, on account of Herod's good will and friendship, he was ready to grant the Jews whatsoever they should ask him, and that their requests seemed to him in themselves just; and that if they requested anything further, he should not scruple to grant it them, provided they were no way to the detriment of the Roman government; but that, while their request was not more than this, that what privileges they had already given them might not be abrogated, he confirmed this to them, that they might continue in the observation of their own customs, without anyone offering them the least injury; and when he had said thus, he dissolved the assembly: [61]upon which Herod stood up and saluted him, and gave him thanks for the kind disposition he showed to them. Agrippa also took this in a very obliging manner, and saluted him again, and embraced him in his arms; [62]after which he went away from Lesbos; but the king determined to sail from Samos to his own country; and when he had taken his leave of Agrippa, he pursued his voyage, and landed at Cesarea in a few days' time, as having favorable winds; from whence he went to Jerusalem, and there gathered all the people together to an assembly, not a few being there out of the country also. [63]So when he came to them, and gave them a particular account of all his journey, and of the affairs of all the Jews in Asia, how by his means they would live without injurious treatment for the time to come. [64]He also told them of the entire good fortune he had met with, and how he had administered the government, and had not neglected anything which was for their advantage; and as he was very joyful, he now remitted to them the fourth part of their taxes for the last year. [65]Accordingly, they were so pleased with his favor and speech to them, that they went their ways with great gladness, and wished the king all manner of happiness.

7.14.2 [338]"Since, therefore," says he, "you were ordained king by God himself before you were born, endeavor to render yourself worthy of this his providence, as in other instances, so particularly in being religious, and righteous, and courageous. Keep also his commands, and his laws, which he has given us by Moses, and do not permit others to break them." . . . [342]He also gave orders, that when the temple should be once built, they should put the ark therein, with the holy vessels; and he assured them, that they ought to have had a temple long ago, if their fathers had not been negligent of God's commands, who had given it in charge, that when they had got the possession of this land they should build him a temple. Thus did David discourse to the governors, and to his son.

7.14.5 [355]. . . This he charged Zadok the high priest, and Nathan the prophet, to do: [356]and commanded them to follow Solomon through the midst of the city, and to sound the trumpets, and to wish aloud that Solomon the king may sit upon the royal throne forever, that so all the people may know that he is ordained king by his father. He also gave Solomon a charge concerning his government, to rule the whole nation of the Hebrews, and particularly the tribe of Judah, religiously and righteously.

7.14.8 [374]And I pray that the promises of God may be fulfilled; and that this happiness which he has promised to bestow upon king Solomon, over all the country, may continue therein for all time to come. And these promises, O son, will be firm, and come to a happy end, if you show yourself to be a religious and a righteous man, and an observer of the laws of your country; but, if not, expect adversity upon your disobedience to them.

7.15.1 [384]On which account I exhort you, while I am still alive, though already very near to death, in the same manner as I have formerly said in my advice to you, to be righteous towards your subjects, and religious towards God, that has given you your kingdom; to observe his commands and his laws, which he has sent us by Moses; and neither do you out of favor nor flattery allow any lust or other passion to weigh with you to disregard them.

9.11.2 [236]Now Jotham, the son of Uzziah, reigned over the tribe of Judah in Jerusalem, being a citizen thereof by his mother, whose name was Jerusha. This king was not defective in any virtue, but was religious towards God, and righteous towards men, and careful of the good of the city.

Josephus, **Jewish War** *2.8.7 §139*

See section 5.6 below for this text.

3.6 Jesus' Baptism (Matt. 3:13–17; Mark 1:9–11; Luke 3:21–22) (JaS 21)

Jerome, **Dialogue against the Pelagians 3.2***

In the *Gospel of the Nazareans,* cited here in Jerome's work, Jesus is said to have had a discussion with his family in which he asserts that he has no need for John's baptism because—unless he is mistaken—he has not committed any sin.

In the Gospel according to the Hebrews, which is written in the Chaldee and Syrian language, but in Hebrew characters, and is used by the Nazarenes to this day (I mean the Gospel according to the Apostles, or, as is generally maintained, the Gospel according to Matthew, a copy of which is in the library at Caesarea), we find, "Behold, the mother of our Lord and His brethren said to Him, John the Baptist baptizes for the remission of sins; let us go and be baptized by him. But He said to them, what sin have I committed that I should go and be baptized by him? Unless, per chance, the very words which I have said are only ignorance." And in the same volume, "If your brother sins against you in word, and make amends to you, receive him seven times in a day." Simon, His disciple, said to Him, "Seven times in a day?" The Lord answered and said to him, "I say unto you until seventy times seven." Even the prophets, after they were anointed with the Holy Spirit were guilty of sinful words. Ignatius, an apostolic man and a martyr, boldly writes, "The Lord chose Apostles who were sinners above all men." It is of their speedy conversion that the Psalmist sings, "Their infirmities were multiplied; afterwards they made haste." If you do not allow the authority of this evidence, at least admit its antiquity, and see what has been the opinion of all good churchmen. Suppose a person who has been baptized to have been carried off by death either immediately, or on the very day of his baptism, and I will generously concede that he neither thought nor said anything whereby, through error and ignorance, he fell into sin. Does it follow that he will, therefore, be without sin, because he appears not to have overcome, but to have avoided sin? Is not the true reason rather that by the mercy of God he was released from the prison of sins

and departed to the Lord? We also say this, that God can do what He wills; and that man of himself and by his own will cannot, as you maintain, be without sin. If he can, it is idle for you now to add the word grace, for, with such a power, he has no need of it. If, however, he cannot avoid sin without the grace of God, it is folly for you to attribute to him an ability which he does not possess. For whatever depends upon another's will, is not in the power of him whose ability you assert, but of him whose aid is clearly indispensable.

we can't be sinless if we need Grace help to do that

Obviously Jesus baptism was an embarrassment [illegible] Xian

4

The Initial Portrait of Jesus' Galilean Ministry

4.1 The Calling of the Disciples (Matt. 4:18–22; Mark 1:16–20) (*JaS* 26)

1QH 5.7–8 (= col. 13)

This text from the Qumran Hymn Scroll closely associates fishing with judgment.

[7]. . . right among lions, intended for the sons of guilt, lions which grind the bones of strong men, and drink the blood of champions. [8]You made my lodging with many fishermen, those who spread the net upon the surface of the sea, those who go hunting the sons of iniquity. And there you established me for the judgment.

4.2 Teaching in the Synagogue in Capernaum (Mark 1:21–22; Luke 4:31–32) (*JaS* 27)

Josephus, **Jewish War** *3.10.8 §§516–519*

Josephus describes the beauty and agricultural wealth of Capernaum.

[516]The country also that lies over against this lake has the same name of Gennesareth; its nature is wonderful as well as its beauty; its soil is so fruitful that all sorts of trees can grow upon it, and the inhabitants accordingly plant all sorts of trees there; for the temper of the air is so well mixed, that it agrees very well with those several sorts, [517]particularly walnuts, which require the coldest air, flourish there in vast plenty; there are palm trees also, which grow best in hot air; fig trees also and olives grow near them, which yet require an air that is more temperate. [518]One may call this place the ambition of nature, where it forces those plants that are naturally enemies to one another to agree together; it is a happy contention of the seasons as if every one of them laid claim to this country; [519]for it not only nourishes different sorts of autumnal fruit beyond men's expectation, but preserves them a great while; it supplies men with the principal fruits, with grapes and figs continually during ten months of the year, and the rest of the fruit as they become ripe together, through the whole year; for besides the good temperature of the air, it is also watered from a most fertile fountain. The people of the country call it Capharnaum.

4.3 The Healing of the Demoniac in the Synagogue (Mark 1:23–28; Luke 4:33–37) (*JaS* 28)

PGM *4.1066–1069, 1239–1247, 3019–3023; 5.44–50; 8.6–8, 13–14; 9.8–12; 36.163–166**

The following citations are from the magical papyri, which date from after the time of Jesus. They reveal the various methods certain exorcists employed in dealing with demons, including the practice of naming the demon(s). (Long e and o appear in brackets; skips in the verse numbering are as they appear in the originals.)

[4.1066]*Dismissal of brightness:* "CH[OO] CH[OO] [O]CH[OO]CH, 'holy brightness.' In order [1067]that the brightness also go away: Go away, holy brightness, go away, beautiful [1068]and holy light of the highest god, AIAONA." Say it one time with closed eyes, [1069]smear yourself with *kohl* (Coptic): smear yourself by means of a golden probe.

[4.1239] . . . I conjure you, daimon, [1240] / whoever you are, by this god, SABARBARBATHI[O]TH SABARBARBATHIOUTH [1241]SABARBARBATHI[O]N[E]TH SABARBARBAPHAI. Come out daimon, whoever you are, and stay [1245]away from him. . . . Come out, daimon, [1246]since I bind you with unbreakable adamantine fetters, and I deliver you into the [1247]black chaos in perdition.

[4.3019]After placing [the patient] opposite [to you], conjure. *This is the conjuration:* [3020]"I conjure you by the god of the Hebrews, Jesus, IABA IAE ABRA[O]TH AIA [3021]TH[O]TH ELE EL[O] A[EO] EOY IIIBAECH ABARMAS IABARAOU ABELBEL L[O]NA ABRA [3022]MAROIA BRAKI[O]N, who appears in fire, who is in the midst of the land, snow, and [3023]fog, TANN[E]TIS."

[5.44]*Dismissal:* Go Lord, to your own world and to your own thrones, to your own [45]vaults, and keep me and / this boy from harm, in the name of the highest god, [46]SAMAS PHR[E]TH. Do this when the moon is in a settled sign, in conjunction with [50]beneficial planets or is in good houses, not when it is full; for it is / better, and in this way the well-ordered oracle is completed.

[8.6]Your names in heaven: LAMPHTHEN [7]OU[O]TH OUASTHEN OU[O]THI OAMEN[O]TH ENTHOMOUCH. These are the [names] in [8]the 4 quarters of heaven. . . . [13]I also know your wood: ebony. I know you, [14]Hermes, who you are and where you come from and what your city is: Hermopolis.

[9.8]*On the back of the lamella:* "EULAM[O] SISIRBBAI[E]RSESI PHERMOU CHNOU[O]R ABRASAX. [9]Bring into subjection, enslave, and put to silence the soul, the wrath [of [10]him, NN], because I adjure you by the / awful Necessity MASKELLI MASKELL[O] [11]PHMOUKENTABA[O]TH OREOBAZAGRA R[E]XICHTH[O]N HIPPOCHTH[O]N PYRIP[E]GANYX [12]LEPETAN LEPETAN PHNOUNOBO[E]."

[36.163]*Charm to restrain anger and charm for success.* (No charm is greater, and it is [164]to be performed by means of words alone:) Hold your thumbs and repeat the spell [165]7 times: "ERMALL[O]TH ARCHIMALL[O]TH stop the mouths / that speak against me, [166]because I glorify your sacred and honored names which are in heaven."

P. London 121.396, 967

These texts exist only in Greek. They contain magical texts with formulae and symbols.

Sirach 45:6

Aaron is referred to in Sirach as a "holy man" like Moses. Both were set apart for special service to God.

He exalted Aaron, a holy man like Moses who was his brother, of the tribe of Levi.

1QapGen 20.27–29

This text from the Genesis Apocryphon contributes to a cache of texts in Judaism demonstrating that it was not uncommon to deal with demons. In this scenario, the demon departed in response to prayer.

[27] . . . Depart from [28]all the cities of Egypt! But now pray for me and for my household so that this evil spirit will be banished from us. I prayed for [. . .] [29]and laid my hands upon his head. The plague was removed from him; [the evil spirit] was banished [from him] and he lived.

4.4 Summary: Jesus' Tour of Galilee (Matt. 4:23; Mark 1:39; Luke 4:44) (JaS 32)

Writers such as Pliny the Elder, Strabo, and Dio Cassius use the term *Judea* in its widest sense, that is, to include the region of Galilee.

Pliny the Elder, Natural History 5.15.70

Beyond Idumaea and Samaria stretches the wide expanse of Judaea. The part of Judaea adjoining Syria is called Galilee, and next to Arabia and Egypt Peraea. Peraea is covered with rugged mountains, and is separated from the other parts of Judaea by the river Jordan. The rest of Judaea is divided into ten Local Government Areas in the following order: the district of Jericho, which has numerous palm-groves and springs of water, and those of Emmaus, Lydda, Joppa, Accrabim, Jufna, Timnath-Serah, Beth-lebaoth, the Hills, the district that formerly contained Jerusalem, by far the most famous city of the East and not of Judaea only, and Herodium with the celebrated town of the same name.

Strabo, Geographica 16.4.21

The first people above Syria who dwell in Arabia Felix are the Nabataeans and the Sabaeans. They often overran Syria before they became subject to the Romans; but at present both they and the Syrians are subject to the Romans. The metropolis of the Nabataeans is Petra, as it is called; for it lies on a site which is otherwise smooth and level, but it is fortified all round by a rock, the outside parts of the site being precipitous and sheer, and the inside parts having springs in abundance, both for domestic purposes and for watering gardens. Outside the circuit of the rock most of the territory is desert, in particular that towards Judaea. Here, too, is the shortest road to Hiericus, a journey of three or four days, as also to the grove of palm trees, a journey of five days. Petra is always ruled by some king from the royal family; and the king has as Administrator one of his companions, who is called "brother." It is exceedingly well-governed; at any rate, Athenodorus, a philosopher and companion of mine, who had been in the city of the Petraeans, used to describe their government with admiration, for he said that he found both many Romans and many other foreigners sojourning there, and that he saw that the foreigners often engaged in lawsuits, both with one another and with the natives, but that none of the natives prosecuted one another, and that they in every way kept peace with one another.

Dio Cassius, Roman History 37.15.2–17.3*

In this text, there is a description of the situation that led Rome to take over Israel (called *Palestine* in this text). Note the allusion to the Sabbath as a day on which the Jews do not fight. Dio Cassius also makes reference to other ("peculiar") Jewish practices, to monotheism, and to the temple. The Hyrcanus referred to here is Hyrcanus II.

Thence he proceeded against Syria Palaestinia, because its inhabitants had ravaged Phoenicia. There rulers were two brothers, Hyrcanus and Aristobulus, who were quarrelling themselves, as it chanced, and were creating factions in the cities on account of the priesthood (for so they called their kingdom) of their god, whoever he is. Pompey immediately won over Hyrcanus without a battle, since the latter had no force worthy of note; and by shutting up Aristobulus in a certain place he compelled him to come to terms, and when he would surrender neither the money nor the garrison, he threw him into chains. After this he more easily overcame the rest, but had trouble in besieging Jerusalem. Most of the city, to be sure, he took without any trouble, as he was received by the party of Hyrcanus; but the temple itself, which the other party had occupied, he captured only with difficulty. For it was on high ground and was fortified by a wall of its own, and if they had continued defending it on all days

alike, he could not have gotten possession of it. As it was, they made an exception of what are called the days of Saturn, and by doing no work at all on those days afforded the Romans an opportunity in this interval to batter down the wall. The latter, on learning of this superstitious awe of theirs, made no serious attempts the rest of the time, but on those days, when they came round in succession, assaulted most vigorously. Thus the defenders were captured on the days of Saturn, without making any defense, and all the wealth was plundered. The kingdom was given to Hyrcanus and Aristobulus was carried away.

This was the course of events at that time in Palestine; for this is the name that has been given from of old to the whole country extending from Phoenicia to Egypt along the inner sea. They have also another name that they have acquired: the country has been named Judaea, and the people themselves Jews. I do not know how this title came to be given them, but it applies also to all the rest of mankind, although of alien race, who affect their customs. This class exists even among the Romans, and though often repressed has increased to a very great extent and has won its way to the right of freedom in its observances. They are distinguished from the rest of mankind in practically every detail of life, and especially by the fact that they do not honor any of the usual gods, but show extreme reverence for one particular divinity. They never had any statue of him even in Jerusalem itself, but believing him to be unnamable and invisible, they worship him in the most extravagant fashion on earth. They built to him a temple that was extremely large and beautiful, except in so far as it was open and

75

roofless, and likewise dedicated to him the day called the day of Saturn, on which, among many other peculiar observances, they undertake no serious occupation.

4.5 The Healing of the Paralytic (Mark 2:1–12; Luke 5:17–26; Matt. 9:1–8) (JaS 35)

4Q242 frags. 1–3.1–8 (Prayer of Nabonidus)

In this text, it appears that a Jewish exorcist forgave the sin of King Nabonidus, after he prayed.

¹Words of the prayer which Nabonidus, king of the la[nd of Babylon, [the great] king, prayed [when he was afflicted] ²by a malignant inflammation, by decree of the G[od Most] High, in Teiman. [I, Nabonidus,] was afflicted [by a malignant inflammation] ³for seven years, and was banished far [from men, until I prayed to the God Most High] ⁴and an exorcist forgave my sin. He was a Je[w] from [the exiles, who said to me:] ⁵Make a proclamation in writing, so that glory, exal[tation and honour] be given to the name of the G[od Most high. And I wrote as follows: When] ⁶[I was afflicted by a malign[nant] inflammation, [and remained] in Teiman, [by decree of the God Most High, I] ⁷prayed for seven years [to all] the gods of silver and gold, [of bronze and iron,] ⁸of wood, of stone and of clay, because [I thought] that they were gods [. . .].

1 Enoch 37–71 (excerpts)

The figure described in these Old Testament pseudepigraphic texts is "the Son of Man"—one who possesses authority to carry out the great eschatological judgment over all peoples, including governors, kings, high officials, and all those in authority.

⁴⁶·³. . . This is the Son of Man, to whom belongs righteousness, and with whom righteousness dwells . . . ⁴[who] would remove the kings and the mighty ones from their comfortable seats and the strong ones from their thrones and kingdoms. . . .

⁴⁸·⁵All those who dwell upon the earth shall fall and worship before him. . . .

⁴⁹·⁴He shall judge the secret things. And no one will be able to utter vain words in his presence. . . .

⁵⁰·⁴He is righteous in his judgment and in the glory that is before him. Oppression cannot survive his judgment; and the unrepentant in his presence shall perish. . . .

⁵¹·²And he shall choose the righteous and the holy ones from among (the risen dead), for the day when they shall be selected and saved has arrived. . . .

⁶¹·⁸He placed the Elect One [i.e., the Son of Man] on the throne of glory; and he shall judge all the works of the holy ones in heaven above, weighing in the balance their deeds.

4 Ezra (= 2 Esdras) 13:1–58

¹After seven days I dreamed a dream in the night. ²And lo, a wind arose from the sea and stirred up all its waves. ³As I kept looking the wind made something like the figure of a man come up out of the heart of the sea. And I saw that this man flew with the clouds of heaven; and wherever he turned his face to look, everything under his gaze trembled, ⁴and when-

ever his voice issued from his mouth, all who heard his voice melted as wax melts when it feels the fire.

5After this I looked and saw that an innumerable multitude of people were gathered together from the four winds of heaven to make war against the man who came up out of the sea. 6And I looked and saw that he carved out for himself a great mountain, and flew up on to it. 7And I tried to see the region or place from which the mountain was carved, but I could not.

8After this I looked and saw that all who had gathered together against him, to wage war with him, were filled with fear, and yet they dared to fight. 9When he saw the onrush of the approaching multitude, he neither lifted his hand nor held a spear or any weapon of war; 10but I saw only how he sent forth from his mouth something like a stream of fire, and from his lips a flaming breath, and from his tongue he shot forth a storm of sparks. 11All these were mingled together, the stream of fire and the flaming breath and the great storm, and fell on the onrushing multitude that was prepared to fight, and burned up all of them, so that suddenly nothing was seen of the innumerable multitude but only the dust of ashes and the smell of smoke. When I saw it, I was amazed.

12After this I saw the same man come down from the mountain and call to himself another multitude that was peaceable. 13Then many people came to him, some of whom were joyful and some sorrowful; some of them were bound, and some were bringing others as offerings.

Then I woke up in great terror, and prayed to the Most High, and said, 14"From the beginning you have shown your servant these wonders, and have deemed me worthy to have my prayer heard by you; 15now show me the interpretation of this dream also. 16For as I consider it in my mind, alas for those who will be left in those days! And still more, alas for those who are not left! 17For those who are not left will be sad 18because they understand the things that are reserved for the last days, but cannot attain them. 19But alas for those also who are left, and for that very reason! For they shall see great dangers and much distress, as these dreams show. 20Yet it is better to come into these things, though incurring peril, than to pass from the world like a cloud, and not to see what will happen in the last days."

He answered me and said, 21"I will tell you the interpretation of the vision, and I will also explain to you the things that you have mentioned. 22As for what you said about those who survive, and concerning those who do not survive, this is the interpretation: 23The one who brings the peril at that time will protect those who fall into peril, who have works and faith toward the Almighty. 24Understand therefore that those who are left are more blessed than those who have died.

25"This is the interpretation of the vision: As for your seeing a man come up from the heart of the sea, 26this is he whom the Most High has been keeping for many ages, who will himself deliver his creation; and he will direct those who are left. 27And as for your seeing wind and fire and a storm coming out of his mouth, 28and as for his not holding a spear or weapon of war, yet destroying the onrushing multitude that came to conquer him, this is the interpretation: 29The days are coming when the Most High will deliver those who are on the earth. 30And bewilderment of mind shall come over those who inhabit the earth. 31They shall plan to make war against one another, city against city, place against place, people against people, and kingdom against kingdom. [32]When these things take place and the signs occur that I showed you before, then my Son will be revealed, whom you saw as a man coming up from the sea.

[33]"Then, when all the nations hear his voice, all the nations shall leave their own lands and the warfare that they have against one another; [34]and an innumerable multitude shall be gathered together, as you saw, wishing to come and conquer him. [35]But he shall stand on the top of Mount Zion. [36]And Zion shall come and be made manifest to all people, prepared and built, as you saw the mountain carved out without hands. [37]Then he, my Son, will reprove the assembled nations for their ungodliness (this was symbolized by the storm), [38]and will reproach them to their face with their evil thoughts and the torments with which they are to be tortured (which were symbolized by the flames), and will destroy them without effort by means of the law (which was symbolized by the fire).

[39]"And as for your seeing him gather to himself another multitude that was peaceable, [40]these are the nine tribes that were taken away from their own land into exile in the days of King Hoshea, whom Shalmaneser, king of the Assyrians, made captives; he took them across the river, and they were taken into another land. [41]But they formed this plan for themselves, that they would leave the multitude of the nations and go to a more distant region, where no human beings had ever lived, [42]so that there at least they might keep their statutes that they had not kept in their own land. [43]And they went in by the narrow passages of the Euphrates river. [44]For at that time the Most High performed signs for them, and stopped the channels of the river until they had crossed over. [45]Through that region there was a long way to go, a journey of a year and a half; and that country is called Arzareth.

[46]"Then they lived there until the last times; and now, when they are about to come again, [47]the Most High will stop the channels of the river again, so that they may be able to cross over. Therefore you saw the multitude gathered together in peace. [48]But those who are left of your people, who are found within my holy borders, shall be saved. [49]Therefore when he destroys the multitude of the nations that are gathered together, he will defend the people who remain. [50]And then he will show them very many wonders."

[51]I said, "O sovereign Lord, explain this to me: Why did I see the man coming up from the heart of the sea?"

[52]He said to me, "Just as no one can explore or know what is in the depths of the sea, so no one on earth can see my Son or those who are with him, except in the time of his day. [53]This is the interpretation of the dream that you saw. And you alone have been enlightened about this, [54]because you have forsaken your own ways and have applied yourself to mine, and have searched out my law; [55]for you have devoted your life to wisdom, and called understanding your mother. [56]Therefore I have shown you these things; for there is a reward laid up with the Most High. For it will be that after three more days I will tell you other things, and explain weighty and wondrous matters to you."

[57]Then I got up and walked in the field, giving great glory and praise to the Most High for the wonders that he does from time to time, [58]and because he governs the times and whatever

things come to pass in their seasons. And I stayed there three days.

4.6 The Calling of Levi/Matthew (Mark 2:13–17; Luke 5:27–32; Matt. 9:9–13) (JaS 36)

Sirach 35:1–7

In this text, the author states that faithful law-keeping is akin to offering acceptable sacrifices.

¹The one who keeps the law makes many offerings; ²one who heeds the commandments makes an offering of well-being. ³The one who returns a kindness offers choice flour, ⁴and one who gives alms sacrifices a thank offering. ⁵To keep from wickedness is pleasing to the Lord, and to forsake unrighteousness is an atonement. ⁶Do not appear before the Lord empty-handed, ⁷for all that you offer is in fulfillment of the commandment.

Prayer of Azariah 16–17

This text, in similar fashion to Sirach 35:1–7 cited above, closely associates humility and right ethic with proper and acceptable sacrifice.

¹⁶Yet with a contrite heart and a humble spirit may we be accepted, ¹⁷as though it were with burnt offerings of rams and bulls, or with tens of thousands of fat lambs; such may our sacrifice be in your sight today, and may we unreservedly follow you, for no shame will come to those who trust in you.

Diogenes Laertius, Lives of Eminent Philosophers 6.1.5–8 (Life of Antisthenes)*

This text is a variation on the theme of Jesus' remark that physicians treat the sick.

⁵Once, when he was applauded by rascals, he remarked, "I am horribly afraid I have done something wrong."

⁶When brothers agree, no fortress is so strong as their common life, he said. The right outfit for a voyage, he said, is such as, even if you are shipwrecked, will go through the water with you. One day when he was censured for keeping company with evil men, the reply he made was, "Well, physicians are in attendance on their patients without getting the fever themselves." "It is strange," said he, "that we weed out the darnel from the corn and the unfit in war, but do not excuse evil men from the service of the state." When he was asked what advantage had accrued to him from philosophy, his answer was, "The ability to hold converse with myself." Some one having called upon him over the wine for a song, he replied, "Then you must accompany me on the pipe." When Diogenes begged a coat of him, he bade him fold his cloak around him double. ⁷Being asked what learning is the most necessary, he replied, "How to get rid of having anything to unlearn." And he advised that when men are slandered, they should endure it more courageously than if they were pelted with stones.

And he used to taunt Plato with being conceited. At all events when in a procession he spied a spirited charger he said, turning to Plato, "It seems to me that you would have made just such a proud, showy steed." This because Plato was constantly praising horseflesh. And one day he visited Plato, who was ill, and seeing the basin into which Plato had vomited, remarked, "The bile I see, but not the pride." ⁸He used to recommend the Athenians to vote that asses are horses. When they deemed this absurd, his reply was, "But yet generals are found among you who had had no training, but were merely elected." "Many men praise you," said one. "Why, what wrong have I done?" was his rejoinder. When he turned the torn part of his cloak so that it came into view, Socrates no sooner saw this than he said, "I spy your love of fame peeping through your cloak."

4.7 The Question about Fasting (Mark 2:18–22; Luke 5:33–39; Matt. 9:14–17) (JaS 37)

Didache 8.1*

This text from the *Didache* enjoins fasting—among many things—upon its church membership. True Christians, however, were not to fast on the days when the hypocrites (= Pharisees) fasted but on other days.

But do let not your fasts coincide with those of the hypocrites. They fast on Monday and Thursday, so you must fast on Wednesday and Friday.

4.8 The Dispute over the Disciples' Plucking of Grain on the Sabbath (Mark 2:23–28; Luke 6:1–5; Matt. 12:1–8) (JaS 38)

m. Šabbat 7.2*

This passage from the Mishnah, if at all representative of the kinds of prohibitions in Jesus' day, reveals the strictness with which the commandment "to keep the Sabbath holy" was understood.

A. The generative categories of acts of labor [prohibited on the Sabbath] are forty less one:
(1) he who sows, (2) ploughs, (3) reaps, (4) binds sheaves, (5) threshes, (6) winnows, (7) selects

[fit from unfit produce or crops], (8) grinds, (9) sifts, (10) kneads, (11) bakes;
C. (12) who shears wool, (13) washes it, (14) beats it, (15) dyes it;
D. (16) spins, (17) weaves,
E. (18) makes two loops, (19) weaves two threads, (20) separates two threads;
F. (21) ties, (22) unties,
G. (23) sews two stitches, (24) tears in order to sew two stitches;
H. (25) he who traps a dear, (26) slaughters it, (27) flays it, (28) salts it, (29) curds its hide, (30) scrapes it, and (31) cuts it up;
I. (32) he who writes two letters, (33) erases two letters in order to write two letters;
J. (34) he who builds, (35) tears down;
K. (36) he who puts out a fire, (37) kindles a fire;
L. (38) he who hits with a hammer; (39) he who transports an object from one domain to another—
M. lo, these are the forty generative acts of labor less one.

4.9 Synagogue Sabbath Healing: The Man with the Withered Hand (Mark 3:1–6; Luke 6:6–11; Matt. 12:9–14) (JaS 39)

Testament of Simeon 2.12–13

In this passage from the *Testament of Simeon*, we see the respect placed upon healing as a sign of God's forgiveness and blessing (for repentance).

[12]The Lord bound my hands and feet, however, and thus prevented my hands from performing their deeds, because for seven days my right hand became partly withered. [13]I knew, children, that this had happened to me because of Joseph, so I repented and

wept. Then I prayed to the Lord God that my hand might be restored and that I might refrain from every defilement and grudge and from all folly, for I knew that I had contemplated an evil deed in the sight of the Lord and of Jacob, my father, on account of Joseph, my brother, because of my envying him.

m. Šabbat 22.6*

According to this rabbinic tradition, a person was not even allowed to set a broken bone on the Sabbath.

E. . . . And they do not straighten [the limb of] a child or set a broken limb.

m. ʿEduyyot 2.5*

This passage from the Mishnah reveals restrictions placed on medical treatment and healing on the Sabbath. See also m. Šabbat 14.4 and 19.2 below.

A. Three matters did they say about before R. Ishmael, and he did not rule concerning them either to prohibit or to permit, and R. Joshua b. Matya worked them out.

I B. He who cuts open an abscess on the Sabbath—

C. if it is to make an opening for it, he is liable.

D. But if it is to draw out the pus from it, he is exempt.

II E. And concerning him who traps a snake on the Sabbath—

F. if he got involved with it so that it would not bite him, he is exempt.

G. But if it was for purposes of healing, he is liable. . . .

m. Šabbat 14.4*

A. He who is concerned about his teeth may not suck vinegar through them.

B. But he dunks [his bread] in the normal way,

C. and if he is healed, he is healed.

D. He who is concerned about his loins [which give him pain], he may not anoint them with wine or vinegar.

E. But he anoints with oil—

F. not with rose oil.

G. Princes [on the Sabbath], anoint themselves with rose oil on their wounds, since it is their way to do so on ordinary days.

H. R. Simeon says, "All Israelites are princes."

m. Šabbat 19.2*

For the text of 19.2, see m. Šabbat 19.1–2 in section 13.12 below.

t. Šabbat 16.22*

According to this passage from the Tosefta, Shammai did not permit prayer for the sick on the Sabbath, but Hillel did allow it.

A. And so did Rabban Simeon b. Gamaliel say, "The House of Shammai say, 'They do not distribute charity to the poor on the Sabbath in the house of assembly—

B. " 'even funds to marry an orphan boy and an orphan girl.

C. " 'And they do not make a match between a man and his mate.

D. " 'And they do not pray for a sick person on the Sabbath.'

E. "And the House of Hillel permit."

CD 11.5–18

The Damascus Document at Qumran gives certain restrictions for life on the Sabbath within the Qumran community.

[5] . . . No-one should go after an animal to pasture it outside his city, except

for [6]a thousand cubits. . . . He is not to raise his hand to strike with the fist. . . . If [7]it is stubborn, he should not remove it from his house. . . . No-one should remove anything from the house [8]to outside or from outside to the house. Even if he is in a hut, he should remove nothing from it [9]or bring anything into it. He is not to open a sealed vessel on the sabbath. . . . No-one should wear [10]perfumes on the sabbath, to go out or come in. . . . In his dwelling no-one should lift [11]a stone or dust. The wet-nurse should not lift the baby to go out or come in on the sabbath. . . . [12]No-one should press his servant or his maidservant or his employee on the sabbath. . . .

{Not} No-one should help an animal give birth on the sabbath day . . . And if he makes it fall into a well [14]or a pit, he should not take it out on the sabbath. No-one should stay in a place close [15]to gentiles on the sabbath . . . No-one should profane the sabbath by riches or gain on the sabbath . . . [16]And any living man who falls into a place of water or into a place <. . .>, [17]no-one should take him out with a ladder or a rope or a utensil. No-one should offer anything upon the altar on the sabbath, [18]except the sacrifice of the sabbath, for thus it is written: *Lev 23:38* "except your offerings of the sabbath."

5

Jesus' Teaching on Relating to God and Others

5.1 The Beatitudes (Matt. 5:3–12; Luke 6:20b–26) (*JaS* 43)

Isaiah 61:1 functioned within Qumran to give the community hope that God would someday overthrow his enemies in judgment and establish a day of freedom, peace, and comfort. See also *Targum Pseudo-Jonathan* to Numbers 25:12 and *Midrash Ekhah* on Lamentations 3:49–50 below.

11QMelch 2.4–6, 9, 13, 17, 20

⁴[Its inter]pretation for the last days refers to the captives, about whom he said: *Isa 61:1* "To proclaim liberty to the captives." And he will make ⁵their rebels prisoners [. . .] and of the inheritance of Melchizedek, for [. . .] and they are the inheri[tance of Melchi]zedek, who ⁶will make them return. He will proclaim liberty for them, to free them from [the debt of] their iniquities . . . for ⁹it is the time of the "year of grace" for Melchizedek, to exa[lt in the tri]al of the holy ones of God through the rule of judgment . . . ¹³But, Melchizedek will carry out the vengeance of God's judgments [on this day, and they shall be freed from the hands of] Belial and from the hands of all the sp[irits of his lot] . . . ¹⁷Its interpretation: The mountains are the pro[phets . . .] . . . ²⁰"To comfo[rt the afflicted", its interpretation:] to instruct them in all the ages of the worl[d . . .].

Targum Pseudo-Jonathan *to Numbers 25:12**

In an oath I say *to him in my name:* Behold, I have decreed to him my covenant of peace, and *I will make him an angel of the covenant, and he shall live eternally to announce the redemption at the end of days.*

Midrash Ekhah *on Lamentations 3:49–50**

My eyes will flow without ceasing, without respite, until the Lord from heaven looks down and sees: Rabbi Aha in the name of Rabbi Samuel bar Nahmani said, "In three passages we find that immediately following upon a reference to redemption is an allusion to the Holy Spirit, and these are they: 'A joy of wild asses a pasture of flocks' (Isa 32:14), and then: 'Until the spirit us poured out upon us from on high, and the wilderness becomes a fruitful field, and a fruitful field be counted for a forest' (Isa 32:15). 'The smallest shall become a thousand, and the least a mighty nation' (Isa 60:22) and then: 'The spirit of the Lord is upon me, for the Lord has anointed me.' (Isa 61:1). 'My eyes will flow without ceasing, without respite,' and then: 'until the Lord from heaven looks down and sees.'"

5.2 The Light of the World (Matt. 5:14–16; conceptual: Mark 4:21; Luke 8:16) (JaS 45)

Sirach 50:1, 5–7

The high priest Simon, son of Onias, is compared to the splendor of the morning star, the moon, the rainbow, and even the sun that shines on the temple.

[1]The leader of his brothers and the pride of his people was the high priest, Simon son of Onias. . . . [5]How glorious he was, surrounded by the people, as he came out of the house of the curtain. [6]Like the morning star among the clouds, like the full moon at the festal season; [7]like the sun shining on the temple of the Most High, like the rainbow gleaming in splendid clouds. . . .

Testament of Abraham 7.8

The context is of a dream in which the patriarch Isaac sees the sun and the moon, as well as heaven being opened up. He then sees a "light-bearing man" come down from heaven and take away the sun and the moon. Because of this, Isaac was grieving bitterly. In the interpretation of the dream, part of which is given below, we learn that the sun stands for Abraham and the moon for Sarah.

The Commander-in-chief said, "Hear, righteous Abraham: The sun which your child saw is you, his father. And the moon similarly is his mother Sarah. And the light-bearing man who came down from heaven, this is the one sent from God, who is about to take your righteous soul from you."

1 Enoch 48.4

Here the imagery of "light" is related to the Messiah and his work of bringing hope to Gentiles who are spiritually sick. *ha*

He will become a staff for the righteous ones in order that they may lean on him and not fall. He is the light of the gentiles and he will become the hope of those who are sick in their hearts.

Sirach 17:17, 19–20

In this text, God's light exposes sin so that it is evident, another function of light.

[17]He appointed a ruler for every nation, but Israel is the Lord's own portion. . . . [19]All their works are as clear as the sun before him, and his eyes are ever upon their ways. [20]Their iniquities are not hidden from him, and all their sins are before the Lord.

5.3 On the Law and the Prophets (Matt. 5:17–20; conceptual: Luke 16:17) (JaS 46)

1 Maccabees 4:45–46

The Gentiles, under the direction of Antiochus Epiphanes IV, had desolated the sanctuary and profaned the altar. Thus, Judas Maccabeus ordered his men to tear down the altar, carefully placing the stones in a convenient place until a prophet should come who could tell them what to do with the stones. Thus, the idea that Jesus interpreted the law in new and fresh ways has some precedent within Judaism.

[45]And they thought it best to tear it down, so that it would not be a lasting shame to them that the Gentiles had defiled it. So they tore down the altar, [46]and stored the stones in a convenient place on the temple hill until a prophet should come to tell what to do with them. *P ♊73*

5.4 On Adultery (Matt. 5:27–30; Mark 9:43, 45, 47) (JaS 48)

Though Jesus' teaching has a slightly different focus, the following texts from Sirach and Qumran reveal the widespread conviction about the evil of sexual immorality.

Sirach 41:17–18, 20–21

[17]Be ashamed of sexual immorality, before your father or mother; and of a lie, before a prince or a ruler; [18]of a crime, before a judge or magistrate . . . [20]and of silence, before those who greet you; of looking at a prostitute, [21]and of rejecting the appeal of a relative; of taking away someone's portion or gift, and of gazing at another man's wife.

1QS 1.1–6

[1]For [the Instructor . . .] . . . [book of the Rul]e of the Community: in order to [2]seek God . . . to do what is good and just in his presence . . . [5]and to become attached to all good works; to bring about truth, justice and uprightness [6]on earth and not to walk in the stubbornness of a guilty heart and of lecherous eyes. . . .

CD 2.14–16

[14]And now, my sons, listen to me and I shall open your eyes so that you can see and understand . . . [15]so that you can choose what he [God] is pleased with and repudiate what he hates, so that you can walk perfectly [16]on all his paths and not follow after the thoughts of a guilty inclination and lascivious eyes.

5.5 On Divorce (Matt. 5:31–32; conceptual: Luke 16:18) (JaS 49)

The following texts from the Mishnah and Josephus expound certain ideas concerning divorce, i.e., its justifications and causes.

m. Giṭṭin 9.10*

This Mishnah text reveals three different approaches to divorce within Judaism.

A. The House of Shammai say, "A man should divorce his wife only because he has grounds for it in unchastity,

B. "since it is said, *Because he has found her indecency in anything* (Dt. 24:1)."

C. And the House of Hillel say, "Even if she spoiled his dish,

D. "since it is said, *Because he has found her indecency in anything*."

E. R. Aqiba says, "Even if he found someone else prettier than she,

F. "since it is said, *And it shall be if she find no favor in his eyes* (Dt. 24:1)."

m. Yebamot 2.8 F–H*

F. He who is suspected [of having intercourse] with a married woman, and they [the court] dissolve the marriage with her husband,

G. even though he [the suspect] married [the woman],

H. he must put her out.

m. Soṭah 5.1*

A. "Just as the water puts her to the proof, so the water puts him [the lover] to the proof,

B. "since it is said, *And it shall come . . . , And it shall come . . .* (Num. 5:22, 5:24).

C. "Just as she is prohibited to the husband, so she is prohibited to the lover,

D. "since it is said, *And she will be unclean . . . , And she will be unclean . . .* (Num 5:27, 29)," the words of R. Aqiba.

E. Said R. Joshua, "Thus did Zekhariah b. Haqqassab expound [the Scripture]."

F. Rabbi says, "The two times at which, *If she is made unclean . . . , She is made unclean . . .* are stated in the pericope refer, one to the husband and one to the lover."

Josephus, Antiquities 4.8.23 §253

He that desires to be divorced from his wife for any cause whatsoever (and many such causes happen among men), let him in writing give assurance that he will never use her as his wife any more; for by this means she may be at liberty to marry another husband, although before this bill of divorce be given, she is not to be permitted so to do; but if she be misused by him also, or if, when he is dead, her first husband would marry her again, it shall not be lawful for her to return to him.

Josephus, Life of Flavius Josephus 76 §§425–426

[425]However, he could not conceal his being a liar from Vespasian, who condemned him to die; according to which sentence he was put to death. Nay, after that, when those that envied my good fortune did frequently bring accusations against me, by God's providence I escaped them all. I also received from Vespasian no small quantity of land, as a free gift, in Judea; [426]about which time I divorced my wife also, as not pleased with her behavior, though not till she had been the mother of three children, two of whom are dead, and one, whom I named Hyrcanus, is alive.

5.6 On Oaths (Matt. 5:33–37) (JaS 50)

Jesus' teaching on oaths has parallels among the Essenes, as the following texts from Josephus, Qumran, and Philo demonstrate.

Josephus, Jewish War 2.8.6–7 §§135–142

[135]They dispense their anger after a just manner, and restrain their passion. They are eminent for fidelity, and are the ministers of peace; whatsoever they say also is firmer than an oath; but swearing is avoided by them, and they esteem it worse than perjury for they say, that he who cannot be believed without [swearing by] God, is already condemned. [136]They also take great pains in studying the writings of the ancients, and choose out of them what is most for the advantage of their soul and body; and they inquire after such roots and medicinal stones as may cure their distempers.

[137]But now, if any one has a mind to come over to their sect, he is not immediately admitted, but he is prescribed the same method of living which they use, for a year, while he continues excluded; and they give him a small hatchet, and the forementioned girdle, and the white garment. [138]And when he has given evidence, during that time, that he can observe their continence, he approaches nearer to their way of living, and is made a partaker of the waters of purification; yet is he not even now admitted to live with them; for after this demonstration of his fortitude, his temper is tried two more years; and if he appear to be worthy, they then admit him into their society. [139]And before his is allowed to touch their common food, he is obliged to take tremendous oaths, that, in the first place, he will exercise piety towards

86

God, and then that he will observe justice towards men; and that he will do no harm to any one, either of his own accord, or by the command of others; that he will always hate the wicked, and be assistant to the righteous; [140]that he will ever show fidelity to all men, and especially to those in authority, because no one obtains the government without God's assistance; and that if he be in authority, he will at no time whatever abuse his authority, nor endeavor to outshine his subjects, either in his garments, or any other finery; [141]that he will be perpetually a lover of truth, and propose to himself to reprove those that tell lies; that he will keep his hands clear from theft, and his soul from unlawful gains; and that he will neither conceal any thing from those of his own sect, nor discover any of their doctrines to others, no, not though anyone should compel him so to do at the hazard of his life. [142]Moreover, he swears to communicate their doctrines to no one any otherwise than as he received them himself; that he will abstain from robbery, and will equally preserve the books belonging to their sect, and the names of the angels [or messengers]. These are the oaths by which they secure their proselytes to themselves.

Rom 13:1 (handwritten margin)

1QS 5.7–9

[7]Whoever enters the council of the Community [8]enters the covenant of God in the presence of all those who freely volunteer. He shall swear with a binding oath to revert to the Law of Moses with all that it decrees, with whole [9]heart and whole soul. . . .

Philo, Every Good Man Is Free 12 §84

Accordingly, the sacred volumes present an infinite number of instances of the disposition devoted to the love of God, and of a continued and uninterrupted purity throughout the whole of life, of a careful avoidance of oaths and of falsehood, and of a strict adherence to the principle of looking on the Deity as the cause of everything which is good and of nothing which is evil. They also furnish us with many proofs of a love of virtue, such as abstinence from all covetousness of money, from ambition, from indulgence in pleasures, temperance, endurance, and also moderation, simplicity, good temper, the absence of pride, obedience to the laws, steadiness, and everything of that kind; and, lastly, they bring forward as proofs of the love of mankind, goodwill, equality beyond all power of description, and fellowship, about which it is not unreasonable to say a few words.

Jas (handwritten margin)

5.7 On Giving Alms (Matt. 6:1–4) (JaS 53)

The following texts speak about the fundamental religious importance the Jewish people attached to almsgiving.   *Stew.*

Sirach 29:8

Nevertheless, be patient with someone in humble circumstances, and do not keep him waiting for your alms.

Tobit 4:6–7, 16   *Mt 25*

[6]. . . To all those who practice righteousness [7]give alms from your possessions, and do not let your eye begrudge the gift when you make it. Do not turn your face away from anyone who is poor, and the face of God will not be turned away from you. . . . [16]Give some of your food to the hungry, and some of your clothing to the naked. Give all your surplus

as alms, and do not let your eye be-grudge your giving of alms.

Tobit 12:8; 14:10–11

12:8Prayer with fasting is good, but better than both is almsgiving with righteousness. A little with righteousness is better than wealth with wrongdoing.

14:10On whatever day you bury your mother beside me, do not stay over-night within the confines of the city. For I see that there is much wicked-ness within it, and that much de-ceit is practiced within it, while the people are without shame. See, my son, what Nadab did to Ahikar who had reared him. Was he not, while still alive, brought down into the earth? For God repaid him to his face for this shameful treatment. Ahikar came out into the light, but Nadab went into the eternal darkness because he tried to kill Ahikar. Because he gave alms, Ahikar escaped the fatal trap Nadab had set for him, but Nadab fell into it himself, and was destroyed. 11So now, my children, see what almsgiv-ing accomplishes, and what injustice does—it brings death! But now my breath fails me.

Testament of Job 9.7–8

7From all regions people began com-ing to me for a meeting. *The* four *doors* of my house *stood open.* 8And I gave a standing order to my house servants that these doors should stand open, having this in view: Possibly, some would come asking alms and, because they might see me sitting at the door, would turn back ashamed, getting nothing. Instead, whenever they would see me sitting at one door, they could leave through another and take as much as they needed.

m. ʾAbot 5.13*

IV A. There are four traits among people who give charity:
    B. (1) he who wants to give but does not want others to give—he be-grudges what belongs to others;
    C. (2) he wants others to give, but he does not want to give—he begrudges what belongs to himself;
    D. (3) he will give and he wants others to give—he is truly pious;
    E. (4) he will not give and does not want others to give—he is truly wicked.

5.8 On Fasting (Matt. 6:16–18) (JaS 56)

m. Yoma 8.1*

This Mishnah text forbids bathing (i.e., wash-ing the face) when a person is fasting on the Day of Atonement. An exception is made only for a king and a bride.

A. On the Day of Atonement it is forbidden to (1) eat, (2) drink, (3) bathe, (4) put on any sort of oil, (5) put on a sandal, (6) or engage in sexual relations.
    B. But a king and a bride wash their faces.
    C. "And a woman who has given birth may put on her sandal," the words of R. Eliezer.
    D. And sages prohibit.

5.9 Treasures in Heaven (Matt. 6:19–21; Luke 12:33–34) (JaS 57)

Jesus exhorted his followers to store up trea-sure in heaven and not on earth. The term trea-sure was often used in Judaism in connection with pleasing God, especially in light of the final judgment. The following texts reveal this.

Psalms of Solomon *9.5*

The one who does what is right saves up life for himself with the Lord, and the one who does what is wrong causes his own life to be destroyed; for the Lord's righteous judgments are according to the individual and the household.

2 Baruch *24.1*

For behold, the days are coming, and the books will be opened in which are written the sins of all those who have sinned, and moreover, also the treasuries in which are brought together the righteousness of all those who have proven themselves to be righteous.

Testament of Job *18.2–3*

[2]My fellow countrymen, when they saw that what was said truly happened, pursued and attacked me and began to snatch up everything in my house. [3]My eyes witnessed cheap and worthless men at my tables and couches.

5.10 On Serving Two Masters (Matt. 6:24; Luke 16:13) (*JaS* 59)

CD 4.17–19

In this text, three things are likened to a net in which Belial catches Israelites: fornication, wealth, and defilement of the temple.

[17]The first [i.e., the first of Belial's nets to catch Israel] is fornication; the second, wealth; the third, defilement of the temple. He who eludes one is caught in another and he who is freed from that, is caught [19]in another.

CD 6.11–15

Wealth could be a real hindrance to Israel's maintaining her covenant faithfulness to the Lord. In short, wicked wealth defiles, according

to this text from Qumran, and those so defiled are disqualified from serving in the temple.

[11]But all those who have been brought into the covenant [12]shall not enter the temple to kindle his altar in vain. . . . [14]. . . Unless they are careful to act in accordance with the exact interpretation of the law for the age of wickedness: to separate themselves [15]from the sons of the pit; to abstain from wicked wealth which defiles, either by promise or by vow.

1 Enoch *94–103 (excerpts)*

This entire section treats issues tied to judgment of the wicked and the vindication of the righteous. The wicked are too tied to money or its abuse. We note some excerpts from this section.

[94.6]Woe unto those who build op-
    pression and injustice!
Who lay foundations for deceit.
They shall soon be demolished;
and they shall have no peace.
[7]Woe unto those who build their
    houses with sin!
For they shall all be demolished
    from their foundations;
and they shall fall by the sword.
Those who amass gold and silver;
they shall quickly be destroyed.
[8]Woe unto you, O rich people!
For you have put your trust in your
    wealth.
You shall ooze out of your riches,
for you do not remember the Most
    High.
[9]In the days of your affluence, you
    committed oppression,
you have become ready for death,
    and for the day of darkness and
    the day of great judgment.

[96.4]Woe unto you, you sinners!
For your money makes you appear
    like the righteous,

but your hearts do reprimand you
   like real sinners.
this very matter shall be a witness
   against you, as a record of your
   evil deeds.
⁵Woe unto you who eat the best
   bread!
And drink wine in large bowls,
trampling upon the weak people
   with your might.
⁶Woe unto you who have water
   available to you all the time,
for soon you shall be consumed
   and wither away,
for you have forsaken the fountain
   of life.
⁷Woe unto you who carry out oppression, deceit, and blasphemy!
There shall be a record of evil
   against you.
⁸Woe unto you, O powerful people!
You who coerce the righteous with
   your power,
the day of your destruction is coming!
In those days, at the time of your
   condemnation,
many and good days shall come for
   the righteous ones.

⁹⁷·⁷Woe unto you, sinners, who are
   in the midst of the sea and on
   the dry land;
(you) whose records are (both) evil
   (and) against you.
⁸Woe unto you who gain silver and
   gold by unjust means;
you will then say, "We have grown
   rich and accumulated goods,
we have acquired everything that
   we have desired.
⁹So now let us do whatever we like;
for we have gathered silver,
we have filled our treasuries (with
   money) like water.
And many are the laborers in our
   houses."
¹⁰Your lies flow like water.

For your wealth shall not endure
but it shall take off from you
   quickly
for you have acquired it all unjustly,
and you shall be given over to a
   great curse.

¹⁰²·⁹Now I tell you, sinners, you have
satiated yourselves with food and
drink, robbing and sin, impoverishing people and gaining property, and
seeing good days.

¹⁰³·⁵Woe unto you sinners who are
dead! When you are dead in the
wealth of your sins, those who are
like you will say of you, "Happy are
you sinners! (The sinners) have seen
all their days. ⁶They have died now
in prosperity and wealth. They have
not experienced struggle and battle
in their lifetime." ⁷You yourselves
know that they will bring your souls
down to Sheol; and they shall experience evil and great tribulation—in
darkness, nets, and burning flame.
⁸Your souls shall enter into the great
judgment; it shall be a great judgment
in all the generations of the world.
Woe unto you, for there is no peace
for you!

5.11 On Asking God (Matt. 7:7–11; Luke 11:9–13) (JaS 63)

Wisdom of Solomon 6:12

In keeping with biblical, proverbial wisdom,
this text from the Wisdom of Solomon affirms
that wisdom is found by those who seek it.

Wisdom is radiant and unfading, and
she is easily discerned by those who
love her, and is found by those who
seek her.

5.12 The Two Ways (Matt. 7:13–14; Luke 13:23–24) (JaS 65)

The following texts demonstrate that the "doctrine of the two ways" was well known in Judaism.

Testament of Asher 1.3–5

³God had granted two ways to the sons of men, two mind-sets, two lines of action, two models, and two goals. ⁴Accordingly, everything is in pairs, the one over against the other. ⁵The two ways are good and evil; concerning them are two dispositions within our breasts that choose between them.

2 Enoch 30.14–15

¹⁴And I assigned to him four special stars, and called his name Adam. ¹⁵And I gave him his free will; and I pointed out to him the two ways— light and darkness. And I said to him, "This is good for you, but that is bad"; so that I might come to know whether he has love toward me or abhorrence, and so that it might become plain who among his race loves me.

m. ʾAbot 2.9*

A. He said to them, "Go and see what is the straight path to which someone should stick."

B. R. Eliezer says, "A generous spirit."

C. R. Joshua says, "A good friend."

D. R. Yose says, "A good neighbor."

E. R. Simeon says, "Foresight."

F. R. Eleazar says, "Good will."

G. He said to them, "I prefer the option of R. Eleazar b. Arakh, because in what he says is included everything you say."

H. He said to them, "Go out and see what is the bad road, which someone should avoid."

I. R. Eliezer says, "Envy."

J. R. Joshua says, "A bad friend."

K. R. Yose says, "A bad neighbor."

L. R. Simeon says, "Defaulting on a loan." . . .

N. R. Eleazar says, "Bad will."

O. He said to them, "I prefer the option of R. Eleazar b. Arakh, because in what he says is included everything you say."

1QS 3.14–4.26

The entire passage points to the two paths, one of darkness and the other of light. Only 3.17–26 is quoted here, but the contrast continues in chapter 4.

³·¹⁷He created man to rule ¹⁸the world and placed within him two spirits so that he would walk with them until the moment of his visitation: they are the spirits of truth and of deceit. ²⁰In the hand of the Prince of Lights is dominion over all the sons of justice; they walk on paths of light. And in the hand of the Angel ²¹of Darkness is total dominion over the sons of deceit; they walk on paths of darkness. Due to the Angel of Darkness ²²all the sons of justice stray, and all their sins, their iniquities, their failings and their mutinous deeds are under his dominion ²³in compliance with the mysteries of God, until his moment, and all their punishments and periods of grief are caused by the dominion of his enmity; ²⁴and all the spirits of their lot cause the sons of light to fall. However, the God of Israel and the angel of his truth assist all ²⁵the sons of light. He created the spirits of light and of darkness and on them established all his deeds ²⁶[on their p]aths all his labours and on their paths [all] his [labours].

5.13 Houses Built on Rock or Sand (Matt. 7:24–27; Luke 6:47–49) (*JaS* 68)

ʾAbot de Rabbi Nathan 24.1*

The citation of Elisha ben Abuyah in this text shows how the study of Torah was equated to building with stones, but the key was whether Torah was taken to heart and yielded good works.

A. Elisha b. Abuyah says, "One who has good deeds to his credit and has studied the Torah a great deal—to what is he to be likened?

B. To someone who builds first with stones and then with bricks. Even though a great flood of water comes and washes against the foundations, the water does not blot them out of their place.

C. One who has no good deeds to his credit but has studied Torah—to what is he to be likened?

D. To someone who builds first with bricks and then with stones. Even if only a little water comes and washes against the foundations, it immediately overturns them."

6

More Galilean Ministry

6.1 The Healing of the Centurion's Servant (Matt. 8:5–13; Luke 7:1–10) (*JaS* 72)

The following two Mishnah texts reveal the problems Jews had associating with Gentiles. They considered Gentiles unclean, so the centurion's request that Jesus only "speak the word" may reveal his desire not to trample on Jewish scruples.

m. Pesaḥim 8.8*

A. One who has suffered a bereavement of a close relative immerses and eats his Passover offering in the evening,

B. but [he may not eat any other] Holy Things [in that evening].

C. He who hears word [of the death of a close relative], and he who is gathering up bones [for secondary burial] immerses and eats Holy Things.

D. A proselyte who converted on the eve of Passover [the fourteenth of Nisan]—

E. the House of Shammai say, "He immerses and eats his Passover offering in the evening."

F. And the House of Hillel say, "He who takes his leave of the foreskin is as if he took his leave of the grave [and must be sprinkled on the third and seventh day after circumcision as if he had suffered corpse uncleanness]."

m. ʾOhalot 18.7*

A. He who buys a field in Syria, near the Land of Israel, if he can enter it in a state of cleanness, it is clean, and it is subject to the laws of tithes and the seventh year. If he cannot enter it in a state of cleanness, it is unclean, but it [still] is liable to the laws of tithes and of the seventh year.

B. Dwelling places of gentiles [in the Land of Israel] are unclean.

C. How long must [the gentiles] remain in them for them to require examination [to determine their status]? Forty days, even though there is no woman with him.

D. And if a slave or an [Israelite] woman was watching over it, it does not require an examination.

The following texts from 4 Maccabees and *1 Enoch* employ the image of Abraham and the patriarchs in a way similar to Jesus' discussion of the eschatological banquet.

4 Maccabees 13:17

For if we so die, Abraham and Isaac and Jacob will welcome us, and all the fathers will praise us.

1 Enoch 70.4

And there I saw the first (human) ancestors and the righteous ones of old, dwelling in that place.

6.2 The Healing of the Widow of Nain's Son (Luke 7:11–17) (*JaS* 73)

The following texts from the Mishnah and Sirach reveal that burials generally took place on the same day as the death, unless there were special reasons for not doing so. Also, touching the bier rendered one unclean.

m. Šabbat 23.4–5*

[4]A. They wait at the Sabbath limit at twilight to attend to the business of a bride,

B. and the affairs of a corpse,

C. to bring it a coffin and wrappings.

D. A gentile who brought wailing pipes on the Sabbath—an Israelite should not make a lament with them,

E. unless they came from a nearby place.

F. [If] they made for him [a gentile] a coffin and dug a grave for him, an Israelite may be buried therein.

G. But if this was done for an Israelite, he may not ever be buried therein.

[5]A. They prepare all that is needed for a corpse.

B. They anoint and rinse it,

C. on condition that they do not move any limb of the corpse.

D. They remove the mattress from under it.

E. And they put it on [cool] sand so that it will keep.

F. They tie the chin,

G. not so that it will go up, but so that it will not droop [further].

H. And so in the case of a beam which broke—

I. they support it with a bench or the beams of a bed,

J. not so that it will go up, but so that it will not droop further.

K. They do not close the eyes of a corpse on the Sabbath,

L. nor on an ordinary day at the moment the soul goes forth.

M. And he who closes the eyes of a corpse at the moment the soul goes forth, lo, this one sheds blood.

m. Sanhedrin 6.5*

A. Said R. Meir, "When a person is distressed, what words does the Presence of God say? As it were: 'My head is in pain, my arm is in pain.'

B. "If thus is the Omnipresent distressed on account of the blood of the wicked when it is shed, how much the more so on account of the blood of the righteous!"

C. And not this only, but whoever allows his deceased to stay unburied overnight transgresses a negative commandment.

D. But [if] one kept [a corpse] overnight for its own honor, [for example,] to bring a bier for it and shrouds, he does not transgress on its account.

E. And they did not bury [the felon] in the burial grounds of his ancestors.

F. But there were two graveyards made ready for the use of the court, one for those who were beheaded or strangled, and one for those who were stoned or burned.

Sirach 34:30

If one washes after touching a corpse, and touches it again, what has been gained by washing?

6.3 The Sick Healed at Evening (Matt. 8:16–17; Mark 1:32–34; Luke 4:40–41) (*JaS* 75)

Jesus healed with his word and not with the animal parts, smoke, magical incantations, and tricks that we find in these texts from Tobit and Josephus. The second text is a famous one involving traditional beliefs about a son of David, Solomon.

Tobit 6:7–8, 17–18

[7]Then the young man questioned the angel and said to him, "Brother Azariah, what medicinal value is there in the fish's heart and liver, and in the gall?" [8]He replied, "As for the fish's heart and liver, you must burn them to make a smoke in the presence of a man or woman afflicted by a demon or evil spirit, and every affliction will flee away and never remain with that person any longer... [17]When you enter the bridal chamber, take some of the fish's liver and heart, and put them on the embers of the incense. An odor will be given off; [18]the demon will smell it and flee, and will never be seen near her any more. Now when you are about to go to bed with her, both of you must first stand up and pray, imploring the Lord of heaven that mercy and safety may be granted to you. Do not be afraid, for she was set apart for you before the world was made.

Josephus, **Antiquities** 8.2.5 §§45–49

[45]God also enabled him to learn that skill which expels demons, which is a science useful and sanative to men. He composed such incantations also by which distempers are alleviated. And he left behind him the manner of using exorcisms, by which they drive away demons, so that they never return, [46]and this method of cure is of great force unto this day; for I have seen a certain man of my own country, whose name was Eleazar, releasing people that were demoniacal in the presence of Vespasian, and his sons, and his captains, and the whole multitude of his soldiers. The manner of the cure was this:—[47]He put a ring that had a root of one of those sorts

mentioned by Solomon to the nostrils of the demoniac, after which he drew out the demon through his nostrils; and when the man fell down immediately, he abjured him to return into him no more, making still mention of Solomon, and reciting the incantations which he composed. [48]And when Eleazar would persuade and demonstrate to the spectators that he had such a power, he set a little way off a cup or basin full of water, and commanded the demon, as he went out of the man, to overturn it, and thereby to let the spectators know that he had left the man; [49]and when this was done, the skill and wisdom of Solomon was shown very manifestly: for which reason it is, that all men may know the vastness of Solomon's abilities, and how he was beloved of God, and that the extraordinary virtues of every kind with which this king was endowed may not be unknown to any people under the sun; for this reason, I say, it is that we have proceeded to speak so largely of these matters.

6.4 Warning on Following Jesus (Matt. 8:18–22; Luke 9:57–62) (JaS 76)

Taking care of one's parents, even in death, was considered an extremely important obligation in Judaism. The four texts in this section reveal the significance attached to this duty.

Letter of Aristeas 228

(The king) consented to these words, and asked the sixth guest to answer. His question was, "To whom must one show favor?" The answer was, "To his parents, always, for God's very great commandment concerns the honor due to parents. Next (and closely connected) he reckons the honor due to friends, calling the

friend an equal of one's own self.
You do well if you bring all men into
friendship with yourself."

**Josephus, Against Apion 2.27–28
§§205–206**

[205]Our law has also taken care of the
decent burial of the dead, but without
any extravagant expenses for their
funerals, and without the erection of
any illustrious monuments for them;
but has ordered that their nearest
relations should perform their obsequies; and has shown it to be regular,
that all who pass by when anyone
is buried, should accompany the funeral, and join in the lamentation. It
also ordains, that the house and its
inhabitants should be purified after
the funeral is over, that everyone
may thence learn to keep at a great
distance from the thoughts of being
pure, if he has been once guilty of
murder. [206]The law ordains also, that
parents should be honored immediately after God himself, and delivers
that son who does not requite them
for the benefits he has received from
them, but is deficient on any such
occasion, to be stoned. It also says,
that the young men should pay due
respect to every elder, since God is
the eldest of all beings.

Tobit 4:3–4; 6:14–15

[3]Then he called his son Tobias, and
when he came to him he said, "My
son, when I die, give me a proper
burial. Honor your mother and do
not abandon her all the days of her
life. Do whatever pleases her, and
do not grieve her in anything. [4]Re-
member her, my son, because she
faced many dangers for you while
you were in her womb. And when
she dies, bury her beside me in the
same grave."

[6:14]Then Tobias said in answer to Raphael, "Brother Azariah, I have heard
that she already has been married to
seven husbands and that they died
in the bridal chamber. On the night
when they went in to her, they would
die. I have heard people saying that
it was a demon that killed them. [15]It
does not harm her, but it kills anyone who desires to approach her. So
now, since I am the only son my father has, I am afraid that I may die
and bring my father's and mother's
life down to their grave, grieving for
me—and they have no other son to
bury them."

6.5 The Gadarene/Gerasene Demoniac(s) (Matt. 8:28–34; Mark 5:1–20; Luke 8:26–39) (JaS 78)

Josephus, Jewish War 1.7.7 §§155–156

This text shows that Gadara was contended
over by Jews.

[155]He also took away from the nation
all those cities that they had formerly
taken, and that belonged to Celesyria,
and made them subject to him that
was at that time appointed to be the
Roman president there; and reduced
Judea within its proper bounds. He
also rebuilt Gadara, that had been
demolished by the Jews, in order to
gratify one Demetrius, who was of
Gadara, [156]and was one of his own
freedmen.

The following two selections from *m. Nazir*
reveal that Jews regarded cemeteries as unclean and the person who entered it required
cleansing.

m. Nazir 3.5; 7.3*

[3.5]A. He who vowed to be a Nazarite
while in a graveyard,

B. even if he was there for thirty days—

C. those days do not count for him toward the number [of days owing under the vow].

D. Nor does he bring an offering for his uncleanness [for being in the graveyard].

E. [If, however] he went out and then came back [into the graveyard], they do count for him toward the number [of required days].

F. And he does bring an offering for his uncleanness.

G. R. Eliezer says, "That is not the case if it is on the very same day, since it says, *But the former days shall be void* (Num 6:12)—[the offering for uncleanness is brought] only when the former days apply to him."

7.3 A. But as to [uncleanness contracted by overshadowing] (1) interlaced foliage, (2) projecting stones, (3) a grave area, (4) foreign land, (5) the sealing stone and (6) the buttressing stone [of a grave],

B. a quarter-*log* of blood, and a Tent, and a quarter-*qab* of bones, and utensils which touch a corpse,

C. and because of the days of counting [after producing a symptom of *saraat* (Lev. 14:8)] and the days during which he is certified [unclean with *saraat*]—

D. on account of these, the Nazir does not cut his hair or sprinkle himself on the third and seventh days and he does not lose the prior days [observed in cleanness].

E. And he begins to count forthwith [after immersion and sunset].

F. And he is not subject to bringing an offering.

G. Truly did they rule: The days [of uncleanness] by reason of being a *Zab* or a *Zabah* [Lev. 15:2, 25, 28], and the days of being shut up as a *mesora* [Lev. 13:4–5]—lo, these [nonetheless]

go to his credit [in counting out his Nazir days].

PGM 101.1–3   *Mt 8:28-f*

This text from the magical papyri closely associates graveyards with demons, as it is associated with the burial place of prematurely dead infants. Their spirits were often claimed as preferred mediums for magicians.

I bind you with the indissoluble fetters of the underworld Fates and mighty Necessity, for I conjure you, daimons, who lie here and move about here and who keep busy here, and the boys who have died prematurely.

6.6 Jairus's Daughter and the Woman with a Hemorrhage (Matt. 9:18–26; Mark 5:21–43; Luke 8:40–56) (JaS 82)

These two texts from the Mishnah reveal that a hemorrhaging woman was regarded as unclean, and a person had the right to ask if she was in this state.

m. Toharot 5.8*

A. [If there is] one [female] idiot in the village—

B. or [one] gentile woman—

C. or one Samaritan woman—

D. all drops of spit which are in the village are unclean.

E. He on whose garments a woman has stepped,

F. or next to whom a woman sat down on a ship—

G. if she knows him, that he eats heave offering—

H. his utensils are clean.

I. And if not, he will interrogate her.

m. Zabim 5.6*

A. He who touches the *Zab* and the *Zabah* and the menstruating woman and the woman after childbirth and the *mesora*,

B. a bed or a chair [that any of these have lain or sat upon]

C. imparts uncleanness at two removes and renders [heave offering] unfit at one further remove.

D. [If] he separated, he imparts uncleanness at one remove and renders unfit at one further remove.

E. All the same are the one who touches and the one who shifts,

F. and all the same are the one who carries and the one who is carried.

m. Ketubbot 4.4*

M. Ketubbot reveals that even "the poorest man in Israel should not hire fewer than two flutes and one professional wailing woman" for funerals within his family.

A. The father retains control of his daughter [younger than twelve and a half] as to effecting any of the tokens of betrothal; money, document, or sexual intercourse.

B. And he retains control of what she finds, of the fruit of her labor, and of abrogating her vows.

C. And he receives her writ of divorce [from a betrothal].

D. But he does not dispose of the return [on property received by the girl from her mother] during her lifetime.

E. [When] she is married, the husband exceeds the father, for he disposes of the return [on property received by the girl from her mother] during her lifetime.

F. But he is liable to maintain her, and to ransom her, and to bury her.

G. R. Judah says, "Even the poorest man in Israel should not hire fewer

than two flutes and one professional wailing woman."

6.7 Two Blind Men Healed (Matt. 9:27–31 [cf. also Matt. 20:29–34]; Mark 10:46–52; Luke 18:35–43) (JaS 83)

Josephus, Antiquities 8.2.5 §§44–45

This text from Josephus demonstrates a first-century perspective on Solomon (i.e., that he was a man full of wisdom, literary skill, and power to heal). For the rest of this text, see section 6.3 above.

[44]He also composed books of odes and songs, a thousand and five; of parables and similitudes, three thousand; for he spoke a parable upon every sort of tree, from the hyssop to the cedar; and in like manner also about beasts, about all sorts of living creatures, whether upon the earth, or in the seas, or in the air; for he was not unacquainted with any of their natures, nor omitted inquiries about them, but described them all like a philosopher, and demonstrated his exquisite knowledge of their several properties. [45]God also enabled him to learn that skill which expels demons, which is a science useful and sanative to men. He composed such incantations also by which distempers are alleviated. And he left behind him the manner of using exorcisms, by which they drive away demons, so that they never return. . . .

6.8 The Commissioning of the Twelve and the Mission Instruction (Matt. 10:1–16; Mark 3:13–19a; Luke 6:12–16; cf. also

Mark 6:7–11; Luke 9:1–5; 10:3) (*JaS* 86)

These excerpts from *1 Enoch* 90.6–15 likely describe the revolt Judas Maccabeus led against Antiochus Epiphanes IV. In this *vision*, the sheep symbolize the people of God who need protection, deliverance, and guidance.

1 Enoch *90.6–10, 15*

[6]Then, behold lambs were born from those snow-white sheep; and they began to open their eyes and see, and cried aloud to the sheep. [7]But as for the sheep, they (the lambs) cried aloud to them, yet they (the sheep) did not listen to what they (the lambs) were telling them but became exceedingly deafened, and their eyes became exceedingly dim sighted. [8]Then I saw in a vision ravens flying above those lambs, and they seized one of those lambs, and then smashing the sheep, they ate them. [9]I kept seeing till those lambs grew horns; but the ravens crushed their horns. Then I kept seeing till one great horn sprouted on one of those sheep, and he opened their eyes; and they had vision in them and their eyes were opened. [10]He cried aloud to the sheep, and all the rams saw him and ran unto him. . . . [15]And I kept seeing till the Lord of the sheep came upon them in wrath, and all who saw him fled and fell all into darkness, from before his face.

6.9 The Fate of the Disciples (Matt. 10:17–25; Mark 13:9–13; Luke 12:11–12; 6:40; 21:12–19) (*JaS* 87)

m. Makkot *3.10–12**

This text from the Mishnah gives the prescribed Jewish method for flogging.

[10]A. How many times do they flog him?

B. Forty stripes less one,

C. as it is said, *By number, forty* (Dt. 25:2, 3)—a number near [but less than] forty.

D. R. Judah says, "He is flogged a full forty times,"

E. And where does the additional one fall?

F. Between the shoulders.

[11]A. They make an estimate of his capacity to take the flogging [without being irreparably injured or killed] only by a number divisible by three.

I B. [If] they estimated him as able to take forty, [if] he then received part of the flogging, and they said that he cannot take all forty, he is exempt.

II C. [If] they estimated him as able to take eighteen, [and] once he has received the flogging [of eighteen], they said that he can take all forty, he [still] is exempt from the rest.

III D. [If] he committed a transgression on which he is liable on two counts of violating negative commandments, and they make a single estimate [of what he can take, covering both sets],

E. he is flogged and exempt [from the other].

F. And if not, he is flogged and allowed to heal, and then goes and is flogged again.

[12]A. How do they flog him?

B. One ties his two hands on either side of a pillar,

C. and the minister of the community grabs his clothing—

D. if it is torn, it is torn, and if it is ripped to pieces, it is ripped to pieces—

E. until he bares his chest.

F. A stone is set down behind him, on which the minister of the community stands.

G. And a strap of cowhide is in his hand, doubled and redoubled, with two straps that rise and fall [fastened] to it.

6.10 Divisions within Households (Matt. 10:34–36; Luke 12:51–53) (JaS 89)

The following texts refer to the deteriorating moral conditions that will surround Messiah's coming (i.e., "with the footprints of the Messiah") and to the hostility between children and parents.

m. Soṭah 9.15*

A. When R. Meir died, makers of parables came to an end.

B. When Ben Azzai died, diligent students came to an end.

C. When Ben Zoma died, exegetes came to an end.

D. When R. Joshua died, goodness went away from the world.

E. When Rabban Simeon b. Gamaliel died, the locust came, and troubles multiplied.

F. When R. Eleazar b. Azariah died, wealth went away from the sages.

G. When R. Aqiba died, the glory of the Torah came to an end.

H. When R. Hanina b. Dosa died, wonder workers came to an end.

I. When R. Yose Qatnuta died, pietists went away.

J. (And why was he called *Qatnuta*? Because he was the least of the pietists.)

K. When Rabban Yohanan b. Zakkai died, the splendor of wisdom came to an end.

L. When Rabban Gamaliel the Elder died, the glory of the Torah came to an end, and cleanness and separateness perished.

M. When R. Ishmael b. Phabi died, the splendor of the priesthood came to an end.

N. When Rabbi died, modesty and fear of sin came to an end.

O. R. Pinhas b. Yair says, "When the Temple was destroyed, associates became ashamed and so did free men, and they covered their heads.

P. "And wonder workers became feeble. And violent men and big talkers grew strong.

Q. "And none expounds and none seeks [learning] and none asks.

R. "Upon whom shall we depend? Upon our Father in heaven."

S. R. Eliezer the Great says, "From the day on which the Temple was destroyed, sages began to be like scribes, and scribes like ministers, and ministers like ordinary folk.

T. "And the ordinary folk have become feeble.

U. "And none seeks.

V. "Upon whom shall we depend? Upon our Father in heaven."

W. With the footprints of the Messiah: presumption increases, and dearth increases.

X. The vine gives its fruit and wine at great cost.

Y. And the government turns to heresy.

Z. And there is no reproof.

AA. The gathering place will be for prostitution.

BB. And Galilee will be laid waste.

CC. And the Gablan will be made desolate.

DD. And the men of the frontier will go about from town to town, and none will take pity on them.

EE. And the wisdom of scribes will putrefy.

FF. And those who fear sin will be rejected.

GG. And the truth will be locked away.

HH. Children will shame elders, and elders will stand up before children.

II. *For the son dishonors the father and the daughter rises up against her mother, the daughter-in-law against her mother-in-law; a man's enemies are the men of his own house* (Mic. 7:6).

JJ. The face of the generation in the face of a dog.

KK. A son is not ashamed before his father.

III LL. Upon whom shall we depend? Upon our Father in heaven.

MM. R. Pinhas b. Yair says, "Heedfulness leads to cleanliness, cleanliness leads to cleanness, cleanness leads to abstinence, abstinence leads to holiness, holiness leads to modesty, modesty leads to the fear of sin, the fear of sin leads to piety, piety leads to the Holy Spirit, the Holy Spirit leads to the resurrection of the dead, and the resurrection of the dead comes through Elijah, blessed be his memory, Amen."

Jubilees 23.16, 19

These verses can be found in the extended quote from *Jubilees* 23 in section 11.9 below.

1 Enoch 56.7

But the city of my righteous ones will become an obstacle to their horses. And they shall begin to fight among themselves; and (by) their own right hands they shall prevail against themselves. A man shall not recognize his brother, nor a son his mother, until there shall be a (significant) number of corpses from among them. Their punishment is (indeed) not in vain.

6.11 Taking Up the Cross and Finding Life (Matt. 10:37–39; Luke 14:25–27; 17:33) (*JaS* 90)

Josephus, **Against Apion 2.28 §206**

This text from Josephus appears in section 6.4 above. It discusses honoring parents—a commitment that stands at the heart of Jewish belief and practice—but Jesus claims that the one who follows him must take up his cross and put him ahead of commitment to parents and family.

6.12 Jesus Answers John the Baptist (Matt. 11:2–6; Luke 7:18–23) (*JaS* 93)

Josephus, **Antiquities 18.5.2 §§116–119**

This text from Josephus, appearing in section 3.3 above, tells of John the Baptist's fruitful ministry and his untimely and unjust death at the hands of Herod.

6.13 Come to Me (Matt. 11:28–30) (*JaS* 97)

Sirach 40:1; 51:26; 24:19–20

In Sirach 40:1 and 51:26, the "yoke" is used to describe the difficulty of living in a fallen world and the wisdom one needs to live life well. In Sirach 24:19–20, wisdom is seen as something to be pursued, like honey on the honeycomb. This contrasts with Christ's statement that people should pursue him.

40:1Hard work was created for everyone, and a heavy yoke is laid on the children of Adam, from the day they come forth from their mother's womb until the day they return to the mother of all the living.

51:26Put your neck under her [wisdom] yoke, and let your souls receive instruction; it is to be found close by.

24:19"Come to me, you who desire me, and eat your fill of my fruits. 20For the memory of me is sweeter than honey, and the possession of me sweeter than the honeycomb."

6.14 Summary: Jesus Heals the Multitudes by the Sea (Matt. 12:15–21; Mark 3:7–12; Luke 6:17–19) (JaS 100)

Targum Isaiah 42.1, 6–7*

This later targumic text is read messianically. The word (*memra*) of God blesses the servant, an individual to whom God gives the Spirit and through whom he reveals judgment to the nations. In fact, in verses 6–7 the servant is the covenant of God for a people (Israel) and a light to the nations as they watch how the Lord cares for his people by delivering them.

[1]Behold my servant, I will bring him near; my chosen in whom my memra is well pleased: I will set my Holy Spirit upon him; my judgment he shall reveal to the nations. . . . [6]I the Lord have appointed you in truth, and taken you by the hand, and I will establish you and give you for a covenant of a people, for a light to the nations; [7]to open the eyes of the house of Israel who are as it were blind to the law, to bring forth their exiles from among the nations, where they are like prisoners, and to deliver them from the bondage of the kingdoms, where they are imprisoned like them that are bound in darkness.

6.15 The Sinful Woman Anoints Jesus at the Pharisee's Table (Luke 7:36–50; Matt. 26:6–13; Mark 14:3–9; John 12:1–8) (JaS 101)

These two passages indicate other uses of ointment and the sacred contexts in which they can appear.

Josephus, Antiquities 3.8.6 §205; 19.9.1 §§358–359

3.8.6 [205]Now I shall speak of what we do in our sacred offices in my discourse about sacrifices; and therein shall inform men in what cases Moses bid us offer a whole burnt offering, and in what case the law permits us to partake of them as of food. And when Moses had sprinkled Aaron's vestments, himself, and his sons, with the blood of the beasts that were slain, and had purified them with spring waters and ointment, they became God's priests.

19.9.1 [358]They also laid themselves down in public places, and celebrated general feastings, with garlands on their heads, and with ointments and libations to Charon, and drinking to one another for joy that the king was expired. [359]Nay, they were not only unmindful of Agrippa, who had extended his liberality to them in abundance, but of his grandfather, Herod also, who had himself rebuilt their cities, and had raised them havens and temples at vast expenses.

6.16 The Ministering Women (Luke 8:1–3) (JaS 102)

t. Berakot 6.18*

In this passage, women are viewed in a very negative light. This stands in marked contrast to women in the ministry of Jesus as portrayed in the Gospel of Luke.

A. R Judah says, A man must recite three benedictions every day: (1) "Praised [be you, O LORD . . .] who did not make me a Gentile"; (2) "Praised [be you, O LORD . . .] who did not make me a pagan";

(3) "Praised [be you, O Lord . . .] who did not make me a woman."

B. "A Gentile—as Scripture states, 'All the nations are nothing before him, they are accounted by him as less than nothing and emptiness.'"

C. "A pagan—for a pagan does not fear sin."

D. "A woman—For women are not obligated to perform all the commandments."

Josephus, Antiquities 17.2.4 §§41–44

Luke 8:1–3 notes that three women financially supported Jesus' ministry. As this text in Josephus indicates, women providing monetary help for respected religious leaders was not without precedent in the Jewish world.

[41]For there was a certain sect of men that were Jews, who valued themselves highly upon the exact skill they had in the law of their fathers, and made men believe they were highly favored by God, by whom this set of women were inveigled. These are those that are called the sect of the Pharisees, who were in a capacity of greatly opposing kings. A cunning sect they were, and soon elevated to a pitch of open fighting and doing mischief. [42]Accordingly, when all the people of the Jews gave assurance of their good will to Caesar, and to the king's government, these very men did not swear, being above six thousand; and when the king imposed a fine upon them, Pheroras's wife paid their fine for them. [43]In order to requite which kindness of hers, since they were believed to have the foreknowledge of things to come by divine inspiration, they foretold how God had decreed that Herod's government should cease, and his posterity should be deprived of it; but that the kingdom should come to her and Pheroras, and to their children.

[44]These predictions were not concealed from Salome, but were told the king; as also how they had perverted some persons about the palace itself. So the king slew such of the Pharisees as were principally accused, and Bagoas the eunuch, and one Carus, who exceeded all men of that time in comeliness, and one that was his catamite. . . .

6.17 The Cast-Out-by-Beelzebul Charge (Matt. 12:22–30; Mark 3:22–27; Luke 11:14–15, 17–23) (*JaS 104*)

Testament of Solomon 2.8–3.6; 6.1–9 (*excerpts*)

The following material reveals the Jewish belief in a "Prince of Demons" named Beelzeboul. As such, this material provides excellent background for Jesus' controversy with the religious leaders concerning his power to cast out demons and their accusation that he did so by the power of Beelzebul. See also the citations from the magical papyri that follow.

[2.8]The angels commanded sea monsters to arise out of the sea and he withered up their species and cast his fate to the ground. In this same way he also subjected the great demon Ornias to cut stones and to bring to completion the construction of the Temple which I, Solomon, was in the process of building. [9]Again, I glorified the God of heaven and earth and I commanded Ornias to come near according to his fate. Then I gave him the seal and said, "Go and bring here to me the Prince of Demons." [3.1]So Ornias took the ring and went to Beelzeboul, and said to him, "Come! Solomon summons you!" [2]But Beelzeboul said to him, "Tell me, who is the Solomon of whom you speak?" [3]Then Ornias flung the ring into the chest of

Beelzeboul and replied, "Solomon the king summons you!" [4]Beelzeboul cried out like (one who is burned) from a great burning flame of fire, and when he had gotten up, he followed (Ornias) under coercion and came to me. [5]When I saw the Prince of Demons approaching, I glorified God and said, "Blessed are you, Lord God Almighty, who has granted to your servant Solomon wisdom, the attendant of your thrones, and who has placed in subjection all the power of the demons."

[6]Then I interrogated him and said, "Tell me, who are you?" The demon said, "I am Beelzeboul, the ruler of the demons." I demanded that without interruption he sit next to me and explain the manifestations of the demons. Then he promised to bring to me all the unclean spirits bound. Again, I glorified the God of heaven and earth, continually giving thanks to him.

[6.1]Then I summoned Beelzeboul to appear before me again. When he was seated, I thought it appropriate to ask him, "Why are you alone Prince of Demons?" [2]He replied, "Because I am the only one left of the heavenly angels (who fell). [3]I was the highest-ranking angel in heaven, the one called Beelzeboul. . . ."

[4]I said to him, "What are your activities?" He replied, "I bring destruction by means of tyrants; I cause the demons to be worshiped alongside men; and I arouse desire in holy men and select priests. I bring about jealousies and murders in a country, and I instigate wars."

. . . [7]So I said to him, "Tell me in which star you reside." "The one called the Evening Star," he said.

[8]Then I said, "Tell me which angel thwarts you." "The Almighty God," he replied. "He is called by the Hebrews Patike, the one who descends from the heights; he is (called) by the Greeks Emmanouel. I am always afraid of him, and trembling. If anyone adjures me with the oath (called) 'the Elo-i,' a great name for his power, I disappear."

[9]Now when I, Solomon, heard these things, I commanded him to cut blocks of Theban marble. As he was beginning to cut, all the demons cried out with a loud voice because (he was their) king, Beelzeboul.

PGM *1.87–89, 164–66, 181–85, 249–55; 2.52–54*

[1.87–89]And you address the first words to the god: "I shall have you as a friendly assistant, a beneficent god who serves me whenever I say, 'Quickly, by your power now appear on earth to me, yea verily, god!' "

[1.164–66]And this is spoken next: "Hither to me, King, [I call you] God of Gods, mighty, boundless, undefiled, indescribable, firmly established Aion. Be inseparable from me from this day forth through all the time of my life."

The one addressed here who is to do the bidding of the one making request is the spirit of an angel.

[1.181–85]Whenever you wish to do something, speak his name alone into the air [and] say, ["Come!"] and you will see him actually standing near you. And say to him, "Perform this task," and he does it at once, and after doing it he will say to you, "What else do you want? For I am eager for heaven." If you do not have immediate orders, say to him, "Go, lord," and he will depart.

[1.249–55]Rub these with oil of lily, and as you are rubbing them from right to left, say the spell as follows: "I am

ANUBIS, I am OSIR-PHERE, I am OSOT SORONOUIER, I am OSIRIS whom SETH destroyed. Rise up, infernal daimon, I[O] ERB[E]TH I[O] PHOB[E]TH I[O] PAKERB[E]TH I[O] APOMPS; whatever I, NN, order you to do, be obedient to me."

In this text, there is the following invocation of the demon.

2.52–54"ABRI and ABRO EXANTIABIL, God of gods, king of kings, now force a friendly daimon of prophecy to come to me, lest I apply worse tortures to you, the things written on the strips of papyrus."

t. Pisha (= Pesaḥim 2.15)*

A. Rabbi Gamaliel was going along from Akko to Kezib.

B. He found a loaf of cheap bread on the road.

C. He said to his slave, Tabi, "Take the loaf."

D. He saw a Gentile. He said to him, "Mabegai, take this loaf of bread."

E. R Le'ii ran after him [and] said to him, "Who are you?"

F. He said to him, "I come from one of these station-keepers' villages."

G. He said to him, "What is your name?"

H. He said to him, "Mabegai."

I. He said to him, "Now, did Rabbi Gamaliel ever in your life meet you?"

J. He said to him, "No."

K. On the basis of this event we learn that Rabbi Gamaliel divined by the Holy Spirit.

6.18 The Sign of Jonah (Matt. 12:38–42; Mark 8:11–12; Luke

11:16, 29–32; cf. also Matt. 16:1–2a, 4) (JaS 106)

Josephus, Antiquities 8.6.5–6 §§165–175

In the following text, Josephus records the story of how the queen of Egypt and Ethiopia visited Solomon and was thoroughly impressed with his wisdom, concluding that it was even greater than she had earlier been led to believe. She was impressed as well with the king's residence, his servants, and the way in which he conducted his affairs.

165There was then a woman, queen of Egypt and Ethiopia; she was inquisitive into philosophy, and one that on other accounts also was to be admired. When this queen heard of the virtue and prudence of Solomon, she had a great mind to see him; and the reports that went every day abroad induced her to come to him, 166she being desirous to be satisfied by her own experience, and not by a bare hearing (for reports thus heard, are likely enough to comply with a false opinion, while they wholly depend on the credit of the relators); so she resolved to come to him, and that especially, in order to have a trial of his wisdom, while she proposed questions of very great difficulty, and entreated that he would solve their hidden meaning. Accordingly she came to Jerusalem with great splendor and rich furniture; 167for she brought with her camels laden with gold, with several sorts of sweet spices, and with precious stones. Now, upon the king's kind reception of her, he both showed a great desire to please her, and easily comprehending in his mind the meaning of the curious questions she propounded to him, he resolved them sooner than anybody could have expected. 168So she was amazed at the wisdom of Solomon, and discovered that it was more excellent upon trial than what she had heard by report beforehand; and especially she was surprised at the fineness and largeness of his royal palace, and not less so at the good order of the apartments, for she observed that the king had therein shown great wisdom; [169]but she was beyond measure astonished at the house which was called the *Forest of Lebanon*, as also at the magnificence of his daily table, and the circumstances of its preparation and ministration, with the apparel of his servants that waited, and the skillful and decent management of their attendance: nor was she less affected with those daily sacrifices which were offered to God, and the careful management which the priests and Levites used about them. [170]When she saw this done every day, she was in the greatest admiration imaginable, insomuch that she was not able to contain the surprise she was in, but openly confessed how wonderfully she was affected; for she proceeded to discourse with the king, and thereby owned that she was overcome with admiration at the things before related; and said, [171]"All things indeed, O king, that came to our knowledge by report, came with uncertainty as to our belief of them; but as to those good things that to you appertain, both such as you yourself possess, I mean wisdom and prudence, and the happiness you have from your kingdom, certainly the same that came to us was no falsity; it was not only a true report, but it related your happiness after a much lower manner than I now see it to be before my eyes. [172]For as for the report, it only attempted to persuade our hearing, but did not so

make known the dignity of the things themselves as does the sight of them, and being present among them. I, indeed, who did not believe what was reported, by reason of the multitude and grandeur of the things I inquired about, do see them to be much more numerous than they were reported to be. [173]Accordingly, I esteem the Hebrew people, as well as your servants and friends, to be happy, who enjoy your presence and hear your wisdom every day continually. One would therefore bless God, who has so loved this country, and those that inhabit therein, as to make you king over them."

[174]Now when the queen had thus demonstrated in words how deeply the king had affected her, her disposition was known by certain presents, for she gave him twenty talents of gold, and an immense quantity of spices and precious stones. (They say also that we possess the root of that balsam which our country still bears by this woman's gift.) [175]Solomon also repaid her with many good things, and principally by bestowing upon her what she chose of her own inclination, for there was nothing that she desired which he denied her: and as he was very generous and liberal in his own temper, so did he show the greatness of his soul in bestowing on her what she herself desired of him. So when this queen of Ethiopia had obtained what we have already given an account of, and had again communicated to the king what she brought with her, she returned to her own kingdom.

7

From Kingdom Teaching to Confession

7.1 Interpretation of the Parable of the Sower (Matt. 13:18–23; Mark 4:13–20; Luke 8:11–15) (*JaS* 112)

2 Maccabees 15:12

This text refers to Onias the high priest as a "noble and good man," a description used by Jesus in the parable of the sower to refer to spiritual integrity. *cf Barnabas too*

What he saw was this: Onias, who had been high priest, a noble and good man, of modest bearing and gentle manner, one who spoke fittingly and had been trained from childhood in all that belongs to excellence, was praying with outstretched hands for the whole body of the Jews.

7.2 The Parable of the Mustard Seed (Matt. 13:31–32; Mark 4:30–32; Luke 13:18–19) (*JaS* 116)

In these first two Mishnah texts (*m. Niddah* 5.2 and *m. Ṭoharot* 8.8), the mustard seed is considered to be very small and is used to measure the small amount of discharge necessary to render a person unclean. In the final entry, from *m. Kilʾayim*, we learn that the mustard seed was planted not in the garden but only in the field.

m. Niddah 5.2*

A. [If] one was eating heave offering and felt his limbs tremble—

B. he holds on to the penis and swallows the heave offering.

C. And they are made unclean by any amount [of discharge] at all,

D. even though it is like a grain of mustard,

E. and less than that.

m. Ṭoharot 8.8*

A. (1) A kneading trough which lay on an incline,

(2) and the [unclean] dough is above,

(3) and running liquid is below—

B. three pieces of dough [together making up] an egg's bulk—

C. they are not joined together.

D. And two—they are joined together.

E. R. Yose says, "Even two are not joined together,

F. "unless they confine the liquid closely."

G. And if it was standing liquid,

H. even if [the pieces of dough that made up the egg's bulk] were small as a mustard seed—it is joined together.

I. R. Dosa says, "Food broken into crumbs is not joined together [to make up the egg's bulk]."

m. Kil'ayim 2.9; 3.2*

2.9A. He who wishes to lay out his field [in] patches of every kind [with each patch containing a different kind]—

B. (1) he lays out twenty-four patches to a *bet seah*, (2) a patch to a *bet rova*,

C. and sows in any kind that he wishes.

D. "If there were one or two patches [in a field of grain], he sows them with mustard;

E. "[but if there were] three [patches], he shall not sow them [with] mustard,

F. "for [then the field as a whole] looks like a field of mustard,"

G. the words of R. Meir.

H. And the sages say, "Nine patches are permitted, [but] ten are prohibited [it is permitted to lay out no more than nine patches of mustard in a field of grain.]"

I. R. Eliezer b. Jacob says, "Even [if] his entire field is [the size of] a *bet kor*, he shall lay out only one patch in it."

3.2A. No kind of seeds do they sow in a garden bed,

B. but all kinds of vegetables do they sow in a garden bed.

C. Mustard and smooth chick-peas (alt. trans.: small chick-peas) [are considered] kind[s] of seeds,

D. [while] large chick-peas [are considered] a kind of vegetable.

E. A border which was [originally] a handbreadth high and became diminished [in height],

F. is fit,

G. for it was fit from [at] its inception.

H. The furrow and the [dry] water channel which are a handbreadth deep—

I. (1) they sow in them three [kinds of] seeds, (2) one on one [side], one

on the other [side], and one in the middle.

7.3 Interpretation of the Parable of the Wheat and the Darnel (Matt. 13:36–43) (*JaS* 119)

The following three citations show that saints—who are also referred to as "seed"—will shine forth like the sun in the final judgment. We see this same "light" imagery in Jesus' teaching.

Wisdom of Solomon 3:7–8

7In the time of their visitation they will shine forth, and will run like sparks through the stubble. 8They will govern nations and rule over peoples, and the Lord will reign over them forever.

4 Ezra (= 2 Esdras) 7:97

The sixth order, when it is shown them how their face is to shine like the sun, and how they are to be made like the light of the stars, being incorruptible from then on.

2 Baruch 70.2

See section 11.12 below.

7.4 The Parables of the Hidden Treasure and the Pearl (Matt. 13:44–46) (*JaS* 120)

This text indicates what is actually acquired when a person purchases a field.

m. Baba Batra 4.8–9*

8A. He who sells a field has sold (1) the stones which are needed for it, (2) the canes in the vineyard which are needed for it, and (3) the crop which is yet unplucked up from the ground;

B. (4) a partition of reeds which covers less than a quarter-*qab* of space of ground, (5) the watchman's house which is not fastened down with mortar, (6) the carob which was not grafted, and (7) the young sycamores.

⁹A. But he has not sold (1) the stones which are not needed for it, (2) the canes in the vineyard which are not needed for it, (3) the crop which has already been plucked up from the ground.

B. If he had said to him, "It and everything which is in it,"

C. lo, all of them are sold.

D. One way or the other, he has not sold to him (4) a partition of reeds which covers a quarter-*qab* of space of ground, (5) a watchman's house which is fastened down with mortar, (6) a carob which was grafted, and (7) cropped sycamores;

E. (8) a cistern, (9) winepress, or (10) dovecote,

F. whether they are lying waste or in use.

G. "And [the seller] needs to purchase [from the buyer] a right-of-way," the words of R. Aqiba.

H. And sages say, "He does not have to."

I. And R. Aqiba concedes that, when [the seller] said to him, "Except for these," he does not have to buy himself a right-of-way.

J. [If] he sold them to someone else,

K. R. Aqiba says, "[The new purchaser] does not have to buy a right-of-way for himself."

L. And sages say, "He has to buy a right-of-way for himself."

M. Under what circumstances?

N. In the case of one who sells [the aforelisted properties].

O. But in the case of one who gives a gift,

P. he [willingly] hands over all of them.

I Q. Brothers who divided [an estate]—

R. once they have acquired possession of a field, they have acquired possession of all of them [and no longer may retract].

II S. He who lays hold of the property of a deceased proselyte [lacking Israelite heirs],

T. once he has acquired possession of a field, has acquired possession of all of them.

III U. He who declares a field sanctified has declared all of them sanctified.

V. R. Simeon says, "He who declares a field sanctified has declared sanctified only the carob which is grafted, and cropped sycamores."

7.5 Opinions about Jesus (Matt. 14:1–2; Mark 6:14–16; Luke 9:7–9) (JaS 129)

When Jesus appeared on the scene, Herod thought Jesus had a spirit like John the Baptist or that perhaps John had somehow passed on his authority to Jesus. Perhaps the worldview present in this text from Josephus, in which ghosts appear and perform certain activities, provides a backdrop for Herod's thoughts about John and Jesus.

Josephus, Jewish War 1.30.7 §§598–600

⁵⁹⁸When she had said this, she brought the box, which had a small quantity of this potion in it; but the king let her alone, and transferred the tortures to Antiphilus's mother and brother; who both confessed that Antiphilus brought the box out of Egypt, and that they had received the potion from a

brother of his, who was a physician at Alexandria. [599]Then did the ghosts of Alexander and Aristobulus go round all the palace, and became the inquisitors and discoverers of what could not otherwise have been found out, and brought such as were the freest from suspicion to be examined; whereby it was discovered that Mariamne, the high priest's daughter, was conscious of this plot; and her very brothers, when they were tortured, declared it so to be. [600]Whereupon the king avenged this insolent attempt of the mother upon her son, and blotted Herod, whom he had by her, out of his treatment, who had been before named therein as successor to Antipater.

7.6 The Death of John the Baptist (Matt. 14:3–12; Mark 6:17–29; Luke 3:19–20) (JaS 130)

Herod's vow was certainly rash and, in light of *m. Nedarim* 3.1 and 9.4, probably could have been revoked.

m. Nedarim *3.1; 9.4*

[3.1]A. Four [types of] vows did sages declare not binding:

(1) Vows of incitement, (2) vows of exaggeration, (3) vows made in error, and (4) vows [broken] under constraint.

(1) B. *Vows of incitement*: How so?

C. [If] one was selling something and said, "*Qonam* if I chop the price down for you to under a *sela*," and the other says, "*Qonam if* I pay you more than a *shekel*,"

D. [then] both of them agree at three *denars*.

E. R. Eliezer b. Jacob says, "Also: He who wants to force his fellow by a vow to eat with him says, 'Any vow which I am going to vow is null,'—so

long as he is mindful at the moment of his vow."

[9.4]A. And further did R. Meir say, "They unloose his [vow] by reference to what is written in the Torah, saying to him,

B. "'If you had known that you would transgress the commandment, *You shall not take vengeance,* or, *You shall not bear a grudge* (Lev. 19:18), or, *You shall not hate your brother in your heart* (Lev. 19:17), or, *You shall love your neighbor as yourself* (Lev. 19:18), or *That your brother may live with you* (Lev. 25:36), [would you have taken such a vow?] Now what happens if he becomes poor and you will be unable to help him out?'

C. "And he says, 'If I had known that matters were thus, I should never have taken such a vow'—

D. "lo, this [vow] is loosed."

7.7 Disputes over Traditions of the Elders and Defilement (Matt. 15:1–20; Mark 7:1–23) (JaS 135)

The following text reveals the extent to which purification rites and ceremonial washings were performed. The disciples and Jesus apparently show knowledge of, but little concern for, these traditions.

m. Yadayim *1.1–2.4*

[1.1]A. [To render hands clean] a quarter-*log* of water do they pour for hands,

B. for one,

C. also for two.

D. A half-*log* [is to be used] for three or four.

E. A *log* [is to be used] for five and for ten and for a hundred.

F. R. Yose says, "And on condition that for the last among them, there should not be less than a quarter-*log*."

G. They add [to the water used] for the second [pouring], but they do not add [to the water used] for the first [pouring of water over the hands].

2A. With all sorts of utensils do they pour [water] for hands,

B. even with utensils made of dung, utensils made of stone, utensils made of [unbaked] clay.

C. They do not pour [water] for hands either with the sides of [broken] utensils, or the bottom of a ladling jar, or with the plug of a barrel.

D. Nor should a man pour [water] for his fellow with his cupped hands.

E. For they draw, and they mix [water with the ash of the red cow], and they sprinkle purification water, and they pour [water] for hands only with a utensil.

F. And only utensils afford protection with a tightly fitted cover, and nothing affords protection from the power of a clay utensil [in the Tent of a corpse] except utensils.

3A. Water which was unfit for cattle to drink

B. [when it is located] in utensils, is unfit.

C. [When it is located] on the ground, it is fit.

D. [If] there fell into it ink, gum, or copperas, and its color changed, it is unfit.

E. [If] one did work with it,

F. or if he soaked his bread in it,

G. it is unfit.

H. Simeon of Teman says, "Even if he intended to soak [bread] in this and it fell into the second, it [the second] is fit."

4A. [If] he rinsed utensils in it,

B. or scrubbed measures in it,

C. it is unfit.

D. [If] he rinsed in it vessels which had already been rinsed,

E. or new [vessels],

F. it is fit.

G. R. Yose declares unfit in [the case of rinsing] new [vessels in it].

5A. The water in which the baker dips loaves of fine bread is unfit.

B. And when he rinses his hands in it, it is fit.

C. All are fit to pour water on hands, even a deaf-mute, an imbecile, or a minor.

D. One places the jar between his knees and pours [out water on his hands].

E. One sets the jar on its side and pours [out water].

F. And the ape pours water for hands.

G. R. Yose declares unfit in these two cases.

2.1A. [If] one poured water for one hand with a single rinsing, his hand is clean.

B. [If he poured water] for two hands with a single rinsing—

C. R. Meir declares unclean unless he will pour a quarter-*log* [of water].

D. [If] a loaf of heave offering fell [on the water a quarter-*log* in quantity which has been poured on the hands in a single rinsing], it is clean.

E. R. Yose declares unclean.

2A. [If] one poured out the first [water] in one place and the second in another place,

B. and a loaf of heave offering fell on the first, it is unclean.

C. And [if it fell] on the second, it is clean.

D. [If] he poured out the first [water] and the second in one place, and a loaf of heave offering fell [on it], it is unclean.

E. [If] he poured out the first [water], and a splinter or pebble was found on his hands, his hands are unclean,

F. for the second water cleans only the water which is on the hand.

G. Rabban Simeon b. Gamaliel says, "Whatever originates in water is clean."

³A. The hands are susceptible to uncleanness and are rendered clean up to the wrist.

B. How so?

C. [If] one poured the first [water] up to the wrist, and the second beyond the wrist and it went back to the hand—it is clean.

D. [If] he poured out the first and the second [pouring of water] beyond the wrist and it went back to the hand, it is unclean.

E. [If] he poured out the first water onto one hand, and was reminded and poured out the second [water] on to both hands, they are unclean.

F. [If] he poured out the first water on to both hands and was reminded and poured out the second [water] on to one hand, his hand [which has been washed twice] is clean.

G. [If] he poured out water on to one hand and rubbed it on the other, it is unclean.

H. [If he rubbed his hand] on his head or on the wall, it is clean.

I. They pour out [water on the hands of] four or five people side by side, or above one another,

J. on condition that they [the hands] lie loosely so that the water will flow among them.

⁴A. [If it is in] doubt that work has or has not been done with it,

B. [if it is in] doubt that they contain or do not contain the requisite measure,

C. [if it is in] doubt whether it is unclean or clean—

D. a matter of doubt concerning it is clean.

E. For they have said:

A matter of doubt concerning the hands, whether [they are] unclean, or whether [they are deemed] to have imparted uncleanness, or whether

[they are deemed] to have been made clean, is resolved as clean.

F. R. Yose says, "[A matter of doubt concerning whether the hands have] been made clean is resolved as unclean."

G. How so?

H. [If] his hands were clean, and before him were two unclean loaves of bread,

I. [if it is in] doubt whether or not he touched them—

J. [if] his hands were unclean, and before him were two clean loaves of bread,

K. [if] one of his hands was unclean and one of his hands was clean and before him were two clean loaves of bread,

L. [and if] he touched one of them,

M. [if it is in] doubt whether he touched with the unclean or whether he touched with the clean [hand]—

N. [if] his hands were clean, and before him were two loaves of bread, one of them unclean and one of them clean,

O. [and if] he touched one of them,

P. [if it is in] doubt whether he touched the unclean or whether he touched the clean [loaf of bread]—

Q. [if] one of his hands was unclean and one was clean, and before him were two loaves [of bread], one of them unclean and one of them clean,

R. [if] he touched both of them,

S. [if it is in] doubt whether the unclean [hand touched] the unclean [loaf of bread] and the clean [hand touched] the clean [loaf of bread],

T. or [whether] the clean [hand touched] the unclean [loaf of bread] and the unclean [hand touched] the clean [loaf of bread]—

U. the hands remain as they were before [in their former status], and the loaves of bread as they were before [in their former status].

This tractate as a whole deals with the issue of "cleanness." There are even degrees of uncleanness, as 1.4–6 and 2.2–7 show. On issues related to what one has touched, see also 5.2 and 7.8.

m. Ṭoharot *1.4–6; 2.2–7; 5.2; 7.8*

1.4A. And with regard to cattle:

B. (1) The hide, (2) the fat, (3) the sediment, (4) the flesh, (5) the bones, (6) the tendons, (7) and horns, and (8) the hoofs

C. join together to convey the uncleanness of foods

D. but not the uncleanness of carrion.

E. And similarly:

F. He who slaughters an unclean beast for a gentile, and it jerks—it conveys the uncleanness of foods but not the uncleanness of carrion—

G. until it will die,

H. or until one will cut off its head.

I. [The law] has prescribed more [conditions] to convey uncleanness of foods than to convey uncleanness of carrion.

5A. The food which is made unclean by a Father of Uncleanness and that which is made unclean by an Offspring of Uncleanness join together with one another to convey the lighter remove of uncleanness of the two. How so?

B. A half-egg's bulk of food which is unclean in the first remove and a half egg's bulk of food which is unclean in the second remove which one mixed with one another—[the consequent mixture is unclean in the] second [remove of uncleanness].

C. A half-egg's bulk of food unclean in the second remove of uncleanness and a half-egg's bulk of food unclean

in the third remove of uncleanness which one mixed together with one another—[it is unclean in the] first [remove of uncleanness].

D. [But] an egg's bulk of food unclean in the first remove of uncleanness and an egg's bulk of food unclean in the second remove of uncleanness which one mixed together with one another—[it is unclean in the] first [remove of uncleanness.]

E. [If] one divided them up—this is unclean in the second remove of uncleanness, and this is unclean in the second remove of uncleanness.

F. This one fell by itself and this one by itself on a loaf of heave offering—they have rendered it unfit.

G. [If] the two of them fell on it simultaneously—they have made it unclean in the second remove of uncleanness.

6A. An egg's bulk of food unclean in the second remove and an egg's bulk of food unclean in the third remove which one mixed with one another—it is unclean in the second remove.

B. [If] one divided them—

C. this one fell by itself and this by itself on a loaf of heave offering—they have not made it unfit.

D. If the two of them fell simultaneously—they put it into the third remove.

E. An egg's bulk of food unclean in the first remove and an egg's bulk of food unclean in the third remove which one mixed with one another—it is unclean in the first remove.

F. [If] one divided them—this one is unclean in the second remove, and this is unclean in the second remove.

G. For even that which is unclean in the third remove which touched something unclean in the first remove becomes unclean in the second remove.

H. Two eggs' bulk of food unclean in the first remove, two eggs' bulk of food unclean in the second remove which one mixed with one another—it is unclean in the first remove.

I. [If] one divided them—this is unclean in the first remove and this one is unclean in the first remove.

J. [If one divided them into] three or four parts—lo, these are unclean in the second remove.

K. Two eggs' bulk of food unclean in the second remove, two eggs' bulk of food unclean in the third remove, which one mixed together—it is unclean in the second remove.

L. [If] one divided them—this one is unclean in the second remove, and this one is unclean in the second remove.

M. [If one divided them into] three or four parts, lo, these all are in the third remove.

2.2A. R. Eliezer says, "(1) He who eats food unclean in the first remove is unclean in the first remove; (2) [he who eats] food unclean in the second remove is unclean in the second remove; (3) [he who eats) food unclean in the third remove is unclean in the third remove."

B. R. Joshua says, "(1) He who eats food unclean in the first remove and food unclean in the second remove is unclean in the second remove. (2) [He who eats food] unclean in the third remove is unclean in the second remove so far as Holy Things are concerned, (3) and is not unclean in the second remove so far as heave offering is concerned—

C. "in the case of unconsecrated food

D. "which is prepared in conditions of cleanness appropriate to heave offering."

3A. *Unconsecrated food*: in the first remove is unclean and renders [heave offering] unclean.

B. [Unconsecrated food] in the second remove is unfit but does not convey uncleanness.

C. And [unconsecrated food] in the third remove is eaten in pottage of heave offering.

4A. *Heave offering*: in the first and in the second removes is unclean and renders [Holy Things] unclean.

B. [Heave offering] in the third remove is unfit and does not convey uncleanness.

C. And [heave offering] at the fourth remove is eaten in a pottage of Holy Things.

5A. *Holy Things*: in the first and the second and the third removes are susceptible to uncleanness and convey uncleanness.

B. And [Holy Things] in the fourth remove are unfit and do not convey uncleanness.

C. And [Holy Things] in the fifth remove are eaten in a pottage of Holy Things.

6A. *Unconsecrated food*: in the second remove renders unconsecrated liquid unclean and renders unfit foods of heave offering.

B. *Heave offering*: at the third remove renders unclean liquid of Holy Things and renders unfit foods of Holy Things,

C. if it [the heave offering] was prepared in conditions of cleanness pertaining to Holy Things.

D. But if it was prepared in conditions pertaining to heave offering, it renders unclean at two removes and renders unfit at one remove in reference to Holy Things.

7A. R. Eleazar says, "The three of them are equal:

B. "*Holy Things and heave offering and unconsecrated food*: which are at the first remove of uncleanness render unclean at two removes and unfit at one [further] remove in respect to Holy Things,

C. "render unclean at one remove and spoil at one [further] remove in respect to heave offering,

D. "and spoil unconsecrated food.

E. "That which is unclean in the second remove in respect to all of them renders unclean at one remove and unfit at one [further] remove in respect to Holy Things,

F. "and renders liquid of unconsecrated food unclean,

G. "and spoils foods of heave offering.

H. "The third remove of uncleanness in respect to all of them renders liquids of Holy Things unclean,

I. "and spoils foods of Holy Things."

5.2 A. One who said, "I touched this, but I do not know whether it is unclean or whether it is clean"—

B. "I touched, and I do not know which of the two of them I touched"—

C. R. Aqiba declares unclean.

D. And sages declare clean.

E. R. Yose declares unclean in [the case of] all of them but declares clean in the case of the path,

F. for it is the way of men to walk, and it is not their way to touch.

7.8 A. He who was clean, and he changed his mind about eating [heave offering]—

B. R. Judah declares [him] clean,

C. for it is the way of unclean people to separate from him.

D. And sages declare unclean.

E. [If] his hands were clean, and he changed his mind about eating,

F. even though he said, "I know that my hands have not been made unclean,"

G. his hands are unclean,

H. for the hands are busy.

In Sirach 3:6–8, 12–15 and Josephus, *Against Apion* 2.28, we see the importance in Judaism of caring for one's parents.

Sirach 3:6–8, 12–15

[6]Those who respect their father will have long life, and those who honor their mother obey the Lord; [7]they will serve their parents as their masters. [8]Honor your father by word and deed, that his blessing may come upon you. . . . [12]My child, help your father in his old age, and do not grieve him as long as he lives; [13]even if his mind fails, be patient with him; because you have all your faculties do not despise him. [14]For kindness to a father will not be forgotten, and will be credited to you against your sins; [15]in the day of your distress it will be remembered in your favor; like frost in fair weather, your sins will melt away.

Josephus, Against Apion 2.28 §206

See section 6.4 above.

m. Nedarim 1.2–4; 3.2; 9.7*

In these citations from *m. Nedarim*, we learn about the practice of corban (qorban), that is, declaring something dedicated to God and therefore no longer available for any other use.

1.2 A. He who says to his fellow, "*Qonam*," "*Qonah*," "*Qonas*"—lo, these are substitutes for Qorban [a vow to bring a sacrifice, and are valid].

B. [He who says to his fellow,] "*Hereq*," "*Herekh*," "*Heref*," lo, these are substitutes for a *herem* [ban].

C. [He who says to his fellow,] "*Naziq*," "*Naziah*," "*Paziah*,"—lo, these are substitutes for Nazirite vows.

D. [He who says,] "*Shebutah*," "*Shequqah*,"

E. [or if he] vowed [with the word] "Mota,"

F. lo, these are substitutes for *shebuah* [oath].

³A. He who says, "Not-unconsecrated produce shall I not eat with you," "Not-valid [food]," and, "Not pure," "[Not] clean [for the altar]," or "Unclean," or "Remnant," or "Refuse"—

B. is bound.

C. [If he said, "May it be to me] like the lamb [of the daily whole offering]," "Like the [temple] sheds," "Like the wood," "Like the fire," "Like the altar," "Like the sanctuary," "Like Jerusalem"—

D. [if] he vowed by the name of one of any of the utensils used for the altar,

E. even though he has not used the word *qorban*—

F. lo, this one has vowed [in as binding a way as if he had vowed] by *qorban*.

G. R. Judah says, "He who says, 'Jerusalem,' has said nothing."

⁴A. He who says, "An offering," "A whole offering," "A meal offering," "A sin offering," "A thank offering," "Peace offering,"—

B. "be what I eat with you,"

C. he is bound [prohibited from eating with the other party].

D. R. Judah permits [declares him not bound].

E. [If he says, "May what I eat of yours be] the *qorban*," "Like the *qorban*," "[By] a *qorban* [do I vow]"—

F. "be what I eat with you,"

G. he is bound.

H. [If he says,] "For a *qorban* shall be what I eat with you,"

I. R. Meir declares him bound.

J. He who says to his fellow, "*Qonam* be my mouth which speaks with you," or "My hand which works with you," or "My foot which walks with you,"

K. is bound.

³.²(2) A. *Vows of exaggeration:*

B. [If he said, "*Qonam* if I did not see [walking] on this road as many as went out of Egypt,"

C. ". . . if I did not see a snake as big as the beam of an olive press."

(3) D. *Vows made in error:*

E. ". . . if I ate," or ". . . if I drank," and he remembered that he ate or drank;

F. ". . . if I eat," or ". . . if I drink" and he forgot and ate and drank.

G. [If he said, "*Qonam* be any benefit my wife gets from me, for she stole my purse," "for she beat up my son," and he found out that she had not beaten up his son, or he found out that she had not stolen it.

H. [If] he saw people eating figs [belonging to him] and said, "Lo, they are *qorban* to you!" and they turned out to be his father and brothers, and there were others with them—

I. the House of Shammai say, "They are permitted, and those with them are prohibited."

J. And the House of Hillel say, "These and those [men] are permitted [to eat the figs]."

⁹.⁷A. How so?

B. [If] he said, "*Qonam* be what I enjoy from any one of you"—

C. [if] his vow with reference to any one of them was declared not binding, the vow with reference to all of them was declared not binding.

D. [If he said, "*Qonam*] be what I enjoy from this one and from that one,"

E. [if] the vow pertaining to the first was declared not binding, all of them are no longer subject to the vow.

F. [If] the vow pertaining to the last one of them was declared not binding, the last one is permitted [to give benefit to the man] but the rest of them are prohibited.

G. [If the vow] was declared not binding for one in the middle, from him and onward, it is not binding, but from him and backward, it is binding.

H. [If he said,] "Let what I enjoy of this one's be *qorban*, and of that one's be *qorban*," they require an opening [absolution] for each and every one of them.

In the following texts, we see how frequently the image of a plant is used to describe the establishment and flourishing of the people of God.

Jubilees *1.16; 7.34; 21.24*

[1.16]And with all my heart and with all my soul I shall transplant them as a righteous plant. And they will be a blessing and not a curse. And they will be the head and not the tail.

[7.34]And now, my children, hear (and) do justice and righteousness so that you might be planted in righteousness on the surface of the whole earth, and your honor may be lifted up before my God who saved me from the water of the Flood.

[21.24]And he will bless you in all your deeds, and he will raise up from you a righteous plant in all the earth throughout all the generations of the earth; and my name and your name shall not cease from beneath heaven forever.

1 Enoch *10.16; 84.6; 93.2*

For *1 Enoch* 93.2, see section 9.17 below.

[10.16]Destroy injustice from the face of the earth. And every iniquitous deed will end, and the plant of righteousness and truth will appear forever and he will plant joy.

[84.6]Do now destroy, O my Lord, the flesh that has angered you from upon the earth, but sustain the flesh of righteousness and uprightness as a plant of eternal seed; and hide not your face from the prayer of your servant, O Lord.

1QS 8.4–7; 11.8

[8.4]When these things exist in Israel, [5]the Community council shall be founded on truth, *Blank* like an everlasting plantation, a holy house for Israel and the foundation of the holy of [6]holies for Aaron, true witnesses for the judgment and chosen by the will (of God) to atone for the earth and to render [7]the wicked their retribution.

[11.8]He unites their assembly to the sons of the heavens in order (to form) the council of the Community and a foundation of the building of holiness to be an everlasting plantation throughout all future ages.

CD 1.5–8

[5]And at the moment of wrath, three hundred and [6]ninety years after having delivered them up into the hands of Nebuchadnezzar, king of Babylon, [7]he visited them and caused to sprout from Israel and from Aaron a shoot of the planting, in order to possess [8]his land and to become fat with the good things of his soil.

8

Confession and Prediction

8.1 The Transfiguration (Matt. 17:1–9; Mark 9:2–10; Luke 9:28–36) (JaS 145)

The following texts from *2 Baruch* and *1 Enoch* symbolize "glory" through images of light, beauty, and dazzlingly bright garments.

2 Baruch *51.3, 5, 10, 12*

³Also, as for the glory of those who proved to be righteous on account of my law, those who possessed intelligence in their life, and those who planted the root of wisdom in their heart—their splendor will then be glorified by transformations, and the shape of their face will be changed into the light of their beauty so that they may inquire and receive the undying world which is promised to them. . . . ⁵When they, therefore, will see that those over whom they are exalted now will then be more exalted and glorified than they, then both these and those will be changed, these into the splendor of angels and those into startling visions and horrible shapes; and they will waste away even more. . . . ¹⁰For they will live in the heights of that world and they will be like the angels and be equal to the stars. And they will be changed into any shape which they wished, from beauty to loveliness,

and from light to the splendor of glory. . . . ¹²And the excellence of the righteous will then be greater than that of the angels.

1 Enoch *38.1, 4; 62.15–16; 104.2*

³⁸·¹When the congregation of the righteous shall appear, sinners shall be judged for their sins . . . ⁴and from that time, those who possess the earth will neither be rulers nor princes, they shall not be able to behold the faces of the holy ones, for the light of the Lord of the Spirits has shined upon the face of the holy, the righteous, and the elect.

⁶²·¹⁵The righteous and elect ones shall rise from the earth and shall cease being of downcast face. They shall wear the garments of glory. ¹⁶These garments of yours shall become the garments of life from the Lord of the Spirits. Neither shall your garments wear out, nor your glory come to an end before the Lord of the Spirits.

¹⁰⁴·²Be hopeful, because formerly you have pined away through evil and toil. But now you shall shine like the lights of heaven, and you shall be seen; and the windows of heaven shall be opened for you. Your cry shall be heard.

Sirach 48:10

In this text from Sirach, just as in the Gospels, Elijah is anticipated as the end-times prophet. The text appears in section 3.2 above.

2 Maccabees 2:7–8

In keeping with the biblical record concerning Moses and the Israelites, this text from 2 Maccabees also associates the glory of the Lord with the presence of the cloud. It is interesting that God's appearing in a cloud is seen in connection with the gathering of his people and the demonstrations of his mercy.

[7]When Jeremiah learned of it, he rebuked them and declared: "The place shall remain unknown until God gathers his people together again and shows his mercy. [8]Then the Lord will disclose these things, and the glory of the Lord and the cloud will appear, as they were shown in the case of Moses, and as Solomon asked that the place should be specially consecrated."

8.2 About Elijah (Matt. 17:10–13; Mark 9:11–13) (*JaS* 146)

Sirach 48:10

This text from Sirach appears in section 3.2 above and demonstrates the expectation that Elijah would come and reform the nation.

8.3 Jesus Heals a Demon-Possessed Boy (Matt. 17:14–21; Mark 9:14–29; Luke 9:37–43a) (*JaS* 147)

b. Berakot 63[b]*

This text from the Babylonian Talmud shows that the idea of moving a mountain is akin to carrying out the impossible. This text is somewhat obscure, but the image

of uprooting mountains involves someone who exercises great power or does unusual work. Food has precedence over power in this text.

A. Said R. Abin the Levite, "Whoever tries to take advantage of an occasion will find that the occasion takes advantage of him, and whoever forgoes the occasion will find that the occasion is forgone on his account."

B. This [matter derives from the case of] Rabbah and R. Joseph.

C. For R. Joseph was Sinai, and Rabbah was one who uproots mountains. The occasion came on which they were needed [for high office]. They sent over there [to the Land of Israel, to ask], "As between Sinai and one who uproots mountains, which takes precedence?"

D. They replied, "Sinai takes precedence, for everyone needs the sustenance of the one who owns the wheat."

E. Even so, R. Joseph did not accept office, because the Chaldean [astrologers] told him that he would rule for only two years.

F. Rabbah did indeed rule for twenty-two years, and after him, R. Joseph ruled for two and a half years.

G. All the time that Rabbah ruled, he did not call to his house even a blood-letter.

8.4 Payment of the Temple Tax (Matt. 17:24–27) (*JaS* 149)

The first text from Josephus (*Antiquities* 18.9.1) indicates, in keeping with the requirements outlined in Exodus 30:13–16, that each male twenty years and over was to bring a two-drachma (or half-shekel) tax to provide for the temple's upkeep. After the temple was destroyed in AD 70, this fee was exacted by the Romans as state tax.

Josephus, Antiquities 18.9.1 §§312–313

[312]There was also the city Nisibis, situated on the same current of the river. For which reason the Jews, depending on the natural strength of these places, deposited in them that half shekel which everyone, by the custom of our country, offers unto God, as well as they did other things devoted to him; for they made use of these cities as a treasury, [313]whence at a proper time, they were transmitted to Jerusalem; and many ten thousand men undertook the carriage of those donations, out of fear of the ravages of the Parthians, to whom the Babylonians were then subject.

Josephus, Jewish War 7.6.6 §§216–218

[216]About the same time it was that Caesar sent a letter to Bassus, and to Liberius Maximus, who was the procurator [of Judea], and gave order that all Judea should be exposed to sale, [217]for he did not found any city there, but reserved the country for himself. However, he assigned a place for eight hundred men only, whom he had dismissed from his army, which he gave them for their habitation; it is called Emmaus, and is distant from Jerusalem threescore furlongs. [218]He also laid a tribute upon the Jews wheresoever they were and enjoined every one of them to bring two drachmae every year into the Capitol, as they used to pay the same to the Temple at Jerusalem. And this was the state of the Jewish affairs at this time.

8.5 The Parable of the Lost Sheep (Matt. 18:10–14; Luke 15:3–7) (JaS 153)

Both the following texts evidence belief in the concept of guardian angels, both the singular idea (b. Šabbat 119[b]) and the corporate idea (1QSa 2.9–10).

b. Šabbat 119[b]*

Said R. Hisda said Mar Uqba, "Whoever says the Prayer on the eve of the Sabbath and includes the Sabbath verses, 'And the heaven and the earth were finished . . .' (Gen 2:1ff.)—the two angels who accompany a person put their hands on his head and say to him, 'and your iniquity is taken away and your sin atoned for' (Isa. 6:7)."

1QSa 2.5–10

[5]. . . And everyone who is defiled in his flesh . . . [8]these shall not enter to take their place among the congregation of famous men, for the angels [9]of holiness are among their congre[gation]. And if one of these has something to say to the holy council [10]they shall investigate it in private, but the man shall not enter in the midst of [the congregation,] because he is defiled.

8.6 On Reproving a Fellow Disciple (Matt. 18:15–18; Luke 17:3) (JaS 154)

In Matthew 18:15–18, Jesus outlines a process that his disciples are to enter into when dealing with a sinning brother. A somewhat similar process can be seen at Qumran.

1QS 5.24–6.11

[5.24]Each should reproach [25]his fellow in truth, in meekness and in compassionate love for the man. Blank No-one should speak to his brother in anger or muttering, 26or with a hard [neck or with passionate] spiteful intent and he should not detest him [in the stubbornness] of his heart, but instead reproach him that day so as not 6.1to incur a sin for his fault. And in addition, no-one should raise a matter against his fellow in front of the Many unless it is with reproof in the presence of witnesses. In this way, 2shall they behave in all their places of residence. Whenever one fellow meets another, the junior shall obey the senior in work and in money. They shall eat together, 3together they shall bless and together they shall take counsel. In every place where there are ten men of the Community council, there should not be a priest missing amongst them. 4And when they prepare the table to dine or the new wine 5for drinking, the priest shall stretch out his hand as the first to bless the first fruits of the bread {or the new wine for drinking, the priest shall stretch out his hand as the first 6to bless the first fruits of the bread} and of the new wine. And in the place in which the Ten assemble there should not be missing a man to interpret the law day and night, 7always, each man relieving his fellow. And the many shall be on watch together for a third of each night of the year in order to read the book, explain the regulation, 8and bless together. Blank This is the Rule for the session of the Many. Each one by his rank: the priests will sit down first, the elders next and the remainder of 9all the people will sit down in order of rank. And following the same system they shall be questioned with regard to the judgment, the counsel and any matter referred to the Many, so that each can impart his wisdom 10to the council of the Community. No-one should talk during the speech of his fellow before his brother has finished speaking. And

neither should he speak before one whose rank is listed 11before his own. Whoever is questioned should speak in his turn. And in the session of the Many no-one should utter anything without the consent of the Many.

8.7 On Reconciliation (Matt. 18:21–22; Luke 17:4) (JaS 156)

The following three citations indicate that limits were placed on the need to repeatedly forgive someone.

'Abot de Rabbi Nathan 40a*

1. A. He who says, "I shall sin and repent" will never suffice to carry out repentance.

B. "I will sin and the Day of Atonement will accomplish atonement"—the Day of Atonement will not accomplish atonement.

C. "I shall sin and the day of death will wipe away the sin"—the day of death will not wipe away the sin.

D. R. Eliezer b. R. Yose says, "He who sins and repents and then proceeds in an unblemished life does not move from his place before he is forgiven.

E. "He who says, 'I shall sin and repent' is forgiven three times but not more."

b. Yoma 86b; 87a*

86bIt was taught: R. Jose b. Judah said: "If a man commits a transgression, the first, second and third time he is forgiven, the fourth time he is not forgiven, as it is said: 'Thus says the Lord. For three transgressions of Israel, Yea for four, I will not reverse it'; and furthermore it says: 'Lo, all these things does God work, twice, yea, thrice, with a man.' " What does "furthermore" serve for?—One might have assumed that applies only to a community, but not to an individual, therefore: Come and hear [the additional verse]: "Lo, all these things does God wo̲rk, twice, ye̲a̲, thrice with a ma̲n."

[87a]Said R. Yose bar Hanina, "Whoever seeks reconciliation with his neighbor has to do so only three times: 'Forgive I pray you now . . . and now we pray you' (Gen 50:17)."

9

Toward Jerusalem

9.1 On Following Jesus (Luke 9:57–62; Matt. 8:18–22) (*JaS* 160)

Hesiod, Works and Days 441–45

The one who puts his hand to the plow and looks back is not fit for service in the kingdom, according to Christ. This text from Hesiod demonstrates the proverbial nature of Jesus' comment. Here the one who works and "drive[s] a straight furrow" without glancing here and there (i.e., allowing himself to be distracted) is esteemed.

A forty-year-old farmhand should follow your oxen—he needs a loaf of bread that breaks into four and then into eight—he will tend to his labor and drive a straight furrow; too old to look about for companions, he will keep his mind on the job.[1]

9.2 The Return of the Seventy-two (Luke 10:17–20) (*JaS* 162)

In the following texts, there is an explicit connection between the coming of the Messiah (i.e., the Elect One) and the defeat of Satan and evil.

1. *Hesiod: Theogony, Works and Days, Shield*, translation, introduction, and notes by Apostolos N. Athanassakis, 2nd ed. (Baltimore: Johns Hopkins University Press, 2004), 76.

1 Enoch *55.4*

Kings, potentates, dwellers upon the earth. You would have to see my Elect One, how he sits in the throne of glory and judges Azaz'el and all his company, and his army, in the name of the Lord of the Spirits!

Jubilees *23.29*

See section 11.9 below.

Testament of Simeon *6.6*

Then all the spirits of error shall be given over to being trampled underfoot. And men will have mastery over the evil spirits.

Testament of Judah *25.3*

And you shall be one people of the Lord, with one language. There shall no more be Beliar's spirit of error, because he will be thrown into eternal fire.

Testament of Moses *10.1*

Then his kingdom will appear throughout his whole creation. Then the devil will have an end. Yea, sorrow will be led away with him.

Testament of Solomon *20.16–17*

In this text, demons fall from heaven, burn down cities, and set fields on fire.

[16]But we who are demons are exhausted from not having a way station from which to ascend or on which to rest; so we fall down like leaves from the trees and the men who are watching think that stars are falling from heaven. [17]That is not true, King; rather, we fall because of our weaknesses and, since there is nothing on which to hold, we are dropped like flashes of lightning to the earth. We burn cities down and set fields on fire. But the stars of heaven have their foundations laid in the firmament.

Sirach 21:2; 39:28–31

In these two passages from Sirach, the snake is connected with sin and its power to destroy.

we

[21:2]Flee from sin as from a snake; for if you approach sin, it will bite you. Its teeth are lion's teeth, and can destroy human lives.

[39:28]There are winds created for vengeance, and in their anger they can dislodge mountains; on the day of reckoning they will pour out their strength and calm the anger of their Maker. [29]Fire and hail and famine and pestilence, all these have been created for vengeance; [30]the fangs of wild animals and scorpions and vipers, and the sword that punishes the ungodly with destruction. [31]They take delight in doing his bidding, always ready for his service on earth; and when their time comes they never disobey his command.

In the following texts, the book of life is mentioned.

1 Enoch 47.3; 104.1; 108.7

[47.3]In those days, I saw him—the Antecedent of Time, while he was sitting upon the throne of his glory, and the books of the living ones were open before him. And all his power in heaven above and his escorts stood before him.

[104.1]I swear unto you that in heaven the angels will remember you for the good before the glory of the Great One; and your names shall be written before the glory of the Great One.

[108.7]For some of (these things) were written and sealed above in heaven so that the angels may read them (the things that are written) and know that which is about to befall the sinners, the spirits of the ones who err, as well as those who defiled their bodies, revenged themselves on God, and worked together with evil people.

Jubilees 5.12–14; 23.32; 30.19–23

cf Jer 31:31 f

[5.12]And he made for all his works a new and righteous nature so that they might not sin in all their nature forever, and so that they might all be righteous, each in his kind, always. [13]And the judgment of all of them [i.e., all the works of God's creation] has been ordained and written in the heavenly tablets without injustice. And (if) any of them transgress from their way with respect to what was ordained to walk in, or if they do not walk in it, the judgment for every (sort of) nature and every kind has been written. [14]And there is nothing excluded which is in heaven or on earth or in the light or in the darkness or in Sheol or in the depths or in the place of darkness.

[23.32]And you, Moses, write these words because thus it is written and set upon the heavenly tablets as a testimony for eternal generations.

30.19And thus a blessing and righteousness will be written (on high) as a testimony for him in the heavenly tablets before the God of all. 20And we will remember for a thousand generations the righteousness which a man did during his life in all of the (appointed) times of the year. And (it) will be written (on high) and it will come to him and his descendants after him. And he will be written down as a friend and a righteous one in the heavenly tablets. 21All of these words I have written for you, and I have commanded you to speak to the children of Israel that they might not commit sin or transgress the ordinances or break the covenant which was ordained for them so that they might do it and be written down as friends. 22But if they transgress and act in all the ways of defilement, they will be recorded in the heavenly tablets as enemies. And they will be blotted out of the book of life and written in the book of those who will be destroyed and with those who will be rooted out from the land. 23And on the day that the children of Jacob killed Shechem he wrote (on high) for them a book in heaven that they did righteousness and uprightness and vengeance against the sinners and it was written down for a blessing.

1QM 12.1–2

1For there is a multitude of holy ones in heaven and a host of angels in your holy dwelling to [praise] your [name.] And the chosen ones of the holy people 2you have established for yourself in [. . .] The bo[ok] of the names of all their armies is with you in your holy dwelling, [. . .] in the dwelling of your glory.

9.3 The Lawyer's Question and the Good Samaritan (Luke 10:25–37; Matt. 22:34–40; Mark 12:28–34) (*JaS* 164)

Here we see prescriptions for the twice-daily (evening and morning) recitation of the Shema.

m. Berakot 1.1–2*

1A. From what time may they recite the *Shema* in the evening?

B. From the hour that the priests enter [their homes] to eat their heave offering,

C. "until the end of the first watch"—

D. the words of R. Eliezer.

E. But sages say, "Until midnight."

F. Rabban Gamaliel says, "Until the rise of dawn."

G. M'SHŠ His [Gamaliel's] sons returned from a banquet hall [after midnight].

H. They said to him, "We did not [yet] recite the *Shema*."

I. He said to them, "If the dawn has not yet risen, you are obligated to recite [the *Shema*].

J. "And [this applies] not only [in] this [case]. Rather, [as regards] all [commandments] which sages said [may be performed] 'Until midnight,' the obligation [to perform them persists] until the rise of dawn."

K. [For example,] the offering of the fats and entrails—their obligation [persists] until the rise of dawn [see Lev. 1:9; 3:3–5].

L. And all [sacrifices] which must be eaten within one day, the obligation [to eat them persists] until the rise of dawn.

M. If so why did sages say [that these actions may be performed only] until midnight?

N. In order to protect man from sin.

²A. From what time do they recite the *Shema* in the morning?

B. From the hour that one can distinguish between [the colors] blue and white.

C. R. Eliezer says, "Between blue and green."

D. And one must complete it before sunrise.

E. R. Joshua says, "Before the third hour.

F. "For it is the practice of royalty to rise [at] the third hour. [Thus we deem the third hour still to be 'morning.']"

G. One who recites later than this [i.e., the third hour] has not transgressed [by reciting a blessing at the wrong time, for he is viewed simply] as one who recites from the Torah.

The next three texts demonstrate the close connection in Judaism between love for one's neighbor and the proper understanding and application of the law.

Testament of Benjamin 3.3

Fear the Lord and love your neighbor. Even if the spirits of Beliar seek to derange you with all sorts of wicked oppression, they will not dominate you, any more than they dominated Joseph, my brother.

Sipra 200 on Leviticus 19:18 (Akiba)*

CC III 6. A. "You shall not take vengeance or bear any grudge against the sons of your own people":

B. "You may take vengeance and bear a grudge against others."

7. A. "... but you shall love your neighbor as yourself: [I am the Lord]":

B. R. Aqiba says, "This is the encompassing principle of the Torah."

C. Ben Azzai says, "'This the book of the generations of Adam' (Gen. 5:1) is a still more encompassing principle."

b. Šabbat 31ᵃ (Hillel)*

When he went before Hillel, he said to him, "What is hateful to you, do not to your neighbor: that is the whole Torah, while the rest is the commentary thereof; go and learn it."

9.4 Rebuke of the Pharisees and the Lawyers (Luke 11:37–54; Matt. 15:1–9; 23:4, 6–7, 13, 25–32, 34–36; Mark 7:1–9) (JaS 175)

M. Yadayim 1.1–2.3, appearing in section 7.7 above, relates many diverse details regarding the Jewish ritual of hand washing before meals. These details include prescriptions for the source, quantity, and quality of water; the kinds of utensils to be used; and the definition of "clean" and "unclean" hands. Passages from *t. Demai* and *t. Berakot* reveal that the Jews' interest was not in matters of hygiene but in matters of ceremonial uncleanness.

t. Demai 2.11–12*

¹¹E. And they accept [him first] with regard to *knpym*, [meaning uncertain; usually interpreted as "uncleanness of hands"] and afterwards they accept [him] with regard to foodstuffs which require preparation in conditions of cleanness.

F. If he said, "I take upon myself only [the obligations] regarding *knpym*," they accept him.

G. If he took upon himself [the obligations] regarding clean foodstuffs but did not take upon himself [the obligation] regarding *knpym*, he also is not deemed trustworthy [*n'mn*] with respect to clean foodstuffs.

[12]H. How long before they accept [him]? [viz., how long is the probationary period before the prospective *haber* is fully accepted?]

I. The House of Shammai say, "For liquids, thirty days; for clothing, twelve months."

J. And the House of Hillel say, "For both, thirty days."

t. Berakot 5.26*

A. The House of Shammai say, "They wash their hands and then mix the cup [of wine]" [*m. Ber.* 8:2],

B. lest [any] liquids on the outer surface of the cup become unclean through contact with [unclean] hands and in turn render [the contents of] the cup unclean.

C. The House of Hillel say, "The outer surface of the cup [in any case] is always deemed unclean."

D. Another version: "Handwashing must always immediately precede the meal" [cf. *t. Ber.* 4:8, 5:6, 5:13].

m. Demai 2.1*

The following passage from *t. Demai* deals with the Jewish practice of tithing herbs or produce.

A. These items are tithed as *demai* produce in every place [viz., both in and outside the Land of Israel]—

B. (1) pressed figs, and (2) dates, and (3) carobs, and (4) rice, and (5) cumin.

C. Rice which is [grown] outside of the Land—all who make use of it are exempt [from tithing].

m. Ma῾aśer Šeni*

This entire tractate in the Mishnah is taken up with regulations governing the tithing of produce.

y. Berakot 4b*

This text from *y. Berakot* reveals the special greetings that were often given to those recognized as Torah teachers.

[IV. A.] It was taught: [One who wishes to interrupt his recitation of the *Shema*'] to greet his teacher or [to greet] one who is greater than he in Torah-learning—he is permitted to do this. From this rule we deduce that a person must greet one who is greater than he in Torah learning.

[B.] And also from this [next discussion we deduce that same practice.] For it was taught: If one tore [his garment as a sign of mourning for a relative who appeared to have died] and he [the relative] was revived and then died, if this happens right away [after he first tore his garment], he need not tear [his garment again]. If it happens over some time, he must tear [his garment again].

[C.] How long is "right away"? The time it takes to utter [a greeting]. How much time is that? R. Simon in the name of R. Joshua b. Levi, "The time it takes a man to greet his associate."

[D.] Abba bar bar Hannah in the name of R. Yohanan, "The time it takes a student to greet his teacher and say to him, 'May peace be upon you, my teacher.'" [From this we learn that a student must greet his teacher.]

[E.] R. Yohanan was leaning on R. Jacob bar Idi [as they were walking]. R. Eleazar saw them and his from them.

[F.] He [Yohanan] said, "This Babylonian [Eleazar] did two [improper] things to me. First, he did not greet me [even though I am his teacher]. Second, he did not attribute a teaching to me [see *b. Yebamot* 96b]."

[G.] He [Jacob bar Idi] said to him, "This is the way they act towards each other [in Babylonia out of respect]. The lower among them [in status] does not greet the greater [among them in status so as not to bother him to respond]. For they uphold the verse, 'The young men saw me and withdrew.'" [Job 29:8].

Testament of Moses 7.1–4

This text warns those who pass themselves off as righteous but are actually deceitful and please only themselves.

[1]When this has taken place, the times will quickly come to an end. [2][. . .] [3]Then will rule destructive and godless men, who represent themselves as being righteous, [4]but who will (in fact) arouse their inner wrath, for they will be deceitful men, pleasing only themselves, false in every way imaginable, (such as) loving feasts at any hour of the day—devouring, gluttonous.

9.5 Faithfulness in the Midst of Watchfulness (Luke 12:35–48; Matt. 24:42–51; Mark 13:33–37) (JaS 184)

Tobit 11:18

This text indicates that celebrations at wedding feasts could go on for days—hence, the exhortation in Jesus' parable to remain faithful during his prolonged absence.

Ahikar and his nephew Nadab were also present to share Tobit's joy. With merriment they celebrated Tobias's wedding feast for seven days, and many gifts were given to him.

9.6 Mission: To Bring Division (Luke 12:49–53; Matt. 10:34–36; Mark 10:38) (JaS 185)

Texts from *Jubilees* 23.16, 19 (see the extended quote of *Jubilees* 23 in section 11.9 below), *m. Sotah* 9.15 (see section 6.10 above), and *4 Ezra* (2 Esdras) 6:24 (see section 15.2 below) use the image of "division between family members/friends" to illustrate sin, failure to heed the law, and a lack of concern for truth.

9.7 Sabbath Healing of a Crippled Woman (Luke 13:10–17) (JaS 189)

1QapGen 20.16–29

In this text from Qumran, there is a clear connection between physical suffering and the presence of evil spirits.

[16]And I wept and stayed silent. That night, the God Most High sent him a chastising spirit, to afflict him and all the members of his household, an evil spirit [17]that kept afflicting him and all the members of his household. And he was unable to approach her, much less have sexual intercourse with her, in spite of being with her [18]for two years. At the end of the two years, the punishments and plagues, against him and against all the members of his household, increased and intensified. And he sent [19]for all [the wise men] of Egypt to be called, and all the wizards as well as all the healers of Egypt, (to see) whether they could heal him of that disease, [him] and the members [20]of his household. However, all the healers and wizards and all the wise men were unable to rise up and heal him. For the spirit attacked all of them and [21]they fled. *Blank* Then HRKNWS came to me and

asked me to come and pray for [22]the king, and lay my hands upon him so that he would live. For [he had seen me] in a dream. But Lot said to him: Abram my uncle cannot pray for [23]the king while Sarai, his wife, is with him. Go, now, and tell the king to send back his wife to her own husband and he will pray for him and he will live. [24]*Blank* When HRKNWS heard Lot's words, he went and said to the king: All these plagues and punishments [25]with which the king my Lord is afflicted and punished are on account of Sarai, Abram's wife. They should return Sarai, then, I beg you to Abram, her husband, [26]and this plague and the spirit of purulent evils will cease to afflict you. (The Pharaoh) called to him and said to me: What have you done to me with regard to Sarai? You told me: [27]She is my sister, when she is your wife; so that I took her for myself for a consort. Here is your wife; take her away! Go! Depart from [28]all the cities of Egypt! But now pray for me and for my household so that this evil spirit will be banished from us. I prayed for [. . .] [29]and laid my hands upon his head. The plague was removed from him; [the evil spirit] was banished [from him] and he lived.

These texts from the Mishnah go into great detail about how one is to feed, handle, and rescue one's animals on the Sabbath.

m. Šabbat 5.1–4; 15.2*

[5.1]A. With what does a beast [Ex. 20:10] go out [on the Sabbath], and with what does it not go out?

B. (1) A camel goes out with its curb, (2) a female camel with its nose ring, (3) a Libyan ass with its bridle, (4) and a horse with its chain.

C. And all beasts which wear a chain go out with a chain and are led by a chain, and they sprinkle on

the [chains if they become unclean] and immerse them in place [without removing them].

[2]A. An ass goes out with its saddle cloth when it is tied on to him [before the Sabbath].

B. Rams go out strapped up [at the male organ].

C. And female [sheep] go forth (1) strapped over their tails, (2) under their tails, or (3) wearing protective cloths.

D. And goats go forth [with] bound [udders].

E. R. Yose prohibits in the case of all of them,

F. except for the case of ewes wearing protective cloths.

G. R. Judah says, "Goats go forth with bound udders to keep them dry, but not to collect the milk."

[3]A. And with what does [a beast] not go out?

B. (1) A camel does not go out with a pad, nor (2) with forelegs bound together [or: hind legs bound together] or (3) with a hoof tied back to the shoulder.

C. And so is the rule for all other beasts.

D. One should not tie camels to one another and lead them.

E. But one puts the ropes [of all of them] into his hand and leads them,

F. so long as he does not twist [the ropes together].

[4]A. (1) An ass does not go out with its saddle cloth when it is not tied to him [cf. M. 5:2A],

B. or with a bell, even though it is plugged,

C. or with the ladder yoke around its neck,

D. or with a strap on its leg.

E. And (2) fowl do not go forth with ribbons or straps on their legs.

F. And (3) rams do not go forth with a wagon under their fat tail.

G. And (4) ewes do not go forth protected [with the wood chip in their nose (B. Shab. 54b)].

H. And (5) a calf does not go out with its rush yoke.

I. or (6) a cow with a hedgehog skin [tied around the udder], or with a strap between its horns.

J. The cow of R. Eleazar b. Azariah would go out with a strap between its horns,

K. not with the approval of the sages.

15.2A. You have knots on account of which they are not liable, like a camel driver's knot and a sailor's knot.

B. A woman ties (1) the slit of her shift, (2) the strings of her hairnet and of her belt, (3) the thongs of a shoe or sandal, (4) [leather] bottles of wine or oil, and (5) a cover over meat.

C. R. Eliezer b. Jacob says, "They tie a knot before a domestic beast so that it will not go forth."

D. They tie a bucket with a belt but not with a rope.

E. R. Judah permits [tying with a rope].

F. A governing principle did R. Judah state, "On account of any sort of knot which does not last they are not liable."

m. ʿErubin 2.1–4*

1A. They set up boards around wells [in the public domain].

B. "Four cornerpieces appearing like eight [single boards] [are to be set up]," the words of R. Judah.

C. R. Meir says, "Eight appearing like twelve [are to be set up].

D "Four are cornerpieces, and four are flat."

E. Their height is to be ten handbreadths, and their breadth six, and their thickness in any measure at all.

F. "And the space between them is to be enough for two teams of three oxen each," the words of R. Meir.

G. R. Judah says, "For four teams of four oxen each,

H "tied together and not widely apart,

I. "one going in while the other goes out."

2A. It is permitted to bring [the fence] close to the well,

B. so long as the head and greater part of a cow will be inside [the enclosed space] when it drinks.

C. And it is permitted to draw them back any distance at all,

D. so long as one increases the number of boards.

3A. R. Judah says, "They [may draw them back from the well only] so far as to leave two seahs of space."

B. They said to him, "The measure of two seahs space has been stated only in connection with what is required for a garden or an outer area.

C. "But if it was a cattle pen, fold, storeyard, or courtyard, even a space of five kors, even a space of ten kors, is permitted."

D. And it is permitted to draw the boards back any distance at all,

E. so long as one increases the number of boards.

4A. R. Judah says, "If a public path went through them [the boards], one should divert it to the side."

B. And sages say, "It is not necessary [to do so]."

C. "All the same are a cistern serving the public, a well serving the public, and a well serving an individual: they set up boards for them."

D. "But for a cistern serving an individual they set up a partition ten handbreadths high," the words of R. Aqiba.

E. R. Judah b. Baba says, "They set up boards only for a well serving the public alone."

F. "But for the rest they set up a [rope]belt ten handbreadths high" [cf. M. 1:9]

9.8 Exclusion from the Kingdom (Luke 13:22–30; Matt. 7:13–14, 22–23; 8:11–12; 19:30) (JaS 192)

The following texts reveal how few will be allowed to sit at the eschatological banquet table, although it is simply assumed that righteous Jews will be there.

1QSa 2.11–22

[11]This is the assembly of famous men, [those summoned to] the gathering of the community council, when [God] begets [12]the Messiah with them. [The] chief [priest] of all the congregation of Israel shall enter, and all [13][his] brothers, the sons] of Aaron, the priests [summoned] to the assembly, the famous men, and they shall sit [14]befo[re him, each one] according to his dignity. After, [the Me]ssiah of Israel shall ent[er] and before him shall sit the chiefs [15][of the clans of Israel, each] one according to his dignity, according to their [positions] in their camps and in their marches. And all [16]the chiefs of the cl[ans of the congre]gation with the wise [men and the learned] shall sit before them, each one according [17]to his dignity. And [when] they gather at the table of community [or to drink] the new wine, and the table of [18]community is prepared [and] the new wine [is mixed] for drinking, [no-one should stretch out] his hand to the first-fruit of the bread [19]and of the [new wine] before the priest, for [he is the one who bl]esses the first-fruit of bread [20]and of the new wine [and stretches out] his hand towards the bread before them. Afterwards, the Messiah of Israel shall stretch out his hand [21]to-

wards the bread. [And afterwards, shall] bless all the congregation of the community, each [one according to] his dignity. And in accordance with this regulation they shall act [22]at each me[al, when] at least ten m[en are gat]thered.

1 Enoch 62.14–15

[14]The Lord of the Spirits will abide over them; they shall eat and rest and rise with that Son of Man forever and ever. [15]The righteous and elect ones shall rise from the earth and shall cease being of downcast face.

2 Enoch 45.2

He who makes lamps numerous in front of the face of the LORD, the LORD will make his treasure stores numerous.

2 Baruch 29.2; 30.1–5

[29.2]For at that time I shall only protect those found in this land at that time.

[30.1]And it will happen after these things when the time of the appearance of the Anointed One has been fulfilled and he returns with glory, that then all who sleep in hope of him will rise. [2]And it will happen at that time that those treasuries will be opened in which the number of the souls of the righteous were kept, and they will go out and the multitudes of the souls will appear together, in one assemblage, of one mind. And the first ones will enjoy themselves and the last ones will not be sad. [3]For they know that the time has come of which it is said that it is the end of times. [4]But the souls of the wicked will the more waste away when they shall see all these things [i.e., the coming of the Anointed One and the blessing bestowed on those who have hoped in Him]. [5]For they know that their torment has come and that their perditions have arrived.

9.9 The Lament over Jerusalem (Luke 13:34–35; Matt. 23:37–39) (JaS 194)

2 Baruch 41.3–4

God's protection of Israel is often compared to the way a bird shields its young under its wings.

[3]For behold, I see many of your people who separated themselves from your statutes and who have cast away from them the yoke of your Law. [4]Further, I have seen others who left behind their vanity and who have fled under your wings.

9.10 The Healing of the Man with Dropsy (Luke 14:1–6) (JaS 195)

According to CD 11.12–18 (appearing in section 4.9 above), a person was not able to help an animal give birth on the Sabbath, or, if an animal fell into a well, no one was permitted to help it out.

9.11 Teaching on Humility (Luke 14:7–14) (JaS 196)

In this text from 2 Maccabees, those who keep the law, even in the face of imminent death, will be rewarded with resurrection to an "everlasting renewal of life" (7:9). Note how this resurrection is described in very physical, or material, terms. Restoration includes a body.

2 Maccabees 7:1–19, 30–38

[1]It happened also that seven brothers and their mother were arrested and were being compelled by the king, under torture with whips and thongs, to partake of unlawful swine's flesh. [2]One of them, acting as their spokesman, said, "What do you intend to ask and learn from us? For we are ready to die rather than transgress the laws of our ancestors." [3]The king fell into a rage, and gave orders to have pans and caldrons heated. [4]These were heated immediately, and he commanded that the tongue of their spokesman be cut out and that they scalp him and cut off his hands and feet, while the rest of the brothers and the mother looked on. [5]When he was utterly helpless, the king ordered them to take him to the fire, still breathing, and to fry him in a pan. The smoke from the pan spread widely, but the brothers and their mother encouraged one another to die nobly, saying, [6]"The Lord God is watching over us and in truth has compassion on us, as Moses declared in his song that bore witness against the people to their faces, when he said, 'And he will have compassion on his servants.' "

[7]After the first brother had died in this way, they brought forward the second for their sport. They tore off skin of his head with the hair, and asked him, "Will you eat rather than have your body punished limb by limb?" [8]He replied in the language of his ancestors and said to them, "No." Therefore he in turn underwent tortures as the first brother had done. [9]And when he was at his last breath, he said, "You accursed wretch, you dismiss us from this present life, but the King of the universe will raise us up to an everlasting renewal of life, because we have died for his laws."

[10]After him, the third was the victim of their sport. When it was demanded, he quickly put out his tongue and courageously stretched forth his hands, [11]and said nobly, "I got these from Heaven, and because of his laws I disdain them, and from him I hope to get them back again." [12]As a result the king himself and those with him were astonished at the young man's spirit, for he regarded his sufferings as nothing.

[13]After he too had died, they maltreated and tortured the fourth in the same way. [14]When he was near death, he said, "One cannot but choose to die at the hands of mortals and to cherish the hope God gives of being raised again by him. But for you there will be no resurrection to life!"

[15]Next they brought forward the fifth and maltreated him. [16]But he looked at the king, and said, "Because you have authority among mortals, though you also are mortal, you do what you please. But do not think that God has forsaken our people. [17]Keep on, and see how his mighty power will torture you and your descendants!"

[18]After him they brought forward the sixth. And when he was about to die, he said, "Do not deceive yourself in vain. For we are suffering these things on our own account, because of our sins against our own God. Therefore astounding things have happened. [19]But do not think that you will go unpunished for having tried to fight against God!" . . . [30]While she was still speaking, the young man said, "What are you waiting for? I will not obey the king's command, but I obey the command of the law that was given to our ancestors through Moses. [31]But you, who have contrived all sorts of evil against the Hebrews, will certainly not escape the hands of God. [32]For we are suffering because of our own sins. [33]And if our living

Lord is angry for a little while, to rebuke and discipline us, he will again be reconciled with his own servants. [34]But you, unholy wretch, you most defiled of all mortals, do not be elated in vain and puffed up by uncertain hopes, when you raise your hand against the children of heaven. [35]You have not yet escaped the judgment of the almighty, all-seeing God. [36]For our brothers after enduring a brief suffering have drunk of everflowing life, under God's covenant; but you, by the judgment of God, will receive just punishment for your arrogance. [37]I, like my brothers, give up body and life for the laws of our ancestors, appealing to God to show mercy soon to our nation and by trials and plagues to make you confess that he alone is God, [38]and through me and my brothers to bring to an end the wrath of the Almighty that has justly fallen on our whole nation."

9.12 The Parable of the Great Supper (Luke 14:15–24; Matt. 22:1–14) (JaS 197)

Philo, On the Creation 25 §78

Philo uses the imagery of a banquet as a metaphor for the way God created the world and called man into existence to enjoy it. So a banquet pictures celebration of God's provision.

As then, those who make a feast do not invite their guests to the entertainment before they have provided everything for festivity, and as those who celebrate gymnastic or dramatic contests, before they assemble the spectators, provide themselves with an abundance of competitors and spectacles, and sweet sounds, with which to fill the theatres and stadia; so in the same manner did the Ruler of all, as a man proposing games, or giving a banquet and being about to invite others to feast and to behold the spectacle, first provide everything for every kind of entertainment. . . .

9.13 The Parable of the Lost Sheep (Luke 15:1–7; Matt. 18:12–14) (JaS 200)

This passage from the Tosefta indicates that modest herds may have contained up to three hundred sheep.

t. Baba Qamma 6.20*

A. A shepherd who hands over his flock to another shepherd—

B. the first is liable, and the second is exempt.

C. He who hands over his flock to a shepherd,

D. even if it is one who is lame, or even sick, or even if there are under his oversight as many as three hundred sheep,

E. is exempt [cf. M. Q.B. 6:2E]

F. [If] he handed it over to a deaf-mute, an idiot, or a minor, he is liable.

G. [If he handed it over to] a slave or a woman, he is exempt.

H. And they pay compensation after an interval.

I. How [does a woman or a slave pay compensation after an interval]?

J. They call a court into session to deal with their case.

K. The write a writ of debt against them.

L. [If] the woman is divorced or the slave freed, they are then liable to pay compensation.

9.14 The Pharisees Reproved (Luke 16:14–15) (JaS 206)

These passages warn against greed and the love of money and possessions. Greed will be met with the strictest judgment.

1 Enoch 102.9–10

[9]Now I tell you, sinners, you have satiated yourselves with food and drink, robbing and sin, impoverishing people and gaining property, and seeing good days. [10]Have you seen the righteous, how their end comes about, for no injustice is found upon them until their death?

Testament of Moses 7.1–4

This text appears in section 9.4 above.

t. Menahot 13.22*

A. Said R. Yohanan b. Torta, "On what account was Shiloh destroyed? Because of the disgraceful disposition of the Holy Things which were there.

B. "As to Jerusalem's first building, on what account was it destroyed? Because of idolatry and licentiousness and bloodshed which was in it.

C. "But [as to] the latter [building] we know that they devoted themselves to Torah and were meticulous about tithes.

D. "On what account did they go into exile? Because they love money and hate one another.

E. "This teaches you that hatred of one for another is evil before the Omnipresent, and Scripture deems it equivalent to idolatry, licentiousness, and bloodshed."

9.15 The Parable of the Rich Man and Lazarus (Luke 16:19–31) (*JaS* 208)

The following texts reveal images of the afterlife.

4 Ezra (= 2 Esdras) 7:85–98

[85]The fifth way, they shall see how the habitations of the others are guarded by angels in profound quiet. [86]The sixth way, they shall see how some of them will cross over into torments. [87]The seventh way, which is worse than all the ways that have been mentioned, because they shall utterly waste away in confusion and be consumed with shame, and shall wither with fear at seeing the glory of the Most High in whose presence they sinned while they were alive, and in whose presence they are to be judged in the last times. [88]Now this is the order of those who have kept the ways of the Most High, when they shall be separated from their mortal body. [89]During the time that they lived in it, they laboriously served the Most High, and withstood danger every hour so that they might keep the law of the Lawgiver perfectly. [90]Therefore this is the teaching concerning them: [91]First of all, they shall see with great joy the glory of him who receives them, for they shall have rest in seven orders. [92]The first order, because they have striven with great effort to overcome the evil thought that was formed with them, so that it might not lead them astray from life into death. [93]The second order, because they see the perplexity in which the souls of the ungodly wander and the punishment that awaits them.

2 Baruch 51.5–6

[5]When they, therefore, will see that those over whom they are exalted now will then be more exalted and glorified than they, then both these and those will be changed, these into the splendor of angels and those into startling visions and horrible shapes; and they will waste away even more. [6]For they will first see and then they will go away to be tormented.

2 Maccabees 6:23

But making a high resolve, worthy of his years and the dignity of his old age and the gray hairs that he had reached with distinction and his excellent life even from childhood, and moreover according to the holy God-given law, he declared himself quickly, telling them to send him to Hades.

1 Enoch 22.1–11; 39.3–9; 102.4–5 (excerpts)

[22.1]Then I went to another place, and he showed me on the west side a great and high mountain of hard rock [2]and inside it four beautiful corners; it had [in it] a deep, wide, and smooth (thing) which was rolling over; and it (the place) was deep and dark to look at. [3]At that moment, Rufael, one of the holy angels, who was with me, responded to me; and he said to me, "These beautiful corners (are here) in order that the spirits of the souls of the dead should assemble into them—they are created so that the souls of the children of the people should gather here. [4]They prepared these places in order to put them (i.e., the souls of the people) there until the day of their judgment and the appointed time of the great judgment upon them." [5]I saw the spirits of the children of the people who were dead, and their voices were reaching unto heaven until this very moment. [6]I asked Rufael, the angel who was with me, and said to him, "The spirit, the voice of which was reaching (into heaven) like this and is making suit, whose (spirit) is it?" [7]And he answered me, saying, "This is the spirit which had left Abel, whom Cain, his brother had killed; it (continues to) sue him until all of (Cain's) seed is exterminated from the face of the earth, and his seed has disintegrated from among the seed of the people." [8]At that moment, I raised a question regarding him and regarding the judgment of all, "For what reason is one separated from another?" [9]And he replied and said to me, "These three have been made in order that the spirits of the dead might be separated. And in the manner in which the souls of the righteous are separated (by) this spring of water with light upon it, [10]in like manner, the sinners are set apart when they die and are buried in the earth and judgment has not been executed upon them in their lifetime [11]upon this great pain, until the great day of judgment—and to those who curse (there will be) plague and pain forever, and the retribution of their spirits."

[39.3]In those days, whirlwinds carried me off from the earth, and set me down into the ultimate ends of the heavens. [4]There I saw other dwelling places of the holy ones and their resting places too. [5]So there my eyes saw their dwelling places with the holy angels, and their resting places with the holy ones, and they interceded and petitioned and prayed on behalf of the children of the people, and righteousness flowed before them like water, and mercy like dew upon the earth, and thus it is in their midst forever and ever. [6]And in those days my eyes saw the Elect One of righteousness and of faith, and righteousness shall prevail in his days, and

the righteous and elect ones shall be without number before him forever and ever. [7]And I saw a dwelling place underneath the wings of the Lord of the Spirits; and all the righteous and the elect one before him shall be as intense as the light of fire. Their mouth shall be full of blessing; and their lips will praise the name of the Lord of the Spirits, and righteousness before will have no end; and uprightness before him will not cease. [8]There (underneath his wings) I wanted to dwell; and my soul desired that dwelling place. Already my portion is there; for thus has it been reserved for me before the Lord of the Spirits. [9]In those days, I praised and prayed to the name of the Lord of the Spirits with blessings and praises, for he had strengthened me by blessings and praises in accordance with the will of the Lord of the Spirits.

[102.4]But you, souls of the righteous, fear not; and be hopeful, you souls that died in righteousness! [5]Be not sad because your souls have gone down into Sheol in sorrow; or (because) your flesh fared not well the earthly existence in accordance with your goodness; indeed the time you happened to be in existence was (a time of) sinners, a time of curse and a time of plague.

Psalms of Solomon 14.6, 9–10; 15.10

[14.6]But not so are sinners and criminals, who love (to spend) the day in sharing their sin. . . . [9]Therefore their inheritance is Hades, and darkness and destruction; and they will not be found on the day of mercy for the righteous. [10]But the devout of the Lord will inherit life in happiness.

[15.10]And the inheritance of sinners is destruction and darkness, and their lawless actions shall pursue them below into Hades.

b. Beṣah *32^b^**

This text from the Babylonian Talmud provides background showing how destitute Lazarus was according to rabbinic thinking.

VII I. Said R. Hisda, Also: his life is no life."

J. [Developing I], our rabbis have taught on Tannaitic authority:

K. There are three [individuals] whose lives that are no lives, and these are they: 1) one who depends upon his companion's table, 2) one whose wife controls him, and 3) one whose body is subject to sufferings.

9.16 On Forgiveness (Luke 17:3b–4; Matt. 18:15) (*JaS* 210)

Testament of Gad *6.3–7*

In this passage, Jews are exhorted to love one another deeply, including forgiving others and trusting God to deal with those who deny their guilt or who feign repentance.

³Love one another from the heart, therefore, and if anyone sins against you, speak to him in peace. Expel the venom of hatred, and do not harbor deceit in your heart. If anyone confesses and repents, forgive him. ⁴If anyone denies his guilt, do not be contentious with him, otherwise he may start cursing, and you would be sinning doubly. ⁵In a dispute do not let an outsider hear your secrets, since out of hatred for you he may become your enemy, and commit a great sin against you. He may talk to you frequently but treacherously, or be much concerned with you, but for an evil end, having absorbed from you the venom. ⁶Even if he denies it and acts disgracefully out of a sense of guilt, be quiet and do not be upset. For he who denies will repent, and

offending you again; indeed he will honor you, will respect you and be at peace. ⁷But even if he is devoid of shame and persists in his wickedness, forgive him from the heart and leave vengeance to God.

9.17 The Kingdom in the Midst (Luke 17:20–21) (*JaS* 214)

Psalms of Solomon *17–18*

The "kingdom" according to these important texts will come with power, securing victory over any and all detractors.

17.1Lord, you are our King forevermore,
  for in you, O God, does our soul take pride.
²How long is the time of a person's life on the earth?
  As is his time, so also is his hope in him.
³But we hope in God our savior.
  for the strength of our God is forever with mercy.
And the kingdom of our God is forever over the nations in judgment.
⁴Lord, you chose David to be king over Israel,
  and swore to him about his descendants forever,
  that his kingdom should not fail before you.
⁵But (because of) our sins, sinners rose up against us,
  they set upon us and drove us out.
Those to whom you did not (make the) promise,
  they took away (from us) by force;
  and they did not glorify your honorable name.

⁶With pomp they set up a mon-
    archy because of their arro-
    gance;
  they despoiled the throne of
    David with arrogant shout-
    ing.
⁷But you, O God, overthrew them,
    and uprooted their descen-
    dants from the earth,
  for there rose up against them a
    man alien to our race.
⁸You rewarded them, O God, ac-
    cording to their sins;
  it happened to them according
    to their actions.
⁹According to their actions, God
    showed no mercy to them;
  he hunted down their descen-
    dants, and did not let even
    one of them go.
¹⁰The Lord is faithful in all his judg-
    ments
  which he makes in the world.

¹¹The lawless one laid waste our
    land, so that no one inhabited
    it;
  they massacred young and old
    and children at the same time.
¹²In his blameless wrath he ex-
    pelled them to the west,
  and did not spare even the of-
    ficials of the country from
    ridicule.
¹³As the enemy (was) a stranger
    and his heart alien to our God,
    he acted arrogantly.
¹⁴So he did in Jerusalem all the
    things
  that gentiles do for their gods in
    their cities.
¹⁵And the children of the covenant
    (living) among the gentile
    rabble
  adopted these (practices).
  No one among them in Jerusalem
    acted (with) mercy or truth.
¹⁶Those who loved the assemblies
    of the devout fled from them

as sparrows fled from their nest.
¹⁷(They became) refugees in the
    wilderness
  to save their lives from evil.
  The life of even one who was saved
    from them was precious in
    the eyes of the exiles.
¹⁸They were scattered over the
    whole earth by (these) lawless
    ones.

¹⁹For the heavens withheld rain
    from falling on the earth.
  Springs were stopped,
    (from) the perennial (springs)
      far underground
    (to) those in the high mountains.
  For there was no one among them
    who practiced righteousness or
      justice:
²⁰From their leader to the common-
    est of the people,
  (they were) in every kind of sin:
    The king was a criminal
    and the judge disobedient;
    (and) the people sinners.
²¹See, Lord, and raise up for them
    their king,
  the son of David, to rule over
    your servant Israel
  in the time known to you, O
    God.
²²Undergird him with the strength
    to destroy the unrighteous
    rulers,
  to purge Jerusalem from gentiles
    who trample her to destruction;
²³in wisdom and in righ-
    teousness to drive out
  the sinners from the inheritance;
  to smash the arrogance of sinners
    like a potter's jar;
²⁴To shatter all their substance with
    an iron rod;
  to destroy the unlawful nations
    with the word of his mouth;
²⁵At his warning the nations will
    flee from his presence;

and he will condemn sinners by
   the thoughts of their hearts.

[26]He will gather a holy people
   whom he will lead in righteousness;
and he will judge the tribes of the
   people
   that have been made holy by the
   Lord their God.
[27]He will not tolerate unrighteousness (even) to pause among
   them,
   and any person who knows
   wickedness shall not live with
   them.
For he shall know them
   that they are all children of their
   God.
[28]He will distribute them upon the
   land
   according to their tribes;
the alien and the foreigner will no
   longer live near them.
[29]He will judge peoples and nations
   in the wisdom of his righteousness.
Pause.
[30]And he will have gentile nations
   serving him under his yoke,
   and he will glorify the Lord in (a
   place) prominent (above) the
   whole earth.
And he will purge Jerusalem
   (and make it) holy as it was even
   from the beginning,
[31](for) nations to come from the
   ends of the earth to see his
   glory,
to bring as gifts her children *the return*
   who had been driven out,
and to see the glory of the Lord
   with which God has glorified
   her.
[32]And he will be a righteous king
   over them, taught by God.
There will be no unrighteousness
   among them in his days,
   for all shall be holy, *Jer 31*

and their king shall be the Lord
   Messiah.
[33](For) he will not rely on horse and
   rider and bow,
   nor will he collect gold and silver for war.
Nor will he build up hope in a
   multitude for a day of war.
[34]The Lord himself is his king,
   the hope of the one who has a
   strong hope in God.

He shall be compassionate to all *messeat*
   the nations
   (who) reverently (stand) before
   him.
[35]He will strike the earth with the
   word of his mouth forever;
   he will bless the Lord's people
   with wisdom and happiness.
[36]And he himself (will be) free from
   sin, (in order) to rule a great
   people.
He will expose officials and drive
   out sinners
   by the strength of his word.
[37]And he will not weaken in his
   days, (relying) upon his God,
   for God made him
   powerful in the holy spirit
   and wise in the counsel of understanding,
   with strength and righteousness.
[38]And the blessing of the Lord will
   be with him in strength,
   and he will not weaken;
[39]His hope (will be) in the Lord.
Then who will succeed against
   him,
   [40]mighty in his actions
   and strong in the fear of God?
Faithfully and righteously shep-
   herding the Lord's flock,
   he will not let any of them stumble in their pasture.
[41]He will lead them all in holiness
   and there will be no arrogance
   among them,
   that any should be oppressed.

⁴²This is the beauty of the king of
    Israel
  which God knew,
    to raise him over the house of
    Israel
    to discipline it.

⁴³His words will be purer than the
    finest gold, the best.
He will judge the peoples in the
    assemblies,
    the tribes of the sanctified.
His words will be as the words of
    the holy ones,
    among sanctified peoples.
⁴⁴Blessed are those born in those
    days
    to see the good fortune of Israel
    which God will bring to pass in
    the assembly of the tribes.

⁴⁵May God dispatch his mercy
    upon Israel;
    may he deliver us from the pol-
    lution of profane enemies;
⁴⁶The Lord Himself is our king for-
    evermore.

¹⁸·¹O Lord, your mercy is upon the
    works of your hands forever.
(You show) your goodness to Israel
    with a rich gift.
²Your eyes (are) watching over
    them and none of them will
    be in need.
Your ears listen to the hopeful
    prayer of the poor,
³Your compassionate judgments
    (are) over the whole world,
    and your love is for the descen-
    dants of Abraham, an Israel-
    ite.
⁴Your discipline for us (is) as (for) a
    firstborn son, an only child,
to divert the perceptive person
    from unintentional sins.
⁵May God cleanse Israel for the day
    of mercy in blessing,

for the appointed day when his
    Messiah will reign.
⁶Blessed are those born in those
    days,
    to see the good things of the
    Lord
    which he will do for the coming
    generation;
⁷(which will be) under the rod of
    discipline of the Lord
    Messiah,
    in the fear of his God,
    in wisdom of spirit,
and of righteousness and of
    strength,
⁸to direct people in righteousness
    acts, in the fear of God,
    to set them all in the fear of the
    Lord
⁹A good generation (living) in the
    fear of God,
    in the days of mercy.
Pause.

¹⁰Our God is great and glorious
    living in the highest (heavens),
who arranges the stars into orbits
    (to mark) time of the hours from
    day to day.
And they have not deviated from
    their course,
    which he appointed them.
¹¹Their course each day is in the
    fear of God,
    from the day God created them
    forever.
¹²And they have not wandered
    from the day he created them,
    from ancient generations.
They have not veered off their
    course
    except when God directed them
    by the command of his servants.

These texts from *1 Enoch* and *2 Baruch* also
speak of cosmic signs attending the arrival of
the kingdom in its fullness.

1 Enoch 91.1–19; 93.1–14

91.1Now, my son Methuselah, (please) summon all your brothers on my behalf, and gather together to me all the sons of your mother; for the voice calls me, and the spirit is poured over me so that I may show you everything that shall happen to you forever. 2Then Methuselah went and summoned his brothers, and having summoned them to him, gathered his family together. 3Then he (Enoch) spoke to all of them, children of righteousness, and said, "Hear, all you children of Enoch, the talk of your father and listen to my voice in uprightness; 4for I exhort you, (my) beloved, and say to you: Love uprightness, and it alone. Do not draw near uprightness with an ambivalent attitiude, and neither associate with hypocrites! But walk in righteousness, my children, and it shall lead you in the good paths; and righteousness shall be your friend. 5For I know that the state of violence will intensify upon the earth; a great plague shall be executed upon the earth; all (forms of) oppression will be carried out; and everything shall be uprooted; and every arrow shall fly fast. 6Oppression shall recur once more and be carried out upon the earth; every (form of) oppression, injustice, and iniquity shall infect (the world) twofold. 7When sin, oppression, blasphemy, and injustice increase, crime, iniquity, and uncleanliness shall be committed and increase (likewise). Then a great plague shall take place from heaven upon all these; the holy Lord will emerge with wrath and plague in order that he may execute judgment upon the earth. 8In those days, violence shall be cut off from its (sources of succulent) fountain and from its roots—(likewise) oppression together with deceit; they shall be destroyed from underneath heaven. 9All

that which is (common) with the heathen shall be surrendered; the towers shall be inflamed with fire, and be removed from the whole earth. They shall be thrown into the judgment of fire, and perish in wrath and in the force of the eternal judgment. 10Then the righteous one shall arise from his sleep, and the wise one shall arise; and he shall be given unto them (the people), 11and through him the roots of oppression shall be cut off. Sinners shall be destroyed; by the sword they shall be cut off (together with) the blasphemers in every place; and those who design oppression and commit blasphemy shall perish by the knife.

12"Then after that there shall occur the second eighth week—the week of righteousness. A sword shall be given to it in order that judgment shall be executed in righteousness on the oppressors, and sinners shall be delivered into the hands of the righteous. 13At its completion, they shall acquire great things through their righteousness. A house shall be built for the Great King in glory for evermore.

14"Then after that in the ninth week the righteous judgment shall be revealed to the whole world. All the deeds of the sinners shall depart from upon the whole earth, and be written off for eternal destruction; and all people shall direct their sight to the path of uprightness.

15"Then, after this matter, on the tenth week in the seventh part, there shall be the eternal judgment; and it shall be executed by the angels of the eternal heaven—the great (judgment) which emanates from all of the angels. 16The first heaven shall depart and pass away; a new heaven shall appear; and all the powers of heaven shall shine forever sevenfold.

[17]"Then after that there shall be many weeks without number forever; it shall be (a time) of goodness and righteousness, and sin shall no more be heard of forever.

[18]"Now I shall speak unto you, my children, and show you the ways of righteousness and the ways of wickedness. Moreover, I shall make a revelation to you so that you may know that which is going to take place. [19]Now listen to me, my children, and walk in the way of righteousness, and do not walk in the way of wickedness, for all those who walk in the ways of injustice shall perish."

[93.1]Then after that Enoch happened to be recounting from the books. [2]And Enoch said, "Concerning the children of righteousness, concerning the elect ones of the world, and concerning the plant of truth, I will speak these things, my children, verily I, Enoch, myself, and let you know (about it) according to that which was revealed to me from the heavenly vision, that which I have learned from the words of the holy angels, and understood from the heavenly tablets." [3]He then began to recount from the books and said, "I was born the seventh during the first week, during which time judgment and righteousness continued to endure. [4]After me there shall arise in the second week great and evil things; deceit should grow, and therein the first consummation will take place. But therein (also) a (certain) man shall be saved. After it is ended, injustice shall become greater, and he shall make a law for the sinners.

[5]"Then after that at the completion of the third week a (certain) man shall be elected as the plant of the righteous judgment, and after him one (other) shall emerge as the eternal plant of righteousness.

[6]"After that at the completion of the fourth week visions of the old and righteous ones shall be seen; and a law shall be made with a fence, for all the generations.

[7]"After that in the fifth week, at the completion of glory, a house and a kingdom shall be built.

[8]"After that in the sixth week those who happen to be in it shall all of them be blindfolded, and the hearts of them all shall forget wisdom. Therein, a (certain) man shall ascend. And, at its completion, the house of the kingdom shall be burnt with fire; and therein the whole clan of the chosen root shall be dispersed.

[9]"After that in the seventh week an apostate generation shall arise; its deeds shall be many, and all of them criminal. [10]At its completion, there shall be elected the elect ones of righteousness from the eternal plant of righteousness, to whom shall be given sevenfold instruction concerning all his flock.

[11]"For what kind of a human being is there that is able to hear the voice of the Holy One without being shaken? Who is there that is able to ponder his (deep) thoughts? Who is there that can look directly at all the good deeds? [12]What kind of a person is he that can (fully) understand the activities of heaven, so that he can see a soul, or even perhaps a spirit—or, even if he ascended (into the heavens) and saw all (these heavenly beings and) their wings and contemplated them; or, even if he can do (what the heavenly beings) do?—and is able to live? [13]What kind of a person is anyone that is able to understand the nature of the breadth and length of the earth? To whom has the extent of all these been shown? [14]Is there perchance any human being that is able to understand the length of heaven, the extent of its altitude, upon what it is founded, the

number of the stars, and (the place) where all the luminaries rest?"

2 Baruch 53–73 (excerpts)

53.1 And I saw a vision. And behold, a cloud was coming up from the great sea. And I was looking at it, and behold, it was entirely filled with black water and there were many colors in that water. And something like great lightning appeared at its top. 2 And I saw that the cloud was rapidly passing in a quick run and covering the whole earth. 3 And it happened after this that the cloud began to pour the water that it contained upon the earth. 4 And I saw that the water which descended from it was not of the same likeness. 5 For at first, it was very black until a certain time. And then, I saw that the water became bright, but there was not much of it. And after this, I saw black water again, and after this bright again, and black again and bright again. 6 This, now, happened twelve times, but the black were always more than the bright. 7 And it happened at the end of the cloud that, behold, it poured black water and it was much darker than all the water that had come before. And fire was mingled with it. And where that water descended, it brought about devastation and destruction. 8 And after this I saw how the lightning which I had seen at the top of the cloud seized it and pressed it down to the earth. 9 That lightning shone much more, so that it lighted the whole earth and healed the regions where the last waters had descended and where it had brought about destruction. 10 And it occupied the whole earth and took command of it. 11 And after this I saw, behold, twelve rivers came from the sea and surrounded the lightning and became subject to it. 12 And because of my fear I awoke.

56.5 And as you first saw the black waters on the top of the cloud which first came down upon the earth; this is the transgression which Adam, the first man, committed. . . . 9 And from these black waters again black were born, and very darkness originated. 10 For he [i.e., Adam] who was a danger to himself was also a danger to the angels. . . . 12 And some of them came down and mingled themselves with women.

57.1 And after these [i.e., black waters] you saw the bright waters; that is the fountain of Abraham and his generation, and the coming of his son, and the son of his son, and of those who are like them. 2. . . . And the hope of the world which will be renewed was built at that time, and the promise of the life that will come later was planted.

58.1 And the third black waters you have seen; that is the mingling of all sins which the nations committed afterward, after the death of those righteous men, and the wickedness of the land of Egypt. . . .

59.1 And the fourth bright waters which you have seen; that is the coming of Moses, and of Aaron. . . . 3 But also the heaven will be shaken from its place at that time; that is, the heavens which are under the throne of the Mighty One were severely shaken when he took Moses with him.

60.1 And the fifth black waters which you have seen poured down; those are the works which the Amorites have done, and the invocations of their incantations. . . .

61.1 And the sixth bright waters which you have seen; this is the time in which David and Solomon were born.

143

[62.1]And the seventh black waters which you have seen; that is the perversion of the ideas of Jeroboam, who planned to make two golden calves.

[69.1]With regard to the last waters you have seen which are blacker than all those preceding which came after the twelfth, those which were brought together; they apply to the whole world.

[70.2]Behold, the days are coming and it will happen when the time of the world has ripened and the harvest of the seed of the evil ones and the good ones has come that the Mighty One will cause to come over the earth . . . confusion of the spirit and amazement of the heart. [3]And they will hate one another and provoke one another to fight. . . . [6] . . . And some of them will fall in war, and others will perish in tribulations, and again others of them will be troubled by their own. [7]The Most High will then give a sign to those nations which he has prepared before, and they will come and wage war with the rulers who will then remain. [8]And it will happen that everyone who saves himself from the war will die in an earthquake, and he who saves himself from the earthquake will be burned by fire, and he who saves himself from the fire will perish by famine.

[73.1]And it will happen after he has brought down everything which is in the world, and has sat down in eternal peace on the throne of the kingdom, then joy will be revealed and rest will appear. . . . [3]And nobody will again die untimely, nor will any adversity take place suddenly.

Rev.

10

Continuing toward Jerusalem

10.1 The Rich Young Man (Matt. 19:16–22; Mark 10:17–22; Luke 18:18–23) (JaS 221)

The following texts refer to *eternal life*, *endless life*, *inheriting life*, and similar expressions, all of which provide conceptual background to the rich young man's comment about "inheriting eternal life."

1QS 4.6–8

⁶And the visitation of whose [*sic*] who walk in it will be for healing, ⁷plentiful peace in a long life, fruitful offspring with all everlasting blessings, eternal enjoyment with endless life, and a crown of glory ⁸with majestic raiment in eternal light.

CD 3.20

See section 11.1 below.

4Q181 1.3–4

³In accordance with God's compassion and in accordance with his goodness and the wonders of his glory he approaches some from among the sons of world [. . .] so that they can be considered with him in [the community of] ⁴the gods like a holy congregation in the position of eternal life and in the lot of his holy ones [. . .].

2 Maccabees 7:9

See section 9.11 above.

4 Maccabees 15:3

She loved religion more, the religion that preserves them for eternal life according to God's promise.

1 Enoch 37.4; 40.9; 58.3

³⁷·⁴Until now such wisdom, which I have received as I recited (it) in accordance with the will of the Lord of the Spirits, had not been bestowed upon me before the face of the Lord of the Spirits. From him, the lot of eternal life has been given to me.

⁴⁰·⁹And he said to me, "The first one is the merciful and forbearing Michael; the second one, who is set over all disease and every wound of the children of the people, is Raphael; the third, who is set over all exercise of strength, is Gabriel; and the fourth, who is set over all actions of repentance unto the hope of those who would inherit eternal life, is Phanuel by name."

⁵⁸·³The righteous ones shall be in the light of the sun and the elect ones in the light of eternal life which has no end, and the days of the life of the holy ones cannot be numbered.

Psalms of Solomon 3.12

This is the share of sinners forever, but those who fear the Lord shall rise up to eternal life, and their life shall be in the Lord's light, and it shall never end.   *J M*

10.2 The Request for Precedence by the Sons of Zebedee (Matt. 20:20–28; Mark 10:35–45; Luke 22:24–27) (*JaS* 225)

Martyrdom and Ascension of Isaiah 5.13

Just as in the Synoptic Gospels, so here the metaphor of the "cup" is used to refer to suffering.

> And to the prophets who (were) with him he said before he was sawed in half, "Go to the district of Tyre and Sidon, because for me alone the Lord has mixed the cup."

10.3 The Parable of the Pounds (Luke 19:11–27; Matt. 25:14–30; Mark 13:34) (*JaS* 228)

The following texts mention Archelaus and his coming to power and provide background for Jesus' parable of the pounds.

Josephus, Antiquities 17.8.1 §188; 17.9.3 §222; 17.11.4 §317

17.8.1 [188]And now Herod altered his testament upon the alteration of his mind; for he appointed Antipas, to whom he had before left the kingdom, to be tetrarch of Galilee and Berea, and granted the kingdom to Archelaus.

17.9.3 [222]And Sabinus, out of regard to Varus, did neither seize upon any of the castles that were among the Jews, nor did he seal up the treasures in them, but permitted Archelaus to have them, until Caesar should declare his resolution about them; so

that, upon this his promise, he tarried still at Caesarea. But after Archelaus was sailed for Rome, and Varus was removed to Antioch, Sabinus went to Jerusalem, and seized on the king's palace.

17.11.4 [317]When Caesar had heard these pleadings, he dissolved the assembly; but a few days afterwards he appointed Archelaus, not indeed to be the king of the whole country, but ethnarch of one half of that which had been subject to Herod, and promised to give him the royal dignity hereafter, if he governed his part virtuously.

Josephus, Jewish War 2.6.1 §80; 2.6.3 §93

2.6.1 [80]But now came another accusation from the Jews against Archelaus at Rome, which he was to answer to. It was made by those ambassadors who, before the revolt, had come, by Varus's permission, to plead for the liberty of their country; those that came were fifty in number, but there were more than eight thousand of the Jews at Rome who supported them.

2.6.3 [93]So Caesar, after he had heard both sides, dissolved the assembly for that time; but a few days afterward, he gave the one half of Herod's kingdom to Archelaus, by the name of Ethnarch, and promised to make him king also afterward, if he rendered himself worthy of that dignity.

10.4 Entry into Jerusalem (Matt. 21:1–9; Mark 11:1–10; Luke 19:28–40; John 12:12–19) (*JaS* 229)

Josephus, Antiquities 9.6.2 §111

This text from the *Antiquities* comments on 2 Kings 9:13 and shows how the people responded with praise when Jehu was made king. Their response included making a "carpet" from garments and blowing trumpets.

. . . And when they were eager about the matter, and desired he would tell them, he answered, that God had said he had chosen him to be king over the multitude. When he had said this, every one of them put off his garment, and strewed it under him, and blew with trumpets, and gave notice that Jehu was king.

m. Sukkah 3.1, 8–9, 11–12; 4.5, 8*

These texts from *m. Sukkah* indicate that waving palm branches was associated with the Feast of Tabernacles and the recitation of the Hallel Psalms (i.e., 113–118). Some unusual terms in this passage must be defined. An *asherah* is a tree worshiped in idolatry. The *lulab* are branches of palm, myrtle, and willow bound together and carried along during the festival. The *Hallel* is a liturgy drawn from Psalms 113–118, which is recited during festival times and new moons. The *omer* is the first sheaf of the season which is harvested and offered at the temple as a meal offering. A *sofar* is a ram's horn blown at set times at the temple and in the synagogue. A *sukkah* is a temporary dwelling or "booth" in which Israelite men lived during the Feast of Tabernacles.

3.1 I A. A stolen or dried-up palm branch is invalid.

B. And one deriving from an *asherah* or an apostate town is invalid.

C. [If] its tip was broken off, or [if] its leaves were split, it is invalid.

D. [If] its leaves were spread apart, it is valid.

E. R. Judah says, "Let him tie it up at the end."

F. Thorn palms of the Iron Mountain are valid.

G. A palm branch which is [only] three handbreadths long,

H. sufficient to shake,

I. is valid.

⁸A. "They bind up the *lulab* [now: palm branch, willow branch, and myrtle branch] only with [strands of] its own species," the words of R. Judah.

B. R. Meir says, "Even with a rope [it is permitted to bind up the *lulab*]."

C. Said R. Meir, "MᶜSH B: The townsfolk of Jerusalem bound up their palm branches with gold threads."

D. They said to him, "But underneath they [in fact had] tied it up with [strands of] its own species."

⁹A. And at what point [in the *Hallel* Psalms, 113–118] did they shake [the *lulab*]?

B. "At *O give thanks unto the Lord* (Ps. 118), beginning and end; and at, *Save now, we beseech thee, O Lord* (Ps. 118:25)," the words of the House of Hillel.

C. And the House of Shammai say, "Also: At, *O Lord, we beseech thee, send now prosperity* (Ps. 118:25)."

D. Said R. Aqiba, "I was watching Rabban Gamaliel and R. Joshua, for all the people waved their palm branches, but they waved their palm branches only at , *Save now, we beseech thee, O Lord* (Ps. 118:25)."

E. He who was on a trip and had no *lulab* to carry—

F. when he reaches home, should carry the *lulab* at his own table.

G. [If] he did not carry his *lulab* in the morning, he should carry it at dusk,

H. for the entire day is a suitable time for the palm branch.

¹¹A. Where they are accustomed to repeat [the last nine verses of Ps. 118] let one repeat.

B. [Where it is the custom] to say them only once, let one say them only once.

C. [Where it is the custom] to say a blessing after it, let one say a blessing after it.

D. Everything follows the custom of the locality.

E. He who buys a *lulab* [palm branch, myrtle branch, willow branch] from his fellow in the Seventh Year [the seller] gives him a citron as a gift.

F. For one is not permitted to buy [the citron] in the Seventh Year.

¹²A. At first the *lulab* was carried in the Temple for seven days, and in the provinces, for one day.

B. When the Temple was destroyed, Rabban Yohanan b. Zakkai ordained that the *lulab* should be carried in the provinces seven days,

C. as a memorial to the Temple;

D. and that the whole of the day on which the *omer* is waved should be forbidden [for the use of new produce, which may be used only from the waving of the *omer* and thereafter; this had formerly been at noon].

^{4.5}A. The religious requirement of the willow branch: How so?

B. There was a place below Jerusalem, called Mosa. [People] go down there and gather young willow branches. They come and throw them along the sides of the altar, with their heads bent over the altar.

C. They blew on the *shofar* a sustained, a quavering, and a sustained note.

D. Every day they walk around the altar one time and say, "*Save now, we beseech thee, O Lord! We beseech thee, O Lord, send now prosperity* (Ps. 118:25)."

E. R. Judah says, "[They say], '*Ani waho, save us we pray! Ani waho, save us we pray!*'"

F. And on that day [the seventh day of the willow branch] they walk around the altar seven times.

G. When they leave, what do they say?

H. "Homage to you, O altar! Homage to you, O altar!"

I. R. Eliezer says, "For the Lord and for you, O altar! For the Lord and for you, O altar!"

⁸A. *The Hallel Psalms and the rejoicing are for eight days*: How so?

B. This rule teaches that a person is obligated for the *Hallel* Psalms, for the rejoicing, and for the honoring of the festival day, on the last festival day of the Festival, just as he is on all the other days of the Festival.

C. *The obligation to dwell in the sukkah for seven days:* How so?

D. [If] one has finished eating [the last meal of the festival], he should not untie his *sukkah* right away.

E. But he brings down the utensils [only] from twilight onward—

F. on account of the honor due to the last festival day of the Festival.

10.5 Jesus Weeps for Jerusalem (Luke 19:41–44) (*JaS* 230)

1QpHab 9.4–10

Jerusalem—with its priests who steal from the people, promote bloodshed, and act wickedly toward the Teacher of Righteousness—is pictured here in this pesher on Habakkuk as overrun by the Kittim (i.e., the Roman army).

⁴Its interpretation concerns the last priests of Jerusalem, ⁵who will accumulate riches and loot from plundering the peoples. ⁶However, in the last days their riches and their loot will fall into the hands ⁷of the army of the Kittim. *Blank* For they are *Hab 2:8a* "the greatest of the peoples." ⁸*Hab 2:8b* For the human blood [spilt] and the violence done to the country, the city and all its /occupants/. *Blank* ⁹Its

interpretation concerns the Wicked Priest, since for the wickedness against the Teacher of [10]Righteousness and the members of his council God delivered him into the hands of his enemies to disgrace him.

The following texts from Josephus describe Titus's destruction of Jerusalem.

70 AD

Josephus, **Jewish War** *5.11.1 §446; 5.12.2 §§508–510; 7.1.1 §§1–4; 7.8.7 §§375–377*

5.11.1 [446]So now Titus's banks were advanced a great way, notwithstanding his soldiers had been very much distressed from the wall. He then sent a party of horsemen, and ordered they should lay ambushes for those that went out into the valleys to gather food.

5.12.2 [508]Now the length of this wall was forty furlongs, one only abated. Now at this wall without were erected thirteen places to keep garrisons in, the circumference of which, put together, amounted to ten furlongs; [509]the whole was completed in three days: so that what would naturally have required some months, was done in so short an interval as is incredible. [510]When Titus had therefore encompassed the city with this wall, and put garrisons into proper places, he went round the wall, at the first watch of the night, and observed how the guard was kept; the second watch he allotted to Alexander; the commanders of legions took the third watch.

7.1.1 [1]Now, as soon as the army had no more people to slay or to plunder, because there remained none to be the objects of their fury (for they would not have spared any, had there remained any other such work to be done) Caesar gave orders

that they should now demolish the entire city and temple, but should leave as many of the towers standing as were of the greatest eminency; that is, Phasaelus, and Hippicus, and Mariamne, and so much of the wall as enclosed the city on the west side. [2]This wall was spared, in order to afford a camp for such as were to lie in garrison; as were the towers also spared, in order to demonstrate to posterity what kind of city it was, and how well fortified, which the Roman valor had subdued; [3]but for all the rest of the wall, it was so thoroughly laid even with the ground by those that dug it up to the foundation, that there was left nothing to make those that came thither believe it had ever been inhabited. [4]This was the end which Jerusalem came to by the madness of those that were for innovations; a city otherwise of great magnificence, and of mighty fame among all mankind.

7.8.7 [375]And where is now that great city, the metropolis of the Jewish nation, which was fortified by so many walls round about, which had so many fortresses and large towers to defend it, which could hardly contain the instruments prepared for the war, and which had so many ten thousands of men to fight for it? [376]Where is this city, that was believed to have God himself inhabiting therein? It is now demolished to the very foundations; and has nothing but that monument of it preserved, I mean the camp of those that has destroyed it, which still dwells upon its ruins; [377]some unfortunate old men also lie upon the ashes of the temple, and a few women are there preserved alive by the enemy, for our bitter shame and reproach.

149

11

The Passion Week

11.1 The Cleansing of the Temple and the Cursing of the Fig Tree (Mark 11:11–17; Matt. 21:10–19; Luke 19:45–46; John 2:13–17) (*JaS* 231)

These two texts from *m. Šeqalim* deal with the issue of "changing money," including both where and from whom it can be exacted.

m. Šeqalim 1.3; 3.1*

1.3A. On the fifteenth of that same month [Adar] they set up money changers' tables in the provinces.

B. On the twenty-fifth [of Adar] they set them up in the Temple.

C. Once they were set up in the Temple, they began to exact pledges [from those who had not paid the tax in specie].

D. From whom do they exact a pledge?

E. Levites, Israelites, proselytes, and freed slaves,

F. but not from women, slaves, and minors.

G. Any minor in whose behalf the father began to pay the *sheqel* does not again cease [to pay].

H. And they do not exact a pledge from priests,

I. for the sake of peace.

3.1A. At three times in the year do they take up the heave offering of the [coins collected in the] [*sheqel*] chamber:

B. half a month before Passover, half a month before Aseret [Pentecost], and half a month before the Festival [of Sukkot].

C. "And these are the 'threshing floors' [the times at which the obligation to tithe becomes operative] for tithing cattle," the words of R. Aqiba.

D. Ben Azzai says, "On the twenty-ninth of Adar, on the first of Sivan, and on the twenty-ninth of Ab."

E. R. Eleazar and R. Simeon say, "On the first of Nisan, on the first of Sivan, and on the twenty-ninth of Elul."

F. On what account did they rule, "On the twenty-ninth of Elul," instead of saying, "on the first of Tishre"?

G. Because it is a festival day, and it is not possible to give tithe on a festival day.

H. Therefore they set it a day earlier, on the twenty-ninth of Elul.

m. Berakot 9.5*

In this text, the rabbis recognize the problem of commercialism and discuss their ongoing concern for the temple's sanctity.

A. A man is obligated to recite a blessing over evil just as he recites a blessing over good.

B. As it is said, *And you shall love the Lord your God with all your heart, with all your soul, and with all your might* (Dt. 6:5).

C. *With all your heart*—[this means] with both of your inclinations, with the good inclination and with the evil inclination.

D. *And with all your soul*—even if He takes your soul.

E. *And with all your might*—with all of your money.

F. Another matter: *With all your might*—with each and every measure that he measures out for you, thank him much.

G. One should not act silly while facing the Eastern Gate [of the Temple in Jerusalem] for it faces toward the Chamber of the Holy of Holies.

H. One should not enter the Temple mount with his walking stick, his overshoes, his money bag, or with dust on his feet.

I. And one should not use [the Temple mount] for a shortcut.

J. And spitting [there likewise is forbidden, as is proven by an argument] *a minori ad majus* [if you may not use it for a shortcut, you obviously may not spit there].

K. [At one time] all blessings in the Temple concluded with "forever."

L. When the heretics corrupted [the practice] and said, "There is but one world [but no world to come],"

M. they ordained that they should say, "forever and ever" [thus suggesting the existence of a world to come].

N. And they ordained that an individual should greet his fellow with [God's] name,

O. in accordance with what is said, *And behold Boaz came from Bethlehem; and he said to the reapers, "The Lord be with you!" And they answered, "The Lord bless you"* (Ruth 2:4).

P. And it says, *The Lord is with you you mighty man of valor* (Judges 6:12).

Q. And it says, *Do not despise your mother when she is old* (Prov. 23:22).

R. And it says, *It is the time for the Lord to act, for thy law has been broken* (Ps. 119:126).

Josephus, Antiquities 12.3.4 §145; 15.11.5 §417

These two texts from Josephus discuss temple sanctity in terms of restricting access to foreigners and to ceremonially defiled Jews. The second text (15.11.5 §417) appears in section 11.9 below.

12.3.4 [145] And these were the contents of this epistle. He also published a decree through all his kingdom, in honor of the temple, which contained what follows:—"It shall be lawful for no foreigner to come within the limits of the temple round about; which thing is forbidden also to the Jews, unless to those who, according to their own custom, have purified themselves."

The following texts discuss Messiah's participation in renewed temple worship at the end. They declare God's ultimate "coming" to his temple, future sacrifices, and the role of the nations.

Shemoneh Esreh, *benediction 14**

And to Jerusalem, your city, return with mercy and dwell in its midst as you have spoken; and build it soon in our days to be an everlasting building; and raise up quickly in its midst the throne of David. *Blessed are You, Lord, who builds Jerusalem.*

Josephus, Antiquities 18.4.1 §§85–87

[85] But the nation of the Samaritans did not escape without tumults. The man

who excited them to it, was one who thought lying a thing of little consequence, and who contrived everything so, that the multitude might be pleased; so he bade them get together upon Mount Gerizzim, which is by them looked upon as the most holy of all mountains, and assured them that, when they were come thither, he would show them those sacred vessels which were laid under that place, because Moses put them there. [86]So they came thither armed, and thought the discourse of the man probable; and as they abode at a certain village, which was called Tirathaba, they got the rest together to them, and desired to go up the mountain in a great multitude together. [87]But Pilate prevented their going up, by seizing upon the roads with a great band of horsemen and footmen, who fell upon those that were gotten together in the village; and when it came to an action, some of them they slew, and others of them they put to flight, and took a great many alive, the principal of whom, and also the most potent of those that fled away, Pilate ordered to be slain.

Josephus, Jewish War 6.5.2 §§283–285

[283]The soldiers also came to the rest of the cloisters that were in the outer [court of the] temple, whither the women and children, and a great mixed multitude of the people fled, in number about six thousand. [284]But before Caesar had determined anything about these people, or given the commanders any orders relating to them, the soldiers were in such a rage, that they set that cloister on fire; by which means it came to pass that some of these were destroyed by throwing themselves down headlong, and some were burnt in the cloisters themselves. Nor did any one of them

escape with his life. [285]A false prophet was the occasion of these people's destruction, who had made a public proclamation in the city that very day, that God commanded them to get upon the temple, and that there they should receive miraculous signs of their deliverance.

Tobit 14:5

But God will again have mercy on them, and God will bring them back into the land of Israel; and they will rebuild the temple of God, but not like the first one until the period when the times of fulfillment shall come. After this they all will return from their exile and will rebuild Jerusalem in splendor; and in it the temple of God will be rebuilt, just as the prophets of Israel have said concerning it.

2 Maccabees 2:7

See section 8.1 above.

1 Enoch 24–25; 89–90 (excerpts)

[24.1]From there I went to another place of the earth, and he showed me a mountain of fire which was flaming day and night. [2]And I went in its direction and saw seven dignified mountains . . . of precious and beautiful stones. . . . [4]And among them, there was one tree . . . its leaves, its flowers, and its wood would never wither forever; its fruit is beautiful and resembles the clustered fruits of a palm tree. . . . [25.3]He [Michael, the archangel] answered [Enoch], saying, "This tall mountain which you saw whose summit resembles the throne of God is (indeed) his throne, on which the Holy and Great Lord of Glory, the Eternal King, will sit when he descends to visit the earth with goodness. [4]And as for this fragrant tree. . . . [5]This is for the righteous and the pious. . . . *. . . They shall enter into the holy (place); its fragrance shall (penetrate) their bones."

89.50Then that house [i.e., Solomon's temple] became great and spacious; a lofty building was built upon it for that sheep, as well as a tall and great tower upon it for the Lord of the sheep; that house was low but the tower was really elevated and lofty. Then the Lord of the sheep stood upon that tower, and they offered a full table before him.

51Again I saw those sheep, how they went astray, going in diverse ways and abandoning that house of his. Then the Lord of the sheep called some from among the sheep and sent them to the sheep, but the sheep began to slay them. 52However, one of them was not killed but escaped alive and fled away; he cried aloud to the sheep, and they wanted to kill him, but the Lord of the sheep rescued him from the sheep and caused him to ascend to me and settle down. 53He sent many other sheep to those sheep to testify to them and to lament over them. 54Thereafter I saw that, when they abandoned the house of the Lord and his tower, they went astray completely, and their eyes became blindfolded. Then I saw the Lord of the sheep, how he executed much slaughter upon them, in their flocks, until those sheep (began to) invoke that slaughter, and he vindicated his place. 55He left them in the hands of the lions, leopards, and wolves, hyenas, as well as in the hands of the foxes and to all the wild beasts; and these wild beasts of the wilderness began to tear those sheep into pieces. 56I saw how he left that house of theirs and that tower of theirs and cast all of them into the hands of the lions—(even) into the hands of all the wild beasts—so that

they may tear them into pieces and eat them.

90.20Then I kept seeing till a throne was erected in a pleasant land; and he sat upon it for the Lord of the sheep; and he took all the sealed books and opened those very books in the presence of the Lord of the sheep. 21Then the Lord called those people, the seven first snow-white ones, and ordered them to bring before him (some) from among the first star(s) that arose, and from among those stars whose sexual organs were like those of the horses, as well as (that) first star which had fallen down earlier. And they brought them all before him. 22He spoke to the man who was writing in his presence—that (man) being one of those seven snow-white ones—saying, "Take those seven shepherds to whom I had handed over the sheep, but who decided to kill many more than they were ordered." 23Behold, I saw all of them bound; and they all stood before him. 24Then his judgment took place. First among the stars, they received their judgment and were found guilty, and they went to the place of condemnation; and they were thrown into an abyss, full of fire and flame and full of the pillar of fire. 25Then those seventy shepherds were judged and found guilty; and they were cast into that fiery abyss. 26In the meantime I saw how another abyss like it, full of fire, was opened wide in the middle of the ground; and they brought those blinded sheep, all of which were judged, found guilty, and cast into this fiery abyss, and they were burned—the abyss is to the right of that house; 27thus I saw those sheep while they were burning—their bones also were burning.

[28]Then I stood still, looking at that ancient house being transformed: All the pillars and all the columns were pulled out; and the ornaments of that house were packed and taken out together with them and abandoned in a certain place in the South of the land. [29]I went on seeing until the Lord of the sheep brought about a new house, greater and loftier than the first one, and set it up in the first location which had been covered up—all its pillars were new, the columns new; and the ornaments new as well as greater than those of the first, (that is) the old (house) which was gone. All the sheep were within it.

[30]Then I saw all the sheep that had survived as well as all the animals upon the earth and the birds of heaven, falling down and worshiping those sheep, making petition to them and obeying them in every respect. [31]Thereafter, those three who were wearing snow-white (clothes), the former ones who had caused me to go up, grabbed me by my hand—also the hand of that ram holding me—and I ascended; they set me down in the midst of those sheep prior to the occurrence of this judgment. [32]Those sheep were all snow-white, and their wool considerable and clean. [33]All those which have been destroyed and dispersed, and all the beasts of the field and the birds of the sky were gathered together in that house; and the Lord of the sheep rejoiced with great joy because they had all become gentle and returned to his house.

Jubilees 1.15–17

[15]And afterward they will turn to me from among the nations with all their heart and with all their soul and with all their might. And I shall gather them from the midst of all the nations. And they will seek me so that I might be found by them. When they seek me with all their heart and with all their soul, I shall reveal to them an abundance of peace in righteousness. [16]And with all my heart and with all my soul I shall transplant them as a righteous plant. And they will be a blessing and not a curse. And they will be the head and not the tail. [17]And I shall build my sanctuary in their midst, and I shall dwell with them. And I shall be their God and they will be my people truly and rightly.

CD 3.19–4.2

[3.19]And he built for them a safe home in Israel, such as there has not been since ancient times, not even till [20]now. Those who remained steadfast in it will acquire eternal life, and all the glory of Adam is for them. As [21]God established for them by means of Ezekiel the prophet, saying, *Ez 44:15* "The priests and the levites and the sons of [4.1]Zadok who maintained the service of my temple when the children of Israel strayed [2]far from me, shall offer fat and the blood."

1QM 12.12–18; 19.3b–8

[12.12]Fill the land with glory and your inheritance with blessing: herds of flocks in your fields, gold, /silver,/ and precious stones in your palaces! [13]Rejoice, Sion, passionately! Shine with jubilation, Jerusalem! Exult, all the cities of Judah! [14]Open the gates for ever so that the wealth of the nations can come in! Their kings shall wait on you, all your oppressors lie prone before you, [15][and they shall lick] the dust [of your feet]. [Daughters] of my people, shout with jubilant voice! Deck yourselves with splendid finery! Rule over the gover[nment of . . .] [16][. . .] Israel, in order to reign for ever. *Blank* [17]the heroes of the war, Jerusalem [. . .] [18][. . .] above the heavens, the Lord [. . .].

[19.3b]Place your hand on the neck of your foes and your foot [on the piles of the dead! [4]Strike the nations, your enemies,] and may your sword consume flesh! Fill your land with glory and your inheritance with blessing: [a herd of flocks in your fields, [5]gold, silver, and precious stones in] your palaces! Rejoice, Zion, passionately! Exult, all the cities of Ju[dah! Open the gates for ever [6]so that] the wealth of the nations [can go in to you!] Their kings shall wait on you, [all your oppressors] lie prone in front of you, and they shall lick the dust of your feet]. [7][Daughters] of my people, shout with jubilant voice! Deck yourselves with splendid finery! Rule over the gover[nment of . . .] [8][. . .] Israel, in order to reign for ever.

11QTemple[a] 29.8–10

[8]I shall sanctify my temple with my glory, for I shall make my glory reside [9]over it until the day of creation, when I shall create my temple, [10]establishing it for myself for ever, in accordance with the covenant which I made with Jacob at Bethel.

1QpHab 9.2–5

[2]. . . And what [3]it says: *Hab 2:8a* "Since you pillaged many countries the rest of the people will pillage you." *Blank* Its interpretation concerns the last priests of Jerusalem, [5]who will accumulate riches and loot from plundering the peoples.

CD 5.5–8

According to this text from the Damascus Document at Qumran, this sect regarded the temple in their day as corrupt.

[5]And David's deeds were praised, except for Uriah's blood, [6]and God allowed them to him. And they also defiled the temple, for they did not [7]keep apart in accordance with the law, but instead lay with her who sees the blood of her menstrual flow. And each man takes as a wife [8]the daughter of his brother and the daughter of his sister.

m. Ḥagigah 1.1*

The significance of Jesus' healing of the lame, blind, mute, and deaf is accentuated by this text from the Mishnah in which such people were thought to be excluded from the temple.

A. All are liable for *an appearance offering [before the Lord]* (Ex. 23:14, Dt. 16:16)

B. except for (1) a deaf-mute, (2) an idiot, (3) a minor,

C. (4) one without pronounced sexual characteristics, (5) one who exhibits the sexual traits of both sexes,

D. (6) women, (7) slaves who have not been freed,

E. (8) the lame, (9) the blind, (10) the sick, (11) the old,

F. (12) and one who cannot go up on foot.

I.G. What is the definition of a minor?

H. "Any who cannot ride on the shoulder of his father to go up from Jerusalem to the Temple mount," the words of the House of Shammai.

I. And the House of Hillel say, "Any who cannot hold his father's hand to go up from Jerusalem to the Temple mount,

J. "as it is written, *Three regalim* (Ex. 23:14)."

11.2 The Parable of the Great Supper (Matt. 22:1–14; Luke 14:15–24) (*JaS* 237)

This passage in Sirach shows that to decline an invitation or "to stand aloof" when an important person requests your presence may be taken as an insult. According to two texts from Josephus, refusing a king may result in an extremely harsh response. See also the text from *Ruth Rabbah*.

Sirach 13:9–10

[9]When an influential person invites you, be reserved, and he will invite you more insistently. [10]Do not be forward, or you may be rebuffed; do not stand aloof, or you will be forgotten.

Ruth Rabbah *proem 7**

A parable. A king sent a proclamation to his country. What did the inhabitants of the country do with it? They took it, tore it up, and burnt it. Then they said, "Woe unto us when the king hears of this!"

Josephus, **Jewish War** *2.17.10* §§450–456

[450]It is true, that when the people earnestly desired that they would leave off besieging the soldiers, they were the more earnest in pressing it forward, and this till Metilius, who was the Roman general, sent to Eleazar, and desired that they would give them security to spare their lives only; but agreed to deliver up their arms, and what else they had with them. [451]The others readily complied with their petition, sent to them Gorion, the son of Nicodemus,

and Ananias, the son of Sadduk, and Judas, the son of Jonathan, that they might give them the security of their right hands, and of their oaths; after which Metilius brought down his soldiers; [452]which soldiers, while they were in arms, were not meddled with by any of the seditious, nor was there any appearance of treachery; but as soon as, according to the articles of capitulation, they had all laid down their shields and their swords, and were under no further suspicion of any harm, but were going away, [453]Eleazar's men attacked them after a violent manner, and encompassed them round, and slew them, while they neither defended themselves, nor entreated for mercy, but only cried out upon the breach of their articles of capitulation and their oaths. [454]And thus were all these men barbarously murdered, excepting Metilius; for when he entreated for mercy, and promised that he would turn Jew, and be circumcised, they saved him alive, but none else. This loss to the Romans was but light, there being no more than a few slain out of an immense army; but still it appeared to be a prelude to the Jews' own destruction, [455]while men made public lamentation when they saw that such occasions were afforded for a war as were incurable; that the city was all over polluted with such abominations, from which it was but reasonable to expect some vengeance even though they should escape revenge from the Romans; so that the city was filled with sadness, and every one of the moderate men in it were under great disturbance, as likely themselves to undergo punishment for the wickedness of the seditious; [456]for indeed it so happened that this murder was perpetrated on the Sabbath day, on which day the

Jews have a respite from their works on account of divine worship.

Josephus, **Antiquities 9.13.2 §§264–267**

[264]He also sent to the Israelites, and exhorted them to leave off their present way of living, and to return to their ancient practices, and to worship God, for that he gave them leave to come to Jerusalem, and to celebrate, all in one body, the feast of unleavened bread; and this he said was by way of invitation only, and to be done of their own good will, and for their own advantage, and not out of obedience to him, because it would make them happy. [265]But the Israelites, upon the coming of the ambassadors, and upon their laying before them what they had in charge from their own king, were so far from complying therewith, that they laughed the ambassadors to scorn, and mocked them as fools: as also they affronted the prophets, which gave them the same exhortations, and foretold what they would suffer if they did not return to the worship of God, insomuch that at length they caught them, and slew them; [266]nor did this degree of transgressing suffice them, but they had more wicked contrivances than what have been described: nor did they leave off, before God, as a punishment for their impiety, brought them under their enemies:—but of that more hereafter. [267]However, many there were of the tribe of Manasseh, and of Zebulon, and of Issachar, who were obedient to what the prophets exhorted them to do, and returned to the worship of God. Now all these came running to Jerusalem, to Hezekiah, that they might worship God [there].

11.3 On Paying Tribute to Caesar (Matt. 22:15–22; Mark 12:13–17; Luke 20:20–26) (*JaS* 238)

Josephus, **Antiquities 18.1.1 §§1–10**

This text from Josephus tells how the Jews hated paying the poll tax to Rome and how a certain Jew named Judas tried to engineer a revolt against it.

[1]Now Cyrenius, a Roman senator, and one who had gone through other magistracies, and had passed through them till he had been consul, and one who, on other accounts, was of great dignity, came at this time into Syria, with a few others, being sent by Caesar to be a judge of that nation, and to take an account of their substance; [2]Coponius also, a man of the equestrian order, was sent together with him, to have the supreme power over the Jews. Moreover, Cyrenius came himself into Judea, which was now added to the province of Syria, to take an account of their substance, and to dispose of Archelaus's money; [3]but the Jews, although at the beginning they took the report of a taxation heinously, yet did they leave off any further opposition to it, by the persuasion of Joazar, who was the son of Boethus, and high priest. So they, being overpersuaded by Joazar's words, gave an account of their estates, without any dispute about it; [4]yet was there one Judas, a Gaulonite, of a city whose name was Gamala, who, taking with him Sadduc, a Pharisee, became zealous to draw them to a revolt, who both said that this taxation was no better than an introduction to slavery, and exhorted the nation to assert their liberty; [5]as if they could procure them happiness and security for what they possessed, and an assured enjoyment of a still greater good, which was that of the honor and glory they would

thereby acquire for magnanimity. They also said that God would not otherwise be assisting to them, than upon their joining with one another in such counsels as might be successful, and for their own advantage; and this especially, if they would set about great exploits, and not grow weary in executing the same; ⁶so men received what they said with pleasure, and this bold attempt proceeded to a great height. All sorts of misfortunes also sprang from these men, and the nation was infected with this doctrine to an incredible degree; ⁷one violent war came upon us after another, and we lost our friends, who used to alleviate our pains; there were also very great robberies and murders of our principal men. This was done in pretense indeed for the public welfare, but in reality for the hopes of gain to themselves; ⁸whence arose seditions, and from them murders of men, which sometimes fell on those of their own people (by the madness of these men towards one another, while their desire was that none of the adverse party might be left), and sometimes on their enemies; a famine also coming upon us, reduced us to the last degree of despair, as did also the taking and demolishing of cities; nay, the sedition at last increased so high, that the very temple of God was burnt down by their enemy's fire. ⁹Such were the consequences of this, that the customs of our fathers were altered, and such a change was made, as added a mighty weight toward bringing all to destruction, which these men occasioned by their thus conspiring together; for Judas and Sadduc, who excited a fourth philosophic sect among us, and had a great many followers therein, filled our civil government with tumults at present, and laid the foundations of our future miseries, by this system of philosophy, which

we were before unacquainted withal; ¹⁰concerning which I shall discourse a little, and this the rather, because the infection which spread thence among the younger sort, who were zealous for it, brought the public to destruction.

11.4 Question about Resurrection (Matt. 22:23–33; Mark 12:18–27; Luke 20:27–40) (JaS 239)

According to Josephus, the Sadducees did not believe in physical resurrection from the dead.

Josephus, Antiquities 18.1.4 §16

But the doctrine of the Sadducees is this: That souls die with the bodies; nor do they regard the observation of anything besides what the law enjoins them; for they think it an instance of virtue to dispute with those teachers of philosophy whom they frequent; but this doctrine is received but by a few, yet by those still of the greatest dignity; but they are able to do almost nothing of themselves; for when they become magistrates, as they are unwillingly and by force sometimes obliged to be, they addict themselves to the notions of the Pharisees, because the multitude would not otherwise bear them.

Josephus, Jewish War 2.8.14 §§164–165

¹⁶⁴But the Sadducees are those that compose the second order, and take away fate entirely, and suppose that God is not concerned in our doing or not doing what is evil; ¹⁶⁵and they say, that to act what is good, or what is evil, is at men's own choice, and that the one or the other belongs so to every one, that they may act as they

please. They also take away the belief of the immortal duration of the soul, and the punishments and rewards in Hades.

m. Yebamot*

The Mishnah tractate *Yebamot* deals with levirate marriage, as does Josephus, *Antiquities* 4.8.23 §§254–256. We forgo quoting from *Yebamot* since the entire tractate is relevant to the practice.

Josephus, **Antiquities** *4.8.23 §§254–256*

[254]If a woman's husband die, and leave her without children, let his brother marry her; and let him call the son that is born to him by his brother's name, and educate him as the heir of his inheritance, for this procedure will be for the benefit of the public, because thereby families will not fail, and the estate will continue among the kindred; and this will be for the solace of wives under their affliction, that they are to be married to the next relation of their former husbands; [255]but if the brother will not marry her, let the woman come before the senate, and protest openly that this brother will not admit her for his wife, but will injure the memory of his deceased brother, while she is willing to continue in the family, and to hear him children; and when the senate have inquired of him for what reason it is that he is averse to this marriage, whether he gives a bad or a good reason, the matter must come to this issue, [256]That the woman shall loose the sandals of the brother, and shall spit in his face and say, He deserves this reproachful treatment from her, as having injured the memory of the deceased;—and then let him go away out of the senate, and bear this reproach upon him all his life long; and

let her marry to whom she pleases, of such as seek her in marriage.

In the following texts, we learn that holy angels have no need of marriage, while wicked angels (following a common Jewish reading of the story in Genesis 6) left heaven and cohabited with women. Generally speaking, angels have no need to eat, drink, or propagate, though there are exceptions in Jewish literature.

1 Enoch *15.6–7; 51.4; 104.4–6*

[15.6]Indeed you, formerly you were spiritual, (having) eternal life, and immortal in all the generations of the world. [7]That is why (formerly) I did not make wives for you, for the dwelling of the spiritual beings of heaven is heaven.

[51.4]In those days, mountains shall dance like rams, and the hills shall leap like kids satiated with milk. And the faces of all the angels in heaven shall glow with joy, because on that day the Elect One has arisen.

[104.4]Be hopeful, and do not abandon your hope, because there shall be a fire for you; you are about to be making a great rejoicing like the angels of heaven. [5]You shall not have to hide on the day of the great judgment, and you shall not be found as the sinners; but the eternal judgment shall be (far) away from you for all the generations of the world. [6]Now fear not, righteous ones, when you see the sinners waxing strong and flourishing; do not be partners with them, but keep far away from those who lean onto their own injustice; for you are to be partners with the good-hearted people of heaven.

Testament of Abraham 4.5–7

[5]Then the Commander-in-chief rose up and went outside, as if he needed

to urinate; and he ascended into heaven in the twinkling of an eye and stood before God and said to him, [6]"Master, Lord, let your might know that I cannot announce the mention of death to that righteous man, because I have not seen upon earth a man like him—merciful, hospitable, righteous, truthful, God-fearing, refraining from every evil deed. And so now know, Lord, that I cannot announce the mention of death." [7]Then the Lord said, "Michael, Commander-in-chief, go down to my friend Abraham, and whatever he should say to you, this do; and whatever he should eat you also eat with him."

1QH 3.20–23 (= col. 11)

[20]And I know that there is hope [21]for someone you fashioned out of clay to be an everlasting community. The corrupt spirit you have purified from the great sin so that he can take his place [22]with the host of the holy ones, and can enter in communion with the congregation of the sons of heaven. You cast eternal destiny for man with the spirits of knowledge, [23]so that he praises your name together in celebration, and tells of your wonders before all your works.

1 Enoch 6–9 (excerpts)

[6.1]In those days when the children of man had multiplied, it happened that there were born unto them handsome and beautiful daughters. [2]And the angels, the children of heaven, saw them and desired them; and they said to one another, "Come let us choose wives for ourselves from among the daughters of man and beget us children." [3]And Semyaz, being their leader, said unto them, "I fear that perhaps you will not consent that this deed should be done, and I alone will become (responsible) for this great sin."

[7.1]And they took wives unto themselves, and everyone (respectively) chose one woman for himself, and they began to go unto them. And they taught them magical medicine, incantations, the cutting of roots, and taught them (about) plants. [2]And the women became pregnant and gave birth to great giants whose heights were three hundred cubits.

[8.2]And there were many wicked ones and they committed adultery and erred, and all their conduct became corrupt.

[9.1]Then Michael, Surafel, and Gabriel observed carefully from the sky and they saw much blood being shed upon the earth, and all the oppression being wrought upon the earth.

In Judaism, righteous people were often compared with the angels of heaven. This is true in the following passages from 1 Enoch and 2 Baruch. The second quote from 1 Enoch (104.4–6) appears earlier in this section.

1 Enoch 39.5; 104.4–6

[39.5]So there my eyes saw their
    dwelling places with the holy
    angels,
and their resting places with the
    holy ones,
and they interceded and petitioned
    and prayed on behalf of the chil-
    dren of the people,
and righteousness flowed before
    them like water,
and mercy like dew upon the earth,
and thus it is in their midst forever
    and ever.

2 Baruch 51.10–11

[10]For they will live in the heights of that world and they will be like the angels and be equal to the stars. And they will be changed into any shape

which they wished, from beauty to loveliness, and from light to the splendor of glory. [11]For the extents of Paradise will be spread out for them, and to them will be shown the beauty of the majesty of the living beings under the throne, as well as all the hosts of the angels, those who are held by my word now lest they show themselves, and those who are withheld by my command so that they may stand at their places until their coming has arrived.

11.5 The Great Commandment (Matt. 22:34–40; Mark 12:28–34; Luke 10:25–28) (JaS 240)

These texts from *Genesis Rabbah* and *m. Ḥagigah* show that the question of the greatest commandment was discussed in Judaism. The text from *Mekilta* shows the focus on the Torah and the need to keep its every teaching, that is, to "make a fence around the Torah."

Genesis Rabbah 24.7*

Ben 'Azzai said: THIS IS THE BOOK OF THE DESCENDENTS OF ADAM is a great principle of the Torah. R. Akiba said: *But you shall love your neighbor as yourself* (Lev. 19:18) is even a greater principle.

m. Ḥagigah 1.8*

A. The absolution of vows hovers in the air, for it has nothing [in the Torah] upon which to depend.

B. The laws of the Sabbath, festal offerings, and sacrilege—lo, they are like mountains hanging by a string,

C. for they have little Scripture for many laws.

D. Laws concerning civil litigations, the sacrificial cult, things to be kept cultically clean, sources of cultic uncleanness, and prohibited consanguineous marriages have much on which to depend.

E. And both these and those [equally] are the essentials of the Torah.

Mekilta de Rabbi Ishmael, Pisha 6 on Exodus 12:8*

Why then have the sages said: "Up to midnight?" To prevent the possibility of a transgression of the Law, and to make a fence around the Torah. And thus they fulfilled the words of the men of the Great Synagogue, who had said three things: Be deliberate in judgment, raise up many disciples, and make a fence around the Torah.

11.6 The Question about David's Son (Matt. 22:41–46; Mark 12:35–37a; Luke 20:41–44) (JaS 241)

Although there were various views about the messiah in first-century Judaism, there was a widespread belief in the Judaism of Jesus' day that the Christ would be a "son" of David. Both of the following texts testify to this.

Psalms of Solomon 17.21–25

See section 9.17 above.

4QFlor 1.11–13

See section 13.2 below.

Justin Martyr, First Apology 45*

Justin uses Psalm 110:1 to explain why the Christ must wait in heaven until the time of the consummation.

And that God the Father of all would bring Christ to heaven after He had raised Him from the dead, and would keep Him there until He has subdued His enemies the devils, and until the number of those who are foreknown by Him as good and virtuous is complete, on whose account he has still delayed the consummation—hear what was said by the prophet David. These are his words: "The Lord said to My Lord, Sit at My right hand, until I make your enemies your footstool. The Lord shall send to you the rod of power out of Jerusalem; and you will rule in the midst of your enemies. With you is the government in the day of your power, in the beauties of your saints: from the womb of morning have I begotten you." That which he says, "He shall send to you the rod of power out of Jerusalem," is predictive of the mighty word, which His apostles, going forth from Jerusalem, preached everywhere; and though death is decreed against those who teach or at all confess the name of Christ, we everywhere both embrace and teach it. And if you also read these words in a hostile spirit, you can do no more, as I said before, than kill us, which indeed does no harm to us, but to you and all who unjustly hate us, and do not repent, brings eternal punishment by fire.

11.7 Woe to the Scribes and Pharisees (Matt. 23:1–36; Mark 12:37b–40; Luke 20:45–47; Luke 11:46, 52; 6:39; 11:42, 39–41, 44, 47–48, 49–51, 43) (JaS 242)

t. Sanhedrin 7.8; 8.1*

In these texts from t. Sanhedrin, there is a ranking, or order, to those who served in the Sanhedrin.

7.8A. When the patriarch enters, everyone rises and does not sit down until he says to them, "Sit down."

B. And when the head of the court enters, they set up for him two rows,

one on one side, one on the other side, through which he goes, and he sits down in his place.

C. A sage who comes in—one rises as another sits down, until he comes in and sits down in his place.

D. Younger sages and disciples of sages, when the public requires their services, even step over the heads of the people.

E. And even though they have said, "It is no praise for a disciple of a sage to come in last," if he went out for need, he comes back and sits down in his place.

8.1A. Any sanhedrin in which there are two who know how to engage in argument, and in which all of them are suitable to listen, is suitable to be constituted into a sanhedrin.

B. [If] there are three, it is average, [and if there are] four, it is one of wisdom.

C. The sanhedrin was set in the shape of a half of a round threshing-floor so that [the judges] should be able to see one another [M. San. 4:3A]

D. The patriarch sits in the middle and the elders sit on his right and left.

E. Said R. Eleazar b. R. Sadoq, "When Rabban Gamaliel sat in session in Yavneh, my father and one other were at his right hand, and elders were at his left hand."

F. And on what account does one sit in rank of age at his right hand? Because of the honor owing to age.

1QS 2.19–23

In this text from Qumran, a clearly defined seating order reveals a person's standing in God's order.

19Blank They shall act in this way year after year, all the days of Belial's dominion. The priests shall enter 20the

Rule foremost, one behind the other, according to their spirits. And the levites shall enter after them. [21]In third place all the people shall enter the Rule, one after another, in thousands, hundreds, [22]fifties and tens, so that all the children of Israel may know their standing in God's Community [23]in conformity with the eternal plan. And no-one shall move down from his rank nor move up from the place of his lot.

t. Mo'ed Qatan 2.17*

This text from the Tosefta indicates the honor due a sage at his death.

A. A sage who died—

B. all are deemed his relations [cf. M. M.Q. 3:7A].

C. All tear their garments.

D. And all bear [their shoulders].

E. And all lament.

F. And all receive a mourner's meal on his account,

G. even in the street of the town.

H. They do not bring waling pipes to the house of mourning but to the banquet-house,

I. and to the house of rejoicing, in the place in which that was the custom.

J. What is lamentation [M. M.Q. 3:8A–B]?

K. This is one which is upon the heart,

L. as it is said, *Beat upon your breasts* (Is. 32:12).

M. Clapping is with the hands.

N. A gesture of praise [QYLWS]— this is the spreading open of the arms.

m. Soṭah 3.4*

M. Soṭah 3.4.J identifies the type of people God might judge. It appears within a text on determining if a woman has been unfaithful.

A. She hardly has sufficed to drink it before her face turns yellow, her eyes bulge out, and her veins swell.

B. And they say, "Take her away! Take her away!"

C. so that the Temple court will not be made unclean [by her corpse].

D. [But if nothing happened], if she had merit, she would attribute [her good fortune] to it.

E. There is the possibility that merit suspends the curse for one year, and there is the possibility that merit suspends the curse for two years, and there is the possibility that merit suspends the curse for three years.

F. On this basis Ben Azzai says, "A man is required to teach Torah to his daughter."

G. "For if she should drink the water, she should know that [if nothing happens to her], merit is what suspends [the curse from taking effect]."

H. R. Eliezer says, "Whoever teaches Torah to his daughter is as if he teaches her sexual satisfaction."

I. R. Joshua says, "A woman wants a *qab* [of food] with sexual satisfaction more than nine *qabs* with abstinence."

J. He would say, "A foolish saint, a smart knave, an abstemious woman,

K. "and the blows of abstainers (*perushim*)—

L. "lo, these wear out the world."

ʾAbot de Rabbi Nathan 37a and 40a*

In these two passages from ʾ*Abot de Rabbi Nathan*, hypocrisy and pride are spoken against. In ʾ*Abot de Rabbi Nathan* 40a, which appears in section 8.7 above, the sin of pride is evidenced in one's presumption concerning divine forgiveness.

[37a]IV 1. A. There are seven types of Pharisee:

B. the shoulder-Pharisee [ostentatiously carrying his good deeds on his shoulder, for show], the "excuse-me-I-have-to-do-a-religious-duty"-Pharisee, the . . . -Pharisee, the Pharisee who had a trade, the "what-is-my-duty-that-I-may-do-it"-Pharisee; the Pharisee who separates from his evil impulse; the Pharisee out of fear.

The following four texts illustrate the emphasis placed on scrupulous tithing.

m. Demai 2.1*

This text appears in section 9.4 above.

m. Maʿaśerot 4.5*

A. One who husks barley removes the husks [from the kernels] one by one, and eats [without tithing].

B. But if he husked [a few kernels] and placed [them] in his hand, he is required [to tithe].

C. One who husks parched kernels of wheat sifts [the kernels] from hand to hand, and eats [without tithing].

D. But if he sifted [the kernels] and placed [them] inside his shirt, he is required [to tithe].

E. Coriander which [the farmer] sowed [in order to harvest its] seed [for future sowing]—its leaves are exempt [from the removal of tithes if they are eaten].

F. [If he] sowed it [in order to harvest its] leaves [for use as an herb]—[both] the seeds and the leaves are subject to the law of tithes.

G. R. Eliezer says, "Dill is subject to the law of tithes [in regard to its] seeds, leaves and pods."

H. But Sages say, "Nothing is subject to the law of tithes [in regard to both its] seeds and leaves save cress and field rocket alone."

m. ʿUqṣin 3.6*

A. Unripe figs and grapes—

B. R. Aqiba declares susceptible to uncleanness as food.

C. R. Yohanan b. Nuri says, "[That is the case] when they reach the time of liability to tithes."

D. Olives and grapes which have turned hard—

E. The House of Shammai declare susceptible to uncleanness.

F. And the House of Hillel declare insusceptible to uncleanness.

G. Black cumin—

H. The House of Shammai declare insusceptible.

I. And the House of Hillel declare susceptible.

J. And so [with regard to the question of whether it is liable to] tithes [do they disagree].

m. Šebiʿit 9.1*

A. Rue, goosefoot, wild coriander, water parsley, and eruca of the field are exempt from [separation of] tithes and may be bought from anyone during the Sabbatical year,

B. because produce of their type is not cultivated [but grows wild].

C. R. Judah says, "Aftergrowths of mustard are permitted [may be bought during the Sabbatical year],

D. "because transgressors are not suspect concerning them [they are not suspected of cultivating mustard and then claiming that it is an aftergrowth]."

E. R. Simeon says, "All aftergrowths are permitted, except aftergrowths of cabbage,

F. "because produce of this type does not [grow uncultivated] among wild vegetables."

G. And sages say, "All aftergrowths are forbidden."

ʾAbot de Rabbi Nathan 41a*

I A. Whoever accepts upon himself responsibility to carry out four matters is accepted as a fellow [in a commensal group]:

B. Not to go to a cemetery, not to raise small cattle, not to hand over priestly rations and tithes to a priest who is a common person, not to prepare with a common person food requiring conditions of cultic cleanness.

C. and eating unconsecrated food in a condition of cultic cleanness.

m. Berakot 8.2*

According to m. Berakot 8.2, the rabbis debated the proper way to maintain external purity through washings. The whole ritual of washing and cleanliness is addressed by Jesus in Mark 12:37b–40 (and parallels).

A. The house of Shammai say, "They wash the hands and then mix the cup [of wine]."

B. But the House of Hillel say, "They mix the cup and then wash the hands."

The following texts depict Abel as a martyr, killed unjustly by his own brother Cain.

Pseudo-Philo, Biblical Antiquities 16.2

And God was angry and said, "I commanded the earth, and it gave me man; and to him two sons were born first of all, and the older rose up and killed the younger, and the earth quickly swallowed up his blood. But I drove Cain out and cursed the earth and spoke to the parched land, saying, 'You will swallow up blood no more.'"

Jubilees 4.1–3

[1]And in the third week in the second jubilee, she bore Cain. And in the fourth she bore Abel. And in the fifth she bore Awan, his daughter. [2]And at the beginning of the third jubilee, Cain killed Abel because the sacrifice of Abel was accepted, but the offering of Cain was not accepted. [3]And he killed him in the field, and his blood cried out from the earth to heaven, making accusation because he killed him.

1 Enoch 22.6–7

See section 9.15 above for this text.

11.8 Jesus' Lament over Jerusalem (Matt. 23:37–39; Luke 13:34–35) (JaS 243)

In 1 Enoch 39.7 (see section 9.15 above for the text) and 2 Baruch 41.4 (see section 9.9 above), God's "wings" are symbols of refuge, safety, and blessing.

11.9 Prediction of the Temple's Destruction (Matt. 24:1–2; Mark 13:1–2; Luke 21:5–6) (JaS 245)

There were also others in Jesus' day who regarded the Jewish leadership and the temple service as unfaithful and in danger of God's severe judgment. The following four passages reflect this belief.

Testament of Levi 15.1

Therefore the sanctuary which the Lord chose shall become desolate through your uncleanness, and you will be captives in all the nations.

Testament of Moses 6.8–9

[8]After his death there will come into their land a powerful king of the West who will subdue them; [9]and he will take away captives, and a part of

their temple he will burn with fire. He will crucify some of them around their city.

1QpHab 9.6–7

See section 10.5 above.

Josephus, Jewish War 6.5.3 §§300–301

[300] . . . "Let us remove hence." But, what is still more terrible there was one Jesus, the son of Ananus, a plebeian and a husbandman, who, four years before the war began, and at a time when the city was in very great peace and prosperity, came to that feast whereon it is our custom for everyone to make tabernacles to God in the temple, [301]began on a sudden cry aloud, "A voice from the east, a voice from the west, a voice from the four winds, a voice against Jerusalem and the holy house, a voice against the bridegrooms and the brides, and a voice against this whole people!" This was his cry, as he went about by day and by night, in all the lanes of the city.

Jubilees 23.11–32

This passage from *Jubilees* reflects a "pattern" reading of earlier events that will characterize a later time.

[11]And all of the generations which will arise henceforth and until the day of the great judgment will grow old quickly before they complete two jubilees, and their knowledge will forsake them because of their old age. And all of their knowledge will be removed. [12]And in those days if a man will live a jubilee and a half, they will say about him, "He prolonged his life, but the majority of his days were suffering and anxiety and affliction. And there was no peace, [13]because plague (came) upon plague, and wound upon

wound, and affliction upon affliction, and evil report upon evil report, and sickness upon sickness, and every evil judgment of this sort one with another: sickness, and downfall, and sleet, and hail, and frost, and fever, and chills, and stupor, and famine, and death, and sword, and captivity, and all plagues, and suffering."

[14]And all of this will come in the evil generation which sins in the land. Pollution and fornication and contamination and abomination are their deeds. [15]Then they will say, "The days of the ancients were as many as one thousand years and good. But behold, (as for) the days of our lives, if a man should extend his life seventy years or if he is strong (for) eighty years, then these are evil. And there is not any peace in the days of this evil generation."

[16]And in this generation children will reproach their parents and their elders on account of sin, and on account of injustice, unrighteousness, and on account of the words of their mouth, and on account of great evil which they will do, and on account of their forsaking the covenant which the LORD made between them and himself so that they might be careful and observe all his commandments and his ordinances and all of his law without turning aside to the right or left. [17]For they all did evil and every mouth speaks of sin and all of their deeds (are) polluted and abominable. And all of their ways (are) contamination and pollution and corruption.

[18]Behold, the land will be corrupted on account of all their deeds, and there will be no seed of the vine, and there will be no oil because their works are entirely faithless. And all of them will be destroyed together: beast, cattle, birds, and all of the fish of the sea on account of the sons of men. [19]Some of these shall strive with others, youths

will old men and old men with youths, the poor with the rich, the lowly with the great, and the beggar with the judge concerning the Law and the Covenant because they have forgotten the commandments and covenant and festivals and months and sabbaths and jubilees and all of the judgments. ²⁰And they will stand up with bow and swords and war in order to turn them to "the way," but they will not be returned until much blood is shed upon the earth by each (group). ²¹And those who escape will not be turned back from their evils to the way of righteousness because they will lift themselves up deceit and wealth so that one shall take everything of his neighbor; and they will pronounce the great name but not in truth or righteousness. And they will pollute the holy of holies with their pollution and with the corruption of their contamination.

²²And there will be a great plague upon the deeds of that generation from the LORD and he will give them to the sword and to judgment and to captivity and pillage and destruction. ²³And he will rouse up against them the sinners of the nations who have no mercy or grace for them and who have no regard for any persons old or young or anyone. For (they will be) cruel and powerful so that they will act more evilly than any of the sons of men.

And they will cause turmoil in Israel and sin against Jacob;
and much blood will be shed upon the earth;
and there will be no one who will gather and no one who will bury.
²⁴In those days, they will cry out and call and pray
to be saved from the hand of sinners, the gentiles,

but there will be none who will be saved,
²⁵and the heads of children will be white with gray hairs,
and an infant three weeks old will look aged
like one whose years (are) one hundred,
and their stature will be destroyed by affliction and torment.
²⁶And in those days, children will begin to search the law,
and to search the commandments and to return to the way of righteousness.
²⁷And the days shall begin to increase and grow longer
among those sons of men, generation by generation,
and year by year, until
their days approach a thousand years,
and to a greater number of years than days.
²⁸And there (will be) no old men and none who is full of days.
Because all of them will be infants and children.
²⁹And all of their days they will be complete
and live in peace and rejoicing
and there will be no Satan and no evil (one) who will destroy,
because all of their days will be days of blessing and healing.
³⁰And then the LORD will heal his servants,
and they will rise up and see great peace.
And they will drive out their enemies
and the righteous ones will see and give praise,
and rejoice forever and ever with joy;
and they will see all their judgments and all of their curses among their enemies.

[31]And their bones will rest in the
    earth,
and their spirits will increase joy,
and they will know that the LORD is
    an executor of judgment;
but he will show mercy to hun-
    dreds and thousands,
to all who love him.

[32]And you, Moses, write these words
because thus it is written and set upon
the heavenly tablets as a testimony for
eternal generations.

Both Josephus and Tacitus describe the
magnificence of the temple in Jerusalem.

Josephus, Jewish War 5.5.1–6 §§184–227

[184]Now this temple, as I have already
said, was built upon a strong hill. At
first the plain at the top was hardly
sufficient for the holy house and the
altar, for the ground about it was very
uneven, and like a precipice; [185]but
when king Solomon, who was the
person that built the temple, had built
a wall to it on its east side, there was
then added one cloister founded on
a bank cast up for it, and on the other
parts the holy house stood naked; but
in future ages the people added new
banks, and the hill became a larger
plain. [186]They then broke down the
wall on the north side, and took in
as much as sufficed afterward for the
compass of the entire temple; [187]and
when they had built walls on three
sides of the temple round about, from
the bottom of the hill, and had performed a work that was greater than
could be hoped for (in which work
long ages were spent by them, as well
as all their sacred treasures were exhausted, which were still replenished
by those tributes which were sent to
God from the whole habitable earth),
they then encompassed their upper
courts with cloisters, as well as they
[afterward] did the lowest [court of
the] temple. [188]The lowest part of this
was erected to the height of three
hundred cubits, and in some places
more; yet did not the entire depth
of the foundations appear, for they
brought earth, and filled up the valleys, as being desirous to make them
on a level with the narrow streets of
the city; [189]wherein they made use of
stones of forty cubits in magnitude;
for the great plenty of money they
then had, and the liberality of the
people, made this attempt of theirs to
succeed to an incredible degree; and
what could not be so much as hoped
for as ever to be accomplished, was,
by perseverance and length of time,
brought to perfection.
    [190]Now, for the works that were
above these foundations, these were
not unworthy of such foundations;
for all the cloisters were double, and
the pillars to them belonging were
twenty-five cubits in height, and
supported the cloisters. These pillars
were of one entire stone each of them,
and that stone was white marble;
[191]and the roofs were adorned with
cedar, curiously graven. The natural
magnificence, and excellent polish,
and the harmony of the joints in these
cloisters, afforded a prospect that was
very remarkable; nor was it on the
outside adorned with any work of the
painter or engraver. [192]The cloisters [of
the outmost court] were in breadth
thirty cubits, while the entire compass
of it was, by measure, six furlongs,
including the tower of Antonia; those
entire courts that were exposed to the
air were laid with stones of all sorts.
[193]When you go through these [first]
cloisters, unto the second [court of
the] temple, there was a partition
made of stone all round, whose height
was three cubits: its construction was
very elegant; [194]upon it stood pillars,

at equal distances from one another, declaring the law of purity, some in Greek, and some in Roman letters, that "no foreigner should go within that sanctuary"; for that second [court of the] temple was called "the Sanctuary"; [195]and was ascended to by fourteen steps from the first court. This court was foursquare, and had a wall about it peculiar to itself: [196]the height of its buildings, although it were on the outside forty cubits, was hidden by the steps, and on the inside that height was but twenty-five cubits; for it being built over against a higher part of the hill with steps, it was no farther to be entirely discerned within, being covered by the hill itself. [197]Beyond these fourteen steps there was the distance of ten cubits; this was all plain, [198]whence there were other steps, each of five cubits a piece, that led to the gates, which gates on the north and south sides were eight, on each of those sides four, and of necessity two on the east; for since there was a partition built for the women on that side, as the proper place wherein they were to worship, there was a necessity of a second gate for them: this gate was cut out of its wall, over against the first gate. [199]There was also on the other sides one southern and one northern gate, through which was a passage into the court of the women; for as to the other gates, the women were not allowed to pass through them; nor when they went through their own gate could they go beyond their own wall. This place was allotted to the women of our own country, and of other countries, provided they were of the same nation, and that equally; [200]the western part of this court had no gate at all, but the wall was built entire on that side; but then the cloisters which were betwixt the gates, extended from the wall inward, before the chambers;

for they were supported by very fine and large pillars. These cloisters were single, and, excepting their magnitude, were no way inferior to those of the lower court.

[201]Now nine of these gates were on every side covered over with gold and silver, as were the jambs of their doors and their lintels; but there was one gate that was without [the inward court of] the holy house, which was of Corinthian brass, and greatly excelled those that were only covered over with silver and gold. [202]Each gate had two doors, whose height was severally thirty cubits, and their breadth fifteen. [203]However, they had large spaces within of thirty cubits, and had on each side rooms, and those, both in breadth and in length, built like towers, and their height was above forty cubits. Two pillars did also support these rooms, and were in circumference twelve cubits. [204]Now the magnitudes of the other gates were equal one to another; but that over the Corinthian gate, which opened on the east over against the gate of the holy house itself, was much larger; [205]for its height was fifty cubits; and its doors were forty cubits; and it was adorned after a most costly manner, as having much richer and thicker plates of silver and gold upon them than the other. These nine gates had that silver and gold poured upon them by Alexander, the father of Tiberius. [206]Now there were fifteen steps, which led away from the wall of the court of the women to this greater gate; whereas those that led thither from the other gates were five steps shorter.

[207]As to the holy house itself, which was placed in the midst [of the inmost court], that most sacred part of the temple, it was ascended to by twelve steps; and in front its height and its breadth were equal, and each

a hundred cubits, though it was behind forty cubits narrower; for on its front it had what may be styled shoulders on each side, that passed twenty cubits farther. [208]Its first gate was seventy cubits high, and twenty-five cubits broad; but this gate had no doors; for it represented the universal visibility of heaven, and that it cannot be excluded from any place. Its front was covered with gold all over, and through it the first part of the house, that was more inward did all of it appear; which, as it was very large, so did all the parts about the more inward gate appear to shine to those that saw them; [209]but then, as the entire house was divided into two parts within, it was only the first part of it that was open to our view. Its height extended all along to ninety cubits in height, and its length was fifty cubits, and its breadth twenty; [210]but that gate which was at this end of the first part of the house was, as we have already observed, all over covered with gold, as was its whole wall about it; it had also golden vines above it, from which clusters of grapes hung as tall as a man's height; [211]but then this house, as it was divided into two parts, the inner part was lower than the appearance of the outer, and had golden doors of fifty-five cubits altitude, and sixteen in breadth; [212]but before these doors there was a veil of equal largeness with the doors. It was a Babylonian curtain, embroidered with blue, and fine linen, and scarlet, and purple, and of a contexture that was truly wonderful. Nor was this mixture of colors without its mystical interpretation, but was a kind of image of the universe; [213]for by the scarlet there seemed to be enigmatically signified fire, by the fine flax the earth, by the blue the air, and by the purple the sea; two of them having their colors the foundation of this

resemblance; but the fine flax and the purple have their own origin for that foundation, the earth producing the one, and the sea the other. [214]This curtain had also embroidered upon it all that was mystical in the heavens, excepting that of the [twelve] signs, representing living creatures.

[215]When any person entered into the temple, its floor received them. This part of the temple therefore was in height sixty cubits, and its length the same; whereas its breadth was but twenty cubits: [216]but still that sixty cubits in length was divided again, and the first part of it cut off at forty cubits, and had in it three things that were very wonderful and famous among all mankind; the candlestick, the table [of shew bread], and the altar of incense. [217]Now, the seven lamps signified the seven planets; for so many there were springing out of the candlestick. Now, the twelve loaves that were upon the table signified the circle of the zodiac and the year; [218]but the altar of incense, by its thirteen kinds of sweet-smelling spices with which the sea replenished it, signified that God is the possessor of all things that are both in the uninhabitable and habitable parts of the earth, and that they are all to be dedicated to his use. [219]But the inmost part of the temple of all was of twenty cubits. This was also separated from the outer part by a veil. In this there was nothing at all. It was inaccessible and inviolable, and not to be seen by any; and was called the Holy of Holies. [220]Now, about the sides of the lower part of the temple there were little houses, with passages out of one into another; there were a great many of them, and they were of three stories high; there were also entrances on each side into them from the gate of the temple. [221]But the superior part of the temple had no such little houses any farther, because the

temple was there narrower, and forty cubits higher, and of a smaller body than the lower parts of it. Thus we collect that the whole height, including the sixty cubits from the floor, amounted to a hundred cubits.

²²²Now the outward face of the temple in its front wanted nothing that was likely to surprise either men's minds or their eyes, for it was covered all over the plates of gold of great weight, and, at the first rising of the sun, reflected back a very fiery splendor, and made those who forced themselves to look upon it to turn their eyes away, just as they would have done at the sun's own rays. ²²³But this temple appeared to strangers, when they were at a distance, like a mountain covered with snow; for, as to those parts of it that were not gilt, they were exceeding white. ²²⁴On its top it had spikes with sharp points, to prevent any pollution of it by birds sitting upon it. Of its stones, some of them were forty-five cubits in length, five in height, and six in breadth. ²²⁵Before this temple stood the altar, fifteen cubits high, and equal both in length and breadth; each of which dimensions was fifty cubits. The figure it was built in was a square, and it had corners like horns; and the passage up to it was by an insensible acclivity. It was formed without any iron tool, nor did any such iron tool so much as touch it at any time. ²²⁶There was a wall of partition, about a cubit in height, made of fine stones, and so as to be grateful to the sight; this encompassed the holy house, and the altar, and kept the people that were on the outside off from the priests. ²²⁷Moreover those that had the gonorrhea and the leprosy were excluded out of the city entirely; women also, when their courses were upon them were shut out of the temple; nor when they were free from that impurity, were they al-lowed to go beyond the limit before-mentioned; men also, that were not thoroughly pure, were prohibited to come into the inner court of the temple; nay, the priests themselves that were not pure, were prohibited to come into it also.

Tacitus, **History 5.8***

A great part of Judea is covered with scattered villages, but there are some towns also; Jerusalem is the capital of the Jews. In it was a temple possessing enormous riches. The first line of fortifications protected the city, the next the palace, and the innermost wall the temple. Only a Jew might approach its doors, and all save the priests were forbidden to cross the threshold.

The temple was central to the Herodian family's rebuilding program, as the following selections from Josephus indicate.

Josephus, **Antiquities 15.11.1–7** §§380–425

³⁸⁰And now Herod, in the eighteenth year of his reign, and after the acts already mentioned, undertook a very great work, that is, to build of himself the temple of God, and make it larger in compass, and to raise it to a most magnificent altitude, as esteeming it to be the most glorious of all his actions, as it really was, to bring it to perfection, and that this would be sufficient for an everlasting memorial of him; ³⁸¹but as he knew the multitude were not ready nor willing to assist him in so vast a design, he thought to prepare them first by making a speech to them, and then set about the work itself; so he called them together, and spake thus to them:—³⁸²"I think I need not speak to you, my countrymen, about such other works as I have done since I came to the kingdom, although I may say they have

been performed in such a manner as to bring more security to you than glory to myself; [383]for I have neither been negligent in the most difficult times about what tended to ease your necessities, nor have the buildings I have made been so proper to preserve me as yourselves from injuries; and I imagine that, with God's assistance, I have advanced the nation of the Jews to a degree of happiness which they never had before; [384]and for the particular edifices belonging to your own country, and to your own cities, as also to those cities that we have lately acquired, which we have erected and greatly adorned, and thereby augmented the dignity of your nation, it seems to me a needless task to enumerate them to you, since you well know them yourselves; but as to that undertaking which I have a mind to set about at present, and which will be a work of the greatest piety and excellence that can possibly be undertaken by us, I will now declare it to you. [385]Our fathers, indeed, when they were returned from Babylon, built this temple to God Almighty, yet does it want sixty cubits of its largeness in altitude; for so much did that first temple which Solomon built exceed this temple: [386]nor let anyone condemn our fathers for their negligence or want of piety herein, for it was not their fault that the temple was no higher; for they were Cyrus, and Darius the son of Hystaspes, who determined the measures for its rebuilding; and it has been by reason of the subjection of those fathers of ours to them and to their posterity, and after them to the Macedonians, that they had not the opportunity to follow the original model of this pious edifice, nor could raise it to its ancient altitude; [387]but since I am now, by God's will, your governor, and I have had peace a long time, and have gained

great riches and large revenues, and, what is the principal thing of all, I am at amity with and well regarded by the Romans, who, if I may so say, are the rulers of the whole world, I will do my endeavor to correct that imperfection, which has arisen from the necessity of our affairs, and the slavery we have been under formerly, and to make a thankful return, after the most pious manner to God, for what blessings I have received from him, by giving me this kingdom, and that by rendering his temple as complete as I am able."

[388]And this was the speech which Herod made to them: but still this speech affrighted many of the people, as being unexpected by them, and because it seemed incredible, it did not encourage them, but put a damp upon them, for they were afraid that he would pull down the whole edifice, and not be able to bring his intentions to perfection for its rebuilding; and this danger appeared to them to be very great, and the vastness of the undertaking to be such as could hardly be accomplished. [389]But while they were in this disposition, the king encouraged them, and told them he would not pull down their temple till all things were gotten ready for building it up entirely again. And as he promised them this beforehand, so he did not break his word with them, [390]but got ready a thousand wagons, that were to bring stones for the building, and chose out ten thousand of the most skillful workmen, and bought a thousand sacerdotal garments for as many of the priests, and had some of them taught the arts of stone cutters, and others of carpenters, and then began to build; but this not till every thing was well prepared for the work.

[391]So Herod took away the old foundations, and laid others, and erected

the temple upon them, being in length a hundred cubits, and in height twenty additional cubits, which [twenty], upon the sinking of their foundations, fell down: and this part it was that we resolved to raise again in the days of Nero. [392]Now the temple was built of stones that were white and strong, and each of their length was twenty-five cubits, their height was eight, and their breadth about twelve; [393]and the whole structure, as also the structure of the royal cloister, was on each side much lower, but the middle was much higher, till they were visible to those that dwelt in the country for a great many furlongs, but chiefly to such as lived over against them and those that approached to them. [394]The temple had doors also at the entrance, and lintels over them, of the same height with the temple itself. They were adorned with embroidered veils, with their flowers of purple, and pillars interwoven: [395]and over these, but under the crown-work, was spread out a golden vine, with its branches hanging down from a great height, the largeness and fine workmanship of which was a surprising sight to the spectators, to see what vast materials there were, and with what great skill the workmanship was done. [396]He also encompassed the entire temple with very large cloisters, contriving them to be in a due proportion thereto; and he laid out larger sums of money upon them than had been done before him, till it seemed that no one else had so greatly adorned the temple as he had done. There was a large wall to both the cloisters, which wall was itself the most prodigious work that was ever heard of by man. [397]The hill was a rocky ascent, that declined by degrees towards the east parts of the city, till it came to an elevated level. [398]This hill it was which Solomon, who was the first of our kings, by divine revela-

tion, encompassed with a wall; it was of excellent workmanship upwards, and round the top of it. He also built a wall below, beginning at the bottom, which was encompassed by a deep valley; and at the south side he laid rocks together and bound them one to another with lead, and included some of the inner parts, till it proceeded to a great height, [399]and till both the largeness of the square edifice and its altitude were immense, and till the vastness of the stones in the front were plainly visible on the outside, yet so that the inward parts were fastened together with iron, and preserved the joints immovable for all future times. [400]When this work [for the foundation] was done in this manner, and joined together as part of the hill itself to the very top of it, he wrought it all into one outward surface, and filled up the hollow places which were about the wall, and made it a level on the external upper surface, and a smooth level also. This hill was walled all round, and in compass four furlongs, [the distance of] each angle containing in length a furlong: [401]but within this wall, and on the very top of all, there ran another wall of stone also, having, on the east quarter, a double cloister, of the same length with the wall; in the midst of which was the temple itself. This cloister looked to the gates of the temple; and it had been adorned by many kings in former times; [402]and round about the entire temple were fixed the spoils taken from barbarous nations; all these had been dedicated to the temple by Herod, with the addition of those he had taken from the Arabians.

[403]Now on the north side [of the temple] was built a citadel, whose walls were square, and strong, and of extraordinary firmness. This citadel was built by the kings of the Asamonean race, who were also high priests

before Herod, and they called it the Tower, in which were reposited the vestments of the high priest, which the high priest only put on at the time when he was to offer sacrifice. [404]These vestments king Herod kept in that place; and after his death they were under the power of the Romans, until the time of Tiberius Caesar; [405]under whose reign Vitellius, the president of Syria, when he once came to Jerusalem, and had been most magnificently received by the multitude, he had a mind to make them some requital for the kindness they had shown him; so, upon their petition to have those holy vestments in their own power, he wrote about them to Tiberius Caesar, who granted his request: and this their power over the sacerdotal vestments continued with the Jews till the death of king Agrippa; [406]but after that, Cassius Longinus, who was president of Syria, and Cuspius Fadus, who was procurator of Judea, enjoined the Jews to reposit those vestments in the tower of Antonia, [407]for that they ought to have them in their power, as they formerly had. However, the Jews sent ambassadors to Claudius Caesar, to intercede with him for them; upon whose coming, king Agrippa, junior, being then at Rome, asked for and obtained the power over them from the emperor; who gave command to Vitellius, who was then commander in Syria, to give it them accordingly. [408]Before that time they were kept under the seal of the high priest, and of the treasurers, of the temple; which treasurers, the day before a festival, went up to the Roman captain of the temple guards, and viewed their own seal, and received the vestments; and again, when the festival was over, they brought it to the same place, and showed the captain of the temple guards their seal, which corresponded with his seal,

and reposited them there. [409]And that these things were so, the afflictions that happened to us afterwards [about them] are sufficient evidence; but for the tower itself, when Herod the king of the Jews had fortified it more firmly than before, in order to secure and guard the temple, he gratified Antonius, who was his friend, and the Roman ruler, and then gave it the name of the Tower of Antonia. [410]Now, in the western quarter of the enclosures of the temple there were four gates; the first led to the king's palace, and went to a passage over the intermediate valley; two more led to the suburbs of the city; and the last led to the other city, where the road descended down into the valley by a great number of steps, and thence up again by the ascent; for the city lay over against the temple in the manner of a theater, and was encompassed with a deep valley along the entire south quarter; [411]but the fourth front of the temple, which was southward, had indeed itself gates in its middle, as also it had the royal cloisters, with three walks, which reached in length from the east valley unto that on the west, for it was impossible it should reach any farther; [412]and this cloister deserves to be mentioned better than any other under the sun; for while the valley was very deep, and its bottom could not be seen, if you looked from above into the depth, this farther vastly high elevation of the cloister stood upon that height, insomuch that if anyone looked down from the top of the battlements, or down both those altitudes, he would be giddy, while his sight could not reach to such an immense depth. [413]This cloister had pillars that stood in four rows one over against the other all along, for the fourth row was interwoven into the wall, which [also was built of stone]; and the thickness of each pillar was such, that three men might, with their arms extended, fathom it round, and join their hands again, while its length was twenty-seven feet, with a double spiral at its basis; [414]and the number of all the pillars [in that court] was a hundred and sixty-two. Their chapiters were made with sculptures after the Corinthian order, and caused an amazement [to the spectators], by reason of the grandeur of the whole. [415]These four rows of pillars included three intervals for walking in the middle of this cloister; two of which walks were made parallel to each other, and were contrived after the same manner; the breadth of each of them was thirty feet, the length was a furlong, and the height fifty feet; but the breadth of the middle part of the cloister was one and a half of the other, and the height was double, for it was much higher than those on each side; [416]but the roofs were adorned with deep sculptures in wood, representing many sorts of figures: the middle was much higher than the rest, and the wall of the front was adorned with beams, resting upon pillars, that were interwoven into it, and that front was all of polished stone, insomuch that its fineness, to such as had not seen it, was incredible, and to such as had seen it, was greatly amazing. [417]Thus was the first enclosure. In the midst of which, and not far from it, was the second, to be gone up to by a few steps; this was encompassed by a stone wall for a partition, with an inscription, which forbade any foreigner to go in, under pain of death. [418]Now this inner enclosure had on its southern and northern quarters three gates [equally] distant one from another; but on the east quarter, towards the sun-rising, there was one large gate through which such as were pure came in, together with their wives; [419]but the temple farther inward in that gate was not allowed to the women; but still more inward was there a third [court of the] temple, whereinto it was not lawful for any, but the priests alone to enter. The temple itself was within this; and before that temple was the altar, upon which we offer our sacrifices and burnt offerings to God. [420]Into none of these three did king Herod enter, for he was forbidden, because he was not a priest. However, he took care of the cloisters and the outer enclosures; and these he built in eight years.

[421]But the temple itself was built by the priests in a year and six months,—upon which all the people were full of joy; and presently they returned thanks, in the first place, to God; and in the next place for the alacrity the king had shown. They feasted and celebrated this rebuilding of the temple: [422]and for the king, he sacrificed three hundred oxen to God; as did the rest, everyone according to his ability: the number of which sacrifices is not possible to set down, for it cannot be that we should truly relate it; [423]for at the same time with this celebration for the work about the temple, fell also the day of the king's inauguration, which he kept of an old custom as a festival, and it now coincided with the other; which coincidence of them both made the festival most illustrious.

[424]There was also an occult passage built for the king; it led from Antonia to the inner temple, at its eastern gate, over which he also erected for himself a tower, that he might have the opportunity of a subterraneous ascent to the temple, in order to guard against any sedition which might be made by the people against their kings. [425]It is also reported, that during the time that the temple was building, it did not rain in the daytime, but that the showers fell in the nights, so that the

work was not hindered. And this our fathers have delivered to us; nor is it incredible, if any have regard to the manifestations of God. And thus was performed the work of the rebuilding of the temple

Josephus, Jewish War 1.21.1 §401

Accordingly, in the fifteenth year of his reign, Herod rebuilt the temple, and encompassed a piece of land about it with a wall; which land was twice as large as that before enclosed. The expenses he laid out upon it were vastly large also, and the riches about it were unspeakable. A sign of which you have in the great cloisters that were erected about the temple, and the citadel which was on its north side. The cloisters he built from the foundation, but the citadel he repaired at a vast expense; nor was it other than a royal palace, which he called Antonia, in honor of Antony.

11.10 Persecutions (Matt. 24:9–14; Mark 13:9–13; Luke 21:12–19) (JaS 247)

The use of the imagery of birth pangs in connection with the fulfillment of eschatological events is common in Judaism. The first two texts illustrate this idea. The last text does not employ the figure of birth pangs in connection with eschatology but uses it simply as a metaphor for being in distress and danger. In the targum excerpt, italic indicates where the targum becomes more explanatory and departs from the biblical text.

1 Enoch 62.4

Then pain shall come upon them as on a woman in travail with birth pangs—when she is giving birth (the child) enters the mouth of the womb and she suffers from childbearing.

4 Ezra (= 2 Esdras) 4:42–43

[42]For just as a woman who is in labor makes haste to escape the pangs of birth, so also do these places hasten to give back those things that were committed to them from the beginning. [43]Then the things that you desire to see will be disclosed to you.

Targum Psalms 18.5*

Distress has surrounded me, like a woman who sits on the birthstool and has no strength to give birth and so is in danger of death; a band of abusive men has terrified me.

11.11 The Desolation (Matt. 24:15–22; Mark 13:14–20; Luke 21:20–24) (JaS 248)

The following texts from the Old Testament Apocrypha refer to the desecration of the temple carried out by Antiochus Epiphanes IV.

1 Maccabees 1:54–55; 4:38; 6:5–7

[1:54]Now on the fifteenth day of Chislev, in the one hundred forty-fifth year, they erected a desolating sacrilege on the altar of burnt offering. They also built altars in the surrounding towns of Judah, [55]and offered incense at the doors of the houses and in the streets.

[4:38]There they saw the sanctuary desolate, the altar profaned, and the gates burned. In the courts they saw bushes sprung up as in a thicket, or as on one of the mountains. They saw also the chambers of the priests in ruins.

[6:5]Then someone came to him in Persia and reported that the armies that had gone into the land of Judah had been routed; [6]that Lysias had gone first with a strong force, but had turned and fled before the Jews; that the Jews had grown strong from the arms, supplies, and abundant spoils that they had taken from the armies they had cut down; [7]that they had torn down the abomination that he had erected on the altar in Jerusalem; and that they had surrounded the sanctuary with high walls as before, and also Beth-zur, his town.

Eusebius, Ecclesiastical History 3.5.3–4*

This text from Eusebius refers to Christians fleeing from the city in AD 70 when Titus invaded. *an Jesus advised,*

[3]But the people of the church in Jerusalem had been commanded by a revelation, vouchsafed to approved men there before the war, to leave the city and to dwell in a certain town of Perea called Pella. And when those that believed in Christ had come thither from Jerusalem, then, as if the royal city of the Jews and the whole land of Judea were entirely destitute of holy men, the judgment of God at length overtook those who had committed such outrages against Christ and his apostles, and totally destroyed that generation of impious men. [4]But the number of calamities which everywhere fell upon the nation at that time, the extreme misfortunes to which the inhabitants of Judea were especially subjected, the thousands of men, as well as women and children, that perished by the sword, by famine, and by other forms of death innumerable,—all these things, as well as the many great sieges which were carried on against the cites of Judea, and the excessive sufferings endured by those that fled to Jerusalem itself, as to a city of perfect safety, and finally the general course of the whole war, as well as its particular occurrences in detail, and how at last the abomination of desolation, proclaimed by the prophets, stood in the very temple of God, so celebrated of old, the temple which was now awaiting its total and final destruction by fire,—all these things any one that wishes may find accurately described in the history written by Josephus.

11.12 The Coming of the Son of Man (Matt. 24:29–31; Mark 13:24–27; Luke 21:25–28) (*JaS* 250)

The following texts use vivid imagery, including that of light and darkness, in connection with the end of time.

1 Enoch *80.1–8*

[1]In those days, the angel Uriel responded and said to me, "Behold, I have shown you everything, Enoch, and I have revealed everything to you (so that) you might see this sun, this moon, and those that guide the stars of heaven as well as all those who interchange their activities and their seasons and rotate their processions. [2]In respect to their days, the sinners and the winter are cut short. Their seed(s) shall lag behind in their lands and in their fertile fields, and in all their activities upon the earth. He will turn and appear in their time, and withhold rain; and the sky shall stand still at that time. [3]Then the vegetable shall slacken and not grow in its season, and the fruit shall not be born in its (proper) season. [4]The moon shall alter its order, and will not be seen according to its (normal) cycles. [5]In those days it will appear in the sky and it shall arrive in the evening in the extreme ends of the great lunar path, in the west. And it shall shine (more brightly), exceeding the normal degree of light. [6]Many

of the chiefs of the stars shall make errors in respect to the orders given to them; they shall change their courses and functions and not appear during the seasons which have been prescribed for them. [7]All the orders of the stars shall harden (in disposition) against the sinners and the conscience of those that dwell upon the earth. They (the stars) shall err against them (the sinners); and modify all their courses. Then they (the sinners) shall err and take them (the stars) to be gods. [8]And evil things shall be multiplied upon them; and plagues shall come upon them, so as to destroy all."

Testament of Moses 10.5

The sun will not give light. And in darkness the horns of the moon will flee. Yea, they will be broken in pieces.

2 Baruch 70.1–10; 72.2

[70.1]Therefore, hear the exposition of the last black waters which will come after the black waters. This is the word. [2]Behold, the days are coming and it will happen when the time of the world has ripened and the harvest of the seed of the evil ones and the good ones has come that the Mighty One will cause to come over the earth and its inhabitants and its rulers confusion of the spirit and amazement of the heart. [3]And they will hate one another and provoke one another to fight. And the despised will rule over the honorable, and the unworthy will raise themselves over the illustrious. [4]And many will be delivered to the few, those who were nothing will rule over the strong, the poor will be greater in number than the rich, and the impious will exalt themselves over the brave. [5]The wise will

be silent, and the foolish will speak. And the thought of men shall not be realized then, nor the counsel of the strong, and the hope of those who hope will not be realized. [6]Then it will happen when those things occur which have been said before will come to pass, that confusion will fall upon all men. And some of them shall fall in war, and others will perish in tribulations, and again others of them will be troubled by their own. [7]The Most High will then give a sign to those nations which he has prepared before, and they will come and wage war with the rulers who will then remain. [8]And it will happen that everyone who saves himself from the war will die in an earthquake, and he who saves himself from the earthquake will be burned by fire, and he who saves himself from the fire will perish by famine. [9]And it will happen that everyone who will save himself and escape from all things which have been said before—both those who have won and those who have been overcome—that all will be delivered into the hands of my Servant, the Anointed One. [10]For the whole earth will devour its inhabitants.

[72.2]After the signs have come of which I have spoken to you before, when the nations are moved and the time of my Anointed One comes, he will call all nations, and some of them he will spare, and others he will kill.

In these texts, the Son of Man is presented as a powerful figure of judgment coming at the end of time. Fulfilling the Davidic office, he will come on the clouds, as Daniel predicted, and sit on a throne.

1 Enoch 37–71 (*excerpts*)

45.3On that day, my Elect One shall
 sit on the seat of glory
and make a selection of their deeds,
 their resting places will be without
 number,
 their souls shall be firm within
 them when they see my Elect
 One,
 those who have appealed to my
 glorious name.

51.3In those days, (the Elect One) shall
sit on my throne, and from the conscience of his mouth shall come out
all the secrets of wisdom, for the Lord
of the Spirits has given them to him
and glorified him.

55.4Kings, potentates, dwellers upon
the earth: You would have to see my
Elect One, how he sits in the throne of
glory and judges Azaz'el and all his
company, and his army, in the name
of the Lord of the Spirits!

61.8He placed the Elect One on the
throne of glory; and he shall judge all
the works of the holy ones in heaven
above, weighing in the balance their
deeds.

62.2The Lord of the Spirits has sat
down on the throne of his glory, and
the spirit of righteousness has been
poured out upon him. The word of
his mouth will do the sinners in; and
all the oppressors shall be eliminated
from before his face. . . . 9On that day,
all the kings, the governors, the high
officials, and those who rule the earth
shall fall down before him on their
faces, and worship and raise their
hopes in that Son of Man; they shall
beg and plead for mercy at his feet.

69.27(Then) there came to them a great
joy. And they blessed, glorified, and
extolled (the Lord) on account of the
fact that the name of that (Son of) Man
was revealed to them. He shall never
pass away or perish from before the
face of the earth. 28But those who have
led the world astray shall be bound
with chains; and their ruinous congregation shall be imprisoned; all their
deeds shall vanish from before the
face of the earth. 29Thenceforth nothing that is corruptible shall be found;
for that Son of Man has appeared and
has seated himself upon the throne of
his glory; and all evil shall disappear
from before his face; he shall go and
tell to that Son of Man, and he shall be
strong before the Lord of the Spirits.

4 Ezra (2 Esdras) 13 (*excerpts*)

1After seven days I dreamed a dream
in the night. 2And lo, a wind arose
from the sea and stirred up all its
waves. 3And I kept looking, the wind
made something like the figure of a
man come up out of the heart of the
sea. And I saw that this man flew with
the clouds of heaven; and wherever
he turned his face to look, everything
under his gaze trembled, 4and whenever his voice issued from his mouth,
all who heard his voice melted as wax
melts when it feels the fire.

5After this I looked and saw that
an innumerable multitude of people
were gathered together from the four
winds of heaven to make war against
the man who came up out of the sea.
. . . 9When he saw the onrush of the
approaching multitude, he neither
lifted his hand nor held a spear or
any weapon of war; 10but I saw only
how he sent forth from his mouth
something like a stream of fire, and
from his lips a flaming breath, and
from his tongue he shot forth a storm
of sparks . . . 11. . . and burned up all
of them. . . .

²⁵This is the interpretation of the vision: As for your seeing a man come up from the heart of the sea, ²⁶this is he whom the Most High has been keeping for many ages, who will himself deliver his creation; and he will direct those who are left. ²⁷And as for your seeing wind and fire and a storm coming out of his mouth, ²⁸and as for him not holding spear or weapon of war, yet destroying the onrushing multitude which came to conquer him, this is the interpretation: ²⁹The days are coming when the Most High will deliver those who are on the earth. ³⁰And bewilderment of mind shall come over those who inhabit the earth. ³¹They shall plan to make war against one another, city against city. . . . ³²When these things take place and the signs occur which I showed you before, then my Son will be revealed, whom you saw as a man coming from the sea. . . . ³⁷Then he, my Son, will reprove the assembled nations for their ungodliness (this was symbolized by the storm), ³⁸and will reproach them to their face with their evil thoughts and the torments with which they are to be tortured (which were symbolized by the flames), and will destroy them without effort by means of the law (which was symbolized by the fire).

³⁹And as for your seeing him gather to himself another multitude that was peaceable, ⁴⁰these are the nine tribes that were taken away from their own land into exile in the days of King Hoshea, whom Shalmaneser, the king of the Assyrians, made captives; he took them across the river, and they were taken into another land.

b. Sanhedrin 38ᵇ*

. . . E. " 'And what great nation is there that has God so nigh unto it, as the Lord our God is unto us whenever we call upon him [singular]' (Deut. 4:7)

F. " 'And what one nation in the earth is like your people, Israel, whom God have gone [plural] to redeem for a people unto himself [singular]' (2 Sam. 7:23).

G. " 'Till thrones were placed and one that was ancient did sit' " (Dan. 7:9).

H. And what need was there for all these passages?

I. The answer accords with what R. Yohanan said.

J. For R. Yohanan said, "The Holy One, blessed be he, does nothing unless he consults with the heavenly family.

K. "For it is said, 'The matter is by the decree of the watchers and the sentence by the word of the holy ones.' "

L. Now all of the others are suitably [explained], but how shall we explain "Till thrones were placed" (Dan. 7:9)?

M. One is for him, the other for David.

N. As it has been taught on Tannaite authority:

O. "One is for him, the other for David," the words of R. Aqiba.

P. Said to him R. Yose, "Aqiba, how long are you going to treat in a profane way the Presence of God?"

Q. "Rather, one is for bestowing judgment, the other for bestowing righteousness."

R. Did he accept this answer or not?

S. Come and take note for it has been taught on Tannaite authority:

T. "One is for bestowing judgment and the other for bestowing righteousness," the words of R. Aqiba.

U. Said to him R. Eleazar b. Azariah, "Aqiba, what business have you in matters of lore? Go over to rules governing the skin disease [of Lev.

13] and uncleanness imparted though overshadowing of the corpse" [in Ohalot M. Num. 19:1ff.].

V. "Rather, one is a throne for a seat, the other for a footstool for his feet."

b. Sanhedrin 98ᵃ*

98ᵃ101. A. Said R. Alexandri, "R. Joshua b. Levi contrasted verses as follows:

B. 'It is written; "In its time [will the messiah come]," and it is also written; "I [the Lord] will hasten it."

C. [What is the meaning of the contrast?]

D. If [the Israelites] have merit, I will hasten it, if they do not, [the messiah] will come in due course.

E. It is written, "And behold, one like a son of man came with the clouds of heaven" (Dan 7:13), and it is written, "Behold your king comes to you . . . lowly and riding upon a an ass" (Zech. 9:7). [What is the meaning of the contrast?]

F. If [the Israelites] have merit, it will be "with the clouds of heaven" (Dan. 7:13), and if they do not have merit, it will be "lowly and riding upon an ass" (Zech 9:7).' "

The following texts indicate that the theme of God "gathering" his people is often connected to events at the end.

1 Enoch 62.13–14

¹³The righteous and elect ones shall be saved on that day; and from thenceforth they shall never see the faces of the sinners and the oppressors. ¹⁴The Lord of the Spirits will abide over them; they shall eat and rest and rise with that Son of Man forever and ever.

Psalms of Solomon 8.28; 11.2–5; 17.26

⁸·²⁸Bring together the dispersed of Israel with mercy and goodness, for your faithfulness is with us.

¹¹·²Stand on a high place, Jerusalem, and look at your children, from the east and the west assembled together by the Lord. ³From the north they come in the joy of their God; from far distant islands God has assembled them. ⁴. . . The hills fled at their coming. ⁵The forests shaded them as they passed by; God made every fragrant tree to grow for them.

¹⁷·²⁶He will gather a holy people whom he will lead in righteousness; and he will judge the tribes of the people that have been made holy by the Lord their God.

4 Ezra (= 2 Esdras) 13:39–40

See section 4.5 above.

11.13 The Parable of the Ten Virgins (Matt. 25:1–13) (JaS 255)

The following passages from *ʾAbot de Rabbi Nathan* and *t. Berakot* demonstrate that doing good deeds—such as attending a wedding or a funeral or releasing those imprisoned—is more important than mere contemplation of the Torah. Good works in combination with study of the Torah is the goal, not just study by itself.

ʾAbot de Rabbi Nathan 4a, 8, and 22b*

⁴ᵃ1. A. When two disciples of sages are in session and occupied with the Torah, if before them came a bride [to whom they owe the honor of bringing rejoicing] or the bier of a corpse [to whom they are obligated to attend], if the one or the other has adequate provision for the need of the occasion,

let not the disciples interrupt the repetition of their traditions.

B. But if not, then let them go and [Goldin:] cheer and praise the bride or accompany the corpse.

2. A. There was the case of R. Judah b. Ilai who was in session and repeating Mishnah-traditions to his disciples, and a bride came by.

B. He took in his hand myrtle twigs and cheered her until the bride had gone by him.

[8]2. A. In the case of two disciples in session and occupied with study of the Torah, their reward is received on high,

B. as it is said, *Then they who feared the Lord spoke one with another, and the Lord heard . . . and a book of remembrance was written before him for those who feared the Lord and who gave thought to his name* (Mal. 3:16).

C. Who are those referred to as "those who feared the Lord?"

D. They are the ones who reach a decision, saying, "Let us go and free those who are imprisoned and redeem those who have been kidnapped for ransom," and the Holy One, blessed be he, gave sufficient power in their hands to do so, and they go and do it right away.

E. And who are those referred to as "they who have thought to his name"?

F. They are the ones who reckon in their hearts, saying, "Let us go and free those who are imprisoned and redeem those who have been kidnapped for ransom," and the Holy One, blessed be he, did not give sufficient power in their hands to do so, so an angel came and beat them down to the ground.

[22b]A. R. Eleazar b. Azariah says, If there is no learning of Torah, there is no proper conduct, If there is no

proper conduct, there is no learning in Torah. If there is no wisdom, there is no reverence. If there is no reverence, there is no wisdom.

B. He would say, A person who has good works and has studied much in Torah—to what is he likened? To a tree that stands by water, with few branches but deep roots. Even though the four winds of the world come, they cannot move it from its place.

C. as it is said, *He shall be a tree planted by the waters, and that spreads out its roots by the river, and shall not fear when heat comes, and his leaf shall be green, and shall not be careful in the year of drought, neither shall cease from yielding fruit* (Jer. 17:8).

D. A person in whom are no good deeds but who has studied much Torah—to what is he compared? To a tree that stands in the wilderness, with abundant branches but shallow roots. When the winds blow, they will uproot it and blow it down.

E. as it is said, *He shall be like a tamarisk in the desert and shall not see when good comes but shall inhabit the parched places in the wilderness* (Jer. 17:6).

t. Berakot 2.10*

A. The attendants [at a wedding] and all the members of the wedding party are exempt from [the obligation to recite] the Prayer and from [the obligation to don] phylacteries for the entire seven days [of the wedding celebration].

B. [But] they are obligated to recite the *shema*.

C. R. Shila says, "The bridegroom is exempt, but all the members of the wedding party are obligated" [cf. M. Ber. 2:5].

11.14 The Parable of the Talents (Matt. 25:14–30; Luke 19:11–27) (JaS 256)

m. Baba Meṣiᶜa 3.11*

The idea of keeping money safe by depositing it somewhere was not uncommon in Judaism.

A. He who deposits coins with a money changer—

B. if they are wrapped up, [the money changer] should not make use of them.

C. Therefore if they got lost, he is not liable to make them up [as an unpaid bailee (M. 2:7)].

D. [If they were] loose, he may make use of them.

E. Therefore if they got lost, he is liable to make them up.

F. [He who deposits coins] with a householder,

G. whether they are wrapped up or whether they are loose—

H. [the householder] should not make use of them.

I. Therefore if they got lost, he is not liable to make them up.

J. "The storekeeper is subject to the same rule as the householder," the words of R. Meir.

K. R. Judah says, "The storekeeper is subject to the same rule as the money changer."

11.15 The Sheep and the Goats (Matt. 25:31–46) (JaS 257)

The following three citations show that some in Judaism placed "end-time judgment" into the hands of a representative appointed by God.

1 Enoch 9.4; 60.2

9.4 And they said to the Lord of the potentates, "For he is the Lord of lords, and the God of gods, and the King of kings, and the seat of his glory (stands) throughout all the generations of the world. Your name is holy, and blessed, and glorious throughout the whole world."

60.2 And the Antecedent of Time was sitting on the throne of his glory surrounded by his angels and the righteous ones.

Testament of Abraham 13 (rec. A); 11 (rec. B)

13.1 And Abraham said, "My lord Commander-in-chief, who is this all-wondrous judge? And who are the angels who are recording? And who is the sunlike angel who holds the balance? And who is the fiery angel who holds the fire?" 2 The Commander-in-chief said, "Do you see, all-pious Abraham, the frightful man who is seated on the throne? This is the son of Adam, the first-formed, who is called Abel, whom Cain the wicked killed. 3 And he sits here to judge the entire creation, examining both righteous and sinners. For God said, 'I do not judge you, but every man is judged by man.' 4 On account of this he gave him judgment, to judge the world until his great and glorious Parousia. And then, righteous Abraham, there will be perfect judgment and recompense, eternal and unalterable, which no one can question. 5 For every person has sprung from the first-formed, and on account of this they are first judged here by his son. 6 And at the second Parousia they will be judged by the twelve tribes of Israel, both every breath and every creature. 7 And, thirdly, they shall be judged by the Master God of all; and then thereafter the fulfillment of that judgment will be near, and fearful will be the sentence and there is none who can release. [8]And thus the judgment and recompense of the world is made through three tribunals. And therefore a matter is not ultimately established by one or two witnesses, but *every matter shall be established by three witnesses.*

[9]"The two angels, the one on the right and the one on the left, these are those who record sins and the righteous deeds. The one on the right records righteous deeds, while the one on the left (records) sins. [10]And the sunlike angel, who holds the balance in his hand, this is the archangel Dokiel, the righteous balance-bearer, and he weighs the righteous deeds and the sins with the righteousness of God. [11]And the fiery and merciless angel, who holds the fire in his hand, this is the archangel Purouel, who has authority over fire, and he tests the work of men through fire. [12]And if the fire burns up the work of anyone, immediately the angel of judgment takes him and carries him away to the place of sinners, a most bitter place of punishment. [13]But *if the fire tests the work of anyone* and does not touch it, this person is justified and the angel of righteousness takes him and carries him up to be saved in the lot of the righteous. And thus, most righteous Abraham, all things in all people are tested by fire and balance."

[11.1]And Abraham said to Michael, "Lord, who is this judge? And who is the other one who brings the charges of sins?" [2]And Michael said to Abraham, "Do you see the judge? This is Abel, who first bore witness, and God brought him here to judge. [3]And the one who produces (the evidence) is the teacher of heaven and earth and the scribe of righteousness, Enoch. [4]For the Lord sent them here in order that they might record the

sins and the righteous deeds of each person." [5]And Abraham said, "And how can Enoch bear the weight of the souls, since he has not seen death? Or how can he give the sentence of all the souls?" [6]And Michael said, "If he were to give sentence concerning them, it would not be accepted. But it is not Enoch's business to give sentence; [7]rather, the Lord is the one who gives sentence, and it is this one's (Enoch's) task only to write. [8]For Enoch prayed to the Lord saying, 'Lord, I do not want to give the sentence of the souls, lest I become oppressive to someone.' [9]And the Lord said to Enoch, 'I shall command you to write the sins of a soul that makes atonement, and it will enter into life. [10]And if the soul has not made atonement and repented, you will find its sins (already) written, and it will be cast into punishment.' "

The following four texts depict God as a faithful and long-suffering shepherd, teaching, training, and guiding his people, the sheep of his pasture.

Sirach 18:13

The compassion of human beings is for their neighbors, but the compassion of the Lord is for every living thing. He rebukes and trains and teaches them, and turns them back, as a shepherd his flock.

1 Enoch 89.18

The sheep then went to the wolves in accordance with the word of the Lord, together with another sheep which he had met, so the two of them went on and arrived together into the assembly of those wolves, and spoke to them and warned them not to touch the sheep.

Pseudo-Philo, Biblical Antiquities 28.5; 30.5

28.5 And Kenaz and the elders and all the people lifted up their voices and wept with great lamentation until evening and said, "Will the Shepherd destroy his flock for any reason except that it has sinned against him? And now he is the one who will spare us according to the abundance of his mercy, because he has toiled so much among us."

30.5 And when the people had fasted seven days and sat in sackcloth, the LORD sent to them on the seventh day Deborah, who said to them, "Can the sheep to be slaughtered give answer to its slaughterer? But both the slaughterer and the slaughtered are silent even though he is sorrowful over it. And now you were like a flock before our LORD, and he led you into the height of the clouds and set the angels beneath your feet and established for you the Law and commanded you through the prophets and corrected you through the leaders and showed you not a few wonders; and on your account he commanded the luminaries, and *they stood still in their* assigned *places*; and when your enemies came against you, he rained down *hailstones on them* and destroyed them. And Moses and Joshua and Kenaz and Zebul commanded you, and you did not obey them."

11.16 The Desire to Kill Jesus (Matt. 26:1–5; Mark 14:1–2; Luke 22:1–2) (JaS 259)

The following texts from Josephus show that the Feast of Unleavened Bread and Passover were often united together and referred to as a single event.

Josephus, Antiquities 3.10.5 §249; 14.2.1 §21; 17.9.3 §213

3.10.5 249 The feast of unleavened bread succeeds that of the passover, and falls on the fifteenth day of the month, and continues seven days, wherein they feed on unleavened bread; on every one of which days two bulls are killed, and one ram, and seven lambs. Now these lambs are entirely burnt, besides the kid of the goats which is added to all the rest, for sins; for it is intended as a feast for the priest on every one of those days.

14.2.1 21 So Aretas united the forces of the Arabians and of the Jews together, and pressed on the siege vigorously. As this happened at the time when the feast of unleavened bread was celebrated, which we call the Passover, the principal men among the Jews left the country, and fled into Egypt.

17.9.3 213 Now, upon the approach of that feast of unleavened bread which the law of their fathers had appointed for the Jews at this time, which feast is called the Passover, and is a memorial of their deliverance out of Egypt (when they offer sacrifices with great alacrity; and when they are required to slay more sacrifices in number than at any other festival . . .).

11.17 The Last Supper (Matt. 26:26–29; Mark 14:22–25; Luke 22:15–20) (JaS 264)

This text from the Mishnah indicates that there were four cups in the Passover meal.

m. Pesaḥim 10.6–7*

6A. To what point does one say [Hallel]?

185

B. The House of Shammai say, "To *A joyful mother of children* (Ps. 113:9)."

C. And the House of Hillel say, "To *A flintstone into a springing well* (Ps. 114:8)."

D. And he concludes with [a formula of] Redemption.

E. R. Tarfon says, ". . . 'who redeemed us and redeemed our forefathers from Egypt.'

F. "And he did not say a concluding benediction."

G. R. Aqiba says, "'. . . So, Lord, our God, and God of our fathers, bring us in peace to other appointed times and festivals, rejoicing in the rebuilding of your city and joyful in your Temple worship, where may we eat of the animal sacrifices and Passover offerings,' etc., up to, 'Blessed are you, Lord, who has redeemed Israel.'"

IIIA. They mixed the third cup for him.

B. He says a blessing for his food.

IV C. [And at] the fourth, he completes the *Hallel* and says after it the grace of song.

D. Between these several cups of wine, if he wants to drink, he may drink wine.

E. But between the third and the fourth cup of wine, he may not drink.

11.18 Peter's Denial Predicted (Matt. 26:30–35; Mark 14:26–31; Luke 22:31–34; John 13:36–38) (*JaS* 267)

In the following selections, we see the importance attached to the Hallel psalms, some associated with the general Passover celebration and some used during the meal. (The mishnaic texts are not cited in *Jesus according to Scripture*.)

m. Pesaḥim 5.7; 9.3*

5.7A. The first group went out and the second group came in.

B. The second group went out and the third group came in.

C. In accord with the rite of the first group were the rites of the second and third.

D. [The Levites meanwhile] proclaimed the Hallel psalms [113–118].

E. If they completed [the recitation], they repeated it, and if they completed the second time, they repeated it for a third—

F. even though they never in all their days had to repeat it a third time.

G. R. Judah says, "In all the days of the third group they never even reached the verse, *I love the Lord because he has heard my voice* (Ps. 116:1),

H. "because its numbers were small."

9.3A. What is the difference between the first Passover and the second?

B. The first Passover is subject to the prohibition about leaven: *It shall not be seen* and *It shall not be found* (Ex. 12:19, 13:7).

C. As to the second, unleavened bread and leaven may be in the house right alongside one another.

D. The first Passover requires the recitation of the *Hallel* Psalms when it is eaten, but the second Passover does not require the recitation of *Hallel* Psalms when it is eaten.

E. This and that require a *Hallel* Psalm to be sung while they are being prepared.

F. And [both Passover offerings] are eaten roasted, with unleavened bread and bitter herbs.

G. And [both Passover offerings] override [the prohibitions of the] Sabbath.

m. Pesaḥim 10.7*

See section 11.17 above.

t. Pesaḥim 10.8*

A. Townsfolk who have no one to pronounce the *Hallel*-Psalms for them to go to the synagogue and read the first part.

B. Then they go home and eat and drink, and come back and complete the entire thing.

C. And if it is not possible for them [to go home and come back], they complete the whole thing [the first time around].

D. As to the *Hallel*, they leave nothing out of it, and they add nothing to it.

Antiphonal Song.

Midrash Psalms 118 §22*

This is the day which the Lord has made (Ps. 118:24). After all the redemptions that came to Israel, enslavement followed, but from now on no more enslavement will follow, as is said *Sing unto the Lord; for He hath done gloriously . . . For great is the Holy One of Israel in the midst of thee* (Isa. 12:5–6).

We beseech Thee, O Lord, save now! (Ps. 118:25). From inside the walls, the men of Jerusalem will say, *We beseech Thee, O Lord, save now.* And from outside, the men of Judah will say, *We beseech Thee, O Lord, make us now to prosper! (ibid.).*

From inside, the men of Jerusalem will say, *Blessed be he that comes IN the name of the Lord* (Ps. 118:26). And from outside, the men of Judah will say, *We bless you OUT of the house of the Lord (ibid.).*

From inside, the men of Jerusalem will say, *The Lord is God, and has given us light (ibid. 118:27).* And from outside, the men of Judah will say *Order the festival procession with boughs, even unto the horns of the altar (ibid.).*

From inside the men of Jerusalem will say, *Thou art my God, and I will give thanks unto Thee (ibid. 118:28).* And from outside, the men of Judah will say, *Thou art my God, and I will exalt Thee (ibid.).*

Then the men of Jerusalem and the men of Judah, together, opening their mouths in praise of the Holy One, blessed be He, will say: *O give thanks to the Lord, for He is good, for His mercy endureth for ever (ibid. 118:29).*

11.19 Gethsemane (Matt. 26:36–46; Mark 14:32–42; Luke 22:39–46) (JaS 269)

Justin Martyr, **Dialogue with Trypho 103.8***

This text from Justin Martyr demonstrates that he knew of the textual reading that asserts that Jesus' sweat became like drops of blood falling to the ground.

. . . Moreover, the statement, "All my bones are poured out and dispersed like water; my heart has become like wax, melting in the midst of my belly," was a prediction of that which happened to Him on that night when men came out against Him to the Mount of Olives to seize Him. For in the memoirs which I say were drawn up by His apostles and those who followed them, [it is recorded] that His sweat fell down like drops of blood while He was praying, and saying, "If it be possible, let this cup pass:" His heart and also His bones trembling; His heart being like wax melting in His belly: in order that we may perceive that the Father wished His Son really to undergo such sufferings for our sakes, and may not say that He, being the Son of God, did not feel what was happening to Him and inflicted on Him. Further,

re the truly suffered Pain   187

the expression, "My strength is dried up like a potsherd, and my tongue has cleaved to my throat," was a prediction, as I previously remarked, of that silence, when He who convicted all your teachers of being unwise returned no answer at all.

11.20 Jesus Examined before the Council and Peter's Denials (Matt. 26:57–75; Mark 14:53–72; Luke 22:54–71; John 18:13–28) (JaS 271)

Josephus, Antiquities 20.9.1 §§197–203

In this text, which appears in section 1.1 above, Josephus describes how Annas abused his authority (from a Roman, legal-cultural perspective) by unjustly putting James the brother of Jesus to death. *Acts 12*

Josephus, Jewish War 2.8.1 §§117–118

The following text indicates that the power to impose the death penalty rested with the Roman procurator.

[117]And now Archelaus's part of Judea was reduced into a province, and Coponius, one of the equestrian order among the Romans, was sent as a procurator, having the power of [life and] death put into his hands by Caesar. [118]Under his administration it was that a certain Galilean, whose name was Judas, prevailed with his countrymen to revolt; and said they were cowards if they would endure to pay a tax to the Romans, and would, after God, submit to mortal men as their lords. This man was a teacher of a peculiar sect of his own, and was not at all like the rest of those their leaders.

Mishnah tractate *Sanhedrin* 4.1 and 11.2 outline the proper procedure to follow in capital trials.

m. Sanhedrin 4.1; 11.2*

[4.1]A. All the same are property cases and capital cases as to examination and interrogation [of witnesses],

B. as it is said, *You will have one law* (Lev. 24:22).

C. What is the difference between property cases and capital cases?

D. (1) Property cases [are tried] by three [judges], and capital cases by twenty-three.

E. (2) In property cases they begin [argument] with the case either for acquittal or for conviction, while in capital cases they begin only with the case for acquittal, and not with the case for conviction.

F. (3) In property cases they decide by a majority of one, whether for acquittal or for conviction, while in capital cases they decide by a majority of one for acquittal, but only with a majority of two [judges] for conviction.

G. (4) In property cases they reverse the decision whether in favor of acquittal or in favor of conviction, while in capital cases they reverse the decision in favor of acquittal, but they do not reverse the decision in favor of conviction.

H. (5) In property cases all [judges and even disciples] argue either for acquittal or conviction. In capital cases all argue for acquittal, but all do not argue for conviction.

I. (6) In property cases one who argues for conviction may argue for acquittal, and one who argues for acquittal may also argue for conviction. In capital cases the one who argues for conviction may argue for acquittal, but the one who argues for acquittal has not got the power to retract and to argue for conviction.

J. (7) In property cases they try the case by day and complete it by night. In capital cases, they try the case by day and complete it [by] day.

K. (8) In property cases they come to a final decision on the same day [as the trial itself], whether it is for acquittal or conviction. In capital cases they come to a final decision for acquittal on the same day, but on the following day for conviction.

L. (Therefore they do not judge [capital cases] either on the eve of the Sabbath or on the eve of a festival.)

11.2A. *An elder who defies the decision of a court* [M. 11:1B3]—

B. as it is said, *If there arise a matter too hard for you in judgment, between blood and blood, between plea and plea* (Dt. 17:8)—

C. there were three courts there.

D. One was in session at the gate of the Temple mount, one was in session at the gate of the courtyard, and one was in session in the hewn-stone chamber.

E. They come to the one which is at the gate of the Temple mount and say, "Thus I have explained the matter, and thus my colleagues have explained the matter.

F. "Thus I have ruled in the matter, and thus my colleagues have ruled."

G. If they had heard a ruling, they told it to them, and if not, they come along to that court which was at the gate of the courtyard.

H. And he says, "Thus I have explained the matter, and thus my colleagues have explained the matter.

I. "Thus I have ruled in the matter, and thus my colleagues have ruled."

J. If they had heard a ruling, they told it to them, and if not, these and

those come along to the high court which was in the hewn-stone chamber,

K. from which Torah goes forth to all Israel,

L. as it is said, *From that place which the Lord shall choose* (Dt. 17:12).

M. [If] he went back to his town and again ruled just as he had ruled before, he is exempt.

N. But if he instructed others to do it in that way, he is liable,

O. as it is said, *And the man who does presumptuously* (Dt. 17:12).

P. He is liable only if he will give instructions to people actually to carry out the deed [in accord with the now-rejected view].

Q. A disciple of a sage who gave instruction to carry out the deed [wrongly] is exempt.

R. It turns out that the strict ruling concerning him [that he cannot give decisions] also is a lenient ruling concerning him [that he is not punished if he does give decisions].

m. Sanhedrin 7.5*

The rules defining blasphemy are outlined in *m. Sanhedrin* 7.5. Here blasphemy is narrowly defined as requiring pronunciation of the divine name.

A. *He who blasphemes* [M. 7:4D1] [Lev. 24:10] is liable only when he will have fully pronounced the divine Name.

B. Said R. Joshua b. Qorha, "On every day of a trial they examine the witnesses with a substituted name, [such as], 'May Yose smite Yose.'

C. "[Once] the trial is over, they would not put him to death [on the basis of evidence given] with the euphemism, but they put out everyone and ask the most important of the witnesses, saying to him, 'Say, what exactly did you hear [in detail]?'

D. "And he says what he heard.

189

E. "And the judges stand on their feet and tear their clothing, and never sew them back up.

F. "And the second witness says, 'Also I [heard] what he heard.'

G. "And the third witness says, 'Also I [heard] what he heard.'"

m. Beṣah 5.2*

This Mishnah text prohibits examining the accused on a feast day.

A. For (1) any act for which [people] are liable on grounds of Sabbath rest, for (2) optional acts, or for (3) acts of religious duty, on the Sabbath,

B. are they liable in regard to the festival day.

C. And these are the acts for which people are liable by reason of Sabbath rest:

D. (1) they do not climb a tree, (2) ride a beast, (3) swim in water, (4) clap hands, (5) slap the thigh, (6) or stamp the feet.

E. And these are the acts [for which people are liable] by reason of optional acts:

F. (1) they do not sit in judgment, (2) effect a betrothal, (3) carry out a rite of halisah (4) or enter into levirate marriage.

G. And these are the acts [for which people are liable] by virtue of acts of religious duty:

H. (1) they do not declare objects to be sanctified, (2) make a vow of valuation, (3) declare something to be herem, (4) or raise up heave offering or tithe.

I. All these actions on the festival have they declared [to be culpable], all the more so [when they are done] on the Sabbath.

J. The sole difference between the festival and the Sabbath is in the preparation of food alone.

m. Sanhedrin 11.4*

There were exceptions to the rules laid down in m. Beṣah 5.2 (above); in important cases, examinations could be carried out.

A. "They put him to death not in the court in his own town or in the court which is in Yabneh, but they bring him up to the high court in Jerusalem.

B. "And they keep him until the festival, and they put him to death on the festival,

C. "as it is said, *And all the people shall hear and fear and no more do presumptuously* (Dt. 17:13)," the words of R. Aqiba.

D. R. Judah says, "They do not delay the judgment of this one, but they put him to death at once.

E. "And they write messages and send them with messengers to every place:

F. "'Mr. So-and-so, son of Mr. So-and-so, has been declared liable to the death penalty by the court.'"

Both *1 Enoch* 77.2 and *m. Berakot* 7.3 refer to God as "blessed."

1 Enoch 77.2

The second is called the South, because the Most High will descend there, indeed because the Eternally Blessed will descend there.

m. Berakot 7.3*

A. How do they invite [others for the grace after the meal]?

B. (1) For three [who ate together, the leader] says, "Let us bless."

(2) For three [others] and himself [four] he says, "Bless."

C. (3) For ten he says, "Let us bless our God."

(4) For ten and himself he says, "Bless."

D. The same [rule applies for] ten and for ten thousand.

E. (5) For one hundred he says, "Let us bless the Lord our God."

(6) For one hundred and himself he says, "Bless."

F. (7) For one thousand he says, "Let us bless the Lord our God, God of Israel."

(8) For one thousand and himself he says, "Bless."

G. (9) For ten thousand he says, "Let us bless the Lord our God, God of Israel, God of the Hosts who sits upon the Cherubim, for the food we have eaten."

(10) For ten thousand and himself he says, "Bless."

H. As he blesses, so they answer after him:

I. "Blessed is the Lord our God, God of Israel, God of the Hosts, who sits upon the Cherubim, for the food we have eaten."

J. R. Yose the Galilean says, "According to the size of the congregation [so] they bless. As it says, *In* [accordance with the size of your] *gatherings, bless God, the Lord, [you who are] from Israel's fountain* (Ps. 68:27)."

K. Said R. Aqiba, "What do we find in the synagogue? It is the same whether there are many or few present. [The reader] says, 'Bless the Lord.'"

L. R. Ishmael says, "Bless the Lord who is blessed."

In the following two texts, the term *power* is used as a circumlocution for God.

1 Enoch 62.7

For the Son of Man was concealed from the beginning, and the Most High One preserved him in the presence of his power; then he revealed him to the holy and the elect ones.

Targum Job 5.8*

But as for me I would seek out *instruction* from the *Powerful One*, and to God I would state my case.

1 Enoch 70.1–71.14 (excerpts)

In this text, Enoch himself receives authority to enter into the "heaven of heavens" and directly into the presence of the Antecedent of Time.

70.1 And it happened after this that his living name was raised up before that the Son of Man and to the Lord from among those who dwell upon the earth; 2 it was lifted up in a wind chariot and it disappeared from among them. 3 From that day on, I was not counted among them. But he placed me between two winds, between the northeast and the west, where the angels took a cord to measure for me the places for the elect and righteous ones. 4 And there I saw the first (human) ancestors and the righteous ones of old, dwelling in that place.

71.1 (Thus) it happened after this that my spirit passed out of sight and ascended into the heavens. And I saw the sons of the holy angels walking upon the flame of fire; their garments were white—and their overcoats—and the light of their faces was like snow. 2 Also, I saw two rivers of fire, the light of which fire was shining like hyacinth. Then I fell upon my face before the Lord of the Spirits. 3 And the angel Michael, one of the archangels, seizing me by my right hand and lifting me up; led me out into all the secrets of mercy; and he showed me all the secrets of righteousness. 4 He also showed me all the secrets of the extreme ends of heaven and all the reservoirs of the stars and the luminaries—from where they come out (to shine) before the faces of the holy ones. ⁵He carried off my spirit, and I, Enoch was in the heaven of heavens. There I saw . . . a structure built of crystals [and] . . . tongues of fire. ⁶And my spirit saw a ring which encircled this structure of fire. On its four sides were rivers of living fire which encircled it. ⁷Moreover, seraphim, cherubim, and ophanim—the sleepless ones who guard the throne of his glory—also encircled it. ⁸And I saw countless angels [and]. . . . ¹⁰With them is the Antecedent of Time: His head is white and pure like wool and his garment is indescribable. ¹¹I fell on my face, my whole body mollified and my spirit transformed. Then I cried with a great voice by the spirit of the power, blessing, glorifying, and extolling. . . . ¹³Then the Antecedent of Time came with Michael, Gabriel, Raphael, Phanuel, and a hundred thousand and ten million times a hundred thousand angels that are countless. ¹⁴Then an angel came to me and greeted me and said to me, "You, son of man, who art born in righteousness and upon whom righteousness has dwelt, the righteousness of the Antecedent of Time will not forsake you."

Ezekiel the Tragedian, Exagōgē 68–89

In this text, Moses has a dream about his authority to produce the plagues, which allows him to sit in heaven as he is "God to Pharaoh" (Exod. 7:1).

⁶⁸On Sinai's peak I saw what
    seemed a throne
⁶⁹so great in size it touched the
    clouds of heaven.
⁷⁰Upon it sat a man of noble mien,
⁷¹becrowned, and with a scepter in
    one hand

⁷²while with the other he did
    beckon me.
⁷³I made approach and stood before
    the throne.
⁷⁴He handed o'er the scepter and
    he bade
⁷⁵me mount the throne, and gave to
    me the crown;
⁷⁶then he himself withdrew from off
    the throne.
⁷⁷I gazed upon the whole earth
    round about;
⁷⁸things under it, and high above
    the skies.
⁷⁹Then at my feet a multitude of
    stars
⁸⁰fell down, and I their number
    reckoned up.
⁸¹They passed by me like armèd
    ranks of men.
⁸²Then I in terror wakened from the
    dream.
And his father interprets the dream
as follows:
⁸³My friend, God gave you this as
    sign for good.
⁸⁴Would I might live to see these
    things transpire.
⁸⁵For you shall cause a mighty
    throne to rise,
⁸⁶and you yourself shall rule and
    govern men.
⁸⁷As for beholding all the peopled
    earth,
⁸⁸and things below and things
    above God's realm:
⁸⁹things present, past, and future
    you shall see.

According to 1 Maccabees 2:14 and *b. Sanhedrin* 60ᵃ, men tore their garments because of blasphemy or shameful acts.

1 Maccabees 2:12–14

¹²"And see, our holy place, our beauty, and our glory have been laid waste; the Gentiles have profaned them. ¹³Why should we live any longer?"

[14]Then Mattathias and his sons tore their clothes, put on sackcloth, and mourned greatly.

b. Sanhedrin 60[a]*

A. Our rabbis have taught on Tannaite authority:

B. All the same are the one who actually hears [the blasphemy] and the one who hears it from the one heard it. Both are liable to tear their garments.

C. But the witnesses are not liable to tear their garments, for they already did so at the moment when they heard the original blasphemy.

D. But if they did so at the moment when they heard the original blasphemy, what difference does that make? Lo, they are now hearing it again!

E. Do not let that argument enter your mind, for it is written, "And it came to pass, when King Hezekiah heard it, that he tore his clothes" (2 Kgs. 18:37).

F. King Hezekiah tore his clothes, buy they did not tear their clothes.

G. Said R. Judah said Samuel, "He who hears the name of God [blasphemed] by an idolater does not have to tear his clothes,

H. And should you ask about Rab Shakeh [who was an idolater, and on account of whose blasphemy the king and court tore their clothes], in point of fact, he was an Israelite apostate."

I. And R. Judah said Samuel said, "People tear their clothes only on account of the four-lettered name of God [used as a curse]."

J. That then would exclude a hearing a euphemism, on account of which one does not [tear clothes].

K. And this differs from the view of R. Hiyya in two matters.

L. For R. Hiyya said, "He who hears the name of God blasphemed these days is not liable to tear his clothes, for if you do not take that position, it will result that peoples' entire garments will be full of rents."

M. Now from whom [would one hear these curses?] Should you say that it is from Israelites, are the Israelites so wanton?

N. Rather, it is clear that he assumes the curses come from idolaters.

O. And if you should propose that what they are saying is that four-lettered name of God, do they know it?

P. Does it not, rather mean, that they curse by using a euphemism?

Q. And it further follows that he speaks of the present age, in which one is not liable, but in olden times, one was liable.

R. That proves it.

11.21 The Examination before Pilate (Matt. 27:11–14; Mark 15:2–5; Luke 23:2–5; John 18:29–38) (JaS 274)

Josephus and Philo indicate that Pilate had problems with the Jews early in his tenure.

Josephus, Jewish War 2.9.2–4 §§169–177

[169]Now Pilate, who was sent as procurator into Judea by Tiberius, sent by night those images of Caesar that are called Ensigns, into Jerusalem. [170]This excited a very among great tumult among the Jews when it was day; for those that were near them were astonished at the sight of them, as indications that their laws were trodden underfoot; for those laws do not permit any sort of image to be brought into the city. Nay, besides the indignation

193

which the citizens had themselves at this procedure, a vast number of people came running out of the country. [171]These came zealously to Pilate to Caesarea, and besought him to carry those ensigns out of Jerusalem, and to preserve them their ancient laws inviolable; but upon Pilate's denial of their request, they fell down prostrate upon the ground, and continued immovable in that posture for five days and as many nights.

[172]On the next day Pilate sat upon his tribunal, in the open market place, and called to him the multitude, as desirous to give them an answer; and then gave a signal to the soldiers that they should all by agreement at once encompass the Jews with their weapons; [173]so the band of soldiers stood round about the Jews in three ranks. The Jews were under the utmost consternation at that unexpected sight. Pilate also said to them, that they should be cut in pieces, unless they would admit of Caesar's images, and gave intimation to the soldiers to draw their naked swords. [174]Hereupon the Jews, as it were at one signal, fell down in vast numbers together, and exposed their necks bare, and cried out that they were sooner ready to be slain, than that their law should be transgressed. Hereupon Pilate was greatly surprised at their prodigious superstition, and gave order that the ensigns should be presently carried out of Jerusalem.

[175]After this he raised another disturbance, by expending that sacred treasure which is called Corban upon aqueducts, whereby he brought water from the distance of four hundred furlongs. At this the multitude had great indignation; and when Pilate was come to Jerusalem, they came about his tribunal, and made a clamor at it. [176]Now when he was apprised aforehand of this disturbance, he mixed his own soldiers in their armor with the multitude, and ordered them to conceal themselves under the habits of private men, and not indeed to use their swords, but with their staves to beat those that made the clamor. He then gave the signal from his tribunal (to do as he had bidden them). [177]Now the Jews were so sadly beaten, that many of them perished by the stripes they received, and many of them perished as trodden to death, by which means the multitude was astonished at the calamity of those that were slain, and held their peace.

Josephus, Antiquities 18.3.1 §§55–59

[55]But now Pilate, the procurator of Judea, removed the army from Cesarea to Jerusalem, to take their winter quarters there, in order to abolish the Jewish laws. So he introduced Caesar's effigies, which were upon the ensigns, and brought them into the city; whereas our law forbids us the very making of images; [56]on which account the former procurators were wont to make their entry into the city with such ensigns as had not those ornaments. Pilate was the first who brought those images to Jerusalem, and set them up there; which was done without the knowledge of the people, because it was done in the nighttime; [57]but as soon as they knew it, they came in multitudes to Cesarea, and interceded with Pilate many days, that he would remove the images; and when he would not grant their requests, because it would tend to the injury of Caesar, while yet they persevered in their request, on the sixth day he ordered his soldiers to have their weapons privately, while he came and sat upon his judgment seat, which seat was so prepared in the open place of the city, that it concealed the army that lay ready

to oppress them: [58]and when the Jews petitioned him again, he gave a signal to the soldiers to encompass them round, and threatened that their punishment should be no less than immediate death, unless they would leave off disturbing him, and go their ways home. [59]But they threw themselves upon the ground, and laid their necks bare, and said they would take their death very willingly, rather than the wisdom of their laws should be transgressed; upon which Pilate was deeply affected with their firm resolution to keep their laws inviolable, and presently commanded the images to be carried back from Jerusalem to Caesarea.

Philo, **Embassy to Gaius 38 §§301–302**

[301]But when he steadfastly refused this petition (for he was a man of very inflexible disposition, and very merciless as well as very obstinate) they cried out: "Do not cause a sedition; do not make war upon us; do not destroy the peace which exists. The honor of the emperor is not identical with dishonor to the ancient laws; let it not be to you a pretence for heaping insult on our nation. Tiberius is not desirous that any of our laws or customs shall be destroyed. And if you yourself say that he is, show us either some command from him, or some letter, or something of the kind, that we, who have been sent to you as ambassadors, may cease to trouble you, and may address our supplications to your master." [302]But this last sentence exasperated him in the greatest possible degree, as he feared lest they might in reality go on an embassy to the emperor, and might impeach him with respect to other particulars of his government, in respect of

his corruption, and his acts of insolence, and his rapine, and his habit of insulting people, and his cruelty, and his continual murders of people untried and uncondemned, and his never ending, and gratuitous, and most grievous inhumanity.

11.22 Jesus or Barabbas (Matt. 27:15–23; Mark 15:6–14; Luke 23:17–23; John 18:39–40) (*JaS* 277)

The following two passages from Josephus indicate that there were times when an official would release prisoners, although there are no extrabiblical examples of a release at festival time. The *sicarii* are Jewish zealots.

Josephus, **Antiquities 20.9.3 §§208–210; 20.9.5 §215**

20.9.3 [208]But now the *sicarii* went into the city by night, just before the festival, which was now at hand, and took the scribe belonging to the governor of the temple, whose name was Eleazar, who was the son of Ananus (Ananias) the high priest, and bound him, and carried him away with them; [209]after which they sent to Ananias, and said that they would send the scribe to him, if he would persuade Albinus to release ten of those prisoners which he had caught of their party; so Ananias was plainly forced to persuade Albinus, and gained his request of him. [210]This was the beginning of greater calamities; for the robbers perpetually contrived to catch some of Ananias's servants; and when they had taken them alive, they would not let them go till they thereby recovered some of their own *sicarii*; and as they were again become no small number, they grew bold, and were a great affliction to the whole country.

20.9.5 [215]But when Albinus heard that Gessius Florus was coming to succeed him, he was desirous to appear to do somewhat that might be grateful to the people of Jerusalem; so he brought out all those prisoners who seemed to him to be most plainly worthy of death, and ordered them to be put to death accordingly. But as to those who had been put into prison on some trifling occasion, he took money of them, and dismissed them; by which means the prisons were indeed emptied, but the country was filled with robbers.

11.23 Pilate Delivers Jesus to be Crucified (Matt. 27:24–26; Mark 15:15; Luke 23:24–25) (*JaS* 278)

These texts describe the horrors of punishment by whipping.

Suetonius, **Domitian 11***

His savage cruelty was not only excessive, but also cunning and sudden. He invited one of his stewards to his bed-chamber the day before crucifying him, made him sit beside him on his couch, and dismissed him in a secure and happy state of mind, even deigning to send him a share of his dinner. When he was on the point of condemning the ex-consul Arrecinius Clemens, one of his intimates and tools, he treated him with as great favor as before, if not greater, and finally, as he was taking a drive with him, catching sight of his accuser he said: "Pray, shall we hear this base slave tomorrow?"

To abuse men's patience the more insolently, he never pronounced an unusually dreadful sentence without a preliminary declaration of clemency, so that there came to be no more

certain indication of cruel death than leniency of his preamble.

He had brought some men charged with treason into the senate, and when he had introduced the matter by saying that he would find out that day how dear he was to the members, he had no difficulty in causing them to be condemned to suffer the ancient method of punishment. Then appalled at the cruelty of the punishment, he interposed a veto, to lessen the odium, in these words (for it will be of interest to know his exact language): "Allow me, Fathers of the senate, to prevail on you by your love for me to grant a favor which I know I shall obtain with difficulty, namely, that you allow the condemned free choice of the manner of their death; for thus you will spare your own eyes and all men will know that I was present at the meeting of the senate."

Josephus, **Jewish War 2.14.9 §§305–308; 6.5.3 §§302–304**

2.14.9 [305]Florus was more provoked at this, and called out aloud to the soldiers to plunder that which was called the Upper Market Place, and to slay such as they met with. So the soldiers, taking this exhortation of their commander in a sense agreeable to their desire of gain, did not only plunder the place they were sent to, but forcing themselves into every house, they slew its inhabitants; [306]so the citizens fled along the narrow lanes, and the soldiers slew those that they caught, and no method of plunder was omitted; they also caught many of the quiet people, and brought them before Florus, whom he first chastised with stripes, and then crucified. [307]Accordingly, the whole number of those that were destroyed that day, with their wives and children, (for they did not spare even the infants themselves), was about three thousand and six hundred; [308]and what made this calamity the heavier, was this new method of Roman barbarity; for Florus ventured then to do what no one had done before, that is, to have men of the equestrian order whipped, and nailed to the cross before his tribunal; who, although they were by birth Jews, yet were they of Roman dignity notwithstanding.

6.5.3 [302]However, certain of the most eminent among the populace had great indignation at this dire cry of his, and took up the man, and gave him a great number of severe stripes; yet did not he either say anything for himself, or anything peculiar to those that chastised him, but still went on with the same words which he cried before. [303]Hereupon our rulers supposing, as the case proved to be, that this was a sort of divine fury in the man, brought him to the Roman procurator; [304]where he was whipped till his bones were laid bare; yet he did not make any supplication for himself, nor shed any tears, but turning his voice to the most lamentable tone possible, at every stroke of the whip his answer was, "Woe, woe to Jerusalem!"

Philo, **Against Flaccus 10 §75**

And then he commanded them all to stand in front of their enemies, who were sitting down, to make their disgrace the more conspicuous, and ordered them all to be stripped of their clothes and scourged with stripes, in a way that only the most wicked of malefactors are usually treated, and they were flogged with such severity that some of them the moment they were carried out died of their wounds, while others were rendered

so ill for a long time that their recovery was despaired of.

11.24 Jesus Mocked by Soldiers (Matt. 27:27–31a; Mark 15:16–20a; John 19:2–3) (*JaS* 279)

Jesus' mocking finds parallels in events mentioned by Philo, Dio Cassius (note the apparent sarcasm in these texts), and Plutarch, who speaks of Romans being mocked by others.

Philo, **Against Flaccus 6 §§36–39**

[36]There was a certain madman named Carabbas, afflicted not with a wild, savage, and dangerous madness (for that comes on in fits without being expected either by the patient or by bystanders), but with an intermittent and more gentle kind; this man spent all this [*sic*] days and nights naked in the roads, minding neither cold nor heat, the sport of idle children and wanton youths; [37]and they, driving the poor wretch as far as the public gymnasium, and setting him up there on high that he might be seen by everybody, flattened out a leaf of papyrus and put it on his head instead of a diadem, and clothed the rest of his body with a common door mat instead of a cloak and instead of a scepter they put in his hand a small stick of the native papyrus which they found lying by the way side and gave to him; [38]and when, like actors in theatrical spectacles, he had received all the insignia of royal authority, and had been dressed and adorned like a king, the young men bearing sticks on their shoulders stood on each side of him instead of spear-bearers, in imitation of the bodyguards of the king, and then others came up, some as if to salute him, and others making as though they wished to plead their causes before him, and others pre-

tending to wish to consult with him about the affairs of the state. [39]Then from the multitude of those who were standing around there arose a wonderful shout of men calling out Maris; and this is the name by which it is said that they call the kings among the Syrians; for they knew that Agrippa was by birth a Syrian, and also that he was possessed of a great district of Syria of which he was the sovereign.

Dio Cassius, Roman History 37/15.2; 37.17.1–3*

[37.15.2]Thence he proceeded against Syria Palaestina, because its inhabitants had ravaged Phoenicia. Their rulers were two brothers, Hyrcanus and Aristobulus, who were quarrelling with themselves, as it chanced, and were creating factions in the cities on account of the priesthood (for so they called their kingdom) of their god, whoever he is.

[37.17.1–3]This was the course of events at that time in Palestine; for this is the name that has been given from of old to the whole country extending from Phoenicia to Egypt along the inner sea. They have also another name that they have acquired; the country has been named Judaea, and the people themselves Jews. I do not know how this title came to be given to them, but it applies also to all the rest of mankind, although of alien race, who affect their customs. This class exits even among the Romans, and though often repressed has increased to a very great extent and has won its way to the right of freedom in its observances. They are distinguished from the rest of mankind in practically every detail of life, and especially by the fact that they do not honor any of the usual gods, but show extreme reverence for one particular divinity.

They never had any statue of him even in Jerusalem itself, but believing him to be unnamable and invisible, they worship him in the most extravagant fashion on earth. They built to him a temple that was extremely large and beautiful, except in so far as it was open and roofless, and likewise dedicated to him the day called the day of Saturn, on which, among many other most peculiar observances, they undertake no serious occupation.

Plutarch, Pompey 24

But they heaped most insults upon the Romans, even going up from the sea along their roads and plundering there, and sacking the neighboring villas. Once, too, they seized two praetors, Sextillius and Bellinus, in their purple edged robes, and carried them away, together with their attendants and lectors. They also captured a daughter of Antonius, a man who had celebrated a triumph, as she was going into the country, and exacted a large ransom for her. But their crowning insolence was this. Whenever a captive cried out that he was a Roman and gave his name, they would pretend to be frightened out of their senses, and would smite their thighs, and fall down before him entreating him to pardon them; and he would be convinced of their sincerity, seeing them so humbly suppliant. Then some would put Roman boots on his feet, and others would throw a toga around him, in order, forsooth, that there might be no mistake about him again. And after thus mocking the man for a long time and getting their fill of amusement from him, at last they would let down a ladder in mid-ocean and bid him disembark and go on his way rejoicing; and if he did not wish to go, they would push him overboard themselves and drown him.

11.25 The Crucifixion (Matt. 27:33–37; Mark 15:22–26; Luke 23:33–34; John 19:17b–27) (JaS 281)

These two texts from *Jubilees* indicate that a loincloth might remain on an executed person.

Jubilees *3.30–31; 7.20*

3.30But from all the beasts and all the cattle he granted to Adam alone that he might cover his shame. 31Therefore it is commanded in the heavenly tablets to all who will know the judgment of the Law that they should cover their shame and they should not be uncovered as the gentiles are uncovered.

7.20And in the twenty-eighth jubilee Noah began to command his grandsons with ordinances and commandments and all of the judgments which he knew. And he bore witness to his sons so that they might do justice and cover the shame of their flesh and bless the one who created them and honor father and mother, and each one love his neighbor and preserve themselves from fornication and pollution and from all injustice.

The following texts from Josephus demonstrate that the title "King of the Jews" was a perfectly common title.

Josephus, **Jewish War** *1.14.4 §282*

Hereupon Antony was moved to compassion at the change that had been made in Herod's affairs, and this both upon his calling to mind how hospitably he had been treated by Antipater, but more especially on account of Herod's own virtue; so he then resolved to get him made king of the Jews, whom he had himself formerly made tetrarch. The contest also that he had with Antigonus was another inducement, and that of no less weight than the great regard he had for Herod; for he looked upon Antigonus as a seditious person, and an enemy of the Romans.

Josephus, **Antiquities** *15.10.5 §373; 15.11.4 §409; 16.9.3 §291; 16.10.2 §311*

15.10.5 373Now there was one of these Essenes, whose name was Manahem, who had this testimony, that he not only conducted his life after an excellent manner, but had the foreknowledge of future events given him by God also. This man once saw Herod when he was a child, and going to school, and saluted him as king of the Jews.

15.11.4 409And that these things were so, the afflictions that happened to us afterwards [about them] are sufficient evidence; but for the tower itself, when Herod the king of the Jews had fortified it more firmly than before, in order to secure and guard the temple, he gratified Antonius, who was his friend, and the Roman ruler, and then gave it the name of the Tower of Antonia.

16.9.3 291Sylleus also wrote an account of this to the Arabians; who were so elevated with it, that they neither delivered up the robbers that had fled to them, nor paid the money that was due: they retained those pastures also which they had hired, and kept them without paying their rent, and all this because the king of Jews was now in a low condition by reason of Caesar's anger at him.

16.10.2 [311]But as for the king of the Jews, he was not now in the temper he was in formerly towards Alexander and Aristobulus, when he had been content with the hearing their calumnies when others told him of them; but he was now come to that pass as to hate them himself, and to urge men to speak against them, though they did not do it of themselves.

11.26 The Emmaus Road (Luke 24:13–35) (*JaS* 291)

1 Maccabees 3:40, 57; 4:3

These texts from 1 Maccabees link the traditional site for Emmaus with a Maccabean battleground.

[3:40]So they set out with their entire force, and when they arrived they encamped near Emmaus in the plain.

[3:57]Then the army marched out and encamped to the south of Emmaus.

[4:3]But Judas heard of it, and he and his warriors moved out to attack the king's force in Emmaus.

The following texts from Josephus and the Mishnah tie Emmaus to a fort site where Vespasian once stationed troops. Emmaus was also known as Motza (or Mosa). A *shofar*, mentioned in the Mishnah reading, is a ram's horn. It was blown like a bugle to signal an event.

Josephus, Jewish War 7.6.6 §§216–218

See section 8.4 above.

m. Sukkah 4.5*

See section 10.4 above.

11.27 Jesus' Last Words and Ascension (Luke 24:44–53) (*JaS* 294)

The prologue to Sirach and the text from 4QMMT 10 speak of a threefold division of the Old Testament.

Sirach, prologue

Many great teachings have been given to us through the Law and the Prophets and the others that followed them, and for these we should praise Israel for instruction and wisdom. Now, those who read the scriptures must not only themselves understand them, but must also as lovers of learning be able through the spoken and written word to help the outsiders. So my grandfather Jesus, who had devoted himself especially to the reading of the Law and the Prophets and the other books of our ancestors, and had acquired considerable proficiency in them, was himself also led to write something pertaining to instruction and wisdom, so that by becoming familiar also with his book those who love learning might make even greater progress in living according to the law.

You are invited therefore to read it with goodwill and attention, and to be indulgent in cases where, despite our diligent labor in translating, we may seem to have rendered some phrases imperfectly. For what was originally expressed in Hebrew does not have exactly the same sense when translated into another language. Not only this book, but even the Law itself, the Prophecies, and the rest of the books differ not a little when read in the original.

When I came to Egypt in the thirty-eighth year of the reign of Euergetes and stayed for some time, I found opportunity for no little instruction. It seemed highly necessary that I should myself devote some diligence and labor to the translation of this book. During that time I have applied my skill day and night to complete and publish the book for those living abroad who wished to gain learning and are disposed to live according to the law.

4QMMT (4QHalakhic Letter[d] [4Q397/ 4QMMT[d]]) 10 (Frags. 7 + 8)

. . . to you we have wr[itten] that you must understand the book of Moses [and the words of the] prophets and of David [and the annals]. . . .

Jesus according to John

12

Introducing Jesus
in John's Gospel

12.1 The Prologue: The Word Became Flesh (John 1:1–18) (JaS J1)

cf Prov —

In the following texts from Wisdom of Solomon, "wisdom" is likened to God as fashioner of all things, creator, and judge. Wisdom also possesses the attributes of God, including power, glory, and light. In the targum, the Word (*memra* in Aramaic) often expresses the mind of God. In Targum Onqelos, *memra* occurs frequently (197 times), often substituting for "God" or "Yahweh."

Wisdom of Solomon 7:21–22; 9:9; 7:25–29; 9:1–2; 18:14–16

7:21I learned both what is secret and what is manifest, 22for wisdom, the fashioner of all things, taught me. *Jn 1*

9:9With you is wisdom, she who knows your works and was present when you made the world; she understands what is pleasing in your sight and what is right according to your commandments. *Wisdom we did*

7:25For she is a breath of the power of God, and a pure emanation of the glory of the Almighty; therefore nothing defiled gains entrance into her. 26For she is a reflection of eternal light, a spotless mirror of the working of God, and an image of his goodness. 27Although she is but one, she can do

all things, and while remaining in herself, she renews all things; in every generation she passes into holy souls and makes them friends of God, and prophets; 28for God loves nothing so much as the person who lives with wisdom. 29She is more beautiful than the sun, and excels every constellation of the stars. Compared with the light she is found to be superior.

9:1O God of my ancestors and Lord of mercy, who have made all things by your word, 2and by your wisdom have formed humankind to have dominion over the creatures you have made.

18:14For while gentle silence enveloped all things, and night in its swift course was now half gone, 15your all-powerful word leaped from heaven, from the royal throne, into the midst of the land that was doomed, a stern warrior 16carrying the sharp sword of your authentic command, and stood and filled all things with death, and touched heaven while standing on the earth.

Targum Onqelos *to Exodus 4:12**

Now go and my Word (*memra*) shall be with your mouth.

205

b. Pesaḥim *54*[a]*

Yet was the fire of the Gehenna created on the eve of the Sabbath? Surely it was taught: Seven things were created before the world was created, and these are they: The Torah, repentance, the Garden of Eden, Gehenna, the Throne of Glory, the Temple, and the name of the Messiah. The Torah, for it is written, The Lord made me [sc. the Torah] as the beginning of his way. Repentance, for it is written, Before the mountains were brought forth, and it is written, You turn man to contrition, and say, Repent, you children of men. The Garden of Eden, as it is written, And the Lord planted a garden in Eden from aforetime. The Gehenna, for it is written, For Tophet [i.e., Gehenna] is ordered of old. The Throne of Glory and the Temple, for it is written, You throne of glory, on high from the beginning, you place of our sanctuary. The name of the Messiah, as it is written, His [sc. the Messiah's] name shall endure for ever, and has exited before the sun!—I will tell you: only its [i.e., Gehenna's] cavity was created before the world was created, but its fire [was created] on the eve of the Sabbath.

12.2 The Witness of John the Baptist (John 1:19–34) (*JaS* J2)

The following three texts reveal the Jewish expectation that Elijah would return to the earth near the end.

1 Enoch *90.31; 89.52*

[90.31]Thereafter, those three who were wearing snow-white (clothes), the former ones who had caused me to go up, grabbed me by my hand—also the hand of that ram holding me—and I ascended; they set me down in the midst of those sheep prior to the occurrence of this judgment.

[89.52]However, one of them was not killed but escaped alive and fled away; he cried aloud to the sheep, and they wanted to kill him, but the Lord of the sheep rescued him from the sheep and caused him to ascend to me and settle down.

Sirach *48:10*

See section 3.2 above for the text.

b. Ketubbot *96*[a]*

According to *b. Ketubbot* 96[a], untying a sandal was a task below that of a slave.

R. Jose b. Hanina ruled: All manner of work which a wife must render to her husband a widow must render to the orphans, with the exception of serving one's drinks, making ready one's bed and washing one's face, hands or feet. R. Joshua b. Levi ruled: All manner of service that a slave must render to his master a student must render to his teacher, except that of taking off his shoe.

The following texts mention the Jewish conception of a warring and victorious lamb.

Testament of Joseph *19.8–9*

[19.8]And I saw that a virgin was born from Judah, wearing a linen stole; and from her was born a spotless lamb. At his left there was something like a lion, and all the wild animals rushed against him, but the lamb conquered them, and destroyed them, trampling them underfoot. [9]And the angels and mankind and all the earth rejoiced over him.

Testament of Benjamin *3.8*

Through you will be fulfilled the heavenly prophecy concerning the

Lamb of God, the Savior of the world, because the unspotted one will be betrayed by lawless men, and the sinless one will die for impious men by the blood of the covenant for the salvation of the gentiles and of Israel and the destruction of Beliar and his servants.

1 Enoch 90.9–12, 38

90.9I kept seeing till those lambs grew horns; but the ravens crushed their horns. Then I kept seeing till one great horn sprouted on one of those sheep, and he opened their eyes; and they had vision in them and their eyes were opened. 10He cried aloud to the sheep, and all the rams saw him and ran unto him. 11In spite of this, all those eagles, vultures, ravens, and kites until now continue to rip the sheep, swooping down upon them and eating them. As for the sheep, they remain silent; but the rams are lamenting and crying aloud. 12Those ravens gather and battle with him (the horned ram) and seek to remove his horn, but without any success. . . . 38I went on seeing till all their kindred were transformed, and became snow-white cows; and the first among them became something, and that something became a great beast with huge black horns on its head. The Lord of the sheep rejoiced over it and over all the cows.

13

The Book of Signs

13.1 The First Sign: The Water to Wine at a Wedding in Cana (John 2:1–12) (*JaS* J4)

Wine was often associated with end-time expectations of celebration and rejoicing, which is reflected in these texts.

1 Enoch *10.19*

And they shall plant pleasant trees upon her—vines. And he who plants a vine upon her will produce wine for plentitude. And every seed that is sown on her, one measure will yield a thousand (measures) and one measure of olives will yield ten measures of presses of oil.

2 Baruch *29.5*

The earth will also yield fruits ten thousandfold. And on one vine will be a thousand branches, and one branch will produce a thousand clusters, and one cluster will produce a thousand grapes, and one grape will produce a cor of wine.

Tobit 11:18

According to Tobit 11:18, the text of which appears in section 9.5 above, a wedding party may last seven days.

m. Beṣah *2.3**

M. Beṣah 2.3 indicates that water could be clean or unclean and was often kept in stone containers.

A. And they concur that they effect surface contact between water [which is unclean], contained in a stone utensil [which is insusceptible to uncleanness, with the water of an immersion pool] in order to render [the unclean water] clean.

B. But they do not immerse [unclean water in an unclean utensil which contains it].

C. And they immerse [utensils if they are to be changed] from one use to another use,

D. or [at Passover] from one association [joined to make use of a single Passover lamb] to another [such] association.

Josephus, **Life of Flavius Josephus 16 *§86; 41 §207***

In the following two citations from Josephus, Khirbet Cana is referred to as a place in Galilee.

16 [86] Accordingly, I did not hinder him, as having no suspicion of any wicked designs of his; and I wrote to those to

whom I had committed the administration of the affairs of Tiberius by name, that they should provide a lodging for John, and for such as should come with him, and should procure him what necessaries soever he should stand in need of. Now at this time my abode was in a village of Galilee, which is named Cana.

41 [207]Whereupon, as soon as they heard it, they got together in great numbers, from all parts, with their wives and children; and this they did, as it appeared to me, not more out of their affection to me, than out of their fear on their own account; for, while I staid with them, they supposed that they should suffer no harm. So they all came into the great plain, wherein I lived, the name of which was Asochis.

13.2 The Cleansing of the Temple and an Allusion to Resurrection, the Great Sign (John 2:13–25) (JaS J5)

According to the following two passages from the Talmud, a warning (rather than stricter punishment) for blasphemy was given in certain cases.

b. Šebuʿot 36[a]*

HE WHO BLASPHEMES BY ANY OF THEM IS LIABLE: THIS IS THE OPINION OF R. MEIR; BUT THE SAGES EXEMPT HIM. Our Rabbis taught: Whosoever curses his God shall bear his sin. Why is it written? Is it not already said: And he that blasphemes the name of the Lord shall surely be put to death?—I might think he should be liable only for the actual Name; whence do we know to include the substitutes? Therefore it is said: Whosoever curses his God—in any manner; this is the opinion of R.

Meir; but the Sages say: for the actual Name, [the penalty is] death; for the substitutes, there is a warning.

b. Sanhedrin 38[b]*

See section 11.12 above.

m. Bekorot 8.7*

This Mishnah text indicates that Tyrian coinage was acceptable currency with which to pay the half-shekel temple tax.

A. The five *selas* for redeeming the firstborn son are in Tyrian coinage.
   B. (1) The thirty for the slave [Ex. 21:32], and (2) the fifty to be paid by the rapist and seducer [Ex. 22:15–16 , Dt. 22:28–29], and (3) the hundred to be paid by the gossip [Dt. 22:19]—
   C. all are to be paid in the value of *shekels* of the sanctuary,
   D. in Tyrian coinage.
   E. And everything which is to be redeemed [is redeemed] in silver or its equivalent, except for *shekel* dues.

m. Šeqalim 7.2*

M. Šeqalim 7.2 implies that animals were provided for travelers going to pilgrim festivals.

A. Money which was found before cattle dealers—
   B. throughout the year, it is deemed money in the status of second tithe.
   C. [If it is found] on the Temple mount, it is assumed to be unconsecrated money.
   D. [If it is found] in Jerusalem during a pilgrim festival, it is assumed to be money in the status of second tithe.
   E. And at all other times of the year, it is deemed to be unconsecrated.

The following two texts reflect the belief that righteousness and purity would flourish at Messiah's coming.

Shemoneh Esreh, *benediction 14**

See section 11.1 above.

4QFlor 1.6–17

[6]And he commanded to build for himself a temple of man, to offer him in it, [7]before him, the works of thanksgiving. And as for what he said to David: *2 Sam 7:11* "I shall obtain for you rest from all your enemies": (it refers to this,) that he will obtain for them rest from all [8]the sons of Belial, those who make them fall, to destr[oy them from their s]ins, when they come with the plans of Belial to make the s[ons of] [9]light fall, and to plot against them wicked plans so that they are trapped by Belial in their guilty error. *Blank* [10]And *2 Sam 7:12–14* "YHWH de[clares] to you that he will build you a house. I will raise up your seed after you and establish the throne of his kingdom [11][for ev]er. I will be a father to him and he will be a son to me." This (refers to the) "branch of David," who will arise with the Interpreter of the law who [12][will rise up] in Zi[on in] the last days, as it is written: *Amos 9:11* "I will raise up the hut of David which has fallen," This (refers to) "the hut of [13]David which has fallen," who will arise to save Israel. *Blank* [14]Midrash of "Blessed the man who does not walk in the counsel of the wicked." The interpretation of this sa[ying: they are those who turn] aside from the path [of the wicked,] [15]as it is written in the book of Isaiah, the prophet, for the last days: *Isa 8:11* "And it happened that with a strong [hand he turned me aside from walking on the path of] [16]this people." And this (refers to) those about whom it is written in the book of Ezekiel, the prophet, that *Ez 44:10* "[they should] not [defile themselves any more with all] [17]their filth." This (refers to) the sons of Zadok and to the men of his

council, those who seek jus[tice] eagerly, who will come after them to the council of the community.

Mekilta de Rabbi Ishmael *on Exodus 16:32 (tractate* **Vayassa**[c] *6, lines 60–64)**

What is in one person's heart, according to the later rabbis, was hidden from another person. In fact, seven things are hidden from people.

There are seven things hidden from men, and they are these: The day of death; the day of comfort; the depths of judgment. No man knows by what he can make profit. No man knows what is in the heart of his fellow man. No one knows when the Kingdom of David will be restored to its former position, nor when this wicked kingdom will be uprooted.

13.3 What Do the Signs Show? Jesus and Nicodemus (John 3:1–21) (*JaS* J6)

1QS 6.6–8

This text from Qumran, which appears in section 8.6 above, indicates that the Torah was supposed to be studied at night. Perhaps this tradition lies behind Nicodemus's decision to come to Jesus at night.

Jubilees *1.23–25*

This text from Jubilees anticipates a powerful work of the Spirit with the coming of the final age.

[23]But after this they will return to me in all uprightness and with all of (their) heart and soul. And I shall cut off the foreskin of their heart and the foreskin of the heart of their descendents. And I shall create for them a holy spirit, and I shall purify them so

that they will not turn away from following me from that day and forever. [24]And their souls will cleave to me and to all my commandments. And they will do my commandments. And I shall be a father to them, and they shall be sons to me. [25]And they will all be called "sons of the living God." And every angel and spirit will know and acknowledge that they are my sons and I am their father in uprightness and righteousness. And I shall love them.

1QS 4.19–22

Note the focus on holiness in the Qumran community.

[19]Meanwhile, truth shall rise up forever in the world which has been defiled in paths of wickedness during the dominion of deceit until [20]the time appointed for judgment. Meanwhile, God will refine, with his truth, all man's deeds, and will purify for himself the configuration of man, ripping out all spirit of deceit from the innermost part [21]of his flesh, and cleansing him with the spirit of holiness from every irreverent deed. He will sprinkle over him the spirit of truth like lustral water (in order to cleanse him) from all the abhorrences of deceit and from the defilement [22]of the unclean spirit.

13.4 Jesus and John the Baptist—The Bridegroom, the Christ, the One from Above Must Increase (John 3:22–36) (*JaS* J7)

m. Sanhedrin 3.5*

Perhaps John is referring to the role of the *shoshbin* when he talks about the Baptist's role in preparing the way for Jesus. Compare this text from the Mishnah.

A. "One known to be a friend and one known to be an enemy—

B. "one known to be a friend—this is the one who served as his groomsman;

C. "one known to be an enemy—this is one who has not spoken with him for three days by reason of outrage."

D. They said to [Judah], "Israelites are not suspect for such a factor."

13.5 Jesus and the Samaritan Woman—Worship in Spirit and Truth (John 4:1–42) (*JaS* J8)

The following texts from Josephus indicate that the route Jesus took through Samaria was a common one.

Josephus, Antiquities 20.6.1 §118

Now there arose a quarrel between the Samaritans and the Jews on the occasion following:—It was the custom of the Galileans, when they came to the holy city at the festivals, to take their journeys through the country of the Samaritans; and at this time there lay, in the road they took, a village that was called Ginea, which was situated in the limits of Samaria and the great plain, where certain persons thereto belonging fought with the Galileans, and killed a great many of them.

Josephus, Jewish War 2.12.3 §232

After this there happened a fight between the Galileans and the Samaritans; it happened at a village called Geman, which is situated in the great plain of Samaria; where, as a great number of Jews were going up to Jerusalem to the feast [of tabernacles,] a certain Galilean was slain. . . .

Josephus, Life of Flavius Josephus
52 §269

I then wrote to my friends in Samaria, to take care that they might safely pass through the country: for Samaria was already under the Romans, and it was absolutely necessary for those that go quickly [to Jerusalem] to pass through that country; for in that road you may, in three days' time, go from Galilee to Jerusalem.

m. Niddah *4.1**

This text from the Mishnah indicates that Samaritan women were considered perpetually unclean.

A. Samaritan women are deemed menstruants from their cradle.

B. And the Samaritans convey uncleanness to a couch beneath as to a cover above,

C. because they have intercourse with menstruating women,

D. and continue unclean for any sort of blood.

E. But those [who have contact] with them are not liable for entering the sanctuary and do not burn heave offering on their account,

F. because their uncleanness is a matter of doubt.

m. ʾAbot *1.5**

In this passage from *m. ʾAbot*, it is argued that too much talk with a woman, even one's wife, may bring trouble on a man, distract him from studying the Torah, and ultimately lead him to Gehenna.

A. Yose b. Yohanan of Jerusalem says,

(1) "Let your house be wide open.

(2) "And seat the poor at your table ["make . . . members of your household"].

(3) "And don't talk too much with women."

B. (He spoke of a man's wife, all the more so is the rule to be applied to the wife of one's fellow. In this regard did sages say, "So long as a man talks too much with a woman, (1) he brings trouble on himself, (2) wastes time better spent on studying Torah, and (3) ends up an heir of Gehenna.")

m. Soṭah *3.4**

This passage, which appears in section 11.7 above, indicates that there was debate as to whether a father ought to teach the Torah to his daughter.

13.6 The Second Sign: The Healing of a Royal Official's Son (John 4:43–54) (*JaS* J9)

These two texts from Josephus show that the term *royal official* was used of a person who was connected to the king.

Josephus, Jewish War *1.1.5 §45*

Nay, this disappointment proved an omen to his brother [Judas] how the entire battle would end. It is true that the Jews fought it out bravely for a long time; but the king's forces, being superior in number, and having fortune on their side, obtained the victory; and when a great many of his men were slain, Judas took the rest with him, and fled to the toparchy of Gophna.

Josephus, Life of Flavius Josephus 72 §§400–402

[400]But on the next day, when I had laid an ambush in a certain valley, not far from the banks, I provoked those that belonged to the king to come to a battle, and gave orders to my own soldiers to turn their backs

upon them, until they should have drawn the enemy away from their camp, and brought them out into the field, which was done accordingly; [401]for Sylla, supposing that our party did really run away, was ready to pursue them, when our soldiers that lay in ambush took them on their backs, and put them all into great disorder. [402]I also immediately made a sudden turn with my own forces, and met those of the king's party, and put them to flight. And I had performed great things that day, if a certain fate had not been my hindrance.

b. Berakot 34[b]*

In this text from the Talmud, we have an example of "healing from a distance" that in certain ways parallels the account of Jesus' healing the official's son.

Our Rabbis taught: Once the son of R. Gamaliel fell ill. He sent two scholars to R. Hanina b. Dosa to ask him to pray for him. When he saw them he went up to an upper chamber and prayed for him. When he came down he said to them: Go, the fever has left him. They said to him: Are you a prophet? He replied: I am neither a prophet nor the son of a prophet, but I learned this from experience. If my prayer is fluent in my mouth, I know that he is accepted: but if not, I know that he is rejected. They sat down and made a note of the exact moment. When they came to R. Gamaliel, he said to them: By the temple service! You have not been a moment too soon or too late, but so it happened: at that very moment the fever left him and he asked for water to drink.

13.7 The Third Sign: A Controversial Sabbath Healing in Jerusalem (John 5:1–18) (*JaS* J10)

Two selections from *m. Šabbat* (7.2; 10.5) outline various limitations on what could be done on the Sabbath. The first passage, *m. Šabbat* 7.2, appears in section 4.8 above.

m. Šabbat 10.5*

I A. He who takes out a loaf of bread into the public domain is liable.

II B. [If] two people took it out, they are exempt.

III C. [If] one person could not take it out, but two people took it out, they are liable.

D. And R. Simeon declares [them exempt].

I E. He who takes out food in a volume less than the specified measure in a utensil is exempt even on account of [taking out] the utensil,

F. for the utensil is secondary to it [the food].

II G. [He who takes out] a living person in a bed is exempt even on account of [taking out] the bed,

H. for the bed is secondary to him.

III I. [If he took out] a corpse in a bed, he is liable.

J. And so [one who takes out] an olive's bulk of corpse matter and olive's bulk of carrion and a lentil's bulk of a dead creeping thing is liable.

K. And R. Simeon declares [him] exempt.

3Q15 11.9–13

This Qumran text contains an obscure reference to Bethsaida as Beth Esdatain.

[9]In the grave of the sons of Ha'amata of Jericho (?), [10]there are vessels of myrtle (?) there, and of the tithe of pine (?) (resin). [11]*Blank* Very close by,

[12]in Beth Esdatain, in the cistern [13]at the entrance to the smallest water basin. . . .

Philo, Allegorical Interpretation 1.2–3 §§5–6

In this text from *Allegorical Interpretation*, it is quite clear that Philo believes God continues his work of creating after the initial seven days of creation narrated in Genesis 1–2.

1.2 [5]First, therefore, having desisted from the creation of mortal creatures on the seventh day, he began the formation of other and more divine beings.

1.3 For God never ceases from making something or other; but, as it is the property of fire to burn, and of snow to chill, so it is the property of God to be creating. And much more so, in proportion as he himself is to all other beings the author of their working. [6]Therefore, the expression, "he caused to rest," is very appropriately employed here, not "he rested." For he makes things to rest which appear to be producing others, but which in reality do not affect anything; but he himself never ceases from creating. On which account Moses says, "He caused to rest the things which he had begun." For all the things that are made by our arts when completed stand still and remain; but all those which are accomplished by the knowledge of God are moved at subsequent times. For their ends are the beginnings of other things; as, for instance, the end of day is the beginning of night. And in the same way we must look upon months and years when they come to an end as the beginning of those which are just about to follow them.

Exodus Rabbah *30.9**

In this passage from *Exodus Rabbah*, it is said that God need not rest, for the world is his home and he can roam through it as he wills. In the excerpt below, the small capital letters indicate the biblical phrase being expounded, and italic type is used for other biblical quotations and allusions.

Another explanation of NOW THESE ARE THE ORDINANCES. It is written, *He declares His word unto Jacob* (Ps. CXLVII, 19)— these are the [Ten] Commandments; *His statutes and His ordinances unto Israel (ib.)*— these are the ordinances. The ways of God differ from those of man; whereas man directs others to do a thing while he does nothing, God only tells Israel to do and observe those things which He himself does. It is related of Rabban Gamaliel, R. Joshua, R. Eliezer b. 'Azariah, and R. Akiba that they went to Rome and taught there: The ways of God are not as those of man, who makes a decree enjoining others to do a thing while he does nothing; God not being so. There happened to be a sectarian there, who accosted them as they were going out with the taunt: "Your words are only falsehood. Did you not say that God says a thing and fulfils it? Then why does He not observe the Sabbath?" They replied: "Wretch! Is not a man permitted to carry on the Sabbath in his own courtyard?" He replied: "Yes." Whereupon they said to him: "Both the higher and lower regions are the courtyard of God, as it says, *The whole earth is full of His glory* (Isa. vi, 3), and even if a man carries a distance of his own height, does he transgress?" The other agreed. "Then," said they, "it is written, *Do not I fill heaven and earth?*" (Jer. xxiii, 24). Another explanation of *"He declares His word unto Jacob."* R. Abbahu, in the name of R. Jose b. Hanina, said: It can be compared to a king who had an orchard in which he planted all kinds of trees and in which only he entered, because he was its keeper. When his children became of age, he said: "My children, hitherto I guarded this orchard, not allowing any to enter it. I want you now to look after it as I did." This is what God said to Israel: Prior to My creation of the world, I prepared the Torah, for it says, *Then I was by Him, as a nursling*—amon (Prov. viii, 30). What is the meaning of *"amon"*—"a tutor," as it says, *As a nursing father* (omen) *carries the sucking child* (Num. xi, 12). I did not give it to the heathen, but to Israel, who, as soon as they responded—"*All that the Lord has spoken will we do, and obey*" (Ex. xxiv, 7)—were given the Torah. Hence, "*He declares His word unto Jacob, His statutes and His ordinances unto Israel.*" *He has not dealt so with any nation* (Ps. CXLVII, 20f), only with Jacob, whom He chose from all the heathen people, giving to the latter only part [of the Commandments]. He gave Adam six Commandments, and added one to Noah, Abraham had eight and Jacob nine, but to Israel He gave *all*.

13.8 The Discourse Defending the Sabbath Healing—"The Son Does Nothing of His Own Accord" (John 5:19–47) (JaS J11)

Sirach 48:1

In this text from Sirach, the words of Elijah are said to burn "like a torch," an apt metaphor for the ministry of John the Baptist as well.

Then Elijah arose, a prophet like fire, and his word burned like a torch.

b. Šabbat 116ᵇ*

This passage from the Talmud uses the metaphor of light in a manner similar to that in Matthew 5:16. Light in the biblical and extrabiblical texts refers to what illumines darkness.

Said he [R. Gamaliel] to him, "It is decreed for us, Where there is a son, a daughter does not inherit." [He replied], "Since the day that you were exiled from your land the Law of Moses has been superseded and another book given, wherein it is written, 'A son and a daughter inherit equally.' " The next day, he [R. Gamaliel] brought him a Lybian donkey. Said he to them, "Look at the end of the book, wherein it is written, 'I came not to destroy the Law of Moses nor to add to the Law of Moses,' and it is written therein, 'A daughter does not inherit where there is a son.' " Said she to him, "Let your light shine forth like a lamp." Said R. Gamaliel to him, "A donkey came and knocked the lamp over!"

13.9 The Fourth Sign: The Feeding of the Five Thousand (John 6:1–15) (JaS J12)

Josephus also refers to the Sea of Galilee as the Sea/Lake of Tiberius in two passages from *War*.

*Josephus, **Jewish War** 3.3.5 §§57–58; 4.8.2 §§455–456*

3.3.5 [57] This [last] country begins at Mount Libanus, and the fountains of Jordan, and reaches breadthways to the lake of Tiberias; and in length is extended from a village called Arpha, as far as Julias. Its inhabitants are a mixture of Jews and Syrians.—[58] And thus have I, with all possible brevity, described the country of Judea, and those that lie round about it.

4.8.2 [455]Now the region that lies in the middle between these ridges of mountains, is called the Great Plain; it reaches from the village Ginnabris, as far as the lake Asphaltitis; [456]its length is two hundred and thirty furlongs, and its breadth a hundred and twenty, and it is divided in the midst by Jordan. It has two lakes in it; that of Asphaltitis, and that of Tiberias, whose natures are opposite to each other; for the former is salt and unfruitful, but that of Tiberias is sweet and fruitful.

asphalt
Dead Sea

Tobit 6:11–14

In this passage from Tobit, the term παιδά-ριον is used to refer to a man of marriageable age. In other texts, the term can refer to any boys needing circumcision. So the term in John 5:9 can cover a potentially wide age range.

[11]Raphael said to the young man [τῷ παιδαρίῳ], "Brother Tobias." "Here I am," he answered. Then Raphael said to him, "We must stay this night in the home of Raguel. He is your relative, and he has a daughter named Sarah. [12]He has no male heir and no daughter except Sarah only, and you, as next of kin to her, have before all other men a hereditary claim on her. Also it is right for you to inherit her father's possessions. Moreover, the girl is sensible, brave, and very beautiful, and her father is a good man." [13]He continued, "You have every right to take her in marriage. So listen to me, brother; tonight I will speak to her father about the girl, so that we may take her to be your bride. When we return from Rages we will celebrate her marriage. For I know that Raguel can by no means keep her from you or promise her to another man without incurring the penalty of death according to the decree of the book of Moses. Indeed he knows that you, rather than any other man, are entitled to marry his daughter. So now listen to me, brother, and tonight we shall speak concerning the girl and arrange her engagement to you. And when we return from Rages we will take her and bring her back with us to your house."

[14]Then Tobias [LXX MSS B and A: τὸ παιδάριον, the young man] said in answer to Raphael, "Brother Azariah, I have heard that she already has been married to seven husbands and that they died in the bridal chamber. On the night when they went in to her, they would die. I have heard people saying that it was a demon that killed them."

1 Enoch 62.14

This text from *1 Enoch*, which appears in section 9.8 above, speaks of Messiah's provision of manna and blessing in the end time.

13.10 The Discourse on the Bread of Life Come Down from Above (John 6:22–59) (*JaS* J14)

Both of these quotations claim that God's provision of manna will be renewed (by Messiah) in the end time.

2 Baruch 29.8

And it will happen at that time that the treasury of manna will come down again from on high, and they will eat of it in those years because these are they who will have arrived at the consummation of time.

Sibylline Oracles 3.49 (*fragment 3*)

But those who honor the true eternal God inherit life, dwelling in the luxurious garden of Paradise for the time of eternity, feasting on sweet bread from starry heaven.

Ecclesiastes Rabbah 1.9*

The "latter redeemer" in Ecclesiastes Rabbah 1.9 is said to restore the provision of manna in the eschaton.

R. Berekiah said in the name of R. Isaac: As the first redeemer was, so shall the latter Redeemer be. What is stated of the former redeemer? *And Moses took his wife and his sons, and set them upon an ass* (Ex. 4:20). Similarly will it be with the latter Redeemer, as it is stated, *Lowly and riding upon an ass* (Zech. 9:9). As the former redeemer caused a manna to descend, as it is stated, *Behold, I will cause to rain bread from heaven for you* (Ex. 16:4), so will the latter Redeemer cause manna to descend, as it is stated. *May he be as a rich cornfield in the land* (Ps. 72:16). As the former redeemer made a well to rise, so will the latter Redeemer bring up water, as it is stated, *And a fountain shall come forth of the house of the Lord, and shall water the valley of Shittim* (Joel 4:18).

Two texts from Sirach speak about perpetual hunger and thirst for wisdom, but Jesus speaks of the permanence and value of the manna he offers.

Sirach 24:21, 23

[21]Those who eat of me will hunger for more, and those who drink of me will thirst for more. . . . [23]All this is the book of the covenant of the Most High God, the law that Moses commanded us as an inheritance for the congregations of Jacob.

13.11 Jesus Goes from Galilee to Jerusalem (John 7:1–13) (JaS J16)

Josephus, Antiquities 8.4.1 §§99–100

This text from *Antiquities* describes Solomon's building of the temple and suggests that the Jews regarded the Feast of Tabernacles as the most sacred and prominent of the feasts.

[99]When king Solomon had finished these works, these large and beautiful buildings, and had laid up his donations in the temple, and all this in the interval of seven years, and had given a demonstration of his riches and alacrity therein; insomuch that anyone who saw it would have thought that it must have been an immense time ere it could have been finished, and [would be surprised] that so much should be finished in so short a time;—short, I mean, if compared with the greatness of the work: he also wrote to the rulers and elders of the Hebrews, and ordered all the people to gather themselves together to Jerusalem, both to see the temple which he had built, and to remove the ark of God into it; [100]and when this invitation of the whole body of the people to come to Jerusalem was everywhere carried abroad, it was the seventh month before they came together; which month is, by our countrymen, called *Thisri;* but by the Macedonians *Hyperberetaeus.* The Feast of Tabernacles happened to fall at the same time, which was kept by the Hebrews as a most holy and most eminent feast.

The Feast of Tabernacles celebrated God's provision during the exodus which, according to the following four quotations from the Mishnah, was to be tithed (according to R. Judah, the festival hut fell under the law of tithes as well).

m. Maʿaśerot 3.7*

A. Storage huts, watchtowers, and field sheds are exempt [from the law of tithes].

B. A hut [such as those used in the area of] Gennesar,

C. even though it contains millstones and poultry,

D. is exempt [from the law of tithes].

E. A potter's hut—

F. the inner part is subject [to the law]

G. and the outer part is exempt.

H. R. Yose says, "Any [structure] which does not [serve] as [both] a summer dwelling and a winter dwelling is exempt."

I. A festival hut during [the week of] the Festival [of Tabernacles]—

J. R. Judah declares it subject [to the law during that week],

K. but Sages declare it exempt [for that week].

m. Bikkurim 1.6, 10*

⁶A. He who buys two trees [that are growing] on [the property] of his fellow

B. brings [firstfruits from those trees] but does not recite [over them].

C. R. Meir says, "He brings and recites."

D. [If] the spring [which irrigated the field] became dry, [or] the tree was cut down,

E. he brings [firstfruits that were picked from that tree before it was cut down] but does not recite.

F. R. Judah says, "He brings and recites."

G. From Pentecost until the Festival [of Sukkot],

H. he brings and recites.

I. From the Festival until Hanukkah,

J. he brings but does not recite.

K. R. Judah b. Beterah says, "He brings and recites."

¹⁰A. And these [people] bring [firstfruits] and recite:

B. [Those who bring firstfruits] (1) from Pentecost until the Festival [of Sukkot],

(2) from the seven kinds [of produce native to the Land of Israel],

(3) from fruit of the hill country,

(4) from dates of the valley, [and]

(5) from olives [used] for oil [that grow] in Transjordan.

C. R. Yose the Galilean says, "They do not bring firstfruits from [produce grown in] Transjordan, for [Transjordan] is not a land flowing with milk and honey [Dt. 26:15]." *Ra*

m. Šeqalim 3.1*

See section 11.1 above.

13.12 Jesus Teaches in the Temple to Mixed Reaction (John 7:14–52) (JaS J17)

m. Šabbat 19.1–2*

This citation from *m. Šabbat* deals with restrictions and concessions concerning circumcision and the Sabbath.

¹A. R. Eliezer says, "If one did not bring a utensil [used for circumcision] on the eve of the Sabbath, he brings it openly on the Sabbath."

B. And in the time of the danger, one covers it up in the presence of witnesses.

C. And further did R. Eliezer state, "They cut wood to make coals to prepare an iron utensil [for circumcision]."

D. An operative principle did R. Aqiba state, "Any sort of labor [in connection with circumcision] which it is possible to do on the eve of the Sabbath does not override [the restrictions of the Sabbath, and that which it is not possible to do on the eve of the Sabbath does override [the prohibitions of] the Sabbath."

²A. They do prepare all that is needed for circumcision on the Sabbath:

B. they (1) cut [the mark of] circumcision], (2) tear, (3) suck [out the wound].

C. And they put on it a poultice and cummin.

I D. If one did not pound it on the eve of the Sabbath, he chews it in his teeth and puts it on.

II E. If one did not mix wine and oil on the eve of the Sabbath, let this be put on by itself and that by itself.

F. And they do not make a bandage in the first instance.

G. But they wrap a rag around [the wound of the circumcision].

III H. If one did not prepare [the necessary rag] on the eve of the Sabbath, he wraps [the rag] around his finger and brings it, and even from a different courtyard.

The following apocalyptic texts suggest that the Messiah has been hidden from before creation and will only be revealed when he acts.

1 Enoch 48.6

For this purpose he became the Chosen One; he was concealed in the presence of (the Lord of the Spirits) prior to the creation of the world, and for eternity.

2 Baruch 29.3

And it will happen that when all that which should come to pass in these parts has been accomplished, the Anointed One will begin to be revealed.

4 Ezra (= 2 Esdras) 7:28; 13:51–52

For *4 Ezra* (= 2 Esdras) 7:28, see section 13.21 below; for *4 Ezra* (= 2 Esdras) 13:51–52, see section 4.5 above.

Justin Martyr, Dialogue with Trypho 8.7*

This text from *Dialogue with Trypho* mentions another Jewish view claiming that Messiah would be born of flesh and blood and would not be revealed until he is anointed and manifested to all.

. . . When I had said this, my beloved friends those who were with Trypho laughed; but he, smiling, says, "I approve of your other remarks, and admire the eagerness with which you study divine things; but it were better for you still to abide in the philosophy of Plato, or of some other man, cultivating endurance, self-control, and moderation, rather than be deceived by false words, and follow the opinions of men of no reputation. For if you remain in that mode of philosophy, and live blamelessly, a hope of a better destiny were left to you; but when you have forsaken God, and reposed confidence in man, what safety still awaits you? If, then, you are willing to listen to me (for I have already considered you a friend), first be circumcised, then observe what ordinances have been enacted with respect to the Sabbath, and the feasts, and the new moons of God; and, in a word, do all things which have been written in the law: and then perhaps you shall obtain mercy from God. But Christ—if He has indeed been born, and exists anywhere—is unknown, and does not even know Himself, and has no power until Elias come to anoint Him, and make Him manifest to all. And you, having accepted a groundless report, invent a Christ

219

for yourselves, and for his sake are inconsiderately perishing."

m. Sukkah 4.1*

This text from *m. Sukkah* indicates that the Feast of Tabernacles went on for only seven days, but compare also the subsequent citation from *b. Sukkah* 48[b].

A. [The rites of] the *lulab* and the willow branch [carried by the priests around the altar, M. 5:5] are for six or seven [days].

B. The recitation of the *Hallel* Psalms and the rejoicing are for eight [days].

C. [The requirement of dwelling in the] *sukkah* and the water libation are for seven days.

D. And the flute playing is for five or six.

b. Sukkah 48[b]*

THEY HAD EACH A HOLE LIKE A SLENDER SNOUT etc. Must we say that our Mishnah agrees with R. Judah and not with the Rabbis seeing that we have learned, R. JUDAH STATED, WITH ONE LOG HE PERFORMED THE CEREMONY OF THE WATER-LIBATION ALL EIGHT DAYS; for if it agrees with the Rabbis, could they not both pour together?—[No,] You may say that it agrees even with the Rabbis, [the reason for the different sizes of the holes being that] wine is viscous and water is fluid.

m. Sukkah 5.6*

This text from *m. Sukkah* indicates that the eighth day of the Feast of Tabernacles was considered part of the feast as well.

A. On the first festival day of the Festival there were there thirteen bullocks, two rams, and one goat [Num. 29:13, 16].

B. There remained fourteen lambs for the eight priestly watches.

C. On the first day, six offer two each, and the remaining two, one each.

D. On the second day, five offer two each, and the rest, one each.

E. On the third day, four offer two each, and the rest, one each.

F. On the fourth day, three offer two each, and the rest offer one each.

G. On the fifth day, two offer two each, and the rest offer one each.

H. On the sixth day, one offers two, and the rest offer one each.

I. On the seventh, all of them are equal.

J. On the eighth, they go back to drawing lots, as on the [other] festivals.

K. They ruled: Whoever offered a bullock one day should not offer one the next day.

L. But they offer them in rotation.

These texts from *Antiquities* and 2 Maccabees indicate that the Feast of Tabernacles went on for eight days.

Josephus, Antiquities 3.10.4 §§244–245

[244]Upon the fifteenth day of the same month, when the season of the year is changing for winter, the law enjoins us to pitch tabernacles in every one of our houses, so that we preserve ourselves from the cold of that time of the year; [245]as also that when we should arrive at our own country, and come to that city which we should have then for our metropolis, because of the temple therein to be built, and keep a festival for eight days, and offer burnt offerings, and sacrifice thank offerings, that we should then carry in our hands a branch of myrtle, and willow, and a bough of the

palm tree, with the addition of the pomecitron.

2 Maccabees 10:6

They celebrated it for eight days with rejoicing, in the manner of the festival of booths, remembering how not long before, during the festival of booths, they had been wandering in the mountains and caves like wild animals.

m. Sukkah 4.9*

This text from the Mishnah reveals how the priest would gather water from the pool of Siloam and bring it to the temple amid trumpets and rejoicing.

A. *The water libation*: How so?

B. A golden flask, holding three *logs* in volume, did one fill with water from Siloam.

C. [When] they reached the Water Gate, they blow a sustained, a quavering, and a sustained blast on the *shofar*.

D. [The priest] went up on the ramp [at the south] and turned to his left [southwest].

E. There were two silver bowls there.

F. R. Judah says, "They were of plaster, but they had darkened because of the wine."

G. They were perforated with holes like a narrow snout,

H. one wide, one narrow,

I. so that both of them would be emptied together [one of its wine, flowing slowly, the other of its water, flowing quickly].

J. The one on the west was for water, the one on the east was for wine.

K. [If] he emptied the flask of water into the bowl for wine, and the flask of wine into the bowl for water, he has nonetheless carried out the rite.

L. R. Judah says, "A *log* [of water] would one pour out as the water libation all eight days."

M. And to the one who pours out the water libation they say, "Lift up your hand [so that we can see the water pouring out]!"

N. For one time one [priest] poured out the water on his feet.

O. And all the people stoned him with their citrons.

b. Sukkah 27[b]*

For the religious leaders to argue that "a prophet does not arise from Galilee" may have overstated the case. Jonah was from Galilee and, according to this tradition in the Talmud, every tribe in Israel produced prophets.

Our Rabbis have taught: It once happened that R. Ila'i went to pay his respects to R. Eliezer his master in Lydda on a Festival. He said to him, "Ila'i, you are not of those that rest on the Festival," for R. Eliezer used to say, "I praise the indolent who do not emerge from their houses on the Festival since it is written, And you shall rejoice, you and your household." But it is not so? For did not R. Isaac say, "From where do we know that a man is obliged to pay his respects to his teacher on the Festival? From Scripture which said, 'Wherefore will you go to him to-day? It is neither New Moon nor Sabbath' from which it follows that on the New Moon and the Sabbath a man is obliged to pay his respects to his master?"—There is no difficulty. The latter refers to where he can go and return [to his house] on the one day; the former to where he cannot go and return on the same day. Our Rabbis have taught: It happened that R. Eliezer passed the Sabbath in Upper Galilee in the Sukkah of R. Johanan son of R. Ila'i at Caesarea or, as some say, in Caesarea [Philippi], and when the sun reached the Sukkah he said to him, "How if I spread a cloth over it?" He answered him, "There was not a tribe in Israel which did not produce a judge." When the sun reached to the middle of the Sukkah, he said to him, "How if I spread a cloth over it?" He answered him, "There was not a tribe in Israel from which there did not come prophets, and the tribes of Judah and Benjamin appointed their kings at the behest of the prophets." When the sun reached the feet of R. Eliezer, Johanan took a cloth and spread it over [the Sukkah]. R. Eliezer [thereupon] tied up his cloak, threw it over his back, and went out. It was not in order to evade an answer [that he answered as he did] but because he never said anything which he had not heard from his master.

13.13 The Woman Caught in Adultery (John 7:53–8:11)

Gospel of the Hebrews (*as quoted in Eusebius,* Ecclesiastical History 3.39.16)*

The story of the woman caught in adultery, or one very similar, is recorded by Papias and cited later by the church historian Eusebius. See also a reference to the story in the early church document *Apostolic Constitutions* 2.24.

But concerning Matthew he writes as follows: "So then Matthew wrote the oracles in the Hebrew language, and every one interpreted them as he was able." And the same writer uses testimonies from the first Epistle of John and from that of Peter likewise. And he relates another story of a woman, who was accused of many sins before the Lord, which is contained in the Gospel according to the Hebrews. These things we have thought it nec-

essary to observe in addition to what has been already stated.

Apostolic Constitutions 2.24 (= *Syriac* Didascalia 7)*

See then the mercy of the Lord towards Matthew, who was a publican—when he turned unto Him, He made him an evangelist; and towards Peter, who denied Him thrice through fear—when he repented and wept bitterly, He received his repentance, and made him the shepherd of His sheep; and towards Paul, our brother, though he was formerly a persecutor, who blasphemed against the holy Spirit, yet when he turned unto Him, He made him an apostle. And to the woman who was a sinner, who gave alms unto many, He said, "Your sin has been forgiven you." And the other woman also, the adulteress whom the priests set before Him to prove Him, He saved, and said unto her, "Go your way, from henceforth sin no more." It is right for you bishops to set your hope and trust in God, our Lord and our Savior, Jesus Christ the Savior of your souls.

b. Baba Meṣiᶜa 91ᵃ*

Though this text is late, it suggests that adulterers must be seen in the act of adultery in order for adultery charges to stick and the death penalty to be invoked.

The other problem they propounded of me was: May two animals of diverse species [and of opposite sexes] be led into a stable? And I answered them that it is forbidden, this not being in accordance with the law. For Samuel said: In the case of adulterers, they [sc. the witnesses] must have seen them in the posture of adulterers; but in respect to diverse species, they must have seen him assisting [the copulation] even as [one places the] painting stick in the tube.

m. Sanhedrin 7.4*

This text refers to the penalty of stoning for adultery.

A. These are [the felons] who are put to death by stoning:

B. He who has sexual relations with (1) his mother, (2) with the wife of his father, (3) with his daughter-in-law, (4) with a male, and (5) with a cow;

C. (6) and the woman who brings an ox on top of herself;

D. and (1) he who blasphemes, (2) he who performs an act of worship for an idol, (3) he who gives of his seed to Molech, (4) he who has a familiar spirit, and (5) he who is a soothsayer;

E. he who profanes the Sabbath,

F. he who curses his father or his mother,

G. he who has sexual relations with a betrothed maiden,

H. he who beguiles [others to idolatry], and he who leads [a whole town to idolatry],

I. a sorcerer,

J. and a stubborn and incorrigible son.

I K. He who has sexual relations with his mother is liable on her account because of her being his mother and because of her being his father's wife [Lev. 18:6–7, 20:11].

L. R. Judah says, "He is liable only on account of her being his mother alone."

II M. He who has sexual relations with his father's wife is liable on her account because of her being his father's wife and because of her being a married woman,

N. whether this is in the lifetime of his father or after the death of his father,

O. whether she is only betrothed or already married [to the father].

III P. He who has sexual relations with his daughter-in-law is liable on her account because of her being his daughter-in-law and because of her being another man's wife,

Q. whether this is in the lifetime of his son or after the death of his son [Lev. 20:12],

R. whether she is only betrothed or already married [to the son].

S. He who has sexual relations with a male [Lev. 20:13, 15–16], or a cow, and the woman who brings an ox on top of herself—

T. if the human being has committed a sin, what sin has the beast committed?

U. But because a human being has offended through it, therefore the Scripture has said, *Let it be stoned.*

V. Another matter: So that the beast should not amble through the marketplace and people say, "This is the one on account of which Mr. So-and-so got himself stoned."

13.14 The Dispute Deepens as Jesus Claims to Be the Light of the World, the Truth, and Abraham's Superior (John 8:12–59) (JaS J18)

These texts from *m. Šeqalim* tell where to leave contributions for the temple during worship times at feasts.

m. Šeqalim 2.1; 6.1, 5*

2.1A. They change *sheqels* into *darics* because of the burden of the journey.

B. Just as there were *shofar* chests [for receiving the *sheqel* tax] in the Temple, so there were *shofar* chests in the provinces.

C. Townsfolk who sent their *sheqels*, which were stolen or lost—

D. if the heave offering already had been taken up, the [townsfolk] take an oath to the Temple revenuers.

E. And if not, they take an oath before the [other] townsfolk, and the [other] townsfolk pay the *sheqel* in their stead.

F. [If the *sheqels*] were found, or the robbers returned them, both these [coins, paid by the other townsfolk] and those [coins, originally put forth] are in the status *of sheqels*.

G. And they do not go to their credit for the coming year.

6.1 A. (1) Thirteen *shofar* chests, (2) thirteen tables, [and] (3) thirteen acts of prostration were in the sanctuary.

B. The members of the household of Rabban Gamaliel and the members of the household of R. Hananiah, Prefect of the Priests, would do fourteen prostrations.

C. And where was the additional one?

D. Toward the woodshed,

E. for so did they have a tradition) from their forebears that there the ark was stored away.

5 A. Thirteen *shofar* chests were in the sanctuary.

B. And written on them were the following [in Aramaic]:

C. (1) "New *sheqels*" and (2) "old *sheqels*,"

D. (3) "bird offerings," and (4) "young birds for a burnt offering"; (5) "wood" and (6) "frankincense"; (7) "gold for the Mercy seat," and on six, "for freewill offerings."

E. *New sheqels*—those for each year [that is, for the present year].

F. *Old sheqels*—He who did not pay his *sheqel* last year pays his *sheqel* in the coming year.

G. *Bird offerings—these* are for turtledoves.

H. *Young birds for a burnt offering*—these are for pigeons.

I. "And all of them [of D3, 4] are burnt offerings," the words of R. Judah.

J. And sages say, "*Bird offerings*—one is offered as a sin offering and one as a burnt offering [as at Qinnim, for a sin offering].

K. *"Young birds for the whole offering*—all of them are burnt offerings."

m. Sukkah 5.1–4* *I am the Light*

This passage from *m. Sukkah* reveals the great rejoicing that went on all night long. Note the reference to candleholders and, thus, to light that was prominently associated with this feast.

1 A. Flute playing is for five or six days:

B. This refers to the flute playing on *bet hashshoebah*,

C. which overrides the restrictions of neither the Sabbath nor of a festival day.

D. They said: Anyone who has not seen the rejoicing of *bet hashshoebah* in his life has never seen rejoicing.

2 A. At the end of the first festival day of the Festival [the priests and Levites] went down to the women's courtyard.

B. And they made a major enactment [by putting men below and women above].

C. And there were golden candleholders there, with four gold bowls on their tops, and four ladders for each candlestick.

D. And four young priests with jars of oil containing a hundred and twenty *logs*, [would climb up the ladders and] pour [the oil] into each bowl.

³A. Out of the worn-out undergarments and girdles of the priests they made wicks,

B. and with them they lit the candlesticks.

C. And there was not a courtyard in Jerusalem which was not lit up from the light of *bet hashshoebah*.

⁴A. The pious men and wonder workers would dance before them with flaming torches in their hand,

B. and they would sing before them songs and praises.

C. And the Levites beyond counting played on harps, lyres, cymbals, trumpets, and [other] musical instruments,

D. [standing, as they played] on the fifteen steps which go down from the Israelites' court to the women's court—

E. corresponding to the fifteen Songs of Ascents which are in the Book of Psalms—

F. on these the Levites stand with their instruments and sing their song.

G. And two priests stood at the upper gate which goes down from the Israelites' court to the women's court, with two trumpets in their hands.

H. [When] the cock crowed, they sounded a sustained, a quavering, and a sustained note on the *shofar*.

I. [When] they got to the tenth step, they sounded a sustained, a quavering, and a sustained blast on the *shofar*.

J. [When] they reached the courtyard, they sounded a sustained, a quavering, and a sustained blast on the *shofar*.

K. They went on sounding the *shofar* in a sustained blast until they reached the gate which leads out to the east.

L. [When] they reached the gate which goes out toward the east, they turned around toward the west,

M. and they said, "Our fathers who were in this place *turned with their backs toward the Temple of the Lord and their faces toward the east, and they worshipped the sun toward the east* (Ez. 8:16).

N. "But as to us, our eyes are to the Lord."

O. R. Judah says, "They said it a second time, 'We belong to the Lord, our eyes are toward the Lord.' "

Wisdom of Solomon 18:3–4

In this text from Wisdom 18, God's instruction in the law is regarded as "giving light."

³Therefore you provided a flaming pillar of fire as a guide for your people's unknown journey, and a harmless sun for their glorious wandering. ⁴For their enemies deserved to be deprived of light and imprisoned in darkness, those who had kept your children imprisoned, through whom the imperishable light of the law was to be given to the world.

The imagery of light is used in an ethical way in the following citations from Qumran.

1QS 2.3; 3.7–8, 20–21

²·³And may he protect you from everything bad. May he illuminate your heart with the discernment of life and grace you with eternal knowledge.

³·⁷And by the spirit of holiness which links him with his truth he is cleansed of all ⁸his sins. . . . ²⁰In the hand of the Prince of Lights is dominion over all the sons of justice; they walk on paths of light. And in the hand of the Angel ²¹of Darkness is total dominion over the sons of deceit; they walk on paths of darkness. . . .

m. ʾAbot 4.8*

In this passage from m. ʾAbot, Rabbi Ishmael argues that no one should judge alone, for only God can judge alone.

A. He would say, "Do not serve as a judge by yourself, for there is only One who serves as a judge all alone.

B. "And do not say, 'Accept my opinion.'

C. "For they have the choice in that matter, not you."

Josephus, Jewish War 7.8.6 §323

According to Josephus, the Jews denied ever serving Rome, but instead served only God.

Since we, long ago, my generous friends, resolved never to be servants to the Romans, nor to any other than to God himself, who alone is the true and just Lord of mankind, the time is now come that obliges us to make that resolution true in practice.

b. Šabbat 128ᵃ*

In this text, it is claimed that the Jews are royal children.

Abaye said: R. Simeon b. Gamaliel, R. Simeon, R. Ishmael, and R. Akiba, all hold that all Israel are royal children. "R. Simeon R. Gamaliel," as stated. "R. Simeon": for we learned: Royal children may anoint their wounds with oil, since it is their practice to anoint themselves thus on weekdays. R. Simeon said: All Israel are royal children. "R. Ishmael and R. Akiba": for it was taught: If one is a debtor for a thousand zuz, and wears a robe a hundred manehs in value, he is stripped of it and robed with a garment that is fitting for him. It was taught in the name of R. Ishmael, and it was taught in the name of R. Akiba: All Israel are worthy of that robe.

Both of the following texts affirm that in Genesis 15 Abraham had a vision concerning the future of Israel and the Messiah.

Genesis Rabbah 44 (28a)*

Behold a smoking furnace and a flaming torch. Simeon b. Abba said in R. Johanan's same: He [God] showed him four things, viz. Gehenna, the [foreign] kingdoms, Revelation, and the Temple, with the promise: As long as your children occupy themselves with the latter two, they will be saved from the former two; if they neglect the latter two they will be punished by the former two. Would you rather that your children descend into Gehenna or into the power of the [foreign] kingdoms? He asked him. R. Hinena b. Papa said: Abraham himself chose (subjection to foreign) powers. R. Judan, R. Idi, and R. Hama b. R. Hanina said: Abraham chose Gehenna, but the Holy One blessed be He, chose [subjection to foreign] powers for him.

Mekilta de Rabbi Ishmael on Exodus 20:18 (78b)*

R. Nathan says: Whence can you prove that God showed to our father Abraham Gehenna, the giving of the Law, and the division of the Red Sea? From the passage: "And it came to pass, that, when the sun went down, and there was thick darkness, behold a smoking furnace, and flaming torch that passed between these pieces" (Gen. 15:17). "A smoking furnace" refers to Gehenna, as it is said: "And His furnace in Jerusalem" (Isa. 31:9). "And a flaming torch," refers to the giving of the Law, as it is said: "And all the people saw the thunderings and the lightnings." "That passed between these pieces," refers to the division of the Red Sea, as it is said: "To Him who divided the Red Sea into parts"

(Ps. 136.13). He also showed him the Temple with the order of sacrifices. For it is said: "And he said unto him: 'Take me a heifer of three years old,'" etc. (Gen 15.9). He also showed him the four kingdoms that would in the future oppress his children. For it is said: "And it came to pass, that, when the sun was going down, a deep sleep fell upon Abram, and, lo, a dread, even a great darkness, was falling upon" (Gen. 15:12).

13.15 The Sixth Sign: Healing of the Man Born Blind—Jesus, the Light of the World (John 9:1–41) (JaS J19)

Two texts record the tradition that sin causes death and suffering. *Ruth Rabbah* 6.4 teaches that the early death of a scholar can be blamed on his mother's engaging in idolatry during her pregnancy. The other text appears below.

b. Sanhedrin 55ᵃ*

There is no death without sin, and there is no suffering without iniquity.

m. Šabbat 7.2; 24.3; 14.4*

These texts from *m. Šabbat* show that the Jews were not permitted to knead bread on the Sabbath. The text of *m. Šabbat* 7.2 appears in section 4.8 above. According to *m. Šabbat* 14.4, which appears in section 4.9 above, most anointings were prohibited on the Sabbath.

²⁴·³A. They do not stuff food into a camel or cram it [into its mouth].

B. But they put food into its mouth.

C. And they do not fatten calves [with food against their will], but they put food into their mouths [in the normal way].

D. And they force-feed chickens.

E. They put water into the bran, but they do not knead it.

F. And they do not put water before bees or doves which are in dovecotes.

G. But they do put it before geese, chickens, and Herodian doves.

t. Sanhedrin 12.10*

In this passage, it is asserted that anyone who utters charms over a wound or utilizes spit has no place in the world to come.

A. R. 'Aqiba, says, "He who warbles the Song of Songs in a banquet-hall and makes it into a kind of love-song has no portion in the world to come,"

B. Abba Saul says in the name of R. 'Aqiba, "Also *he who whispers over a wound, 'It is written, I will put none of the diseases upon you which I have put on the Egyptians, for I am the Lord who heals you.'* (Ex. 15:26) [M. San. 10:1F], and who [then] spits, has no portion in the world to come."

b. ʿAbodah Zarah 28ᵇ*

This text reveals a debate about the permissibility of anointing eyes on the Sabbath.

Said R. Zutra b. Tobiah in the name of Rab: If one's eye gets out of order, it is permissible to paint it on the Sabbath. He was understood to be of opinion that this only holds good when the medical ingredients had been ground the previous day, but if it is necessary to grind them on the Sabbath and carry them through a public road, it would not be permitted; but one of the Rabbis, R. Jacob by name, remarked to him: It was made plain to me on behalf of Rab Judah that even grinding on the Sabbath and the carrying through the public street are permissible.

Rab Judah declared it as permissible to paint the eye on the Sabbath. Whereupon R. Samuel b. Judah said: He who acts according to Judah profanes the Sabbath. After some time when he himself had a sore eye he sent to ask of Rab Judah: Is it permitted or forbidden? He sent back [the following reply:] "To everyone else it is permitted—but to you it is forbidden. Was it on my own authority [that I permitted it?] It was on that of Mar Samuel." It once happened to a maid-servant in Mar Samuel's house that her eye became inflamed on a Sabbath; she cried, but no one attended her and her eye dropped. On the morrow Mar Samuel went forth and propounded that if one's eye gets out of order it is permissible to paint it on the Sabbath, the reason being because the eyesight is connected with the mental faculties.

The following four texts from the Mishnah describe how one was put out of the synagogue.

m. Taᶜanit 3.8*

A. On account of every sort of public trouble (may it not happen) do they sound the *shofar*,

B. except for an excess of rain.

C. MᶜSH S: They said to Honi, the circle drawer, "Pray for rain."

D. He said to them, "Go and take in the clay ovens used for Passover, so that they not soften [in the rain which is coming]."

E. He prayed, but it did not rain.

F. What did he do?

G. He drew a circle and stood in the middle of it and said before Him, "Lord of the world! Your children have turned to me, for before you I am like a member of the family. I swear by your great name—I'm simply not moving from here until you take pity on your children!"

H. It began to rain drop by drop.

I. He said, "This is not what I wanted, but rain for filling up cisterns, pits, and caverns."

J. It began to rain violently.

K. He said, "This is not what I wanted, but rain of good will, blessing, and graciousness."

L. Now it rained the right way, until Israelites had to flee from Jerusalem up to the Temple Mount because of the rain.

M. Now they came and said to him, "Just as you prayed for it to rain, now pray for it to go away."

N. He said to them, "Go, see whether the stone of the strayers is disappeared."

O. Simeon b. Shatah said to him, "If you were not Honi, I should decree a ban of excommunication against you. But what am I going to do to you? For you importune before the Omnipresent, so he does what you want, like a son who importunes his father, so he does what he wants.

P. "Concerning you Scripture says, *Let your father and your mother be glad, and let her that bore you rejoice* (Prov. 23:25)."

m. Nedarim 1.1*

A. All substitutes for [language used to express] (1) vows are equivalent to vows, and for (2) bans (*herem*) are equivalent to bans, and for (3) oaths are equivalent to oaths, and for (4) Nazirite vows are equivalent to Nazirite vows.

B. He who says to his fellow, (1) "I am forbidden by vow from you," (2) "I am separated from you," (3) "I am distanced from you,"

C. "if I eat your [food]," [or] "if I taste your [food],"

D. is bound [by such a vow].

E. [He who says,] "I am excommunicated from you"—

F. R. Aqiba in this case did incline to impose a stringent ruling.

G. [He who says], "As the vows of the evil folk . . . ," has made a binding vow in the case of a Nazir, or in the case of [bringing] an offering, or in the case of an oath.

H. [He who says,] "As the vows of the suitable folk" has said nothing whatsoever.

I. "As their [suitable folks'] free will offerings" he has made a binding vow in the case of a Nazir or in the case of [bringing] an offering.

m. ʿEduyyot 5.6*

A. Aqabia b. Mahalalel gave testimony in four matters.

B. They said to him, "Aqabia, retract the four rulings which you laid down, and we shall make you patriarch of the court of Israel."

C. He said to them, "It is better for me to be called a fool my whole life but not be deemed a wicked person before the Omnipresent for even one minute,

D. "so that people should not say, 'Because he craved after high office, he retracted.' "

I E. He would declare unclean residual hair [in a leprosy sign] and

II green blood [of a vaginal discharge].

F. And sages declare clean.

III G. He would permit use of the wool which fell out in the case of a firstling which was blemished, and which one put away in a niche, (and [which firstling] one afterward slaughtered.

H. And sages prohibit.

IV I. He would say, "They do not administer bitter water [to test the woman accused of adultery] in the case of a proselyte woman or in the case of a freed slave girl."

J. And sages say, "They do administer the test."

K. They said to him, MʿSH B: "Karkemit, a freed slave girl, was in Jerusalem, and Shemaiah and Abtalion administered the bitter water to her."

L. He said to them, "They administered it to her to make her into an example."

M. They excommunicated him, and he died while he was subject to the excommunication, so the court stoned his bier.

N. Said R. Judah, "God forbid that Aqabia was excommunicated!

O. "For the courtyard is never locked before any Israelite of the wisdom and fear of sin of a man like Aqabia b. Mahalalel.

P. "But whom did they excommunicate? It was Eliezer b. Hanokh, who cast doubt on [the sages' ruling about] the cleanness of hands.

Q. "And when he died, the court sent and put a stone on his bier."

R. This teaches that whoever is excommunicated and dies while he is subject to the excommunication— they stone his bier.

m. Middot 2.2*

A. All those who enter the Temple mount enter at the right, go around, and leave at the left,

B. except for him to whom something happened, who goes around to the left.

C. "What ails you, that you go around to the left?"

D. "For I am a mourner."

E. "May he who dwells in this house comfort you."

F. "That I am excommunicated."

G. " 'May he who dwells in this house put it into their heart that they draw you nigh again,'" the words of R. Meir.

H. Said to him R. Yose, "You have treated the matter as if they have transgressed the law on his account.

I. "But: 'May he who dwells in this house put it into your heart that you listen to the opinion of your fellows, and they draw you nigh again.'"

Shemoneh Esreh, *benediction 12**

This citation shows how judgment was prayed for against those deemed unrighteous.

And for informers let there be no hope; and let all who do wickedness quickly perish; and let them be speedily destroyed; and uproot and crush and hurl down and humble the insolent, speedily in our days. *Blessed are you, Lord, who crushes enemies and humbles the insolent.*

13.16 Jesus, the Good Shepherd with a New Flock (John 10:1–21) (*JaS* J20)

m. Baba Meṣiᶜa 7.9*

In this Mishnah text, a shepherd is supposed to protect the sheep from wolves, but if more than one at a time comes, an "unavoidable accident" might occur.

I A. A single wolf does not count as an unavoidable accident.

B. Two wolves are regarded as an unavoidable accident.

C. R. Judah says, "In a time that wolves come in packs, even a single wolf is an unavoidable accident."

II D. Two dogs do not count as an unavoidable accident.

E. Yadua the Babylonian says in the name of R. Meir, "[If] they come from one direction, they do not count as an unavoidable accident.

F. "If they come from two directions, they count as an unavoidable accident."

III G. A thug—lo, he counts as an unavoidable accident.

IV H. (1) A lion, (2) wolf, (3) leopard, (4) panther, or (5) snake—lo, these count as an unavoidable accident.

I. Under what circumstances?

J. When they come along on their own.

K. But if he took [the sheep] to a place in which there were bands of wild animals or thugs,

L. these do not constitute unavoidable accidents.

13.17 Jesus Declares His Unity with the Father at the Feast of Dedication (John 10:22–42) (*JaS* J21)

1 Maccabees 4:52–59

This text from 1 Maccabees 4 describes the Jewish purification of the temple after the three-year Maccabean revolt.

[52]Early in the morning on the twenty-fifth day of the ninth month, which is the month of Chislev, in the one hundred forty-eighth year, [53]they rose and offered sacrifice, as the law directs, on the new altar of burnt offering that they had built. [54]At the very season and on the very day that the Gentiles had profaned it, it was dedicated with songs and harps and lutes and cymbals. [55]All the people fell on their faces and worshiped and blessed Heaven, who had prospered them. [56]So they celebrated the dedication of the altar for eight days, and joyfully offered burnt offerings; they offered a sacrifice of well-being and a thanksgiving offering. [57]They decorated the front of the temple with golden crowns and

small shields; they restored the gates and the chambers for the priests, and fitted them with doors. [58]There was very great joy among the people, and the disgrace brought by the Gentiles was removed.

[59]Then Judas and his brothers and all the assembly of Israel determined that every year at that season the days of dedication of the altar should be observed with joy and gladness for eight days, beginning with the twenty-fifth day of the month of Chislev.

13.18 The Seventh Sign: Jesus Shows His Power over Life—The Raising of Lazarus and the Jewish Reaction (John 11:1–54) (JaS J22)

Leviticus Rabbah 18.1 and *Ecclesiastes Rabbah* 12.6 both affirm that on the fourth day after death there was no hope for a person to return to life.

Leviticus Rabbah 18.1*

R. Abba b. R. Pappai and R. Joshua of Siknin said in the name of R. Levi: For three days [after death] the soul hovers over the body, intending to re-enter it, but as soon as it sees its appearance change, it departs, as it is written, *When his flesh that is on him is distorted, his soul will mourn over him* (Job 14:22). Bar Kappara said: The full force of mourning lasts for three days. Why? Because [for that length of time] the shape of the face is recognizable, even as we have learnt in the Mishnah: Evidence [to prove a man's death] is admissible only in respect of the full face, with the nose, and only [by one who has seen the corpse] within three days [after death].

Ecclesiastes Rabbah 12.6*

And the pitcher is broken at the fountain: i.e. a man's stomach. Three days after [death] a man's stomach bursts and gives back [its contents] to the mouth saying, "Take what you stole and robbed with violence and placed in me." R. Haggai derived the thought from this verse, *I will spread dung upon your faces, even the dung of your sacrifices* (Mal. 2:3). Bar Kappara said: The full intensity of mourning lasts up to the third day because the appearance of the face is still recognizable, for we have learnt: Evidence [of identity] may be legally tendered only on [proof afforded by] the full face with the nose, etc.

m. Yebamot 16.3*

According to *m. Yebamot* 16.3, a person is identifiable until three days after death.

I A. They derive testimony [concerning the identity of a corpse] only from the appearance of the whole face with the nose,

B. even though there are signs of the corpse's identity on his body or garments.

II C. They derive testimony [that a man has died] only after he has actually died [and has been seen dead],

D. and even if they [the witnesses] saw him mortally wounded, crucified, or being eaten by a wild beast.

III E. They give testimony [about the identity of a corpse] only during a period of three days [after death].

F. R. Judah b. Baba says, "[Decay in corpses] is not alike for all men, all places, and all times."

m. Šabbat 23.4–5*

M. *Šabbat* 23.4–5, which appears in section 6.2 above, indicates that there were times when the need for a quick burial overrode any other law concerning rest on the Sabbath.

m. Ketubbot 4.4*

Even a poor family, according to this mishnaic text appearing in section 6.6 above, ought to "hire no fewer than two flutes and one professional wailing woman" for a funeral.

The reference to "the holy place" in the following two citations is literally "the place" and may refer to Jerusalem with special focus on the temple.

m. Bikkurim 2.2*

A. There are [restrictions which apply] to [second] tithe and to firstfruits which [do] not [apply] to heave offering.

B. For [second] tithe and firstfruits

C. (1) require bringing [to the] place [Jerusalem];

D. (2) and they require [the recitation of the appropriate] confession;

E. (3) and they are prohibited [for consumption] by a mourner [whose dead relative has not yet been buried; Dt. 26:14, M. M.S. 5:8].

F. R. Simeon permits [such mourners to eat firstfruits].

G. (4) And they are subject to [the law of] removal [Dt. 26:12ff., M. M.S. 5:6].

H. R. Simeon exempts [firstfruits from the law of removal] (T. Bik. 1:7, M. M.S. 5:6).

I. (5) And in Jerusalem—[if they are mixed with unconsecrated produce] in any [portion], they [still] are forbidden for consumption [M. Or. 2:1],

J. (6) and in Jerusalem—[if they are used as seed], that which grows from them is prohibited for consumption,

K. [and this prohibition applies] also to commoners [in the case of firstfruits] and to cattle [in the case of second tithe].

L. R. Simeon permits [the consumption, by commoners or cattle, of that which is mixed in Jerusalem with second tithe or firstfruits and that which grows in Jerusalem from second tithe or firstfruits].

M. Lo, these [are restrictions which apply] to [second] tithe and to firstfruits which [do] not [apply] to heave offering.

2 Maccabees 5:19

But the Lord did not choose the nation for the sake of the holy place, but the place for the sake of the nation.

Josephus, Antiquities 11.8.4 §§324–327

The belief that a high priest might utter a prophetic word, as in the case of Caiaphas, was not uncommon in Israel. In this text from Josephus, Jaddua foresaw Alexander the Great's sparing of Jerusalem.

324Whereupon Alexander gave Sanballat leave so to do; who used the utmost diligence, and built the temple, and made Manasseh the priest, and deemed it a great reward that his daughter's children should have that dignity; 325but when the seven months of the siege of Tyre were over, and the two months of the siege of Gaza, Sanballat died. Now Alexander, when he had taken Gaza, made haste to go up to Jerusalem; 326and Jaddua the high priest, when he heard that, was in an agony, and under terror, as not knowing how he should meet the Macedonians, since the king was displeased at his foregoing disobedience. He therefore ordained that the people should make supplications, and should join with him in offering sacrifices to God, whom he besought to protect that nation, and to deliver them from the perils that were coming upon them; 327whereupon God warned him in a dream, which came upon him after he had offered sacrifice, that he should take courage, and adorn the city, and open the gates; that the rest appear in white garments, but that he and the priests should meet the king in the habits proper to their order, without the dread of any ill consequences, which the providence of God would prevent.

Josephus, Antiquities 13.10.7 §299

Note in this passage that the high priest John Hyrcanus prophesied.

But when Hyrcanus had put an end to this sedition, he after that lived happily, and administered the government in the best manner for thirty-one years, and then died, leaving behind him five sons. He was esteemed by God worthy of the three privileges,— the government of his nation, the dignity of the high priesthood, and prophecy.

b. Soṭah 12ᵇ*

In this passage from b. Soṭah 12ᵇ, Pharaoh's daughter "unwittingly" prophesied about Moses.

And the daughter of Pharaoh came down to bathe at the river. R. Johanan said in the name of R. Simeon b. Yohai: It teaches that she went down there to cleanse herself of her father's idols; and thus it says: When the Lord shall have washed away the filth of the daughters of Zion etc. And her maidens walked along etc. R. Johanan said: The word for "walk" means nothing else than death; and thus it says: Behold I am going to die. And she saw the ark among the reeds. When [the maidens] saw that she wished to rescue Moses, they said to her, "Mistress, it is the custom of the world that when a human king makes a decree, though

everybody else does not obey it, at least his children and the members of his household obey it; but you transgress your father's decree!" Gabriel came and beat them to the ground.

And sent her handmaid to fetch it—R. Judah and R. Nehemiah [differ in their interpretation]; one said that the word means "her hand" and the other said that it means "her handmaid." He who said that it means "her hand" did so because it is written ammathah; he who said that it means "her handmaid" did so because the text has not yadah [her hand]. But according to him who said that it means "her handmaid," it has just been stated that Gabriel came and beat them to the ground!—He left her one, because it is not customary for a king's daughter to be unattended. But according to him who said that it means "her hand," the text should have been yadah!—It teaches us that [her arm] became lengthened; for a master has said: You find it so with the arm of Pharaoh's daughter and similarly with the teeth of the wicked, as it is written: You have broken [shibbarta] the teeth of the wicked, and Resh Lakish said: Read not shibbarta but shirbabta [you have lengthened].

She opened it and saw the child—it should have been "and saw." R. Jose b. R. Hanina said: She saw the Shechinah with him.

And, behold, the boy wept—he is called a "child" and then a "boy"!—A Tanna taught: He was a child but his voice was like that of a grown boy; such is the view of R. Judah. R. Nehemiah said to him, If so, you have made our master Moses into one possessed of a blemish; but it teaches that his mother made for him a canopy [such as is used at the marriage] of boys in the ark, saying: "Perhaps I may not be worthy [to be present at] his marriage-canopy."

And she had compassion on him and said: Of the Hebrews' children is this. How did she know it?—R. Jose b. R. Hanina said: Because she saw that he was circumcised. "Is this"—R. Johanan said: It teaches that she unwittingly prophesied that "this" one will fall [into the river] but no other will fall. That is what R. Eleazar said: What means the text: And when they shall say unto you, Seek unto them that have familiar spirits and unto the wizards, that chirp and that mutter? They foresee and know not what they foresee; they mutter and know not what they mutter. They saw that Israel's savior would be punished through water; so they arose and decreed, Every son that is born ye shall cast into the river. After they had thrown Moses [into the water], they said: "We do not see that sign any longer"; they thereupon rescinded their decree. But they knew not that he was to be punished through the water of Meribah. That is what R. Hama b. Hanina said: What means the text: These are the waters of Meribah, because they strove? These are [the waters] about which Pharaoh's magicians saw and erred; and concerning this Moses said: Six hundred thousand footmen etc. Moses said to Israel, "On my account were all of you delivered [from drowning by the edict of Pharaoh]."

b. Baba Batra 119[a–b]*

In this text from the Talmud, "unconscious prophecy" is ascribed to Moses and Israel.

An objection was raised: R. Hidka said: "Simeon of Shikmona was my companion among the disciples of R. Akiba. And thus did R. Simeon of Shikmona say: Moses our Master knew that the daughters of Zelophehad were to be heiresses, but he did not know whether or not they were to take the portion of the birthright—And it was fitting that the [Scriptural] section of the laws of succession should have been written through Moses, but the daughters of Zelophehad merited it, and it was written through them. Moses, furthermore, knew that the man who gathered sticks [on the Sabbath day] was to he put to death, for it is said, Everyone that profanes it shall surely be put to death, but he did not know by which [kind of] death he was to die. And it was fitting that the section of the man who gathered sticks should have been written through Moses, only the gatherer had brought guilt upon himself, and it was written through him. This teaches you that merit is brought about by means of the meritorious and punishment for guilt by means of the guilty. Now, if it be assumed [that] the land of Israel was [regarded as being even before the conquest] in the possession [of those who came out of Egypt], why was he in doubt?—He was in doubt on this very [question]: It is written, and I will give it you for a heritage, I am the Lord, [does this mean]. 'it is for you an inheritance from your fathers' or perhaps [it means] that they would transmit [it] but would not [themselves] he heirs? And it was made clear to him [that the text implies] both: 'It is an inheritance for you from your fathers; yet you would [only] transmit, and not [yourselves] inherit [it].' And this accounts for the Scriptural text, You bring them in, and plant them in the mountain of your inheritance. It is not written, 'You bring us in', but 'You bring them in'; this teaches that they prophesied a nd knew not what they prophesied."

Midrash Psalms *90* §4*

In this text, it is argued that no prophet understood what he prophesied except Moses and Isaiah.

R. Eleazar taught in the name of R. Jose ben Zimra: None of the Prophets, as they uttered their prophecies, knew that they were prophesying, except Moses and Isaiah who did know. Thus Moses said: *My doctrine shall drop as rain* (Deut. 32:1); and Isaiah said: *Behold, I and the children whom the Lord has given me shall be for signs and for wonders in Israel* (Isa. 8:18).

R. Joshua the Priest bar Nehemiah maintained that Elihu also prophesied and knew he was prophesying, for (he said: *My lips shall utter knowledge clearly* (Job 33:3).

R. Eleazar taught in the name of R. Jose ben Zimra: Samuel, the master of prophets, as he uttered his prophecy did not know he was prophesying, as is said *And the Lord sent Jerubbaal, and Bedan, and Jephthah, and Samuel* (1 Sam. 12:11). Samuel did not say "The Lord sent . . . me" but *The Lord sent . . . Samuel,* for he did not know what he was prophesying.

Josephus, Jewish War 4.9.9 §551

Josephus mentions Ephraim here. Most scholars locate it near El-Tayibeh.

So he went up to the mountainous country, and took those two toparchies that were called the Gophnitick and Acrabattene toparchies. After which he took Bethel and Ephraim, two small cities; and when he had put garrisons into them, he rode as far as Jerusalem, in which march he took many prisoners, and many captives.

13.19 The Anointing at Bethany and Opposition Near Passover Time (John 11:55–12:11) (*JaS* J23)

Josephus, Jewish War 1.11.6 §229

According to this text in *Jewish War,* Jews who were purifying themselves should not mix with Gentiles (foreigners) lest they become impure or unclean.

So Herod went to Samaria, which was then in a tumult, and settled the city in peace; after which, at the [Pentecost] festival, he returned to Jerusalem, having his armed men with him; hereupon Hyrcanus, at the request of Malichus, who feared his approach, forbade them to introduce foreigners to mix themselves with the people of the country, while they were purifying themselves; but Herod despised the pretense, and him that gave that command, and came in by night.

13.20 Jesus Enters Jerusalem at Passover (John 12:12–19) (*JaS* J24)

1 Maccabees 13:51

Similar to Jesus' entry into Jerusalem, people spread palm leaves on the ground for Simon of Maccabees when he triumphed over the Syrians.

On the twenty-third day of the second month, in the one hundred seventy-first year, the Jews entered it with praise and palm branches, and with harps and cymbals and stringed instruments, and with hymns and songs, because a great enemy had been crushed and removed from Israel.

2 Maccabees 10:7

According to 2 Maccabees 10:7, palm leaves were used at the rededication of the temple.

Therefore, carrying ivy-wreathed wands and beautiful branches and also fronds of palm, they offered hymns of thanksgiving to him who had given success to the purifying of his own holy place.

13.21 The Son of Man to Be Lifted Up Issues an Explanation and a Warning (John 12:20–50) (*JaS* J25)

In these two texts from *1 Enoch*, reference is made to an extremely exalted role for "the Son of Man" at the end of time. The same is true for the "messianic figure" in *Psalms of Solomon* 17–18.

1 Enoch *49.1; 62.14*

49.1So wisdom flows like water and glory is measureless before him forever and ever.

62.14The Lord of the Spirits will abide over them; they shall eat and rest and rise with that Son of Man forever and ever.

Psalms of Solomon *17–18*

See section 9.17 above.

4 Ezra (= *2 Esdras) 7:27–29*

This text seems to represent another strand in Judaism, which believed that although the Messiah has an exalted role, he does not live or reign forever but perishes after approximately four hundred years.

27Everyone who has been delivered from the evils that I have foretold shall see my wonders. 28For my son the Messiah shall be revealed with those who are with him, and those who remain shall rejoice four hundred years. 29After those years my son the Messiah shall die, and all who draw human breath.

14.1 Jesus Washes the Disciples' Feet (John 13:1–20) (JaS J26)

Mekilta de Rabbi Ishmael 1 on Exodus 21:1–3*

Although generally regarded as an act too menial for even a Hebrew slave, foot washing is here proposed as a humble service that perhaps a son or pupil may perform.

Six Years He Shall Serve. I might understand this to mean in any kind of service, but Scripture says: "You shall not make him to serve as a bondservant" (Lev. 25:39). Hence the sages said: A Hebrew slave must not wash the feet of his master, nor put his shoes on him, nor carry his things before when going to the bathhouse, nor support him by the hips when ascending the steps, nor carry him a litter or a chair or a sedan chair as slaves do. For it is said: "But over your brothers the children of Israel you shall not rule, one over another, with rigor" (Ibid. v. 46). But one's son or pupil may do so.

y. Peʾah 1.15c.14*

In this passage from the Jerusalem Talmud, a woman takes her son, Rabbi Ishmael, before a rabbinic court because he would not allow her to wash his feet. He thought it too demeaning, but she regarded it as an opportunity to honor her son. In the end, the court sides with the mother.

[I] [The Talmud now cites two parallel stories (I–J, K + L–N) as further evidence of the lengths to which one must go in honor of father and mother. R. Tarfon's mother went down for a walk in her courtyard on the Sabbath. (Her slipper came off, and she would not retie it, because that would be a violation of Sabbath laws.) R. Tarfon [not wanting his mother's feet to become sore,] went and placed his two hands under her feet, so that she could walk upon them all the way to her couch.

[J] Some time later, [R. Tarfon] became ill, and the sages came in to visit him. [His mother] said to them, "Pray for Tarfon my son, for he treats me with far too much respect!" They said to her, "What did he do for you?" She told them [the foregoing] story. They said to her, "Even if he were to do so thousands of thousands [of times], still he would not attain even half [the measure] that the Torah commands [for honor of one's mother]!"

[K] R. Ishmael's mother came and complained against [her son] before our rabbis. She said to them, "Rebuke Ishmael my son, for he does not treat me with respect!" At that moment our rabbis' faces flushed [with embarrassment]. They thought, "Is it possible

237

that R. Ishmael would not treat his parents with respect?" [So] they said to her, "What did he do to you?" She said, "When he left the [scholars'] meeting place I wanted to wash his feet and drink the water, but he wouldn't let me, [thereby showing me disrespect]!" They said to [Ishmael], "Since this is her wish, this is [what you must do as a mode of] honoring her."

14.2 Jesus Foretells His Betrayal (John 13:21–30; Matt. 26:21–25; Mark 14:18–21; Luke 22:21–23) (JaS J27)

The following two texts from the Mishnah record the disputed practice of working right up until the Sabbath begins. There seems to have been different customs in different parts of Israel.

m. Pesaḥim 4.5*

V A. Where they are accustomed to do work on the ninth of Ab, they do it.

B. Where they are accustomed not to do work, they do not do it.

C. And in every place disciples of sages refrain [from labor].

D. Rabban Simeon b. Gamaliel says, "Under all circumstances should a man act on his own like a disciple of a sage."

E. And sages say, "In Judah they did work on the eve of Passover up to noon, but in Galilee they did not do so at all."

F. And as to the night [before the fourteenth of Nisan],

G. the House of Shammai prohibit [doing work at that time].

H. And the House of Hillel permit—

I. up to sunrise.

m. Šabbat 23.1*

A. A man [on the Sabbath] asks for jugs of wine or oil from his fellow,

B. provided that he does not say to him, "Lend [them] to me."

C. And so a woman [borrows] loaves of bread from her neighbor.

D. And if one does not trust the other, he leaves his cloak with him and settles with him after the Sabbath.

E. And so is the case on the eve of Passover in Jerusalem when that day coincides with the Sabbath:

F. One leaves his cloak with him and takes his Passover lamb and settles with him after the festival.

m. Pesaḥim 9.11*

This text from m. Pesaḥim may refer to inviting/registering others to share in the Passover.

A. Two people whose Passover offerings were confused—

B. this one takes possession of one of the animals, and that one takes possession of one of the animals.

C. This one registers with himself a third party, and that one registers with himself a third party.

D. This one approaches that, and that one approaches this, and thus do they declare:

E. "If this Passover offering is mine, then you withdraw from yours and register with mine. And if this Passover offering is yours, then I withdraw from mine and register with yours."

Josephus, Antiquities 18.2.2 §§29–30

This text seems to indicate that the Jews were accustomed to allowing Samaritans to enter the temple area during the Passover, until, of course, the Samaritans allegedly committed sacrilege.

²⁹As Coponius, who we told you was sent along with Cyrenius, was exercising his office of procurator, and governing Judea, the following accidents happened. As the Jews were celebrating the feast of unleavened bread, which we call the Passover, it was customary for the priests to open the temple gates just after midnight. ³⁰When, therefore, those gates were first opened, some of the Samaritans came privately into Jerusalem, and threw about dead men's bodies in the cloisters; on which account the Jews afterward excluded them out of the temple, which they had not used to do at such festivals; and on other accounts also they watched the temple more carefully than they had formerly done.

14.3 The Promised Spirit, Love, and Obedience (John 14:15–26) (JaS J30)

Leviticus Rabbah 6.1 on Leviticus 5:1*

This passage from *Leviticus Rabbah* speaks about giving testimony/defense on behalf of another and that when such "witness" is promised it ought to be given and not withheld.

R. Aha said: That [Scriptural passage] represents the Holy Spirit as [Israel's] defender, addressing an appeal first to one and then to another. It says to Israel, *"Be not a witness . . . without cause"* [i.e. a false witness], and afterwards it says to the Holy One, blessed be He, *"Say not: I will do to him as he has done to Me."*

R. Isaac said, It is written, But they like men have transgressed the covenant (Hosea 6:7); [that refers to Israel], but here, [as for You, O God, You have said]: / will not execute the fiercest of

My anger . . . for I am God, and not man (ib. 9:9).

Reuben knew some evidence in favor of Simeon. Said Simeon to him: "Will you come and give this evidence for me?" He answered: "Yes." When he went before the Judge, Reuben withdrew. To the latter does the Holy Spirit say: *"Deceive not with your lips"*; after you beguiled him with your lips, and let him go to Court, you withdrew. On the morrow there arises occasion for Simeon to give evidence on behalf of Reuben. Should Simeon do as Reuben had done to him? [To this the Holy Spirit replies]: *"Say not: I will do to him as he has done to me; I will render to the man according to his deed,"* for the Torah has already given the decree: . . . HE BEING A WITNESS, WHETHER HE HAS SEEN OR KNOWN, IF HE DO NOT UTTER IT, THEN HE SHALL BEAR HIS INIQUITY.

14.4 Hatred of the World (John 15:18–25) (JaS J34)

Psalms of Solomon 7.1

In this text, the writer cries out to God for help against those who have hated the Jews without cause. *PS*

Do not move away from us [i.e., Israel as opposed to Gentiles], O God, lest those who hate us without cause should attack us.

14.5 On Persecutions (John 16:1–4) (JaS J36)

Scandalon

The following three passages indicate that the Greek term σκανδαλίζειν means "to stumble" or even "to depart/fall away" from the faith. (The translation of this verb is shown in italics.)

Didache 16.5*

Then all humanity will come to the fiery test, and "many *will fall away*" and perish; but "those who endure" in their faith "will be saved" by the accursed one himself.

Shepherd of Hermas, Vision 4.1.3*

So, as I was walking by myself, I asked the Lord to complete the revelations and visions which he showed to me through his holy church, in order that he might strengthen me and grant repentance to his servants who *had stumbled*, that his great and glorious name might be glorified, because he considered me worthy to show his wonders to me.

Shepherd of Hermas, Mandate 8.10*

Next here the things that follow these: serving widows, looking after orphans and those in need, delivering God's servants from distress, being hospitable (for the practice of hospitality results in doing good, I presume), opposing no one, being quiet, becoming more needy than all other men, respecting the elderly, practicing righteousness, preserving brotherhood, enduring insults, being patient, bearing no grudges, encouraging those who are sick at heart, not throwing out those who *have stumbled* but returning and encouraging them, admonishing sinners, not oppressing debtors and those in need, and whatever else is like these.

m. Sanhedrin 9.6*

In this passage from *m. Sanhedrin*, several blasphemous acts are said to have led to execution.

III A. He who stole a sacred vessel [of the cult (Num. 4:7)], and he who curses using the name of an idol, and he who has sexual relations with an Aramaean woman—

B. zealots beat him up [on the spot (Num. 25:8, 11)].

IV C. A priest who performed the rite in a state of uncleanness—

D. his brothers, the priests, do not bring him to court.

E. But the young priests take him outside the courtyard and break his head with clubs.

V F. A non-priest who served in the Temple—

G. R. Aqiba says, "[He is put to death] by strangling [Num. 18:7]."

H. And sages say, "[He is put to death] at the hands of Heaven."

14.6 Jesus' Prayer That the Disciples Be Consecrated and Be One, As the Father Is with the Son (John 17:1–26) (JaS J41)

Jubilees 22.7–23

In this passage from *Jubilees*, a farewell discourse is followed by an address to God, which is reproduced here. This is somewhat similar in tone to the discourse in John 14–16, which is followed by Jesus' prayer in John 17:1–26. There is a difference, however. Jesus' concern is for his disciples, while this petitioner (Isaac) defends his own faithfulness and then gives a commission to Jacob, the one who comes after him.

[7]"And now I thank you, my God, because you have let me see this day. Behold, I am one hundred and seventy-five years old, and fulfilled in days. And all of my days were peaceful to me. [8]The sword of the enemy did not triumph over me in anything which you gave to me or my sons all of the days of my life until this day [9]O my God, may your mercy and your peace be upon your servant and upon the seed of his sons so that they might

become an elect people for you and an inheritance from all of the nations of the earth from henceforth and for all the days of the generations of the earth forever."

¹⁰And he called Jacob and said, "My son, Jacob, may the God of all bless you and strengthen you to do righteousness and his will before him. And may he elect you and your seed so that you become a people for him who always belong to his inheritance according to his will. And you, my son, Jacob, draw near and kiss me."

¹¹And he drew near and kissed him. And he said:

"Blessed be my son, Jacob, and all his sons,
unto the LORD, Most High, forever.
May the LORD give you righteous seed,
and may he sanctify some of your sons in the midst of all the earth.
May the nations serve you,
and all the nations bow down before your seed.
¹²Be strong before men;
and rule over all the seed of Seth,
then may your ways be righteous, and the ways of your sons,
in order to be a holy people.
¹³May the Most High God give you all the blessings
(with) which he blessed me,
and (with) which he blessed Noah and Adam;
may they rest upon the holy head of your seed throughout each generation and forever.
¹⁴May he cleanse you from all sin and defilement,
so that he might forgive all your transgressions, and your erring through ignorance.
May he strengthen you and bless you,
and may you inherit all of the earth.

¹⁵And may he renew his covenant with you,
so that you might be a people for him, belonging to his inheritance forever.
And he will be God for you and for your seed in truth and righteousness throughout all the days of the earth.
¹⁶And you also, my son, Jacob, remember my words,
and keep the commandments of Abraham, your father.
Separate yourself from the gentiles,
and do not eat with them,
and do not perform deeds like theirs.
And do not become associates of theirs.
Because their deeds are defiled,
and all of their ways are contaminated, and despicable, and abominable.
¹⁷They slaughter their sacrifices to the dead,
and to the demons they bow down.
And they eat in tombs.
And all their deeds are worthless and vain.
¹⁸And they have no heart to perceive,
and they have no eyes to see what their deeds are,
and where they wander astray,
saying to the tree 'you are my god,'
and to a stone, 'you are my lord, and you are my savior';
and they have no heart.
¹⁹But (as for) you, my son, Jacob,
may God Most High help you,
and the God of heaven bless you.
And may he turn you from their defilement,
and from all their errors.
²⁰Be careful, my son, Jacob, that you do not take a wife from any of the seed of the daughters of Canaan,

because all of his seed is (destined)
for uprooting from the earth;
[21]because through the sin of Ham,
Canaan sinned,
and all of his seed will be blotted
out from the earth,
and all his remnant,
and there is none of his who will be
saved.
[22]And for all of those who worship
idols and for the hated ones,
there is no hope in the land of the
living;
because they will go down into
Sheol.
And in the place of judgment they
will walk,
and they will have no memory
upon the earth.
Just as the sons of Sodom were
taken from the earth,
so (too) all of those who worship
idols shall be taken away.
[23]Do not fear, my son, Jacob,
and do not be in terror, O son of
Abraham.
The Most High God shall protect
you from destruction,
and from all the ways of error he
will deliver you."

14.7 Jesus before Annas and Peter's Denials (John 18:13–28) (JaS J43)

In *m. Horayot* 3.1–2 and Josephus, *Jewish War* 2.12.6, there is precedent for continuing to refer to a *former* high priest by the title "high priest."

m. Horayot 3.1–2*

[1]I A. An anointed [high] priest who
sinned and afterward passed from his
office as anointed high priest,
    B. and so a ruler who sinned and
afterward passed from his position
of greatness—

C. the anointed [high] priest brings
a bullock,
    D. and the patriarch brings a goat
[M. 2:6].
[2]II A. An anointed [high] priest who
passed from his office as anointed
high priest and then sinned,
    B. and so a ruler who passed from
his position of greatness and then
sinned—
    C. a high priest brings a bullock.
    D. But a ruler is like any ordinary
person.

Josephus, Jewish War 2.12.6 §§241–243

[241]But Quadratus put both parties
off for that time, and told them,
that when he should come to those
places he would make a diligent
inquiry after every circumstance.
After which he went to Caesarea,
and crucified all those whom Cu-
manus had taken alive; [242]and when
from thence he was come to the city
Lydda, he heard the affair of the Samaritans, and sent for eighteen of
the Jews, whom he had learned to
have been concerned in that fight,
and beheaded them; [243]but he sent
two others of those that were of the
greatest power among them, and
both Jonathan and Ananias, the
high priests, as also Artanus the son
of this Ananias, and certain others
that were eminent among the Jews,
to Caesar; as he did in like manner by the most illustrious of the
Samaritans.

In the following two texts from Josephus
(the second appears in section 1.1 above), it
is clear that Annas continued to be regarded
as a powerful figure even after completing his
tenure as acting high priest.

Josephus, **Antiquities** *18.2.2 §34;*
20.9.1 §198

18.2.2 [34]This man deprived Ananus of the high priesthood, and appointed Ismael, the son of Phabi, to be high priest. He also deprived him in a little time, and ordained Eleazar, the son of Ananus, who had been high priest before, to be high priest: which office, when he had held for a year, Gratus deprived him of it, and gave the high priesthood to Simon, the son of Camithus.

m. ʾOhalot 18.7, 9*

These Mishnah texts indicate that the dwellings of Gentiles are considered unclean. For *m. ʾOhalot* 18.7, see section 6.1 above.

[9]A. Colonnades are not subject to the law applying to the dwellings of gentiles.

B. Rabban Simeon b. Gamaliel says, "A city of gentiles which was laid waste is not subject to the law applying to the dwellings of gentiles."

C. East of Qisrin and west of Qisarion [Caesarea Phillippi] are graveyards. [The area] east of Akko was in doubt, and sages declared it clean.

D. Rabbi and his court voted concerning Qeni and declared it clean.

14.8 The Trial before Pilate, the Choice, and the Presentation of Jesus for Execution (John 18:29–19:16) (*JaS* J44)

Josephus, **Antiquities** *14.3.1 §36;*
16.10.2 §311

The title "King of the Jews" does appear in Josephus in reference to Hasmonean kings (14.3.1) and Herod the Great (16.10.2; see section 11.25 above).

14.3.1 [36]However, we ourselves saw that present reposited at Rome, in the temple of Jupiter Capitolinus with this inscription, "The Gift of Alexander, the king of the Jews." It was valued at five hundred talents; and the report is, that Aristobulus, the governor of the Jews, sent it.

m. Sanhedrin 7.5*

This text from *m. Sanhedrin* 7.5, which appears in section 11.20 above, indicates that blasphemy requires the use of the divine name, but there is other Jewish evidence suggesting that during the period of Jesus, the grounds for blasphemy were much broader than just the utterance of the divine name.[1]

Philo, **Embassy to Gaius** *38 §302*

This text from Philo, which appears in section 11.21 above, makes clear that Pilate weighed what was and was not politically expedient. His fear of Caesar's reproach demonstrates this.

m. Roš Haššanah 1.2*

M. Roš Haššanah 1.2 shows that the Jews affirmed the unique sovereignty of God over the world in judgment.

A. At four seasons of the year the world is judged:

B. at Passover for grain;

C. at Pentecost for fruit of the tree;

D. at the New Year all who enter the world pass before Him like troops,

E. since it is said, *He who fashions the hearts of them all, who considers all their works* (Ps. 33:15);

F. and on the Festival [of Tabernacles] they are judged in regard to water.

---

1. See Darrell L. Bock, *Blasphemy and Exaltation in Judaism: The Charge against Jesus in Mark 14:53–65*, Biblical Studies Library (Grand Rapids: Baker, 2000).

14.9 Jesus' Crucifixion and Death (John 19:17–30) (*JaS* J45)

The following text from Plutarch says that a criminal must carry his own cross on his back.

Plutarch, The Divine Vengeance 554 A/B

"But hitherto," I said, "the arguments have been our own, and rest on an assumption that the punishment of the wicked is deferred"; what remains to be said we must imagine we hear from Hesiod, who does not say with Plato that punishment is a suffering following upon injustice, but holds it to be a coeval with injustice, springing up with it from the selfsame soil and root. Thus he says that "the evil plan is worst for him that planned it" and "He that devises ill for other men, For his own vitals does the ill devise."

For whereas the blister beetle is reported to contain, mixed with itself, its own remedy, which operates by a sort of counteraction, wickedness engenders with itself pain and punishment, and thus pays the penalty of its wrongdoing not later, but at the very moment of commission; and whereas every criminal who goes to execution must carry his own cross on his back, vice frames out of itself each instrument of its own punishment, cunning artisan that it is of a life of wretchedness containing with infamy a host of terrors, regrets, cruel passions, and never-ending anxieties.

Eusebius, Ecclesiastical History 6.44.1–6*

The following description of martyrdom stands in contrast to Jesus' trial and crucifixion. Jesus was shown no mercy, but Serapion was shown at least some mercy before his execution.

[1]To this same [person] Fabius, who seemed to lean somewhat toward this schism, Dionysius of Alexandria also wrote an epistle. He writes in this many other things concerning repentance, and relates the conflicts of those who had lately suffered martyrdom at Alexandria. After the other account he mentions a certain wonderful fact, which deserves a place in this work. It is as follows:

[2]"I will give you this one example which occurred among us. There was with us a certain Serapion, an aged believer who had lived for a long time blamelessly, but had fallen in the trial. He besought often, but no one gave heed to him, because he had sacrificed. But he became sick, and for three successive days continued speechless and senseless.

[3]Having recovered somewhat on the fourth day he sent for his daughter's son, and said, 'How Long Do You Detain Me, My Child? I beseech you, make haste, and absolve me speedily. Call one of the presbyters to me.' And when he had said this, he became again speechless. And the boy ran to the presbyter. But it was night and he was sick, and therefore unable to come.

[4]But as I had commanded that persons at the point of death, if they requested it, and especially if they had asked for it previously, should receive remission, that they might depart with a good hope, he gave the boy a small portion of the eucharist, telling him to soak it and let the drops fall into the old man's mouth.

[5]The boy returned with it, and as he drew near, before he entered, Serapion again arousing, said, 'You have come, my child, and the presbyter could not come; but do quickly what he directed, and let me depart.' Then the boy soaked it and dropped it into his mouth. And when he had swal-

lowed a little, immediately he gave up the ghost.

[6]Is it not evident that he was preserved and his life continued till he was absolved, and, his sin having been blotted out, he could be acknowledged for the many good deeds which he had done?"

The following two texts from Josephus and Cicero refer to the horrors of death by crucifixion.

Josephus, Jewish War 7.6.4 §203

Whereupon Eleazar besought them not to disregard him, now he was going to suffer a most miserable death, and exhorted them to save themselves, by yielding to the Roman power and good fortune, since all other people were now conquered by them.

Cicero, In Verrum 2.165

Now when I have given your friends and supporters ample proof of all these facts that I undertake to prove, I intend to lay hold of the very point which you yourself concede me, and proclaim myself content with that. What did you say yourself the other day, when you leapt up terrified by the shouts and angry gestures of your countrymen—what did you tell us plainly then? That the man kept calling out that he was a Roman citizen simply in order to delay his execution, but was in fact a mere spy. Very well then, my witnesses are telling the truth. It is precisely this that we are told by Gaius Numitorius, by those two well-known gentlemen Marcus and Publius Cottius who come from the Tauromenium district, by Quintus Lucceius who has been an important banker in Regium, and by all the rest. For until now the witnesses I have called have been chosen not from among those who were to state that they knew Gavius personally, but from those who were to state that they saw him when he was being dragged off to be crucified in spite of his proclaiming himself a Roman citizen. This is exactly what you, Verres, say, this is what you admit, that he kept proclaiming himself a Roman citizen, that this mention of his citizenship had not even so much effect upon you as to produce a little hesitation, or to delay, even for a little, of that cruel and disgusting penalty.

m. Sanhedrin 6.3*

This text from the Mishnah reveals the Jews' concern for propriety in dealing with public nudity.

A. [When] he was four cubits from the place of stoning, they remove his clothes.

B. "In the case of a man, they cover him up in front, and in the case of a woman, they cover her up in front and behind," the words of R. Judah.

C. And sages say, "A man is stoned naked, but a woman is not stoned naked."

Josephus, Antiquities 3.7.4 §161

In this passage from Antiquities, Josephus describes a seamless garment, referred to as a tunic, worn by Jewish men. The garment is not an inner garment but the vestment the high priest wore. Sometimes these garments were seamless.

Now this vesture was not composed of two pieces, nor was it sewed together upon the shoulders and the sides, but it was one long vestment so woven as to have an aperture for the neck; not an oblique one, but parted all along the breast and the back. A border also was sewed to it, lest the aperture should look too indecently:

it was also parted where the hands were to come out.

14.10 Jesus Is Pierced in the Side and Buried (John 19:31–42) (JaS J46)

Philo, Against Flaccus 10 §83

According to Jewish custom, a person executed on a tree was not to be left hanging overnight. Philo seems to concur with this practice.

I have known instances before now of men who had been crucified when this festival and holiday was at hand, being taken down and given up to their relations, in order to receive the honors of sepulture, and to enjoy such observances as are due to the dead; for it used to be considered, that even the dead ought to derive some enjoyment from the natal festival of a good emperor, and also that the sacred character of the festival ought to be regarded.

Josephus, Jewish War 4.5.2 §317

Josephus claims in this passage that the Jews took down the condemned and had them buried before sundown.

Nay, they proceeded to that degree of impiety, as to cast away their dead bodies without burial, although the Jews used to take so much care of the burial of men, that they took down those that were condemned and crucified, and buried them before the going down of the sun.

m. Sanhedrin 11.4*

In this text, which appears in section 11.20 above, the rabbis argue that a rebellious teacher should be put to death during the festival so that others may "hear and fear and no more do presumptuously."

According to Josephus and the Mishnah, criminals were buried in a disgraceful manner, often at night and apart from their ancestors. This would likely involve burial outside the city.

Josephus, Antiquities 5.1.14 §§42–44

[42]These intercessions Joshua put up to God, as he lay prostrate on his face; whereupon God answered him, That he should rise up, and purify his host from the pollution that had got into it; that "things consecrated to me have been imprudently stolen from me," and that this has been the occasion why this defeat had happened to them; and that when they should search out and punish the offender, he would ever take care they should have the victory over their enemies. This Joshua told the people; [43]and calling for Eleazar the high priest and the men in authority, he cast lots, tribe by tribe; and when the lot showed that this wicked action was done by one of the tribe of Judah, he then again proposed the lot to the several families thereto belonging; so the truth of this wicked action was found to belong to the family of Zachar; [44]and when the inquiry was made, man by man, they took Achar, who, upon God's reducing him to a terrible extremity, could not deny the fact; so he confessed the theft, and produced what he had taken in the midst of them, whereupon he was immediately put to death; and attained no more than to be buried in the night in a disgraceful manner, and such as was suitable to a condemned malefactor.

m. Sanhedrin 6.5*

See section 6.2 above.

Josephus, **Antiquities** *17.8.3 §§198–199*

In this text, Josephus indicates that five hundred slaves ("domestics") brought spices to Herod's funeral.

198About the bier were his sons and his numerous relations; next to these was the soldiery distinguished according to their several countries and denominations; and they were put into the following order:—First of all went his guards, then the band of Thracians; and after them the Germans; and next the band of Galatians, everyone in their habiliments of war; and behind these marched the whole army in the same manner as they used to go out to war, 199and as they used to be put in array by their muster-masters and centurions; these were followed by five hundred of his domestics, carrying spices. So they went eight furlongs to Herodium; for there, by his own command, he was to be buried;—and thus did Herod end his life.

Talbab, **Ebel Rabbati (Semaḥot 8.6)***

As the preceding text from Josephus shows, presenting articles at a funeral was one way mourners honored the dead. In the text below, there is debate about who can be honored at a funeral by burning the presented articles. Gamaliel was honored with the burning of materials that probably equaled eighty Tyrian minas in value.

RULE 6. We may burn articles at the funeral of the kings but not at the funeral of princes. When Rabban Gamaliel the Elder died, the proselyte Onkelos burnt after him more than eighty Tyrian *minas.* They asked him, "What was your purpose in doing this?" He replied, "It is written, *You shall die in peace; and with the burnings of your father, the former kings that were there before you so shall they make a burning for you.* And

is not Rabban Gamaliel worth more than a hundred useless kings?"

m. Šabbat *23.5; 24.5*

The text from *m. Šabbat* 23.5, appearing with *m. Šabbat* 23.4 in section 6.2 above, describes how Jews cared for a corpse, while *m. Šabbat* 24.5 speaks of stopping up light holes. Herbert Danby explains that this was done to protect against spreading secondary uncleanness.[2]

24.5A. They abrogate vows on the Sabbath.

B. And they receive questions concerning matters which are required for the Sabbath.

C. They stop up a light hole.

D. And they measure a piece of stuff and an immersion pool.

E. MᶜSH S: In the time of the father of R. Sadoq and of Abba Saul b. Botnit, they stopped up the light hole with a pitcher and tied a pot with reed grass [to a stick] to know whether or not there was in the roofing an opening of a handbreadth square.

F. "And from their deed we learned that they stop up, measure, and tie up on the Sabbath."

14.11 Resurrection Scenes at the Tomb (John 20:1–18) (*JaS* J47)

m. Roš Haššanah *1.8*

According to *Roš Haššanah* 1.8, women were not considered valid witnesses.

A. These are the ones who are invalid [to testify about the appearance of the new moon]:

B. (1) he who plays with dice, (2) they who lend on interest, (3) who race pigeons, (4) and who trade in

2. Herbert Danby, trans., *The Mishnah* (Oxford: Oxford University Press, 1933), 121n10.

produce of the Seventh Year, (5) and slaves.

C. This is the governing principle: Any evidence which a woman is not valid [to offer], also they are not valid [to offer].

In the following two passages, heavenly beings are said to appear as "snow-white," "gloriously beautiful," and "splendidly dressed."

1 Enoch 87.2

And I lifted my eyes up to heaven and saw a vision: And behold, there came forth from heaven (a being) in the form of a snow-white person— one came out of that place and three (others) with him.

2 Maccabees 3:26

Two young men also appeared to him, remarkably strong, gloriously beautiful and splendidly dressed, who stood on either side of him and flogged him continuously, inflicting many blows on him.

14.12 A Johannine Epilogue: At the Sea of Tiberias in Discussion with Peter and a Final Note (John 21:1–25) (JaS J50)

Acts of Peter 37–38*

The relevant portion of Acts of Peter 37–38 is cited to show that there was a tradition affirming that Peter died by crucifixion upside down. This tradition is also attested by paintings displayed at the Vatican in Rome.

37"... But it is time for you, Peter, to surrender your body to those who are taking it. Take it, then, you whose duty this is. I request you therefore, executioners, to crucify me head-downwards—in this way and no other. And the reason, I will tell to those who hear."

38And when they had hanged him up in the way which he requested, he began to speak again, saying "Men whose duty it is to hear, pay attention to what I tell you at this moment that I am hanged up. You must know the mystery of all nature, and the beginning of all things, how it came about. For the first man, whose likeness I have in (my) appearance, in falling head-downwards showed a manner of birth that was not so before; for it was dead, having no movement. He therefore, being drawn down— he who also cast his first beginning down to the earth—established the whole of this cosmic system, being hung up as an image of the calling, in which he showed what is on the right side as on the left, and those on the left as on the right, and changed all the signs of their nature, so as to consider fair those things that were not fair, and take those that were really evil to be good. Concerning this the Lord says in a mystery, 'Unless you make what is on the right hand as what is on the left and what is on the left hand as what is on the right, and what is above as what is below and what is behind as what is before, you will not recognize the Kingdom.' This conception, then, I have declared to you, and the form in which you see me hanging is a representation of that man who first came to birth. You then, my beloved, both those who hear (me) now and those that shall hear in time, must leave your former error and turn back again; for you should come up to the cross of Christ, who is the Word stretched out, the one and only, of whom the Spirit says, 'For what else is Christ but the Word, the sound of God?' So that the Word is this upright tree on which I am crucified; but the sound is the cross-piece, the nature of man; and the nail that holds the cross-piece to the upright in the middle is the conversion (or turning point) and repentance of man."

The early church often connected Isaiah 65:2 with Christ's crucifixion, as the following texts indicate.

Epistle of Barnabas 12.4*

And again in another prophet he says: "All day long I have stretched out my hands to a disobedient unbelieving people who oppose my righteous way." *JC m craw*

Justin Martyr, First Apology 35*

And how Christ after He was born was to escape the notice of other men until He grew to man's estate, which also came to pass, hear what was fore-told regarding this. There are the fol-lowing predictions:—"Unto us a child is born, and unto us a young man is given, and the government shall be upon His shoulders;" which is signifi-cant of the power of the cross, for to it, when He was crucified, He applied His shoulders, as shall be more clearly made out in the ensuing discourse. And again the same prophet Isaiah, being inspired by the prophetic Spirit, said, "I have spread out my hands to a disobedient and gainsaying people, to those who walk in a way that is not good. They now ask of me judgment, and dare to draw near to God." And again in other words, through an-other prophet, He says, "They pierced My hands and My feet, and for My vesture they cast lots." And indeed David, the king and prophet, who ut-tered these things, suffered none of them; but Jesus Christ stretched forth His hands, being crucified by the Jews speaking against Him, and denying that He was the Christ. And as the prophet spoke, they tormented Him,

and set Him on the judgment-seat, and said, Judge us. And the expres-sion, "They pierced my hands and my feet," was used in reference to the nails of the cross which were fixed in His hands and feet. And after He was crucified they cast lots upon His vesture, and they that crucified Him parted it among them. And that these things did happen, you can ascertain from the Acts of Pontius Pilate. And we will cite the prophetic utterances of another prophet, Zephaniah, to the effect that He was foretold expressly as to sit upon the foal of an ass and to enter Jerusalem. The words are these: "Rejoice greatly, O daughter of Zion; shout, O daughter of Jerusalem: be-hold, your King comes to you; lowly, and riding upon an ass, and upon a colt the foal of an ass."

Irenaeus, Demonstration of Apostolic Teaching, 66–69*

This text provides a summary of how the early church of the mid– to late second century read the relationship between Jesus' ministry, the crucifixion, and the Hebrew Scripture (the Old Testament).

[66]Thus, then, did the prophets an-nounce that the Son of God was to be born, and by what manner of birth, and where He was to be born, and that He is Christ, the sole eternal king. And now, how they foretold that when He came He would heal men (and He did heal them), and raise the dead (and He did raise them), and be hated and despised and undergo sufferings and be slain by crucifixion—as He was hated and despised and slain.

[67]Let us now speak of His heal-ings. Isaias says as follows: *He hath taken our infirmities and carried our ills;* that is, "will take" and "will carry," for sometimes the Spirit of God relates through the prophets as a past event

what is to come to pass in the future; for with God, what is approved and determined and decreed to be done is already accounted as done, and the Spirit uses expressions having in view the time in which the outcome of the prophecy is realized. And as for the kinds of cure, he recorded them in these words: *In that day the deaf shall hear the words of the book, and in darkness and obscurity the eyes of the blind shall* see. And again, the same prophet says: *Be strengthened, feeble hands, and palsied knees; be consoled, ye dispirited in mind; be strengthened, fear not; behold our God will render judgment, He will come Himself and save us. Then shall the eyes of the blind be opened, and the ears of the deaf shall hear, then shall the lame man leap as a hart, and the tongue of the stammerer shall be free.* And concerning the raising of the dead he says: So *shall the dead rise again, and those shall rise again who are in the tombs;* and by doing these things He will be believed to be Son of God.

⁶⁸And that He would be despised and tormented and finally slain, Isaias says as follows: *Behold, my son shall understand, and be exalted and extolled greatly; as many shall be astonished at you, so shall your visage be inglorious among men. And many peoples shall be astonished, and kings shall shut their mouths; for they to whom it was not told of Him shall see, and they who heard not shall take notice. Lord, who has believed our report? and, to whom is the arm of the Lord revealed? We have told our tale before His face, like a child, as a root in thirsty ground; and He had no comeliness, and no glory. And we have seen Him, and He had no comeliness, and no beauty. But His look was inglorious, made less than other men, a man in bruises and acquainted with the bearing of torments; because His face was turned away, He was despised and not esteemed. He bears our sins, and for our sake suffers pains, and we esteemed Him to be in* *pains and in bruises and in torments. But He was wounded because of our iniquities, and was tormented because of our sins. The chastisement of our peace is upon Him, by His wounds we are healed.* And thereby it is also declared that He was tormented, as David says too: *and I was tormented.* But David was never tormented, but Christ, when order was given that He be crucified. And again the Word says through Isaiah: *I have given my back to blows, and my cheeks to buffets, and I have not turned away my face from the contumely of spitting.* And the prophet Jeremiah says the same thing, as follows: *He shall give His cheek to him that strikes, He shall be filled with reproaches.* All these things Christ underwent.

⁶⁹Isaiah, then, goes on as follows: *By His wounds we are healed. All we like sheep have gone astray, man has gone astray in his way; and the Lord has delivered Him unto our sins;* so it is clear that it came about by the will of the Father that these things happened to Him, for the sake of our salvation. Then he says: *And through His suffering He opened not the mouth; He was led as a sheep to the slaughter, mute as a lamb before the shearer.* See how he declares His voluntary coming to death. But when the prophet says that *in humility His judgment was taken away* he is speaking of the appearance of His humility: the taking of the judgment was according to the form of abasement. And the taking of the judgment is for some unto salvation, and for others unto torments of perdition; for there is taking *to* a person, and taking *from* a person. So too the judgment has been taken *on* some, and they have it in the torments of their perdition; but *off* others, and they are thereby saved. But those men took judgment on themselves, who crucified Him, and, having thus treated Him, did not believe Him, so that they be brought to perdition with torments through

the judgment which was taken by them. And judgment has been taken off those who believe in Him, and they are no more subject to it; and the judgment, which is to come by fire, will be the perdition of those who did not believe, towards the end of this world.

The following texts affirm Peter's death and that it was by crucifixion upside down.

1 Clement 5.4*

There was Peter, who, because of unrighteous jealousy, endured not one or two but many trials, and thus having given his testimony went to his appointed place of glory.

Tertullian, Scorpion's Sting 15*

Now, then, the epistles of the apostles also are well known. And do *we*, (you say), in all respects guileless souls and doves merely, love to go astray? I should think from eagerness to live. But let it be so, that meaning departs from their epistles. And yet, that the apostles endured such sufferings, we know: the teaching is clear. This only I perceive in running through the Acts. I am not at all on the search. The prisons there, and the bonds, and the scourges, and the big stones, and the swords, and the onsets by the Jews, and the assemblies of the heathen, and the indictments by tribunes, and the hearing of causes by kings, and the judgment-seats of pro-consuls and the name of Caesar, do not need an interpreter. That Peter is struck, that Stephen is overwhelmed *by stones*, that James is slain as is a victim at the altar, that Paul is beheaded has been written in their own blood. And if a heretic wishes his confidence to rest upon a public record, the archives of the empire will speak, as would the stones of Jerusalem. We read the

lives of the Caesars: At Rome Nero was the first who stained with blood the rising faith. Then is Peter girt by another, when he is made fast to the cross. Then does Paul obtain a birth suited to Roman citizenship, when in Rome he springs to life again ennobled by martyrdom. Wherever I read of these occurrences so soon as I do so, I learn to suffer; nor does it signify to me which I follow as teachers of martyrdom, whether the declarations or the deaths of the apostles, save that in their deaths I recall their declarations also. For they would not have suffered ought of a kind they had not previously known they had to suffer. When Agabus, making use of corresponding action too, had foretold that bonds awaited Paul, the disciples, weeping and entreating that he would not venture upon going to Jerusalem, entreated in vain. As for him, having a mind to illustrate what he had always taught, he says, "Why weep ye, and grieve my heart? But for my part, I could wish not only to suffer bonds, but also to die at Jerusalem, for the name of my Lord Jesus Christ." And so they yielded by saying, "Let the will of the Lord be done;" feeling sure, doubtless, that sufferings are included in the will of God. For they had tried to keep him back with the intention not of dissuading, but to show love for him; as yearning for (the preservation of) the apostle, not as counseling against martyrdom. And if even then a Prodicus or Valentinus stood by, suggesting that one must not confess on the earth before men, and must do so the less in truth, that God may not (seem to) thirst for blood, and Christ for a repayment of suffering, as though He besought it with the view of obtaining salvation by it for Himself also, he would have immediately heard from the servant of God what the devil had from the

Lord: "Get behind me, Satan; you are an offense unto me. It is written, You shall worship the Lord your God, and Him only shall you serve." But even now it will be right that he hear it, seeing that, long after, he has poured forth these poisons, which not even thus are to injure readily any of the weak ones, if any one in faith will drink, before being hurt, or even immediately after, this draught of ours.

Eusebius, Ecclesiastical History 3.1.2*

[2]Peter appears to have preached in Pontus, Galatia, Bithynia, Cappadocia, and Asia to the Jews of the dispersion. And at last, having come to Rome, he was crucified head-downwards; for he had requested that he might suffer in this way. . . . These facts are related by Origen in the third volume of his Commentary on Genesis.

Philo, Posterity of Cain 43 §§143b–144

John's expression "the whole world could not contain" has parallels in Judaism, as this text from Philo demonstrates.

[143b]On which account those persons appear to speak with great truth, who say to Moses, "Do you speak to us, and let not God speak to us, lest we die." For they know that they have not in themselves any organ which can be worthy of God who is giving

laws to his church; [144]nor, indeed, could even the whole world, both land and sea, contain his riches if he were inclined to display them, unless we think that the descent of the rains and of the other things that happen in the world are appointed to take place according to the pre-arranged periods of the seasons, and not all at once, because of the scarcity and rarity of the things themselves, and not from any regard to the advantage of those who are benefited by them; who would be injured rather than benefited by a continual enjoyment of such gifts.

t. Soperim 16.8*

The following text contains a variation on the idiom "the world itself could not contain the books that would be written."

Rule 8. It was related of R. Johanan b. Zakkai that he did not neglect the study of a single passage of the Torah. He also studied [all] scripture, Targum, Mishnah, Halakoth and 'aggadoth. He learned everything. It was also related of him that he declared, "If all the heavens were sheets, all the trees quills and all the seas ink, they would not suffice for recording my wisdom which I acquired from my masters; and yet I have gained no more of the wisdom of the Sages than a fly [acquires] which dips in the great sea and deprives it of the tiniest drop."

A Theological Portrait of Jesus

15

Major Themes
in the Evangelists' Portrait
of Jesus' Theology

This final chapter contains readings that give background to the major themes of Jesus' ministry as the Gospel writers present them.

15.1 Jesus Submitting to Baptism: Identifying with John the Baptist's Message and Being Identified by the Divine Voice

Josephus, Antiquities 18.5.2 §§116–119

In this text from *Antiquities*, appearing in section 3.3 above, Josephus makes mention of John the Baptist's ministry and how Herod had him slain.

1QS 8.14; 9.19–21

The following two citations from 1QS demonstrate that the community located near the Dead Sea self-consciously postured itself in light of Isaiah 40:3 (**** stands for the divine name).

8.14As it is written: "In the desert, prepare the way of ****, straighten in the steppe a roadway for our God."

9.19This is the time for making ready the path 20to the desert and he will teach them about all that has been discovered so that they can carry it out in this moment and so they will be detached

from anyone who has not withdrawn his path 21from all wickedness.

15.2 Jesus' Teaching on God as Father and His Program: The Kingdom of God as the Expression of God's Dynamic Rule and Vindication of the Righteous Both Now and Yet to Come

Wisdom of Solomon 10:10

Here is one of the few intertestamental texts that uses the term *kingdom of God*. It appears to refer to a place of righteousness where God and his ways can be found.

When a righteous man fled from his brother's wrath, she guided him on straight paths; she showed him the kingdom of God, and gave him knowledge of holy things; she prospered him in his labors, and increased the fruit of his toil.

1 Enoch 9.4–5; 12.3; 25.3–4; 27.3; 81.3

The following five texts from *1 Enoch* speak of God's comprehensive and all-encompassing rule.

9.4And they said to the Lord of the potentates, "For he is the Lord of lords,

255

and the God of gods, and the King of kings, and the seat of his glory (stands) throughout all the generations of the world. Your name is holy, and blessed, and glorious throughout the whole world. [5]You have made everything and with you is the authority for everything. Everything is naked and open before your sight, and you see everything; and there is nothing *PS139* which can hide itself from you."

[12.3]And I, Enoch, began to bless the Lord of the mighty ones and the King of the universe.

[25.3]He answered, saying, "This tall mountain which you saw whose summit resembles the throne of God is (indeed) his throne, on which the Holy and Great Lord of Glory, the Eternal King, will sit when he descends to visit the earth with goodness. [4]And as for this fragrant tree, not a single human being has the authority to touch it until the great judgment, when he shall take vengeance on all and conclude (everything) forever."

[27.3]There will be upon them the spectacle of the righteous judgment, in the presence of the righteous forever.

[81.3]At that very moment, I blessed the Great Lord, the King of Glory forever, for he has created all the phenomena in the world. I praised the Lord because of his patience; and I wept on account of the children of the people upon the earth.

Assumption of Moses 10 (excerpts)

In these excerpts from the *Assumption of Moses*, Satan is said to be removed when God comes in the fullness of his presence.

[10.1]Then his kingdom will appear throughout his whole creation. Then

the devil will have an end. Yea, sorrow will be led away with him. . . . [3]For the Heavenly One will arise from his kingly throne. Yea, he will go forth from his holy habitation with indignation and wrath on behalf of his sons. . . . [7]For God Most High will surge forth, the Eternal One alone. In full view will he come to work vengeance on the nations. Yea, all their idols will he destroy.

The enemies of God are described in earthly terms in *Psalms of Solomon* 17–18 (i.e., the Romans) and in spiritual terms in *2 Baruch* 36–40. Chapters 36–40 of *2 Baruch* discuss a vision of the end. An enemy kingdom is said to "exalt itself more than the cedars of Lebanon" and to be "polluted with unrighteousness" (39.5–6). The Anointed One comes to judge this kingdom in the end, as described in the first three verses from *2 Baruch* 40 quoted below.

Psalms of Solomon 17–18

See section 9.17 above.

2 Baruch 40.1–3

[1]The last ruler who is left alive at that time will be bound, whereas the entire host will be destroyed. And they will carry him on Mount Zion, and my Anointed One will convict him of all his wicked deeds and will assemble and set before him all the works of his hosts. [2]And after these things he will kill him and protect the rest of my people who will be found in the place that I have chosen. [3]And his dominion will last forever until the world of corruption has ended and until the times which have been mentioned before have been fulfilled.

1QS 3–4 (excerpts)

Belial (mentioned in 1QS 2.19 [see section 11.7 above]) will be defeated in the end, according to this text from Qumran. He is called the Angel of Darkness in 3.21–24, and 4.9–14 describes his defeat and that of all who walk in his wicked ways.

3.21 . . . Due to the Angel of Darkness [22]all the sons of justice stray, and all their sins, their iniquities, their failings and their mutinous deeds are under his dominion [23]in compliance with the mysteries of God, until his moment; and all their punishments and their periods of grief are caused by the dominion of his enmity; [24]and all the spirits of their lot cause the sons of light to fall.

4.9However, to the spirit of deceit belong greed, frailty of hands in the service of justice, irreverence, deceit, pride and haughtiness of heart, dishonesty, trickery, cruelty, [10]much insincerity, impatience, much insanity, impudent enthusiasm, appalling acts performed in a lustful passion, filthy paths for indecent purposes, [11]blasphemous tongue, blindness of eyes, hardness of hearing, stiffness of neck, hardness of heart in order to walk in all the paths of darkness and evil cunning. And the visitation [12]of those who walk in it will be for a glut of punishments at the hands of all the angels of destruction, for eternal damnation for the scorching wrath of the God of revenge, for permanent error and shame [13]without end with the humiliation of destruction by the fire of the dark regions. And all the ages of their generations they shall spend in bitter weeping and harsh evils in the abysses of darkness until [14]their destruction, without there being a remnant or a survivor among them.

The following selections reveal the widespread belief that a time of unprecedented upheaval would precede the appearance of the kingdom.   *Mt 29*

Sibylline Oracles *3.796–808*

[796]I will tell you a very clear sign, so that you may know [797]when the end of all things comes to pass on earth: [798]when swords are seen at night in starry heaven [799]toward evening and toward dawn, [800]and again dust is brought forth from heaven [801]upon the earth and all the light of the sun [802]is eclipsed in the middle from heaven, and the rays [803]of the moon appear and return to the earth. [804]There will be a sign from the rocks, with blood and drops of gore. [805]You will see a battle of infantry and cavalry in the clouds, [806]like a hunt of wild beasts, like a mist. [807]This is the end of war which God, who inhabits heaven, is accomplishing. [808]But all must sacrifice to the great king.

2 Baruch *70.2–8*

See section 11.12 above.

4 Ezra (= *2 Esdras*) *6:24; 9:1–12; 13:29–31*

Mt 24

[6:24]At that time friends shall make war on friends like enemies, the earth and those who inhabit it shall be terrified, and the springs of the fountains shall stand still, so that for three hours they shall not flow.

[9:1]He answered me and said, "Measure carefully in your mind, and when you see that some of the predicted signs have occurred, [2]then you will know that it is the very time when the Most

High is about to visit the world that he has made. ³So when there shall appear in the world earthquakes, tumult of peoples, intrigues of nations, wavering of leaders, confusion of princes, ⁴then you will know that it was of these that the Most High spoke from the days that were of old, from the beginning. ⁵For just as with everything that has occurred in the world, the beginning is evident, and the end manifest; ⁶so also are the times of the Most High: the beginnings are manifest in wonders and mighty works, and the end in penalties and in signs.

⁷"It shall be that all who will be saved and will be able to escape on account of their works, or on account of the faith by which they have believed, ⁸will survive the dangers that have been predicted, and will see my salvation in my land and within my borders, which I have sanctified for myself from the beginning. ⁹Then those who have now abused my ways shall be amazed, and those who have rejected them with contempt shall live in torments. ¹⁰For as many as did not acknowledge me in their lifetime, though they received my benefits, ¹¹and as many as scorned my law while they still had freedom, and did not understand but despised it while an opportunity of repentance was still open to them, ¹²these must in torment acknowledge it after death."

¹³:²⁹The days are coming when the Most High will deliver those who are on the earth. ³⁰And bewilderment of mind shall come over those who inhabit the earth. ³¹They shall plan to make war against one another, city against city, place against place, people against people, and kingdom against kingdom.

1QM 12.9; 19.1–2

¹²·⁹The war hero is in our congregation; the army of his spirits, with our infantry and our cavalry. They are like clouds and dew to cover the earth.

¹⁹·¹For our Glorious is holy and the King of glory is with us. The army [of his spirits is with our infantry and cavalry like clouds and dew] ²to cover the land like torrential rain which pours down justice on every[thing that grows.

2 Maccabees 1:24–29

This text represents a prayerful cry to God for deliverance and the fulfillment of everything good that he has promised for his people.

²⁴The prayer was to this effect: "O Lord, Lord God, Creator of all things, you are awe-inspiring and strong and just and merciful, you alone are king and are kind, ²⁵you alone are bountiful, you alone are just and almighty and eternal. You rescue Israel from every evil; you chose the ancestors and consecrated them. ²⁶Accept this sacrifice on behalf of all your people Israel and preserve your portion and make it holy. ²⁷Gather together our scattered people, set free those who are slaves among the Gentiles, look on those who are rejected and despised, and let the Gentiles know that you are our God. ²⁸Punish those who oppress and are insolent with pride. ²⁹Plant your people in your holy place, as Moses promised."

4 Ezra (= 2 Esdras) 7:28–29; 12:31–34; 13:25–26

In three passages from 4 Ezra, the Messiah is seen to have a mixture of divine and human qualities. Fourth Ezra 7:28–29 appears in section 13.21 above; *4 Ezra* 13:25–26 appears in section 4.5 above.

[12:31]And as for the lion whom you saw rousing up out of the forest and roaring and speaking to the eagle and reproving him for his unrighteousness, and as for all his words that you have heard, [32]this is the Messiah whom the Most High has kept until the end of days, who will arise from the offspring of David, and will come and speak with them. He will denounce them for their ungodliness and for their wickedness, and will display before them their contemptuous dealings. [33]For first he will bring them alive before his judgment seat, and when he has reproved them, then he will destroy them. [34]But in mercy he will set free the remnant of my people, those who have been saved throughout my borders, and he will make them joyful until the end comes, the day of judgment, of which I spoke to you at the beginning.

The following texts suggest an eschatological restoration of the nation of Israel with all twelve tribes represented.

1QM 2.1–3

[1]They shall arrange the chiefs of the priests behind the High Priest and of his second (in rank), twelve chiefs to serve [2]in perpetuity before God. And the twenty-six chiefs of the divisions shall serve in their divisions and after them the chiefs of the levites to serve always, twelve, one [3]per tribe. And the chiefs of their divisions shall each serve in their place. The chiefs of the tribes, and after them the fathers of the congregation, shall have charge of the sanctuary gates in perpetuity.

4QpIsaᵈ frag. 1.1–8

[1][He will trea]t all Israel like "jet" around the eye. *Is 54:11* And your foundations are sapphires. [Its interpretation:] [2]they will found the council of the Community, the priests and the peo[ple . . .] [3]the assembly of their elect, like a sapphire stone in the midst of stones. *Is 54:12* [I will place] [4]all your battlements [of rubies]. Its interpretation concerns the twelve [chiefs of the priests who] [5]illuminate with the judgment of the Urim and Thummim [. . . without] [6]any from among them missing, like the sun in all its light. *Is 54:12* And a[ll your gates of glittering stones.] [7]Its interpretation concerns the chiefs of the tribes of Israel in the las[t d]ays [. . .] [8]of its lot, their functions [. . .].

Testament of Judah 25.1–2

[1]And after this Abraham, Isaac, and Jacob will be resurrected to life and I and my brothers will be chiefs (wielding) our scepter in Israel: Levi, the first; I, second, Joseph, third; Benjamin, fourth; Simeon, fifth; [2]Issachar, sixth; and all the rest in their order. And the Lord blessed Levi; the Angel of the Presence blessed me; the powers of glory blessed Simeon; the heaven blessed Reuben; the earth blessed Issachar; the sea blessed Zebulon; the mountains blessed Joseph; the Tent blessed Benjamin; the lights blessed Dan; luxury blessed Naphtali; the sun blessed Gad; the olive tree blessed Asher.

Testament of Benjamin 10.7

Then shall we also be raised, each of us over our tribe, and we shall prostrate ourselves before the heavenly king.

The following two passages give evidence that the preposition ἐντός with the genitive plural can mean "in the midst" or "within their reach."

Xenophon, Anabasis 1.10.3

The Milesian woman, however, the younger one, after being seized by the King's men made her escape, lightly clad, to some Greeks who had chanced to be standing guard amid the baggage train and, forming themselves in line against the enemy, had killed many of the plunderers, although some of their own number had been killed also; nevertheless, they did not take to flight, but they saved this woman and, furthermore, *whatever else* came *within their lines* [ὁπόσα ἐντὸς αὐτῶν], whether persons or property, they saved all alike.

Herodotus, Histories 7.100

. . . The captains put out as far as four hundred feet from the shore, and there kept the ships anchored in a line, their prows turned landward and the fighting men on them armed as for war; Xerxes viewed them, passing between the prows and the land [ὅ δ᾽ ἐντὸς τῶν πρωρέων πλέων ἐθηεῦτο καὶ τοῦ αἰγιαλοῦ].

Shemoneh Esreh, *benediction 1**

In this passage from *Shemoneh Esreh*, God is known as the one who made promises to the fathers, Abraham, Isaac, and Jacob.

Blessed are you, Lord our God and God of our fathers, God of Abraham, God of Isaac and God of Jacob, great, mighty, and fearful God, most high God, who bestows abundant grace and creates all things and remembers the promises of grace to the fathers and brings a Redeemer to their children's children for your Name's sake out of

love. O King, who brings help and salvation and who is a shield. *Blessed are you, Lord, shield of Abraham.*

Though rare when compared with its frequent occurrence in the New Testament, the name "father" is used for God in some Jewish texts, as illustrated by these excerpts from Sirach, 3 Maccabees, and Wisdom.

Sirach 23:1–2, 4

[1]O Lord, Father and Master of my life, do not abandon me to their designs, and do not let me fall because of them! [2]Who will set whips over my thoughts, and the discipline of wisdom over my mind, so as not to spare me in my errors, and not overlook my sins? . . . [4]O Lord, Father and God of my life, do not give me haughty eyes, and remove evil desire from me.

3 Maccabees 6:1–8

[1]Then a certain Eleazar, famous among the priests of the country, who had attained a ripe old age and throughout his life had been adorned with every virtue, directed the elders around him to stop calling upon the holy God, and he prayed as follows: [2]"King of great power, Almighty God Most High, governing all creation with mercy, [3]look upon the descendants of Abraham, O Father, upon the children of the sainted Jacob, a people of your consecrated portion who are perishing as foreigners in a foreign land. [4]Pharaoh with his abundance of chariots, the former ruler of this Egypt, exalted with lawless insolence and boastful tongue, you destroyed together with his arrogant army by drowning them in the sea, manifesting the light of your mercy on the nation of Israel. [5]Sennacherib exulting in his countless forces, oppressive king of the Assyrians, who had already gained control of the whole world by the spear

and was lifted up against your holy city, speaking grievous words with boasting and insolence, you, O Lord, broke in pieces, showing your power to many nations. ⁶The three companions in Babylon who had voluntarily surrendered their lives to the flames so as not to serve vain things, you rescued unharmed, even to a hair, moistening the fiery furnace with dew and turning the flame against all their enemies. ⁷Daniel, who through envious slanders was thrown down into the ground to lions as food for wild animals, you brought up to the light unharmed. ⁸And Jonah, wasting away in the belly of a huge, sea-born monster, you, Father, watched over and restored unharmed to all his family."

Wisdom of Solomon 14:2–4

²For it was desire for gain that planned that vessel, and wisdom was the artisan who built it; ³but it is your providence, O Father, that steers its course, because you have given it a path in the sea, and a safe way through the waves, ⁴showing that you can save from every danger, so that even a person who lacks skill may put to sea.

15.3 Jesus' Titles, Teachings, and Actions: Who Is Jesus?

These texts describe Solomon as a healer and exorcist. This tradition may stand behind the people's conception of Jesus as both Son of David and healer/exorcist.

Josephus, Antiquities 8.2.5 §§45–46

The text appears in section 6.3 above.

Wisdom of Solomon 7:17–22

¹⁷For it is he who gave me unerring knowledge of what exists, to know

the structure of the world and the activity of the elements; ¹⁸the beginning and end and middle of times, the alternations of the solstices and the changes of the seasons, ¹⁹the cycles of the year and the constellations of the stars, ²⁰the natures of animals and the tempers of wild animals, the powers of spirits and the thoughts of human beings, the varieties of plants and the virtues of roots; ²¹I learned both what is secret and what is manifest, ²²for wisdom, the fashioner of all things, taught me.

Pseudo-Philo, Biblical Antiquities 60.1–3

¹And in that time *the spirit of the Lord* was taken away *from Saul, and* an evil spirit was choking him. And Saul sent and brought David, and *he played a song on his lyre* by night. And this was the song he played for Saul in order that *the evil spirit might depart from him.* ²"Darkness and silence were before the world was made, and silence spoke a word and the darkness became light. Then your name was pronounced in the drawing together of what had been spread out, the upper of which was called heaven and the lower was called earth. And the upper part was commanded to bring down rain according to its season, and the lower part was commanded to produce food for all things that had been made. And after these was the tribe of your spirit made. ³And now do not be troublesome as one created on the second day. But if not, remember Tartarus where you walk. Or is it enough for you to hear that, through what resounds before you, I sing to many? Or do you not remember that you were created from a resounding echo in the chaos? But let the new womb from which I was born rebuke you, from which after a

time one born from my loins will rule over you." And as long as David sang, the spirit spared Saul.

Both *1 Enoch* 37–71 and *4 Ezra* 13 testify to a messianic figure not too different from the one revealed in Daniel 7:13–14.

1 Enoch *37–71*

See sections 4.5 and 11.12 above.

4 Ezra (= 2 Esdras) *13:1–58*

See section 4.5 above.

4Q242 *frags. 1–3.2–5 (Prayer of Nabonidus)*

In this text from Qumran, which appears in section 4.5 above, Nabonidus claims to have been forgiven by a Jewish exorcist.
The following two texts reveal that the Qumran community probably set stricter rules for the Sabbath than did the rabbis.

CD *11.12–14*

[12]. . . No-one should help an animal give birth on the sabbath day. *Blank* And if he makes it fall into a well [14]or a pit, he should not take it out on the sabbath.

m. Šabbat *18.3**

A. They do not deliver the young of cattle on the festival, but they help out.
B. And they do deliver the young of a woman on the Sabbath.
C. They call a midwife for her from a distant place,
D. and they violate the Sabbath on her [the woman in childbirth's] account.
E. And they tie the umbilical cord.
F. R. Yose says, "Also: They cut it."

G. And all things required for circumcision do they perform on the Sabbath.

Philo, **Special Laws** 2.46 §253

Here we see how one Jew views invoking God rashly. This has implications for one who asks God to act on the Sabbath.

On which account we must say this, that him, who swears rashly and falsely, calling God to witness an unjust oath, God, although he is merciful by nature, will yet never release, inasmuch as he is thoroughly defiled and infamous from guilt, even though he may escape punishment at the hands of men. And such a man will never entirely escape, for there are innumerable beings looking on, zealots for and keepers of the national laws, of rigid justice, prompt to stone such a criminal, and visiting without pity all such as work wickedness, unless, indeed, we are prepared to say that a man who acts in such a way as to dishonour his father or his mother is worthy of death, but that he who behaves with impiety towards a name more glorious than even the respect due to one's parents, is to be borne with as but a moderate offender.

b. Sanhedrin *43*[a]*

In the Gospel accounts, Jesus is charged with sorcery (cf. Mark 3:22). Claims were made that he performed his miracles through the power of Beelzebub (Satan) and that he led Israel astray (cf. Luke 23:2). This text from the Talmud also notes such charges and agrees that Jesus was executed for concerns such as these.

This implies only immediately before [the execution], but not previous thereto. [In contradiction to this] it was taught: On the eve of the Passover Yeshu was hanged. For forty days before the execution took place, a herald went forth and cried, "He is going forth to be stoned because he has practiced sorcery and enticed Israel to apostasy. Anyone who can say anything in his favor, let him come forward and plead on his behalf." But since nothing was brought forward in his favor he was hanged on the eve of the Passover.

Though there is some dispute as to whether there are Christian interpolations in these texts, both the *Testament of Dan* 5.3 and *Testament of Issachar* 5.2 and 7.6 reflect the idea that one is to love both God and neighbor. Philo, *Special Laws* 2.15, appeals to the same ethic, which itself is probably rooted in the Old Testament prophetic tradition.

Testament of Dan 5.3

Throughout all your life love the Lord, and one another with a true heart.

Testament of Issachar 5.2; 7.6

5.2Love the Lord and your neighbor; be compassionate toward poverty and sickness.

7.6I acted in piety and truth all my days. The Lord I loved with all my strength; likewise, I loved every human being as I love my children.

Philo, Special Laws 2.15 §63

And there are, as we may say, two most especially important heads of all the innumerable particular lessons and doctrines; the regulating of one's conduct towards God by the rules of piety and holiness, and of one's conduct towards men by the rules of humanity and justice; each of which is subdivided into a great number of subordinate ideas, all praiseworthy.

1 Enoch 90.28–30, 40

In this text from *1 Enoch*, the transformation of the temple is said to be part of eschatological restoration. A similar notion is found in benediction 14 of *Shemoneh Esreh*.

28Then I stood still, looking at the ancient house being transformed: All the pillars and all the columns were pulled out; and the ornaments of that house were packed and taken out together with them and abandoned in a certain place in the South of the land. 29I went on seeing until the Lord of the sheep brought about a new house, greater and loftier than the first one, and set it up in the first location which had been covered up—all its pillars were new, the columns new; and the ornaments new as well as greater than those of the first, (that is) the old (house) which was gone. . . . 30Then I saw all the sheep that had survived as well as all the animals upon the earth and the birds of heaven, falling down and worshipping those sheep, making petition to them and obeying them in every respect. . . . 40This is the vision I saw while I was sleeping. Then I woke up and blessed the Lord of righteousness and gave him glory.

Shemoneh Esreh, *benediction 14**

See section 11.1 above.

Wisdom of Solomon 2:12–20; 5:1–7

Both Wisdom of Solomon 2:12–20 and 5:1–7 speak about God's vindication of the righteous.

2:12"Let us lie in wait for the righteous man, because he is inconvenient to us and opposes our actions; he reproaches us for sins against the law, and accuses us of sins against our training. 13He professes to have knowledge of God, and calls himself a child of the Lord. [14]He became to us a reproof of our thoughts; [15]the very sight of him is a burden to us, because his manner of life is unlike that of others, and his ways are strange. [16]We are considered by him as something base, and he avoids our ways as unclean; he calls the last end of the righteous happy, and boasts that God is his father. [17]Let us see if his words are true, and let us test what will happen at the end of his life; [18]for if the righteous man is God's child, he will help him, and will deliver him from the hand of his adversaries. [19]Let us test him with insult and torture, so that we may find out how gentle he is, and make trial of his forbearance. [20]Let us condemn him to a shameful death, for, according to what he says, he will be protected."

[5:1]Then the righteous will stand with great confidence in the presence of those who have oppressed them and those who make light of their labors. [2]When the unrighteous see them, they will be shaken with dreadful fear, and they will be amazed at the unexpected salvation of the righteous. [3]They will speak to one another in repentance, and in anguish of spirit they will groan, and say, [4]"These are persons whom we once held in derision and made a byword of reproach—fools that we were! We thought that their lives were madness and that their end was without honor. [5]Why have they been numbered among the children of God? And why is their lot among the saints? [6]So it was we who strayed from the way of truth, and the light

of righteousness did not shine on us, and the sun did not rise upon us. [7]We took our fill of the paths of lawlessness and destruction, and we journeyed through trackless deserts, but the way of the Lord we have not known."

15.4 The Vindication to Come: Warning to Israel, Inclusion of Gentiles, and the Return of the Son of Man to Judge the World

The following four passages deal with the theme of darkness and its connection to divine judgment.

1 Enoch 10.4, 8

[4]And secondly the Lord said to Raphael, "Bind Azaz'el hand and foot (and) throw him into the darkness!" And he made a whole in the desert which was in Duda'el and cast him there. . . . [8]And the whole earth has been corrupted by Azaz'el's teaching of his (own) actions; and write upon him all sin.

Jubilees 7.29

And no man who eats blood or sheds the blood of man will remain upon the earth; and neither seed nor posterity will remain alive for him under heaven. For they will go down into Sheol, and into the place of judgment they will descend. And into the darkness of the depths they will all be removed with a cruel death.

Psalms of Solomon 14.9; 15.10

See section 9.15 above.

Works Cited

The following sources were used in compiling this collection of readings. Bibliographic information for sources cited only once is provided in the footnote attached to that reading.

Ante-Nicene Fathers

The Ante-Nicene Fathers. Edited by Alexander Roberts and James Donaldson. 10 vols. 1885–87. Reprint, Grand Rapids: Eerdmans, n.d.

Apostolic Fathers

The Apostolic Fathers: Greek Texts and English Translations. Edited and revised by Michael W. Holmes. Updated edition. Grand Rapids: Baker, 1999.

Greco-Roman Historians

Selected volumes from the Loeb Classical Library

Josephus and Philo

The Works of Josephus: Complete and Unabridged. Translated by William Whiston. New updated ed. Peabody, MA: Hendrickson, 1987.
The Works of Philo: Complete and Unabridged. Translated by C. D. Yonge. New updated ed. Peabody, MA: Hendrickson, 1993.

Midrashim

Lamentations Rabbah: An Analytical Translation. Translated by Jacob Neusner. Brown Judaic Studies 193. Atlanta: Scholars Press, 1989.
Mekilta de-Rabbi Ishmael. Translated by Jacob Z. Lauterbach. 3 vols. JPS Library of Jewish Classics. Philadelphia: Jewish Publication Society of America, 1976.

The Midrash on Psalms. Translated by William G. Braude. Yale Judaica Series 13. New Haven, CT: Yale University Press, 1959.
Midrash Rabbah. Edited by H. Freedman and M. Simon. 3rd ed. 10 vols. London and New York: Soncino, 1983.
Sifra. Translated by Morris Ginsberg. South Florida Studies in the History of Judaism 194. Atlanta: Scholars Press, 1999.
Sifre: A Tannaitic Commentary on the Book of Deuteronomy. Translated by Reuven Hammer. Yale Judaica Series 24. New Haven, CT: Yale University Press, 1986.

Mishnah and Tosefta

The Mishnah: A New Translation. Translated by Jacob Neusner. New Haven, CT: Yale University Press, 1988.
The Tosefta. Translated by Jacob Neusner. New York: Ktav, 1981.

New Testament Apocrypha

New Testament Apocrypha. Edited by Wilhelm Schneemelcher. English translation edited by R. McL. Wilson. Rev. ed. 2 vols. Cambridge: Clarke; Louisville: Westminster/John Knox, 1991–92.

Old Testament Apocrypha

New Revised Standard Version of the Bible

Old Testament Pseudepigrapha

The Old Testament Pseudepigrapha. Edited by James H. Charlesworth. 2 vols. Garden City, NY: Doubleday, 1983–85.

Qumran

García Martínez, Florentino. *The Dead Sea Scrolls Translated: The Qumran Texts in English.* 2nd ed. Translated by Wilfred G. E. Watson. Leiden: Brill; Grand Rapids: Eerdmans, 1996.

Talmuds

The Talmud of Babylonia: An American Translation. Translated by Jacob Neusner. Brown Judaic Studies. Chico, CA: Scholars Press, 1984–.

The Talmud of the Land of Israel: A Preliminary Translation and Explanation. Translated by Jacob Neusner. Chicago Studies in the History of Judaism. Chicago: University of Chicago Press, 1982–94.

Targums

Targum Neofiti 1, Numbers. Translated by Martin McNamara. *Targum Pseudo-Jonathan, Numbers.* Translated by Ernest G. Clarke. Aramaic Bible 4. Collegeville, MN: Liturgical Press, 1995.

For Further Reading

The following bibliography is confined to key commentaries, general studies on Jesus, basic resources for Jewish studies, and patristic sources. English translations of foreign works are cited when available. Monographs dedicated to specific topics or themes related to the Gospels also provide helpful background information and can be found in the bibliographies of the commentaries listed below.

Key Commentaries on the Gospels

Matthew

Blomberg, Craig L. *Matthew.* New American Commentary. Nashville: Broadman, 1992.

Carson, D. A. "Matthew." In vol. 8 of *The Expositor's Bible Commentary*, ed. Frank E. Gaebelein, 1–599. Grand Rapids: Zondervan, 1984.

Davies, W. D., and Dale Allison. *Matthew.* 3 vols. International Critical Commentary. Edinburgh: Clark, 1988–97.

Hagner, Donald. *Matthew.* Word Biblical Commentary. Dallas: Word, 1993–95.

Keener, Craig S. *A Commentary on the Gospel of Matthew.* Grand Rapids: Eerdmans, 1999.

Mark

Cranfield, C. E. B. *The Gospel according to St. Mark.* Cambridge Greek Testament Commentary. Cambridge: Cambridge University Press, 1959.

Evans, Craig A. *Mark 8:27–16:20.* Word Biblical Commentary. Dallas: Word, 2001.

France, R. T. *Commentary on Mark.* New International Greek Testament Commentary. Grand Rapids: Eerdmans, 2002.

Guelich, Robert. *Mark 1:1–8:26.* Word Biblical Commentary. Dallas: Word, 1989.

Gundry, Robert. *Mark: A Commentary on His Apology for the Cross.* Grand Rapids: Eerdmans, 1992.

Hooker, Morna D. *The Gospel according to Saint Mark.* Black's New Testament Commentaries. Peabody, MA: Hendrickson, 1991.

Lane, William. *The Gospel according to Mark.* New International Commentary on the New Testament. Grand Rapids: Eerdmans, 1973.

Marcus, Joel. *Mark 1–8.* Anchor Bible. New York: Doubleday, 2000.

Witherington, Ben, III. *The Gospel of Mark: A Socio-Rhetorical Commentary.* Grand Rapids: Eerdmans, 2001.

Luke

Bock, Darrell L. *Luke 1:1–24:53.* 2 vols. Baker Exegetical Commentary on the New Testament. Grand Rapids: Baker, 1994–96.

Fitzmyer, Joseph A. *The Gospel according to Luke.* 2 vols. Anchor Bible. Garden City, NY: Doubleday, 1981–85.

Green, Joel B. *The Gospel of Luke.* New International Commentary on the New Testament. Grand Rapids: Eerdmans, 1997.

Johnson, Luke Timothy. *The Gospel of Luke.* Sacra Pagina. Collegeville, MN: Liturgical Press, 1991.

Marshall, I. Howard. *Commentary on Luke.* New International Greek Testament Commentary. Grand Rapids: Eerdmans, 1978.

Nolland, John. *Luke.* 3 vols. Word Biblical Commentary. Dallas: Word, 1989–93.

Stein, Robert H. *Luke.* New American Commentary. Nashville: Broadman and Holman, 1992.

John

Barrett, C. K. *The Gospel according to St. John.* 2nd ed. London: SPCK, 1978.

Beasley-Murray, George R. *John*. 2nd ed. Word Biblical Commentary. Nashville: Nelson, 1999.

Brown, Raymond E. *The Gospel according to John*. 2 vols. Anchor Bible. Garden City, NY: Doubleday, 1966–70.

Carson, D. A. *The Gospel according to John*. Pillar New Testament Commentary. Grand Rapids: Eerdmans, 1991.

Keener, Craig S. *The Gospel of John: A Commentary*. 2 vols. Peabody, MA: Hendrickson, 2003.

Köstenberger, Andreas J. *John*. Baker Exegetical Commentary on the New Testament. Grand Rapids: Baker, 2004.

Morris, Leon. *The Gospel according to John*. Rev. ed. New International Commentary on the New Testament. Grand Rapids: Eerdmans, 1995.

Works on Jesus

Allison, Dale C. *Jesus of Nazareth: Millenarian Prophet*. Minneapolis: Fortress, 1998.

Blomberg, Craig. *Jesus and the Gospels*. Nashville: Broadman and Holman, 1997.

Bock, Darrell L. *Blasphemy and Exaltation in Judaism and the Jewish Examination of Jesus*. Wissenschaftliche Untersuchungen zum Neuen Testament 2/106. Tübingen: Mohr, 1998.

Bockmuehl, Marcus. *This Jesus: Martyr, Lord, Messiah*. Edinburgh: Clark, 1994.

Bornkamm, Günther. *Jesus of Nazareth*. New York: Harper & Row, 1960.

Casey, P. M. *From Jewish Prophet to Gentile God: The Origins and Development of New Testament Christology*. Louisville: Westminster/John Knox, 1991.

Chilton, Bruce. *Rabbi Jesus: An Intimate Biography*. New York: Doubleday, 2000.

Crossan, John Dominic. *The Historical Jesus: The Life of a Mediterranean Jewish Peasant*. San Francisco: Harper, 1991.

Dunn, James D. G. "Messianic Ideas and Their Influence on the Jesus of History." In *The Messiah*, ed. James Charlesworth, 365–81. Minneapolis: Augsburg Fortress, 1992.

Ellis, E. Earle. "New Directions in Form Criticism." In *Prophecy and Hermeneutic in Early Christianity*, 237–53. Tübingen: Mohr, 1978.

Evans, Craig A. *Jesus and His Contemporaries: Comparative Studies*. Leiden: Brill, 1995.

Fredriksen, Paula. *From Jesus to Christ: The Origins of the New Testament Images of Jesus*. New Haven, CT: Yale University Press, 1998.

———. *Jesus of Nazareth, King of the Jews: A Jewish Life and the Emergence of Christianity*. New York: Knopf, 1999.

Hengel, Martin. *Studies in Early Christology*. Edinburgh: Clark, 1995.

Jonge, Marinus de. *Jesus, the Servant-Messiah*. New Haven, CT: Yale University Press, 1991.

Kinman, Brent. "The A-triumphal Entry (Luke 19:28–48): Historical Backgrounds, Theological Motifs, and the Purpose of Luke." Th.D. diss., University of Cambridge, 1993.

McKnight, Scot. *A New Vision for Israel: The Teaching of Jesus in National Context*. Grand Rapids: Eerdmans, 1999.

Meier, John P. *A Marginal Jew: Rethinking the Historical Jesus*. 3 vols. New York: Doubleday, 1991–2001.

Osborne, Grant. *The Resurrection Narratives: A Redactional Study*. Grand Rapids: Baker, 1984.

Sanders, E. P. *Jesus and Judaism*. Philadelphia: Fortress, 1985.

Stein, Robert H. *The Method and Message of Jesus' Teachings*. Rev. ed. Louisville: Westminster/John Knox, 1994.

Stuhlmacher, Peter. *Jesus of Nazareth—Christ of Faith*. Peabody, MA: Hendrickson, 1993.

Theissen, Gerd, and Annette Metz. *The Historical Jesus: A Comprehensive Guide*. Minneapolis: Fortress, 1998.

Vermes, Geza. *Jesus the Jew: A Historian's Reading of the Gospels*. 2nd ed. New York: Macmillan, 1983.

Webb, Robert L. *John the Baptizer and Prophet: A Socio-Historical Study*. Sheffield: Sheffield Academic Press, 1991.

Witherington, Ben, III. *The Christology of Jesus*. Philadelphia: Fortress, 1990.

Wright, N. T. *Jesus and the Victory of God*. Minneapolis: Fortress, 1996.

Works on Jewish Literature

General Works

Cowley, A. *Aramaic Papyri of the Fifth Century BC*. Oxford: Clarendon, 1923.

Evans, Craig A. *Noncanonical Writings and New Testament Interpretation*. Peabody, MA: Hendrickson, 1992.

Grisby, Bruce H. "A Proposed Guide for Citing Rabbinic Texts." *Journal of the Evangelical Theological Society* 24 (1981): 83–90.

Jastrow, Marcus. *A Dictionary of the Targumim, the Talmud Babli and Yerushalmi, and the Midrashic Literature*. 1903. Reprint, New York: Judaica, 1992.

Levy, J., H. L. Fleischer, and L. Goldschmidt. *Wörterbuch über die Talmudim und Midrashim*. Darmstadt: Wissenschaftliche Buchgesellschaft, 1963.

Mulder, M. J., ed. *Mikra: Text, Translation, Reading, and Interpretation of the Hebrew Bible in Ancient*

Judaism and Early Christianity. Philadelphia: Fortress; Assen: Van Gorcum, 1988.

Neusner, J. *Introduction to Rabbinic Literature*. New York: Doubleday, 1994.

———. *The Study of Ancient Judaism*. 2 vols. New York: Ktav, 1981.

Rost, L. *Judaism outside the Hebrew Canon: An Introduction to the Documents*. Nashville: Abingdon, 1976.

Stemberger, Günther. *Introduction to the Talmud and Midrash*. Trans. Marcus Bockmuehl. 2nd ed. Edinburgh: Clark, 1996.

Strack, H. L., and Paul Billerbeck. *Kommentar zum Neuen Testament aus Talmud und Midrasch*. 6 vols. Munich: Beck, 1922–28.

Dead Sea Scrolls

Allegro, John M. *Qumran Cave 4.I (4Q 158–4Q186)*. Discoveries in the Judaean Desert of Jordan 5. Oxford: Clarendon, 1968.

Charlesworth, James H. *The Dead Sea Scrolls: Hebrew, Aramaic, and Greek Texts with English Translations*. Vol. 1, *Rule of the Community and Related Documents*. Tübingen: Mohr (Siebeck), 1994.

Davies, P. R. *The Damascus Document: An Interpretation of the Damascus Document*. Journal for the Study of the Old Testament Monograph Series 25. Sheffield: JSOT Press, 1983.

Discoveries in the Judaean Desert of Jordan series. 39 vols. Oxford: Clarendon, 1955–2002.

Dupont-Sommer, A. *The Essene Writings from Qumran*. Trans. Geza Vermes. Gloucester, MA: Smith, 1973.

García Martínez, Florentino. *The Dead Sea Scrolls Translated: The Qumran Texts in English*. Trans. Wilfred G. E. Watson. 2nd ed. Grand Rapids: Eerdmans, 1996.

García Martínez, Florentino, and Eibert J. C. Tigchelaar. *The Dead Sea Scrolls Study Edition*. 2 vols. Grand Rapids: Eerdmans, 1997.

Knibb, Michael A. *The Qumran Community*. Cambridge Commentaries on Writings of the Jewish and Christian World 200 BC to AD 200, vol. 2. Cambridge: Cambridge University Press, 1987.

Maier, Johann. *Die Qumran-Essener: Die Texte vom Toten Meer*. 3 vols. Uni-Taschenbücher. Munich: Reinhardt, 1995–96.

Vermes, Geza. *The Dead Sea Scrolls in English*. 3rd ed. London: Penguin, 1987.

Hebrew Bible and Septuagint

Dos Santos, E. C. *An Expanded Hebrew Index for the Hatch-Redpath Concordance to the Septuagint*. Jerusalem: Dugith, [1974].

Elliger, K., and W. Rudolph, eds. 5th ed. *Biblia Hebraica Stuttgartensia*. Stuttgart: Deutsche Bibelgesellschaft, 1997.

Hatch, Edwin, and Henry A. Redpath. *A Concordance to the Septuagint and the Other Greek Versions of the Old Testament (Including the Apocryphal Books)*. 2nd ed. Grand Rapids: Baker, 1998.

Le Boulluec, A., and P. Sandevoir, eds. *La Bible d'Alexandrie*. Paris: Cerf, 1989.

Muraoka, Takamitsu. *Hebrew/Aramaic Index to the Septuagint (Keyed to the Hatch-Redpath Concordance)*. Grand Rapids: Baker, 1998.

Rahlfs, Alfred, ed. *Septuaginta: Id est Vetus Testamentum graece iuxta LXX interpretes*. Stuttgart: Deutsche Bibelgesellschaft, 1935.

Septuaginta: Vetus Testamentum Graecum. Vols. 1–4, and 8–16 currently available. Göttingen: Vandenhoeck & Ruprecht, 1931–.

Taylor, Bernard A. *The Analytical Lexicon to the Septuagint: A Complete Parsing Guide*. Grand Rapids: Zondervan, 1994.

Jewish Mysticism

Schäfer, Peter, and Hans-Jürgen Becker, eds. *Übersetzung der Hekhalot-Literatur*. 4 vols. Texte und Studien zum antiken Judentum. Tübingen: Mohr, 1987–.

Josephus

Thackeray, H. St. J., Ralph Marcus, Allen Wikgren, and L. H. Feldman, trans. *Josephus*. 10 vols. Loeb Classical Library. Cambridge, MA: Harvard University Press, 1926–65.

Whiston, William, trans. *The Works of Josephus*. New ed. Peabody, MA: Hendrickson, 1987.

Midrash

Bietenhard, Hans. *Midrasch Tanhuma B*. Judaica et Christiana 6. Bern: Peter Lang, 1982.

———. *Sifre Deuteronomium*. Judaica et Christiana 8. Frankfurt: Peter Lang, 1984.

Braude, William G., trans. *The Midrash on Psalms*. 2 vols. Yale Judaica Series 13. New Haven, CT: Yale University Press, 1959.

———. *Pesikta Rabbati*. New Haven, CT: Yale University Press: 1968.

Finkelstein, Louis. *Siphre ad Deuteronomium*. Corpus Tannaiticum: Siphre d'be Rab 3.2. Berlin: Gesellschaft zur Forderung der Wissenschaft des Judentums, 1939. Reprint, New York: Jewish Theological Seminary of America, 1993.

Freedman, H., and M. Simon. *The Midrash Rabbah*. 3rd ed. 10 vols. London and New York: Soncino, 1983.

Goldin, Judah, trans. *The Fathers according to Rabbi Nathan*. Yale Judaica Series 10. New Haven, CT: Yale University Press, 1955.

Hammer, Reuven. *Sifre: A Tannaitic Commentary on the Book of Deuteronomy*. New Haven, CT: Yale University Press, 1986.

Horovitz, Saul. *Siphre ad Numeros adjecto Sipre zutta*. Corpus Tannaiticum: Siphre d'be Rab 3.1. Leipzig: Frock, 1917. Reprint, Jerusalem: Shalem, 1992.

Kuhn, Karl G. *Der tannaitische Midrasch, Sifre zu Numeri*. Rabbinische Texte: Tannaitische Midraschim 2/3. Stuttgart: Kohlhammer, 1959.

Lauterbach, Jacob Z. *Mekilta de-Rabbi Ishmael*. Philadelphia: Jewish Publication Society, 1933–49.

Neusner, J. *Midrash in Context: Exegesis in Formative Judaism*. Philadelphia: Fortress, 1983.

———. *Sifra: An Analytical Translation*. Brown Judaic Studies 140. Atlanta: Scholars Press, 1988.

———. *What Is Midrash?* Philadelphia: Fortress, 1987.

Porton, G. G. *Understanding Rabbinic Midrash*. Hoboken, NJ: Ktav, 1985.

Saldarini, Anthony J. *The Fathers according to Rabbi Nathan: Aboth de Rabbi Nathan Version B*. Studies in Judaism in Late Antiquity 11. Leiden: Brill, 1985.

Schechter, Solomon. *Aboth de Rabbi Nathan*. New York: Feldheim, 1945.

Townsend, John. *Midrash Tanhuma, Genesis: Translated into English with Introduction, Indices, and Brief Notes* (S. Buber Recension). Hoboken, NJ: Ktav, 1989.

Winter, Jakob, and A. Wünsche. *Mechiltha: Ein tannaitischer Midrasch zu Exodus*. Leipzig: Hinrichs, 1909.

Mishnah and Tosefta

Blackman, Philip, ed. *Mishnayoth: Pointed Hebrew Text, English Translation, Introductions, Notes,* etc. 7 vols. 2nd ed., rev., corrected, and enlarged. Gateshead, Eng.: Judaica, 1990.

Danby, Herbert, trans. *The Mishnah: Translated from the Hebrew with Introduction and Brief Explanatory Notes*. Oxford: Oxford University Press, 1933.

Herford, R. Travers, ed. *Pirke Aboth: The Tractate "Fathers," from the Mishnah, Commonly Called "Sayings of the Fathers."* 3rd rev. ed. New York: Jewish Institute of Religion Press, 1945.

Neusner, J. *Mishnah*. New Haven, CT: Yale University Press, 1988.

Taylor, Charles. *Sayings of the Jewish Fathers: Sefer Dibre Aboth Ha-Olam Comprising Pirque Aboth in Hebrew and English with Critical Notes and Excursuses*. Amsterdam: Philo, 1970.

Zuckermandel, M. S., ed. *Tosefta*. Jerusalem: Sifre Vahrman, [1970].

Old Testament Apocrypha and Pseudepigrapha

Black, Matthew. *The Book of Enoch or I Enoch: A New English Edition*. Studia in Veteris Testamenti Pseudepigrapha 7. Leiden: Brill, 1985.

Charles, R. H., ed. *The Apocrypha and Pseudepigrapha of the Old Testament in English*. 2 vols. Oxford: Clarendon, 1913.

Charlesworth, James H., ed. *The Old Testament Pseudepigrapha*. 2 vols. New York: Doubleday, 1983–85.

Denis, A.-M. *Concordance Grecque des Pseudépigraphes d'Ancien Testament*. Louvain-au-Neuve: Université Catholique de Louvain, 1987.

Hollander, H. W., and M. de Jonge. *The Testaments of the Twelve Patriarchs: A Commentary*. Studia in Veteris Testamenti Pseudepigrapha 8. Leiden: Brill, 1985.

Jacobson, Howard. *The Exagoge of Ezekiel*. Cambridge: Cambridge University Press, 1983.

Kee, Howard Clark. *The Cambridge Annotated Study Apocrypha: New Revised Standard Version*. Cambridge: Cambridge University Press, 1994.

Knibb, Michael A, ed. *The Ethiopic Book of Enoch*. Oxford: Clarendon, 1978.

Lechner-Schmidt, Wilfried. *Wortindex der lateinischen erhaltenen Pseudepigraphen zum Alten Testament: Texte und Arbeiten zum neutestamentlichen Zeitalter*. Ed. K. Berger, F. Vouga, M. Wolter, and D. Zeller. Tübingen: Francke, 1990.

Sparks, H. F. D., ed. *The Apocryphal Old Testament*. Oxford: Clarendon, 1984.

Tromp, Johannes. *The Assumption of Moses: A Critical Edition with Commentary*. Studia in Veteris Testamenti Pseudepigrapha 10. Leiden: Brill, 1993.

Uhlig, Siegbert. *Das äthiopische Henochbuch*. Jüdische Schriften aus hellenistisch-römischer Zeit 5.6. Gütersloh: Mohn, 1984.

Wahl, C. A. *Clavis Librorum Veteris Testamenti Apocryphorum Philologica*. Graz: Akademische Druck, 1972.

Philo

Colson, F. H., G. H. Whitaker, J. W. Earp, and R. Marcus, trans. *Philo*. 10 vols. plus 2 supplementary vols. Loeb Classical Library. Cambridge, MA: Harvard University Press, 1929–53.

Yonge, C. D., trans. *The Works of Philo*. New ed. Peabody, MA: Hendrickson, 1993.

Samaritan Pentateuch

Macdonald, John, ed. and trans. *Memar Marqah: The Teaching of Marqah.* Beihefte zur Zeitschrift für die alttestamentliche Wissenschaft 84. Berlin: Töpelmann, 1963.

Talmuds

Epstein, I., ed. *The Babylonian Talmud.* 35 vols. London: Soncino, 1936–48.

Goldschmidt, Lazarus. *Der babylonische Talmud.* 8 vols. Berlin: Calvary, 1897–1909. Reprint, Haag: Nijoff, 1933–35.

Hengel, Martin, Jacob Neusner, Peter Schäfer, Hans-Jürgen Becker, and Frowald Gil Huttenmeister, eds. *Übersetzung des Talmud Yerushalmi.* 16 vols. Tübingen: Mohr, 1975–.

Neusner, J. *The Talmud of the Land of Israel: A Preliminary Translation and Explanation.* 35 vols. Chicago: University of Chicago Press, 1982–89.

Schäfer, Peter, and Hans-Jürgen Becker, eds. *Synopse zum Talmud Yerushalmi.* 4 vols. Texte und Studien zum antiken Judentum. Tübingen: Mohr (Siebeck), 1991–.

Targums

Diez Macho, Alejandro. *Neophyti 1: Levitico.* Textos y Estudios. Madrid: Consejo Superior de Investigaciones Cientificas, 1971.

———. *Neophyti 1: Numeros.* Textos y Estudios. Madrid: Consejo Superior de Investigaciones Cientificas, 1974.

Grossfeld, Bernard. *A Bibliography of Targum Literature.* 2 vols. Bibliographica Judaica 3 and 8. Cincinnati: Hebrew Union College; New York: Ktav, 1972–77.

———, trans. *The Targum Onqelos to Genesis.* Aramaic Bible 6. Wilmington, DE: Glazier, 1988.

———. *The Targum Onqelos to Exodus.* Aramaic Bible 7. Wilmington, DE: Glazier, 1988.

———. *The Targum Onqelos to Leviticus and the Targum Onqelos to Numbers.* Aramaic Bible 8. Wilmington, DE: Glazier, 1988.

———. *The Targum Onqelos to Deuteronomy.* Aramaic Bible 9. Wilmington, DE: Glazier, 1988.

Harrington, Daniel J., and Anthony J. Saldarini, trans. *Targum Jonathan of the Former Prophets.* Aramaic Bible 10. Wilmington, DE: Glazier, 1987.

Maher, Michael, trans. *Targum Pseudo-Jonathan: Genesis.* Aramaic Bible 1B. Collegeville, MN: Liturgical Press, 1992.

McNamara, Martin, Ernest G. Clarke, and Shirley Magder, trans. *Targum Neofiti 1: Numbers and Targum Pseudo-Jonathan: Numbers.* Aramaic Bible 4. Collegeville, MN: Liturgical Press, 1995.

McNamara, Martin, Robert Hayward, and Michael Maher, trans. *Targum Neofiti 1: Exodus and Targum Pseudo-Jonathan: Exodus.* Aramaic Bible 2. Collegeville, MN: Liturgical Press, 1994.

———. *Targum Neofiti 1: Leviticus and Targum Pseudo-Jonathan: Leviticus.* Aramaic Bible 3. Collegeville, MN: Liturgical Press, 1994.

Nickels, P. *Targum and New Testament: A Bibliography Together with a New Testament Index.* Rome: Pontifical Biblical Institute, 1967.

Patristic Sources

Elliott, J. K., ed. *The Apocryphal New Testament: A Collection of Apocryphal Christian Literature in an English Translation.* Oxford: Clarendon; New York: Oxford University Press, 1993.

Fathers of the Church series. 110 vols. to date. Washington, DC: Catholic University of America Press, 1947–.

Holmes, Michael W., ed. *The Apostolic Fathers: Greek Texts and English Translations.* Grand Rapids: Baker, 1999.

Roberts, Alexander, and James Donaldson, eds. *The Ante-Nicene Fathers.* 10 vols. 1885–87. Reprint, Grand Rapids: Eerdmans, n.d.

Schaff, Philip, ed. *A Select Library of Nicene and Post-Nicene Fathers of the Christian Church.* 1st series. 14 vols. New York: Christian Literature Co., 1887–1900. Reprint, Grand Rapids: Eerdmans, 1979.

Schaff, Philip, and Henry Wace, eds. *A Select Library of Nicene and Post-Nicene Fathers of the Christian Church.* 2nd series. 14 vols. New York: Christian Literature Co., 1890–1900. Reprint, Grand Rapids: Eerdmans, 1982.

Schneemelcher, Wilhelm, ed. *New Testament Apocrypha.* Trans. R. McL. Wilson. Rev. ed. 2 vols. Cambridge: Clarke; Louisville: Westminster/John Knox, 1991–92.

Index of Subjects

Index of Scripture
and Other Ancient Writings

The extrabiblical readings appearing in this book are listed below by genre and source. Scripture references included in this index are drawn from the editors' comments and from biblical cross-references appearing in the readings. The primary Gospel passages elucidated by the readings are listed in the front of the book (see "Canonical Guide to the Readings," p. 7).

Old Testament

Genesis

1–2 214
2:1 120
5:1 126
6 159
15 226
15:9 227
15:12 227
15:17 226
50:17 122

Exodus

4:20 217
7:1 192
12:19 186
13:7 186
15:26 227
16:4 217
20:10 129
21:32 209
22:15–16 209
23:14 155, 156
24:7 215
28:9 46
30:13–16 119
32:4 56

Leviticus

1:9 125
3:3–5 125
9:22 46
13 180–81
13:4–5 97
14:8 97
15:2 97
15:25 97
15:28 97
18:6–7 223
19:17 110
19:18 110, 161
20:11 223
20:12 223
20:13 223
20:15–16 223
23:38 82
24:10 189
24:22 188
25:36 110
25:39 66, 237
25:46 237

Numbers

4:7 240
5:14 49
5:18 50
5:22 85
5:24 85
5:27 86
5:29 86

6:12 97
6:24–26 46
11:12 215
15:37–41 44
18:7 240
19:1 181
25:8 240
25:11 240
29:13 220
29:16 220

Deuteronomy

4:7 180
6:4–9 44
6:5 151
11:13–21 44
16:16 155
17:12 189
17:13 190
21:14 50
22:19 209
22:28–29 209
24:1 85
25:2 99
25:3 99
26:12 232
26:14 232
26:15 218
32:1 235

New Testament

Old Testament Apocrypha

80.1–8 177
81.3 255
84.6 117
87.2 248
89–90 152
89.18 184
89.52 206
90.6–10 99
90.9–12 207
90.15 99
90.24–27 66
90.28–30 263
90.31 206
90.38 207
90.40 263
91.1–19 141
93.1–14 141
94–103 89
102.4–5 135
102.9–10 134
104.1 124
104.2 118
104.4–6 159
108.7 124

2 Enoch

30.14–15 91
45.2 131

Ezekiel the Tragedian
Exagōgē
68–89 192

4 Ezra

4:42–43 176
6:24 257
7:27–29 236
7:36–38 66
7:85–93 135
7:97 108
9:1–12 257
12:31–34 258
13 179
13:1–58 76
13:4 66
13:29–31 257

Jubilees

1.15–17 154
1.16 117
1.23–25 210
3.30–31 199
4.1–3 165
5.12–14 124
7.20 199
7.29 264

7.34 117
9.15 66
21.24 117
22.7–23 240
23.11–32 166
23.16 101
23.19 101
23.32 124
30.19–23 124
36.10 66

Letter of Aristeas

1–8 39
95 47
228 95

**Martyrdom and
Ascension of Isaiah**

5.13 146
11.2 49

Psalms of Solomon

3.12 145
7.1 239
8.28 181
9.5 89
11.2–5 181
14.6 136
14.9–10 136
15.4–7 67
15.10 136
17–18 137
17.1–4 49
17.21–23 49
17.25–26 49
17.26 181
17.30 49
17.35–37 49
18.3 49
18.5 49

Pseudo-Philo
Biblical Antiquities
16.2 165
28.5 185
30.5 185
60.1–3 261

Sibylline Oracles

3.49 (frag. 3) 216
3.796–808 257

Testament of Abraham

4.5–7 159

7.8 84
11 (rec. B) 183
13 (rec. A) 183

Testament of Asher

1.3–5 91

Testament of Benjamin

3.3 126
3.8 206
10.7 259

Testament of Dan

5.3 263

Testament of Gad

6.3–7 137

Testament of Issachar

5.2 263
7.6 263

Testament of Job

9.7–8 88
18.2–3 89

Testament of Joseph

19.8–9 206

Testament of Judah

25.1–2 259
25.3 123

Testament of Levi

15.1 165

Testament of Moses

6.8–9 165
7.1–4 128
10.1 123
10.5 178

Testament of Simeon

2.12–13 80
6.6 123

Testament of Solomon

2.8–3.6 103
6.1–9 103
20.16–17 123